Second Edition

BEST 600 SELLING HOME PLANS

table of contents

MW01041778

Cover Design
Josephine Rudyk

Library of Congress No.: 98-75668
ISBN: 0-938708-80-5

Submit all Canadian plan orders to:
The Garlinghouse Co.
60 Baffin Place, Unit #5
Waterloo, Ontario
N2V 127

Canadian Orders Only: 1-800-561-4169
Fax No.: 1-800-719-3219
Customer Service No.: 1-519-746-4169

Victorian Accents

Price Code: B

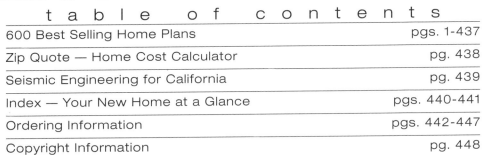

- This plan features:
  — Three bedrooms
  — Two full and one half baths
- Covered Porch and double doors lead into Entry accented by a window seat and curved banister stair case
- Decorative windows overlooking back yard and a large fireplace highlight spacious Great Room
- A hub Kitchen with an island/snack bar and large Pantry access formal Dining Room, Breakfast area and covered side Porch
- Powder Room, Laundry Area, Garage entry and storage nearby Kitchen
- Cathedral ceilings crown Master Bedroom suite with two walk-in closets, two vanities and a whirlpool tub
- Two additional Bedrooms, one with a vaulted ceiling above a window seat, share a full Bath

FIRST FLOOR — 905 SQ. FT.
SECOND FLOOR — 863 SQ. FT.
GARAGE — 487 SQ. FT.
BASEMENT — 905 SQ. FT.

TOTAL LIVING AREA:
1,768 SQ. FT.

PLAN NO. 94907

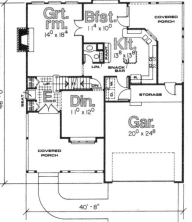

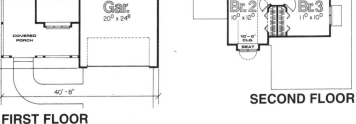

FIRST FLOOR

© design basics, inc.

SECOND FLOOR

ZIP QUOTE
HOME COST CALCULATOR
see order pages for details

Arches Grace
Classic Facade

Price Code: B

- This plan features:
— Three bedrooms
— Two full and one half baths
- Build-in planter and a half wall defines Living Room
- A balcony that connects three upstairs Bedrooms
- Double sinks and a built-in vanity in the Master Bath
- Ample closet space

First floor — 932 sq. ft.
Second floor — 764 sq. ft.
Basement — 920 sq. ft.
Garage — 430 sq. ft.

TOTAL LIVING AREA:
1,696 sq. ft.

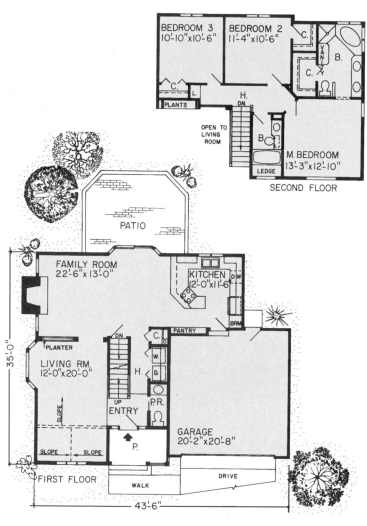

SECOND FLOOR

Br 2
11-6x10

open to below | DN

Br 3
13x9

FIRST FLOOR

38'-8"

Deck

Dining
9x9-6

Kit
12x9

P

Mas. Suite
14x12-8

Living Rm
12-4x17
vaulted

DN

38'-8"

UP

Garage
20x20

Contemporary Traditions

Price Code: A

■ This plan features:

— Three bedrooms

— Two full baths

■ A vaulted ceiling in the Living Room with a half-round transom window and a fireplace

■ A Dining Area flowing into either the Kitchen or the Living Room with sliders to the Deck

■ A main floor Master Suite with corner windows, walk-in closet, and private access to a full Bath

■ Two additional Bedrooms on the second floor, one with a walk-in closet, having use of a full Bath

FIRST FLOOR — 857 SQ. FT.
SECOND FLOOR — 446 SQ. FT.
GARAGE — 400 SQ. FT.

TOTAL LIVING AREA:
1,303 SQ. FT.

Old-Fashioned Porch

Price Code: B

■ This plan features:

— Three bedrooms

— Two full and one half baths

■ A Traditional front Porch, with matching dormers above and a garage hidden below, leading into a open, contemporary layout

■ A Living Area with a cozy fireplace visible from the Dining Room for warm entertaining

■ A U-shaped, efficient Kitchen featuring a corner, double sink and pass-thru to the Dining Room

■ A convenient half bath with a laundry center on the first floor

■ A spacious, first floor Master Suite with a lavish Bath including a double vanity, walk-in closet and an oval, corner window tub

■ Two large bedrooms with dormer windows, on the second floor, sharing a full hall bath

FIRST FLOOR — 1,057 SQ. FT.
SECOND FLOOR — 611 SQ. FT.
BASEMENT — 511 SQ. FT.
GARAGE — 546 SQ. FT.

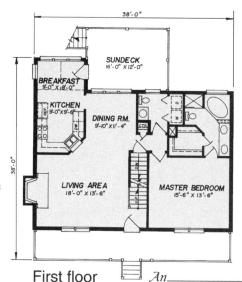

First floor

TOTAL LIVING AREA:
1,668 SQ. FT.

An
EXCLUSIVE DESIGN
By Jannis Vann & Associates, Inc

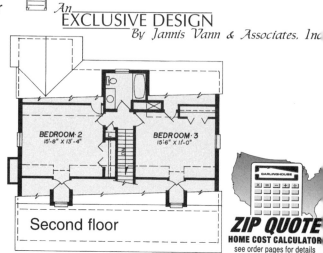

Second floor

ZIP QUOTE
HOME COST CALCULATOR
see order pages for details

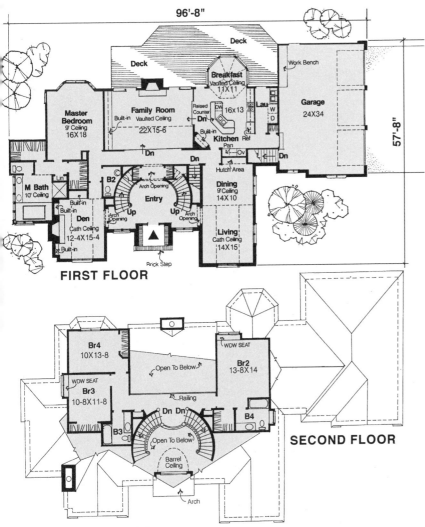

96'-8"

Deck

Deck

Breakfast
Vaulted Ceiling
11X11

Work Bench

**Master
Bedroom**
9' Ceiling
16X18

Family Room
Built-in   Vaulted Ceiling
22X15-6

Raised
Counter
Dn

DW 16 x 13

Lau

W
D

Garage
24X34

57'-8"

Built-in

Kitchen
Pan
Ref

Dn

M Bath
10' Ceiling

Lin

B2

Dn

Dn

Pan
Ov

Dn

Built-in

Hutch Area

Built-in

Den
12-4X15-4

Arch
Opening

Entry

Arch
Opening
Up

Up

Arch
Opening

Dining
9' Ceiling
14X10

Built-in

Brick Step

Living
Cath Ceiling
14X15

FIRST FLOOR

Br4
10X13-8

Open To Below

WDW SEAT

Br2
13-8X14

WDW SEAT
Br3
10-8X11-8

Railing

Dn Dn

B4

B3

Open To Below

SECOND FLOOR

Barrel
Ceiling

Arch

Unusual and Dramatic

Price Code: F

- This plan features:
  — Four bedrooms
  — Three full and one half baths
- Elegant Entry with arched openings and a double curved staircase
- Cathedral ceilings crown arched windows in the Den and Living Room
- Spacious Family Room with a vaulted ceiling and a large fireplace
- Hub Kitchen with a work island/serving counter, Breakfast alcove
- Secluded Master Suite with a lovely bay window, two walk-in closets and a plush bath
- Three second floor bedrooms, one with a private bath, offer ample closets

FIRST FLOOR — 2,646 SQ. FT.
SECOND FLOOR — 854 SQ. FT.

TOTAL LIVING AREA:
3,500 SQ. FT.

Photography Supplied By The Meredith Corporation

Forest Cottage

Price Code: F

- This plan features:
  — Four Bedrooms
  — Four full and one half baths
- The bow shaped front Deck mirrors the eyebrow dormer and large arched window
- Kitchen with an island and a built-in Pantry
- The Great Room is highlighted by a fireplace and access to the screened Porch
- The second floor Master Suite has two walk-in closets and is pampered by a five-piece Bath
- The lower level contains a Media Room, a Play Room, and a Guest Suite
- No materials list is available for this plan

FIRST FLOOR — 1,642 SQ. FT.
SECOND FLOOR — 1411 SQ. FT.
LOWER LEVEL — 1,230 SQ. FT.
BASEMENT — 412 SQ. FT.

TOTAL LIVING AREA:
4283 SQ. FT.

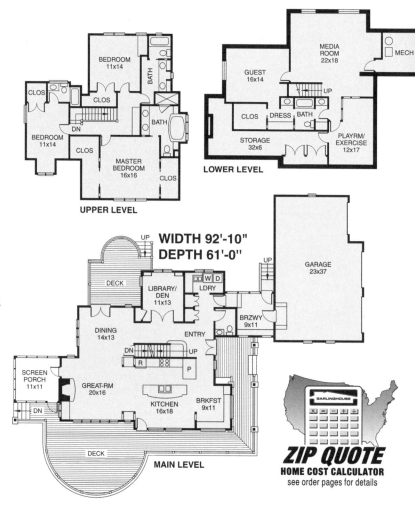

WIDTH 92'-10"
DEPTH 61'-0"

ZIP QUOTE
HOME COST CALCULATOR
see order pages for details

CL
BEDROOM 2
11'4" x 13'2"
BEDROOM 3
11'4" x 12'8"
MASTER BATH
JACCUZI
CL
LN
BATH
HALL
CL
CL
OPTIONAL
W.I.C.
LN
CL
DN
RAILING
BEDROOM 1
11'4" x 13'2"
OPEN
TO
BELOW
MASTER
BEDROOM
15'2" x 18'0"

SECOND FLOOR

WIDTH 69'- 0"
DEPTH 37' - 0"

FIREPLACE
BREAKFAST
10'1" x 14'2"
DW
KITCHEN
12'1" x 14'8"
FAMILY ROOM
15'-2" x 16'-8"
ARCH
REF
CL
P
ARCH
DN
P.R.
2 CAR GARAGE
21'8" x 22'8"
LIVING ROOM
13'2" x 15'2"
ARCH
W D
CL
UP
DINING ROOM
12'2" x 15'2"
FOYER
ARCH
PORCH

FIRST FLOOR

Comfortable Country Porch

Price Code: D

■ This plan features:

— Four bedrooms

— Two full and one half baths

■ Wrap-around Porch leads into two-story Foyer with a lovely banister staircase

■ Formal Living Room with arched opening into Family Room with hearth fireplace

■ Efficient, U-shaped Kitchen with a Pantry, peninsula serving counter, bright Breakfast Area, Garage entry and Laundry facilities

■ Corner Master Bedroom offers two closets, a double vanity and jaccuzi

■ Three additional Bedrooms convenient to a full Bath

■ No materials list is available for this plan

FIRST FLOOR — 1,348 SQ. FT.
SECOND FLOOR — 1,137 SQ. FT.
BASEMENT — 1,348 SQ. FT.

TOTAL LIVING AREA:
2,485 SQ. FT.

Convenient Country

Price Code: B

- This plan features:
— Three bedrooms
— Two full and one half baths
- Full front Porch provides a sheltered entrance
- Expansive Living Room with an inviting fireplace opens to bright Dining Room and Kitchen
- U-shaped Kitchen with peninsula serving counter, Dining Room and nearby Pantry, Laundry and Garage entry
- Secluded Master Bedroom with two closets and a double vanity Bath
- Two second floor Bedrooms with ample closets and dormer windows, share a full Bath
- No materials list is available for this plan

FIRST FLOOR — 1,108 SQ. FT.
SECOND FLOOR — 659 SQ. FT.
BASEMENT — 875 SQ. FT.

TOTAL LIVING AREA:
1,767 SQ. FT.

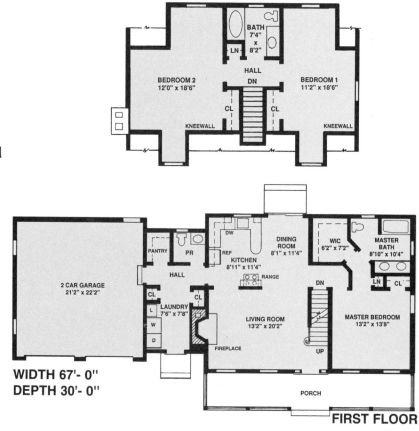

SECOND FLOOR

BATH
7'4" x 8'2"
LN
HALL
DN
BEDROOM 2
12'0" x 18'6"
BEDROOM 1
11'2" x 18'6"
CL
CL
KNEEWALL
KNEEWALL

WIDTH 67'- 0"
DEPTH 30'- 0"

PANTRY
PR
DW
DINING ROOM
8'1" x 11'4"
WIC
6'2" x 7'2"
MASTER BATH
8'10" x 10'4"
2 CAR GARAGE
21'2" x 22'2"
REF
KITCHEN
8'11" x 11'4"
HALL
RANGE
DN
LN
CL
CL
L
LAUNDRY
7'6" x 7'8"
CL
LIVING ROOM
13'2" x 20'2"
MASTER BEDROOM
13'2" x 13'8"
W
D
FIREPLACE
UP
PORCH

FIRST FLOOR

ZIP QUOTE
HOME COST CALCULATOR
see order pages for details

Dynamic Two-Story

Price Code: D

■ This plan features:

— Four bedrooms

— Three full and one half baths

■ Sheltered entry surrounded by glass leads into open Foyer and Great Room with high ceiling, hearth fireplace and atrium door to back yard

■ Columns frame entrance to conveniently located Dining Room

■ Efficient Kitchen with built-in pantry, work island and bright Breakfast area accesses Laundry, backyard and Garage

■ Master Bedroom wing with sitting area, walk-in closet and private bath with corner window tub and double vanity

■ Three additional bedrooms, one with a private bath, located on second floor

■ No materials list available for this plan

FIRST FLOOR — 1,710 SQ. FT.
SECOND FLOOR — 693 SQ. FT.
BASEMENT — 1,620 SQ. FT.
GARAGE — 467 SQ. FT.

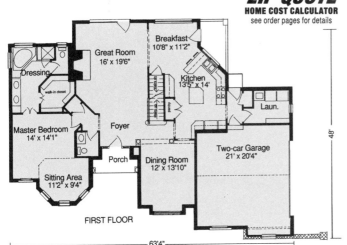

FIRST FLOOR

TOTAL LIVING AREA:
2,403 SQ. FT.

SECOND FLOOR

Southern Traditional

Price Code: B

■ This plan features:

— Three bedrooms

— Two full baths

■ A varied roof line with dormers and a charming colonnaded front Porch

■ Living Room enhanced by nine foot ceilings and a bookcase flanked fireplace

■ Two mullioned French doors leading from the Dining Room to the rear terrace

■ A bayed area in the wrap-around Kitchen

■ Laundry area serving as a Mudroom between the Garage and Kitchen

■ A Master Suite with a walk-in closet, a compartmented Bath with a whirlpool tub, double basin vanity and linen closet

■ Second floor to be finished for future use

FIRST FLOOR — 1,567 SQ. FT.
SECOND FLOOR (BONUS SPACE — 462 SQ. FT.
BASEMENT — 1,567 SQ. FT.
GARAGE — 504 SQ. FT.

TOTAL LIVING AREA:
1,567 SQ. FT.

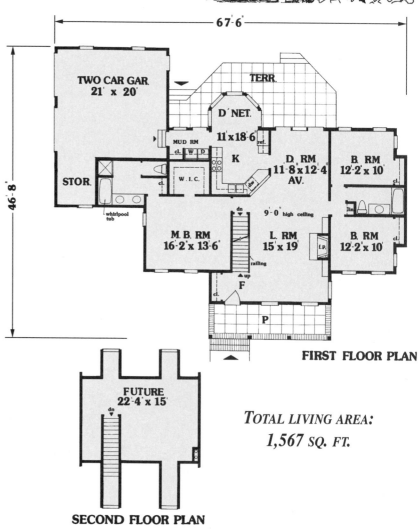

FIRST FLOOR PLAN

TOTAL LIVING AREA:
1,567 SQ. FT.

SECOND FLOOR PLAN

ZIP QUOTE
HOME COST CALCULATOR
see order pages for details

A Touch of Old World Charm

Price Code: D

SECOND FLOOR

TOTAL LIVING AREA:
2,320 SQ. FT.

FIRST FLOOR

- ■ This plan features:
- — Four bedrooms
- — Two full and one half baths
- ■ Authentic balustrade railings and front courtyard greet one and all
- ■ High ceiling in Great Room tops corner fireplace and French doors with arched window
- ■ Formal Dining Room enhanced by a decorative window and furniture alcove
- ■ Country Kitchen with work island, two pantrys, Breakfast area with French door to rear yard, Laundry and Garage entry
- ■ Master Bedroom wing offers a sloped ceiling, plush bath and a huge walk-in closet
- ■ Three additional bedrooms share second floor, balcony and double vanity bath
- ■ No materials list available for this plan

FIRST FLOOR — 1,595 SQ. FT.
SECOND FLOOR — 725 SQ. FT.
GARAGE — 409 SQ. FT.

Neat and Tidy

Price Code: A

■ This plan features:

— Two bedrooms

— Two full baths

■ A two-story Living Room and Dining Room with a handsome stone fireplace

■ A well-appointed Kitchen with a peninsula counter

■ A Master Suite with a walk-in closet and private Master Bath

■ A large utility room with laundry facilities

■ An optional basement or crawl space foundation — please specify when ordering

FIRST FLOOR — 952 SQ. FT.
SECOND FLOOR — 297 SQ. FT.

TOTAL LIVING AREA: 1,249 SQ. FT.

GARLINGHOUSE

ZIP QUOTE
HOME COST CALCULATOR
see order pages for details

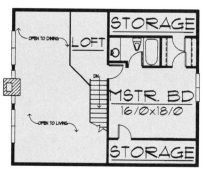

OPEN TO DINING   LOFT   STORAGE

OPEN TO LIVING   MSTR. BD
16/0x18/0

STORAGE

UPPER FLOOR PLAN

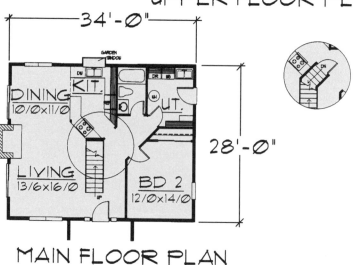

34'-0"

GARDEN WINDOW

DINING
10/0x11/0   KIT.   DR   UT.

LIVING
13/6x16/0   BD 2
12/0x14/0

28'-0"

MAIN FLOOR PLAN

Second floor

First floor

Lower floor

WIDTH 67'-0"
DEPTH 41'-0"

Customized for Sloping View Site

Price Code: C

■ This plan features:

— Three bedrooms

— Two full and one half baths

■ A stone-faced fireplace and vaulted ceiling in the Living Room

■ An island food preparation center with a sink and a Breakfast bar in the Kitchen

■ Sliding glass doors leading from the Dining Room to the adjacent deck

■ A Master Suite with a vaulted ceiling, a sitting room, and a lavish Master Bath with a whirlpool tub, skylights, double vanity, and a walk-in closet

FIRST FLOOR — 1,338 SQ. FT.
SECOND FLOOR — 763 SQ. FT.
LOWER FLOOR — 61 SQ. FT.

TOTAL LIVING AREA:
2,162 SQ. FT.

© 1996 Donald A. Gardner Architects, Inc.

Charm and Personality

Price Code: D

■ This plan features:

— Three bedrooms

— Two full baths

■ Interior columns dramatically open the Foyer and Kitchen to the spacious Great Room

■ Drama is heightened by the Great Room cathedral ceiling and fireplace

■ Master Suite with a tray ceiling combines privacy with access to the rear Deck with spa, while the skylight Bath has all the amenities expected in a quality home

■ Tray ceilings with round-top picture windows bring a special elegance to the Dining Room and the front Swing Room

■ An optional basement or crawl space foundation — please specify when ordering

MAIN FLOOR — 1,655 SQ. FT.
GARAGE — 434 SQ. FT.

TOTAL LIVING AREA:
1,655 SQ. FT.

ZIP QUOTE
HOME COST CALCULATOR
see order pages for details

© 1996 Donald A Gardner Architects, Inc.

Grand Entrance

Price Code: F

FIRST FLOOR

Pool

90' - 0"

Gar 22x23
Covered Patio
Covered Patio
Cathedral Clg.
FamilyRm 18x22
MstrBed 15x21
Kit
Brkfst 10x15
Pwdr
15x15
12'Vaulted Clg.
GolfCart Stor. 15x20
Rear Entry
Entertainment Center
WorkShop
Util
FmlDin 13x15
Bar
LivRm/ Parlor 15x17
Plant Ledge
UP
Ent
21'Clg.
Sloping Clg.
Covered Por

SECOND FLOOR

Bed#4 13x11
16'Clg.
Balcony
Sloping Clg.
Bed#3 13x14
21'Clg.
Ent Below
Bed#2 15x11

FIRST FLOOR — 2,432 SQ. FT.
SECOND FLOOR — 903 SQ. FT.
BASEMENT — 2,432 SQ. FT.
GARAGE — 742 SQ. FT.

**TOTAL LIVING AREA:
3,335 SQ. FT.**

- This plan features:
- — Four bedrooms
- — Two full, one three-quarter and one half baths
- Covered Porch with columns leads to entry hall with a graceful landing staircase
- Fireplaces highlight both the Living Room/Parlor and formal Dining Room
- An efficient Kitchen with an island cooktop, built-in Pantry and open Breakfast Area
- Cathedral ceiling crowns expansive Family Room, accented by a fireplace and a built-in entertainment center
- Lavish Master Bedroom wing
- Three additional Bedrooms, one with a private Bath, on the second floor
- A Garage with Workshop and rear entry to Kitchen and Utility Area
- No materials list is available for this plan

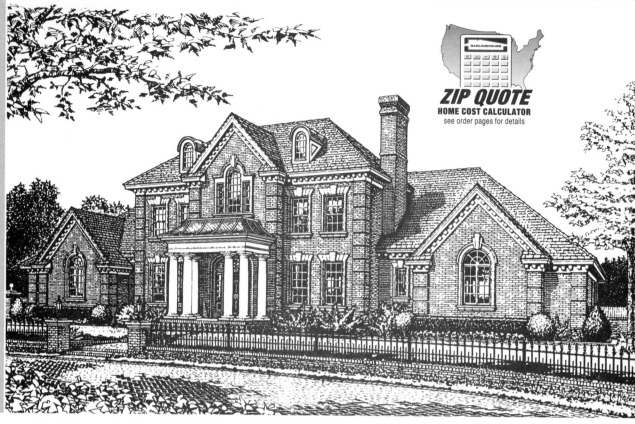

ZIP QUOTE
HOME COST CALCULATOR
see order pages for details

Opulent Luxury

Price Code: F

- **This plan features:**
- — Four bedrooms
- — Three full and one half baths
- Columns frame elegant two-story Entry with a graceful banister staircase
- A stone hearth fireplace and built-in book shelves enhance the Living Room
- Comfortable Family Room with a huge fireplace, cathedral ceiling and access to Covered Veranda
- Spacious Kitchen with cooktop island/ snackbar, built-in pantry and Breakfast Room
- Lavish Master Bedroom wing with a pullman ceiling, sitting area, private Covered Patio and a huge bath with two walk-in closets and a whirpool tub
- Three additional bedrooms on second floor with walk-in closets and private access to a full bath
- No materials list is available

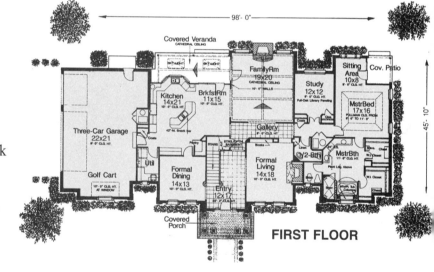

FIRST FLOOR

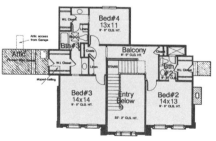

SECOND FLOOR

FIRST FLOOR — 2,804 SQ. FT.
SECOND FLOOR — 979 SQ. FT.
BASEMENT — 2,804 SQ. FT.
GARAGE — 802 SQ. FT.

TOTAL LIVING AREA:
3,783 SQ. FT.

ZIP-QUOTE
HOME COST CALCULATOR
see order pages for details

Efficient and Affordable

Price Code: B

- This plan features:
  - Three bedrooms
  - Two full and one half baths
- Full front porch shelters entrance into open Foyer
- Adjoining Living and Dining Room create great open area for entertaining
- U-shaped Kitchen with serving bar opens to Breakfast Room and Family Room
- Sloped ceiling tops hearth fireplace in Family Room further enhanced by access to rear Deck and yard
- L-shaped stairway leads to laundry facilities and Master Bedroom with two closets and private bath
- Two additional bedrooms on second floor share a full bath

FIRST FLOOR — 980 SQ. FT.
SECOND FLOOR — 728 SQ. FT.
BASEMENT — 972 SQ. FT.
GARAGE — 452 SQ. FT.

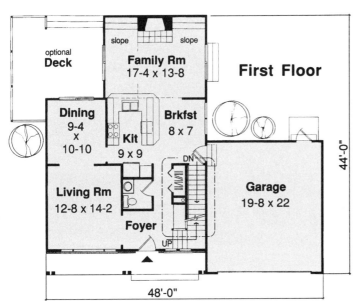

First Floor

optional **Deck**

Family Rm
17-4 x 13-8

slope   slope

Dining
9-4
x
10-10

Brkfst
8 x 7

Kit
9 x 9

Living Rm
12-8 x 14-2

DN

Garage
19-8 x 22

Foyer

UP

44'-0"

48'-0"

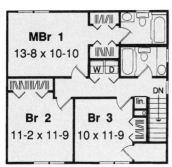

MBr 1
13-8 x 10-10

W D

Br 2
11-2 x 11-9

Br 3
10 x 11-9

DN

lin.

Second Floor

Slab/Crawlspace Option

TOTAL LIVING AREA :
1,708 SQ. FT.

Distinguished Dwelling

Price Code: E

■ This plan features:

— Four bedrooms

— Two full and one half baths

■ Grand two-story Entry into Foyer

■ Formal Living Room with a decorative window and a vaulted ceiling extending into Family Room with cozy fireplace

■ Beautiful bay window in formal Dining Room

■ Convenient Kitchen with cooktop work island, pantry, octagon Dining area, and nearby Study, Laundry and Garage entry

■ Luxurious Master Bedroom offers a glass alcove, walk-in closet and pampering bath with a corner tub

■ Three additional bedrooms with decorative windows, share a full bath

■ No materials list is available

FIRST FLOOR — 1,514 SQ. FT.
SECOND FLOOR —1,219 SQ. FT.

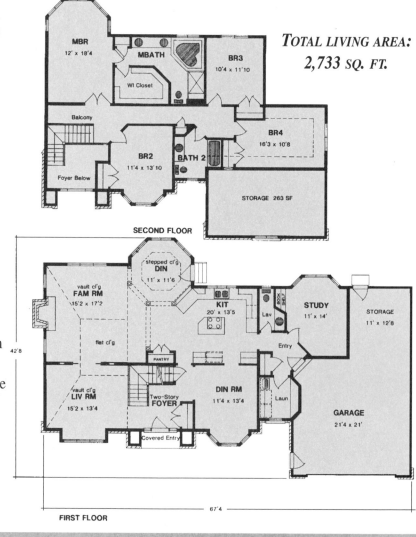

TOTAL LIVING AREA: 2,733 SQ. FT.

SECOND FLOOR

FIRST FLOOR

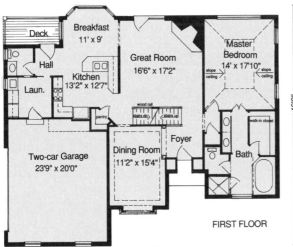

FIRST FLOOR

Deck

Breakfast
11' x 9'

Hall

Kitchen
13'2" x 12'7"

Laun.

Great Room
16'6" x 17'2"

Master
Bedroom
14' x 17'10"
slope ceiling · slope ceiling

pantry

wood rail
stairs dn. · stairs up.

walk-in closet

Two-car Garage
23'9" x 20'0"

Dining Room
11'2" x 15'4"

Foyer

Bath

46'8"

54'8"

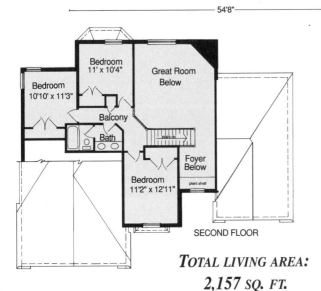

SECOND FLOOR

Bedroom
11' x 10'4"

Bedroom
10'10" x 11'3"

Great Room
Below

Balcony

Bath

Foyer
Below

plant shelf

Bedroom
11'2" x 12'11"

TOTAL LIVING AREA:
2,157 SQ. FT.

A Traditional Two-Story with Character

Price Code: C

■ This plan features:
— Four bedrooms
— Two full and one half baths

■ Front entrance into two-story Foyer with a plant shelf and lovely railing staircase

■ Expansive Great Room with corner fireplace and access to rear yard topped by two-story ceiling

■ Efficient Kitchen with peninsula counter, walk-in pantry, Breakfast bay and access to Deck, Laundry, Garage entry and formal Dining Room

■ Secluded Master Bedroom offers a sloped ceiling and lavish bath with walk-in closet

■ Three additional bedrooms on second floor share a double vanity bath

■ No materials list available for this plan

FIRST FLOOR — 1,511 SQ. FT.
SECOND FLOOR — 646 SQ. FT.
BASEMENT — 1,479 SQ. FT.
GARAGE — 475 SQ. FT.

Luxurious Elegance

Price Code: E

- ■ This plan features:
- — Four bedrooms
- — Three full and one half baths
- ■ Double door leads into two-story entry with an exquisite curved staircase
- ■ Formal Living Room features a marble hearth fireplace, triple window and built-in book shelves
- ■ Formal Dining Room defined by columns and a lovely bay window
- ■ Efficient Kitchen offers cooktop/work island, Utility/Garage entry and serving counter for informal Dining area
- ■ Expansive Great Room with entertainment center, fieldstone fireplace, cathedral ceiling and access to Covered Patio
- ■ Vaulted ceiling crowns Master Bedroom suite offering a plush bath and two walk-in closets
- ■ Three second floor bedrooms, one with a private bath, have walk-in closets
- ■ No materials list available for this plan

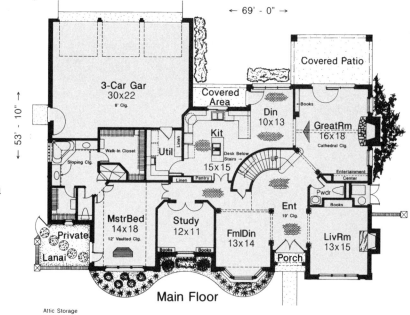

Main Floor

← 69' - 0" →

← 53' - 10" →

3-Car Gar 30x22
Covered Area
Din 10x13
GreatRm 16x18 Cathedral Clg.
Covered Patio
Kit 15x15
Util
Walk-In Closet
Entertainment Center
MstrBed 14x18 12' Vaulted Clg.
Study 12x11
FmlDin 13x14
Ent 19' Clg.
Pwdr
LivRm 13x15
Private
Lanai
Porch

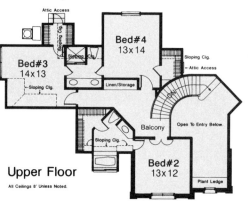

Upper Floor

All Ceilings 8' Unless Noted.

Attic Storage
Attic Access
Bed#3 14x13
Bed#4 13x14
Bed#2 13x12
Balcony
Open To Entry Below
Linen/Storage
Plant Ledge

MAIN FLOOR — 2,190 SQ. FT.
UPPER FLOOR — 920 SQ. FT.
GARAGE — 624 SQ. FT.

TOTAL LIVING AREA: 3,110 SQ. FT.

Plenty of Charm

Price Code: B

■ This plan features:

— Three bedrooms

— Two full and one half baths

■ Double dormer, arched window and covered Porch add light and space

■ Open Foyer graced by banister staircase and Balcony

■ Spacious Activity Room with a pre-fab fireplace opens to formal Dining Room

■ Country-size Kitchen/ Breakfast Area with island counter and access to Sun Deck and Laundry/Garage entry

■ First floor Bedroom highlighted by lovely arched window below a tray ceiling and a pampering Bath

■ Two upstairs Bedrooms share a twin vanity Bath

■ An optional basement or crawl space foundation — please specify when ordering

FIRST FLOOR — 1,165 SQ. FT.
SECOND FLOOR — 587 SQ. FT.
BASEMENT — 1,165 SQ. FT.
GARAGE — 455 SQ. FT.

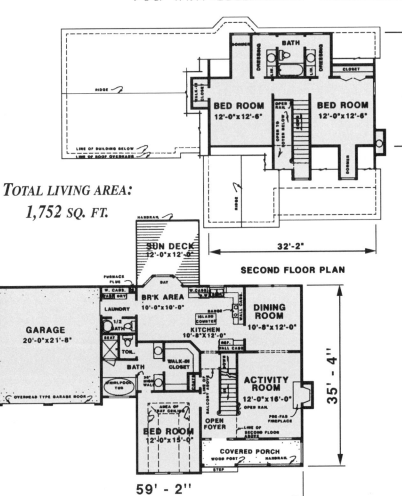

TOTAL LIVING AREA:
1,752 SQ. FT.

SECOND FLOOR PLAN

FIRST FLOOR PLAN

Simple Lines Enhanced by Elegant Window Treatment

Price Code: A

■ This plan features:

— Two bedrooms (optional third)

— Two full baths

■ A huge, arched window that floods the front room with natural light

■ A homey, well-lit Office or Den

■ Compact, efficient use of space

■ An efficient Kitchen with easy access to the Dining Room

■ A fireplaced Living Room with a sloping ceiling and a window wall

■ A Master Bedroom sporting a private master Bath with a roomy walk-in closet

MAIN FLOOR — 1,492 SQ. FT.
BASEMENT — 1,486 SQ. FT.
GARAGE — 462 SQ. FT.

TOTAL LIVING AREA:
1,492 SQ. FT.

An EXCLUSIVE DESIGN
By Karl Kreeger

ZIP QUOTE
HOME COST CALCULATOR
see order pages for details

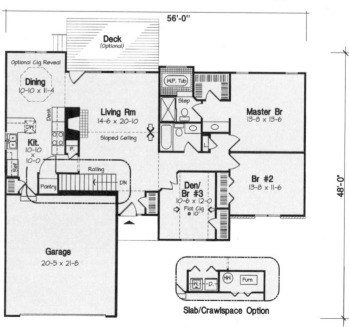

MAIN FLOOR

22

Unique Turret Master Bedroom

Price Code: C

■ This plan features:

— Three bedrooms

— Two full and one half baths

■ Curved glass entry into two-story Foyer with graceful, apron staircase

■ Sunken Great Room with focal point fireplace and atrium door to Deck

■ Efficient U-shaped Kitchen with work island, built-in Pantry, breakfast alcove

■ Sloped ceiling accents window alcove in Master Bedroom suite offering a plush Bath and walk-in closet

■ No materials list is available for this plan

FIRST FLOOR — 1,626 SQ. FT.
SECOND FLOOR — 475 SQ. FT.
BASEMENT — 1,512 SQ. FT.
GARAGE — 438 SQ. FT.

TOTAL LIVING AREA:
2,101 SQ. FT.

ZIP QUOTE
HOME COST CALCULATOR
see order pages for details

Second floor

First floor

WIDTH 59'-0''
DEPTH 60'-8''

Attractive Styling

Price Code: B

- This plan features:
— Three bedrooms
— Two full baths
- Tremendous style and presence created by windows, sidelights and transoms combined with a dramatic entrance
- Formal Dining Room, off the Foyer, enjoying a view of the front yard and access to the Family Room
- A grand fireplace, with windows to either side, serves as a focal point
- Breakfast Room/Kitchen are open to the Family Room
- Secluded Master Suite with walk-in closet, recessed ceiling and five-piece Bath
- No materials list is available for this plan

MAIN FLOOR — 1,849 SQ. FT.
GARAGE — 555 SQ. FT.

TOTAL LIVING AREA:
1,849 SQ. FT.

WIDTH 66'-4"
DEPTH 59'-10"

MAIN FLOOR

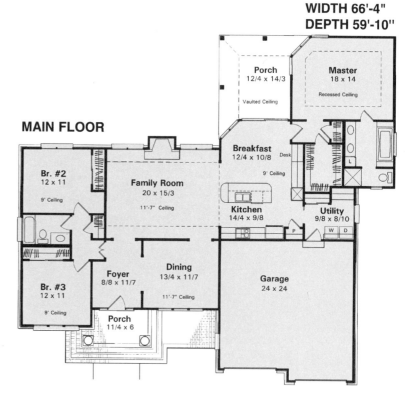

An EXCLUSIVE DESIGN
By Greg Marquis

24

ZIP QUOTE
HOME COST CALCULATOR
see order pages for details

Exciting Impact

Price Code: D

FIRST FLOOR

Great Room
15'6" x 18'1"

high ceiling

Breakfast
11'7" x 12'0"

Laun.

hanging space

entertainment center

walk-in closet

Bath

wood rail   stairs dn

Kitchen
11'9" x 11'

Hall

walk-in pantry

Bath

Master Bedroom
13' x 13'11"

Foyer

Dining Room
11' x 13'

Porch

Two-car Garage
20' x 21'

58'6"

49'

TOTAL LIVING AREA:
2,209 SQ. FT.

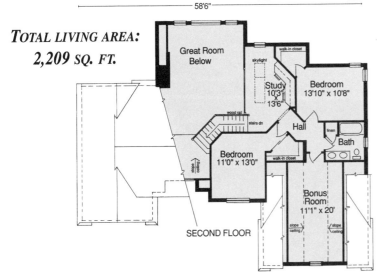

SECOND FLOOR

Great Room
Below

skylight

walk-in closet

Study
10'3" x 13'6"

Bedroom
13'10" x 10'8"

wood rail   stairs dn

Hall

linen

Bath

slope ceiling

Bedroom
11'0" x 13'0"

walk-in closet

Bonus
Room
11'1" x 20'

slope ceiling   slope ceiling

■ This plan features:
— Three bedrooms
— Two full and one half baths

■ Keystone arch accents entrance into open Foyer with lovely angled staircase and sloped ceiling

■ Great Room with entertainment center, hearth fireplace and a wall of windows overlooks the back yard

■ Efficient, angled Kitchen offers work island/snackbar, Breakfast area next to Dining Room, Laundry, and Garage entry

■ Master Bedroom wing features a lavish Bath with two vanities, large walk-in closet and corner window tub

■ Two second floor bedrooms with walk-in closets share a skylit Study, double vanity bath and a Bonus Room

■ No materials list is available

FIRST FLOOR — 1,542 SQ. FT.
SECOND FLOOR — 667 SQ. FT.
BONUS ROOM — 236 SQ. FT.
GARAGE — 420 SQ. FT.

Arches Add Ambiance

Price Code: D

■ This plan features:

— Four bedrooms

— Two full and one half baths

■ Arched two-story entrance highlighted by a lovely arched window

■ Expansive Den offers hearth fireplace between book shelves, raised ceiling and access to rear yard

■ Efficient Kitchen with peninsula counter, built-in pantry, Breakfast bay, Garage entry, laundry and adjoining Dining room

■ Private Master Bedroom enhanced by a large walk-in closet and plush bath

■ Three second floor bedrooms with walk-in closets share a double vanity bath

■ An optional slab or crawl space foundation — please specify when ordering

FIRST FLOOR — 1,250 SQ. FT.
SECOND FLOOR — 783 SQ. FT
GARAGE AND STORAGE — 555 SQ. FT.

TOTAL LIVING AREA:
2,033 SQ. FT.

First floor

Second floor

Towering Windows Enhance Elegance

Price Code: E

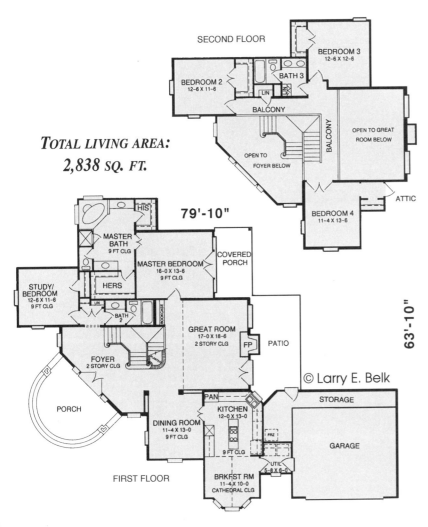

SECOND FLOOR

BEDROOM 3
12-6 X 12-6

BEDROOM 2
12-6 X 11-6

BATH 3

LIN

BALCONY

OPEN TO GREAT
ROOM BELOW

OPEN TO
FOYER BELOW

BALCONY

ATTIC

BEDROOM 4
11-4 X 13-6

TOTAL LIVING AREA:
2,838 SQ. FT.

HIS

MASTER
BATH
9 FT CLG

79'-10"

MASTER BEDROOM
16-0 X 13-6
9 FT CLG

COVERED
PORCH

STUDY/
BEDROOM
12-6 X 11-6
9 FT CLG

HERS

LIN

BATH
2

BOOKCASE

63'-10"

GREAT ROOM
17-0 X 18-6
2 STORY CLG

FP

PATIO

FOYER
2 STORY CLG

© Larry E. Belk

PORCH

PAN

STORAGE

KITCHEN
12-0 X 13-0

FRZ

DINING ROOM
11-4 X 13-0
9 FT CLG

9 FT CLG

GARAGE

UTIL
5-8 X 6-0

FIRST FLOOR

BRKFST RM
11-4 X 10-0
CATHEDRAL CLG

■ This plan features:

— Four bedrooms

— Three full baths

■ Designed for a corner or pie-shaped lot

■ Spectacular split staircase highlights Foyer

■ Expansive Great Room with hearth fireplace opens to formal Dining Room and Patio

■ Quiet Study easily another Bedroom or Home Office

■ Secluded Master Bedroom suite offers private Porch, two walk-in closets, vanity, and a corner whirlpool tub

■ Three second floor Bedrooms with walk-in closets, share a balcony and double vanity Bath

■ No materials list is available for this plan

FIRST FLOOR — 1,966 SQ. FT.
SECOND FLOOR — 872 SQ. FT.
GARAGE — 569 SQ. FT.

ZIP·QUOTE
HOME COST CALCULATOR
see order pages for details

Impressive Two–Story

Price Code: E

■ This plan features:

— Four bedrooms

— Two full and one half baths

■ Two-story Foyer highlighted by lovely, angled staircase and decorative window

■ Bay windows enhance Dining and Living rooms

■ Efficient Kitchen with work island and an open Breakfast area with back yard access

■ Spacious, yet cozy Family Room with a fireplace and Future Sunroom access

■ Private Master Suite offers a walk-in closet and pampering bath

■ Three additional bedrooms share a double vanity bath and large Study

FIRST FLOOR — 1,497 SQ. FT.
SECOND FLOOR — 1,460 SQ. FT.
FUTURE SUNROOM — 210 SQ. FT.
GARAGE — 680 SQ. FT.

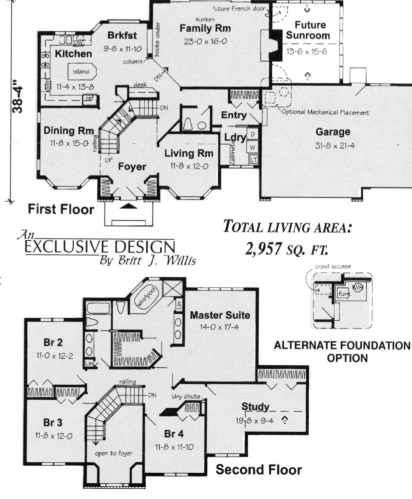

An
EXCLUSIVE DESIGN
By Britt J. Willis

TOTAL LIVING AREA:
2,957 SQ. FT.

ALTERNATE FOUNDATION OPTION

ZIP QUOTE
HOME COST CALCULATOR
see order pages for details

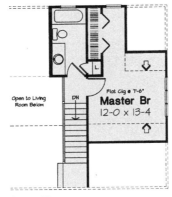

Open to Living
Room Below

DN

Flat Clg @ 7'-6"
Master Br
12-0 x 13-4

Upper Floor

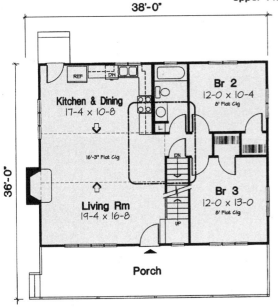

38'-0"

REF DW

Kitchen & Dining
17-4 x 10-8

16'-3" Flat Clg

Living Rm
19-4 x 16-8

UP

DN

L

Br 2
12-0 x 10-4
8' Flat Clg

Br 3
12-0 x 13-0
8' Flat Clg

36'-0"

Porch

Main Floor

FURN HH

Crawl
Space
Access

Crawl Space / Slab Plan

Rustic Exterior;
Complete Home

Price Code: A

■ This plan features:

— Three bedrooms

— Two full baths

■ A two-story, fireplaced Living Room with exposed beams adds to the rustic charm

■ An efficient, modern Kitchen with ample work and storage space

■ Two first floor bedrooms with individual closet space share a full bath

■ A Master Bedroom secluded on the second floor with its own full bath

■ A welcoming front Porch adding to the living space

MAIN FLOOR — 1,013 SQ. FT.
UPPER FLOOR — 315 SQ. FT.
BASEMENT — 1,013 SQ. FT.

TOTAL LIVING AREA:
1,328 SQ. FT.

Comfortable Vacation Living

Price Code: C

- This plan features:
- — Three bedrooms
- — Three full and one half baths

- A wrap-around Deck offering views and access into the Living Room

- A sunken Living Room with a vaulted ceiling, and a raised-hearth fireplace adjoining the Dining area

- An open Kitchen with a corner sink and windows, an eating bar and a walk-in storage/pantry

- Two private Bedroom suites with sliding glass doors leading to a Deck, walk-in closets and plush baths

- A Loft area with a walk-in closet, attic access, and a private bath and a Deck

FIRST FLOOR — 1,704 SQ FT
SECOND FLOOR — 313 SQ. FT.

TOTAL LIVING AREA:
2,017 SQ. FT.

Second floor

WIDTH 58'- 0"
DEPTH 48'- 0"

First floor

ohy Supplied By The Meredith Corporation

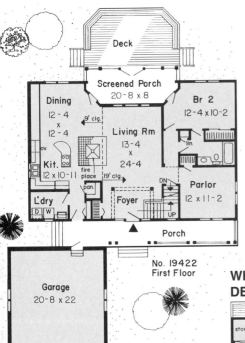

Deck

Screened Porch
20-8 x 8

Dining
12-4
x
12-4

Br 2
12-4 x 10-2

Living Rm
13-4
x
24-4

Kit.
12 x 10-11

fire place

Parlor
12 x 11-2

L'dry
D W

Foyer

Porch

Garage
20-8 x 22

No. 19422
First Floor

TOTAL LIVING AREA:
1,695 SQ. FT.

ZIP QUOTE
HOME COST CALCULATOR
see order pages for details

WIDTH 50'-8"
DEPTH 61'-8"

stor. Balc. seat

deco. box beams

MBr
15-8 x 11-9

beams @ foyer below

DN

make-up

Second Floor   deco. beam

Master Retreat Crowns Spacious Home

Price Code: B

■ This plan features:
— Two bedrooms
— Two full baths

■ An open Foyer leading up an landing staircase with windows above and into a two-story Living Room

■ A unique four-sided fireplace separates the Living Room, Dining area and Kitchen

■ A well-equipped Kitchen featuring a cook island, a walk-in Pantry and access to Dining Area and Laundry Room

■ A three season Screened Porch and Deck beyond adjoining Dining Room, Living Room, and second Bedroom

■ An private second floor Master Suite offering a dormer window seat, private balcony, and relaxing window tub

FIRST FLOOR — 1,290 SQ. FT.
SECOND FLOOR — 405 SQ. FT.
SCREENED PORCH — 152 SQ. FT.
GARAGE — 513 SQ. FT.

Elegant Residence

Price Code: E

■ This plan features:

— Three bedrooms

— Three full and one half baths

■ Central Foyer opens into the Great Room accented by hearth fireplace

■ Formal Dining Room with a bay window

■ Glass Breakfast Area extends from Kitchen

■ Cooktop island/snack bar in the Kitchen

■ Master Bedroom wing has Patio access

■ Two second floor Bedrooms with full Baths

■ An optional basement or crawl space foundation — please specify when ordering

■ No materials list is available for this plan

FIRST FLOOR — 2,214 SQ. FT.
SECOND FLOOR — 884 SQ. FT.
BONUS — 330 SQ. FT.
BASEMENT — 2,150 SQ. FT.
GARAGE — 525 SQ. FT.

TOTAL LIVING AREA:
3,098 SQ. FT.

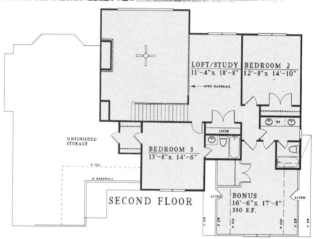

SECOND FLOOR

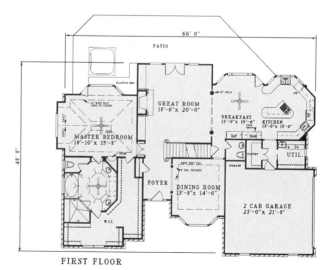

FIRST FLOOR

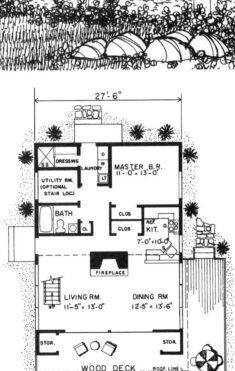

FIRST FLOOR
No. 90028

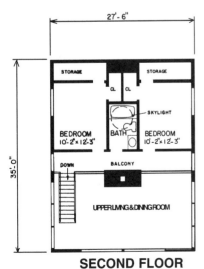

SECOND FLOOR

Modern Design Highlighted by Split Roofline

Price Code: B

■ This plan features:

— Three bedrooms

— Two full baths

■ An energy efficient solar hot water system with solar flat-plate collector panels and double glazed windows

■ A Living/Dining Area accentuated by massive stonefaced, heat-circulating fireplace

■ Upstairs Bedrooms share a skylit full Bath

FIRST FLOOR — 960 SQ. FT.
SECOND FLOOR — 580 SQ. FT.
WOOD DECK — 460 SQ. FT.

TOTAL LIVING AREA:
1,540 SQ. FT.

Country Styled Home

Price Code: C

- ■ This plan features:
- — Three bedrooms
- — Two full and one half baths
- ■ A Country style front Porch provides a warm welcome
- ■ The Family Room is highlighted by a fireplace and front windows
- ■ The Dining Room is separated from the U-shaped Kitchen by only an extended counter
- ■ The first floor Master Suite pampers the owners with a walk-in closet and a five-piece Bath
- ■ There are two additional Bedrooms with a convenient Bath in the hall

FIRST FLOOR — 1,288 SQ. FT.
SECOND FLOOR — 545 SQ. FT.
GARAGE — 540 SQ. FT.

TOTAL LIVING AREA:
1,833 SQ. FT.

An
EXCLUSIVE DESIGN
By Greg Marquis

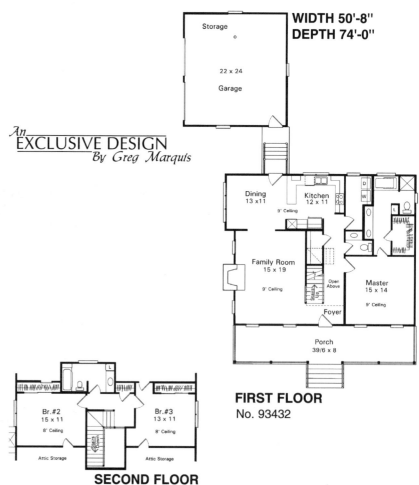

WIDTH 50'-8"
DEPTH 74'-0"

Storage

22 x 24

Garage

Dining 13 x 11
Kitchen 12 x 11
9' Ceiling

Family Room 15 x 19
9' Ceiling

Open Above

Master 15 x 14
9' Ceiling

Foyer

Porch 39/6 x 8

FIRST FLOOR
No. 93432

Br.#2 15 x 11
8' Ceiling

Br.#3 13 x 11
8' Ceiling

Attic Storage

Attic Storage

SECOND FLOOR

A Custom Look
PRICE CODE: E

This plan features:
- Three bedrooms
- Three full and one half baths
- Wonderfully balanced exterior highlighted by triple arched glass in Entry Porch, leading into the Gallery Foyer
- Triple arches lead into Formal Living and Dining Room, Verandah and beyond
- Kitchen, Nook, and Leisure Room area easily flow together
- Owners' wing has a Master Suite with glass alcove to rear yard, a lavish bath and a Study offering many uses
- Two additional bedrooms with corner windows and over-sized closets access a full bath
- No materials list available for this plan

MAIN FLOOR — 2,978 SQ. FT.
GARAGE — 702 SQ. FT.

TOTAL LIVING AREA:
2,978 SQ. FT.

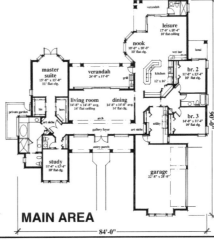

MAIN AREA

One-Story Country Home
PRICE CODE: A

This plan features:
- Three bedrooms
- Two full baths
- A Living Room with an imposing, high ceiling that slopes down to a normal height of eight feet, focusing on the decorative heat-circulating fireplace at the rear wall
- An efficient Kitchen that adjoins the Dining Room that views the front Porch
- A Dinette Area for informal eating in the Kitchen that can comfortably seat six people
- A Master Suite arranged with a large dressing area that has a walk-in closet plus two linear closets and space for a vanity
- Two family bedrooms that share a full hall bath

MAIN AREA — 1,367 SQ. FT.
BASEMENT — 1,267 SQ. FT.
GARAGE — 431 SQ. FT.

TOTAL LIVING AREA:
1,367 SQ. FT.

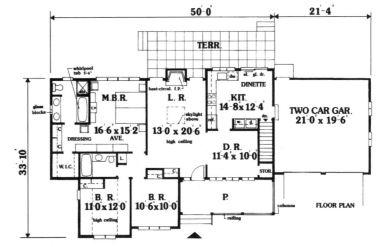

PLAN NO. 96458

Country Charm and Convenience
PRICE CODE: D

■ This plan features:
— Three bedrooms
— Two full baths
■ The open design pulls the Great Room, Kitchen and Breakfast Bay into one common area
■ Cathedral ceilings in the Great Room, Master Bedroom and a secondary bedroom
■ The rear Deck expands the living and entertaining space
■ The Dining Room provides a quiet place for relaxed family dinners
■ Two additional Bedrooms share a full Bath

MAIN FLOOR — 1,512 SQ. FT.
GARAGE & STORAGE — 455 SQ. FT.

TOTAL LIVING AREA:
1,512 SQ. FT.

PLAN NO. 90441

Modest Ranch Has Features of a Larger Plan
PRICE CODE: C

■ This plan features:
— Three bedrooms
— Two full baths
■ A large Great Room with a vaulted ceiling and a stone fireplace with bookshelves on either side
■ A spacious Kitchen with ample cabinet space conveniently located next to the large Dining Room
■ A Master Suite having a large Bath with a garden tub, double vanity and a walk-in closet
■ Two other large Bedrooms, each with a walk-in closet and access to the full Bath
■ An optional basement, slab or crawl space foundation — please specify when ordering

MAIN FLOOR — 1,811 SQ. FT.
BASEMENT — 1,811 SQ. FT.
GARAGE — 484 SQ. FT.

TOTAL LIVING AREA:
1,811 SQ. FT.

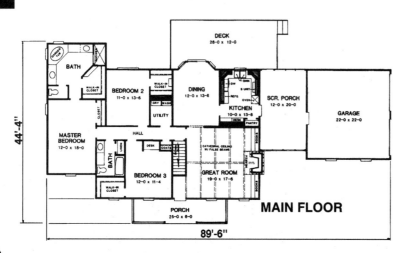

36

To order your Blueprints, call 1-800-235-5700

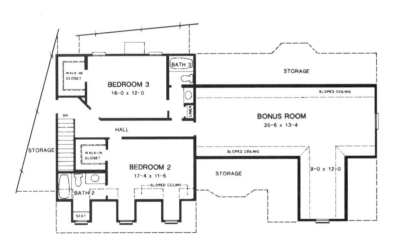

Traditional That Has It All

Price Code: E

- This plan features:
  — Three bedrooms
  — Three full and two half baths
- A Master Suite with two closets and a private bath with separate shower, corner tub and dual vanities
- A large Dining Room with a bay window, adjacent to the Kitchen
- A formal Living Room for entertaining and a cozy Family Room with fireplace for informal relaxation
- Two upstairs Bedrooms with walk-in closets and private Baths
- A Bonus Room to allow the house to grow with your needs
- An optional basement, slab or crawl space foundation — please specify when ordering

FIRST FLOOR — 1,927 SQ. FT.
SECOND FLOOR — 832 SQ. FT.
BONUS ROOM — 624 SQ. FT.
BASEMENT — 1,674 SQ. FT.

TOTAL LIVING AREA:
2,759 SQ. FT.

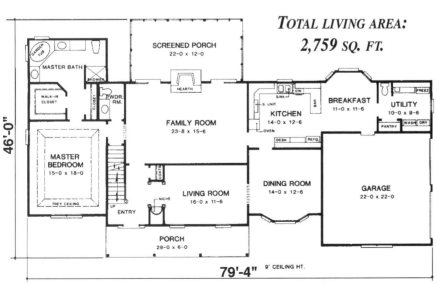

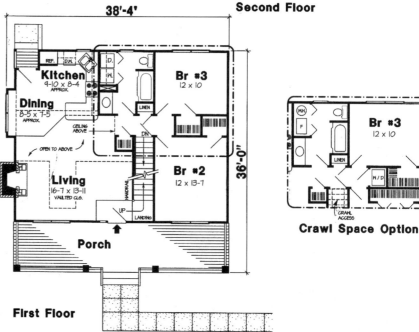

Large Front Porch
Adds a Country Touch

Price Code: A

■ This plan features:

— Three bedrooms

— Two full baths

■ A country-styled front porch

■ Vaulted ceiling in the Living Room which includes a fireplace

■ An efficient Kitchen with double sinks and peninsula counter that may double as an eating bar

■ Two first floor bedrooms with ample closet space

■ A second floor Master Suite with sloped ceiling, walk-in closet and private master Bath

FIRST FLOOR — 1,007 SQ. FT.
SECOND FLOOR — 408 SQ. FT.

TOTAL LIVING AREA:
1,415 SQ. FT.

ZIP·QUOTE
HOME COST CALCULATOR
see order pages for details

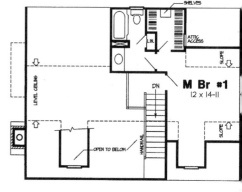

Second Floor

M Br #1
12 x 14-11

SHELVES
LIN.
ATTIC ACCESS
LEVEL CEILING
SLOPE
DN
OPEN TO BELOW
HANDRAIL
SLOPE

38'-4'

36'-0''

REF.   D.W.
D.
W.
Kitchen
9-10 x 8-4
APPROX.
Dining
8-5 x 7-5
APPROX.
CEILING ABOVE
LINEN
Br #3
12 x 10
OPEN TO ABOVE
DN
Living
16-7 x 13-11
VAULTED CLG.
HANDRAIL
UP
LANDING
Br #2
12 x 13-7
Porch

First Floor

Crawl Space Option

M.H.
F
Br #3
12 x 10
LINEN
W/D
CRAWL ACCESS

To order your Blueprints, call 1-800-235-5700

Keystone Arches and Decorative Windows

PRICE CODE: B

- This plan features:
  - Three bedrooms
  - Two full baths
- Brick and stucco enhance the dramatic front elevation and volume entrance
- Inviting Entry leads into expansive Great Room with hearth fireplace framed by transom window
- Bay window Dining Room topped by decorative ceiling convenient to the Great Room and the Kitchen/Breakfast area
- Corner Master Suite enjoys a tray ceiling, roomy walk-in closet and a plush bath with a double vanity and whirlpool window tub
- Two additional bedrooms with large closets, share a full bath

MAIN FLOOR — 1,666 SQ. FT.
BASEMENT — 1,666 SQ. FT.
GARAGE — 496 SQ. FT.

TOTAL LIVING AREA:
1,666 SQ. FT.

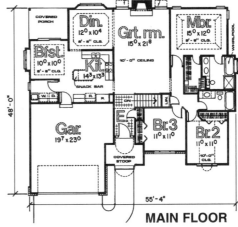

MAIN FLOOR

Bay Windows and a Terrific Front Porch

PRICE CODE: B

- This plan features:
  - Three bedrooms
  - Two full baths
- A country front porch
- An expansive Living Area that includes a fireplace
- A Master Suite with a private Master Bath and a walk-in closet, as well as a bay window view of the front yard
- An efficient Kitchen that serves the sunny Breakfast Area and the Dining Room with equal ease
- A built-in pantry and a desk add to the conveniences in the Breakfast Area
- Two additional bedrooms that share the full hall bath
- A convenient main floor Laundry Room

MAIN AREA — 1,778 SQ. FT.
BASEMENT — 1,008 SQ. FT.
GARAGE — 728 SQ. FT.

TOTAL LIVING AREA:
1,778 SQ. FT.

ZIP QUOTE
HOME COST CALCULATOR
see order pages for details

An
EXCLUSIVE DESIGN
By Jannis Vann & Associates, Inc.

MAIN AREA

PLAN NO. 90398

Interior and Exterior Unity Distinguishes Plan

PRICE CODE: B

- This plan features:
— Three bedrooms
— Two full baths
- A vaulted ceiling Living Room with cozy fireplace
- Columns dividing the Living and Dining Rooms, and half-walls separating the Kitchen and Breakfast Room
- A luxurious Master Suite with a private skylit Bath, double vanity and a generous walk-in closet

MAIN AREA —1,630 SQ. FT.

TOTAL LIVING AREA:
1,630 SQ. FT.

PLAN NO. 92220

Southern Hospitality

PRICE CODE: C

- This plan features:
— Three bedrooms
— Two full baths
- Welcoming covered Veranda catches breezes
- Easy-care, tiled Entry leads into Great Room with fieldstone fireplace and atrium door to another covered Veranda topped by a cathedral ceiling
- A bright Kitchen/Dining Room includes a stovetop island/ snackbar, built-in Pantry and desk and access to covered Veranda
- Vaulted ceiling crowns Master Bedroom that offers a plush Bath and huge walk-in closet
- Two additional Bedrooms with ample closets share a double vanity Bath
- No materials list is available for this plan

MAIN FLOOR — 1,830 SQ. FT.
GARAGE — 759 SQ. FT.

TOTAL LIVING AREA:
1,830 SQ. FT.

ZIP QUOTE
HOME COST CALCULATOR
see order pages for details

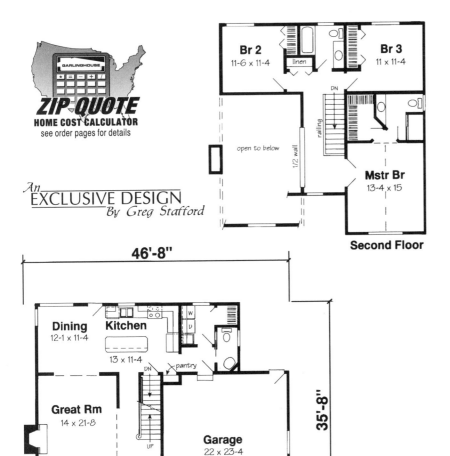

ZIP·QUOTE
HOME COST CALCULATOR
see order pages for details

An
EXCLUSIVE DESIGN
By Greg Stafford

Br 2
11-6 x 11-4

linen

Br 3
11 x 11-4

DN

open to below

1/2 wall

railing

Mstr Br
13-4 x 15

Second Floor

46'-8"

35'-8"

Dining
12-1 x 11-4

Kitchen
13 x 11-4

W D

pantry

DN

Great Rm
14 x 21-8

open to above

UP

Garage
22 x 23-4

First Floor

Second Floor Balcony Overlooks Great Room

Price Code: B

■ This plan features:

— Three bedrooms

— Two full and one half baths

■ A Great Room with a focal point fireplace and a two story ceiling

■ An efficient Kitchen with a work island and built-in pantry

■ A convenient first floor Laundry Room

■ A Dining Room with easy access to both the Kitchen and the outside

■ A Master Suite with a private master Bath and a walk-in closet

■ No materials list is available with this plan

FIRST FLOOR — 891 SQ. FT.
SECOND FLOOR — 894 SQ. FT.
GARAGE — 534 SQ. FT.
BASEMENT — 891 SQ. FT.

TOTAL LIVING AREA:
1,785 SQ. FT.

Wrap-Around Country Porch Provides a Warm Welcome

Price Code: C

■ This plan features:

— Three bedrooms

— Two full and one half baths

■ Living Room with fireplace

■ A U-shaped Kitchen including a breakfast bar, built-in pantry and planning desk and a double sink

■ A Mudroom entry that will help keep the dirt from play or muddy shoes away from the rest of the home

■ A sunny Breakfast Nook providing a cheerful place to start your day

■ A Master Suite highlighted by a walk-in closet and a private Master Bath

■ Two additional bedrooms, one with a built-in desk, share a full hall bath

FIRST FLOOR — 1,113 SQ. FT.
SECOND FLOOR — 970 SQ. FT.
GARAGE — 480 SQ. FT.
BASEMENT — 1,113 SQ. FT.

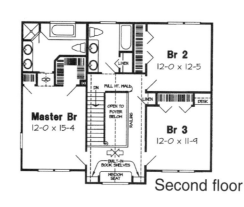

Second floor

TOTAL LIVING AREA:
2,083 SQ. FT.

Crawl Space/Slab Option

First floor

To order your Blueprints, call 1-800-235-5700

Dramatic Ranch

PRICE CODE: B

This plan features:
- Three bedrooms
- Two full baths
- A large Living Room with a stone fireplace and a decorative beamed ceiling
- A Kitchen/Dining Room arrangement which makes the rooms seem more spacious
- A Laundry with a large Pantry located close to the bedrooms and the Kitchen
- A Master Bedroom with a walk-in closet and a private Master Bath
- Two additional Bedrooms, one with a walk-in closet, that share the full hall Bath

FIRST FLOOR — 1,792 SQ. FT.
BASEMENT — 818 SQ. FT.
GARAGE — 857 SQ. FT.

TOTAL LIVING AREA:
1,792 SQ. FT.

ZIP QUOTE
HOME COST CALCULATOR
see order pages for details

An
EXCLUSIVE DESIGN
By Karl Kreeger

56'-0"

Deck

Kitchen 12 x 11-4 | Dining Rm 9 x 11-4 | pantry | Ldry | MBr 1 14-2 x 14-4

Living Rm 21-6 x 19-4 decor. beams

Br 3 12 x 12-6 | Br 2 12 x 12-6

32'-0"

MAIN AREA

Multiple Gables and a Cozy Front Porch

PRICE CODE: B

This plan features:
- Three bedrooms
- Two full baths
- Multiple gables and a cozy front Porch
- A Foyer area that leads to a bright and cheery Great Room capped by a sloped ceiling and highlighted by a fireplace
- The Dining Area includes double hung windows and angles adding light and dimension to the room
- A functional Kitchen providing an abundance of counter space with additional room provided by a breakfast bar
- A rear Porch is accessed from the Dining Area
- A Master Bedroom Suite including a walk-in closet and private Bath
- Two additional Bedrooms share a full Bath in the hall
- No materials list is available

MAIN FLOOR — 1,508 SQ. FT.
BASEMENT — 1,429 SQ. FT.
GARAGE — 440 SQ. FT.

TOTAL LIVING AREA:
1,508 SQ. FT.

ZIP QUOTE
HOME COST CALCULATOR
see order pages for details

MAIN AREA

Porch | Dining Area 11'6" x 14'2" | Great Room 16'6" x 17' | Master Bedroom 14' x 11'9"

Kitchen 18' x 10'10"

Two-car Garage 20' x 22' | Laun. | Foyer | Bath | Hall | Bath

Porch | Bedroom 11' x 10'6" | Bedroom 10'6" x 10'6"

47'

60'

To order your Blueprints, call 1-800-235-5700

Traditional Ranch Plan
PRICE CODE: D

■ This plan features:
— Three bedrooms
— Two full baths
■ Large Foyer set between the formal Living and Dining rooms
■ Spacious Great Room is adjacent to the open Kitchen /Breakfast Area
■ Secluded Master Bedroom highlighted by the Master Bath with a garden tub, separate shower and his-n-her vanity
■ Bay window allows bountiful natural light into the Breakfast Area
■ Two additional Bedrooms sharing a full Bath
■ An optional basement or crawl space foundation — please specify when ordering

MAIN AREA — 2,218 SQ. FT.
BASEMENT — 1,658 SQ. FT.
GARAGE — 528 SQ. FT.

TOTAL LIVING AREA:
2,218 SQ. FT.

MAIN AREA

Attractive Gables and Arches
PRICE CODE: B

■ This plan features:
— Three bedrooms
— Two full baths
■ Easy-care Entry opens to formal Dining Room with arched window
■ Angles and transom windows add interest to the Great Room
■ Bright Hearth area expands Breakfast/Kitchen Area and shares three-sided fireplace
■ Efficient Kitchen offers an angled snack bar, a large Pantry and nearby Laundry/Garage entry
■ Secluded Master Suite crowned by decorative ceiling and has a large walk-in closet and a plush Bath with a whirlpool tub
■ Two secondary Bedrooms in separate wing from Master Suite for added privacy

MAIN FLOOR — 1,782 SQ. FT.
BASEMENT — 1,782 SQ. FT.
GARAGE — 466 SQ. FT.

TOTAL LIVING AREA:
1,782 SQ. FT.

MAIN FLOOR

© design basics, inc.

To order your Blueprints, call 1-800-235-5700

PLAN NO. 92609

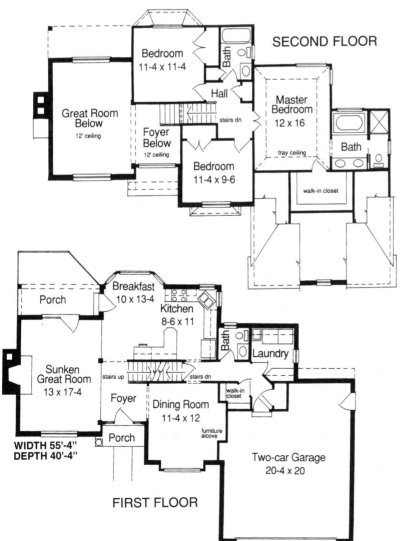

SECOND FLOOR

Bedroom
11-4 x 11-4

Bath

Hall

Master
Bedroom
12 x 16

tray ceiling

Great Room
Below
12' ceiling

Foyer
Below
12' ceiling

stairs dn

Bath

Bedroom
11-4 x 9-6

walk-in closet

Breakfast
10 x 13-4

Kitchen
8-6 x 11

Porch

Bath

Laundry

Sunken
Great Room
13 x 17-4

stairs up

stairs dn

walk-in
closet

Foyer

Dining Room
11-4 x 12

WIDTH 55'-4"
DEPTH 40'-4"

Porch

furniture
alcove

Two-car Garage
20-4 x 20

FIRST FLOOR

A Little Drama

Price Code: B

- ■ This plan features:
- — Three bedrooms
- — Two full and one half baths
- ■ A 12′ high Entry with transom and side-lights, multiple gables and a box window
- ■ A sunken Great Room with a fireplace and access to a rear Porch
- ■ A Breakfast Bay and Kitchen flowing into each other and accessing a rear Porch
- ■ A Master Bedroom with a tray ceiling, walk-in closet and a private Master Bath
- ■ No materials list is available for this plan

FIRST FLOOR — 960 SQ. FT.
SECOND FLOOR — 808 SQ. FT.
BASEMENT — 922 SQ. FT.
GARAGE — 413 SQ. FT.

TOTAL LIVING AREA:
1,768 SQ. FT.

Enticing Two-Story Traditional

Price Code: C

- This plan features:
— Four bedrooms
— Two full and one half baths
- A porch serving as a wonderful, relaxing area to enjoy the outdoors
- A Dining Room including a decorative ceiling and easy access to the Kitchen
- A Kitchen/Utility Area with access to the Garage
- A Living Room with double doors into the Family Room which features a fireplace and access to the Patio
- A Master Bedroom with two enormous walk-in closets, as well as a Dressing Area and private Bath

FIRST FLOOR — 955 SQ. FT.
SECOND FLOOR — 1,005 SQ. FT.
GARAGE — 484 SQ. FT.
BASEMENT — 930 SQ. FT.

TOTAL LIVING AREA:
1,960 SQ. FT.

An
EXCLUSIVE DESIGN
By Karl Kreeger

ZIP QUOTE
HOME COST CALCULATOR
see order pages for details

SECOND FLOOR

Slab/Crawlspace Option

FIRST FLOOR

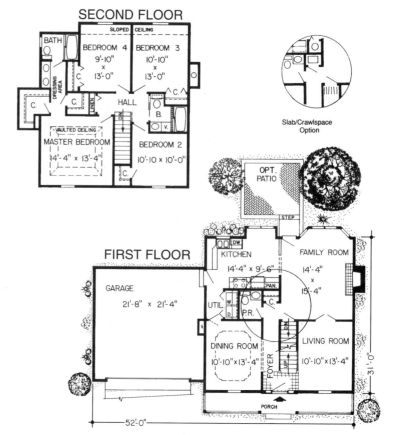

Open Spaces
PRICE CODE: A

This plan features:
- Three bedrooms
- Two full baths
- A Family Room, Kitchen and Breakfast Area that all connects to form a great space
- A double fireplace adding warmth and atmosphere to the Family Room, Kitchen and the Breakfast Area
- An efficient Kitchen that is highlighted by a peninsula counter and doubles as a snack bar
- A Master Suite that includes a walk-in closet, a double vanity, separate shower and tub Bath
- Two additional Bedrooms sharing a full hall Bath
- A wooden Deck that can be accessed from the Breakfast Area
- An optional crawl space or slab foundation — please specify when ordering

MAIN FLOOR — 1,388 SQ. FT.
GARAGE — 400 SQ. FT.

TOTAL LIVING AREA:
1,388 SQ. FT.

ZIP QUOTE
HOME COST CALCULATOR
see order pages for details

An
EXCLUSIVE DESIGN
By Jannis Vann & Associates, Inc.

For the Discriminating Buyer
PRICE CODE: B

This plan features:
- Three bedrooms
- Two full baths
- An attractive, classic brick design, with wood trim, multiple gables, and wing walls
- A sheltered entrance into the Foyer
- A sloped ceiling adding elegance to the formal Dining Room which flows easily into the Great Room
- A sloped ceiling and a corner fireplace enhancing the Great Room
- A Kitchen with a garden window above the double sink
- A peninsula counter joins the Kitchen and the Breakfast Room in an open layout
- A Master Suite, equipped with a large walk-in closet and a private Bath with an oval corner tub, separate shower and double vanity
- Two additional Bedrooms that share a full hall Bath
- No materials list is available for this plan

MAIN AREA — 1,710 SQ. FT.
GARAGE — 455 SQ. FT.
BASEMENT — 1,560 SQ. FT.

TOTAL LIVING AREA:
1,710 SQ. FT.

ZIP QUOTE
HOME COST CALCULATOR
see order pages for details

WIDTH 65'-10"
DEPTH 56'-0"

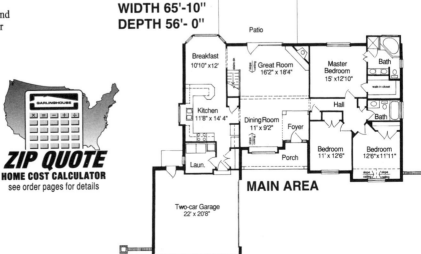

To order your Blueprints, call 1-800-235-5700

47

PLAN NO. 24701

Convenient Floor Plan
PRICE CODE: B

- This plan features:
  — Three bedrooms
  — Two full baths
- Central Foyer leads to Den/Guest Room with arched window below vaulted ceiling and Living Room accented by two-sided fireplace
- Efficient, U-shaped Kitchen with peninsula counter/breakfast bar serving Dining Room and adjacent Utility/Pantry
- Master Suite features large walk-in closet and private Bath with double vanity and whirlpool tub
- Two additional Bedrooms with ample closet space share full Bath

MAIN FLOOR — 1,625 SQ. FT.
BASEMENT — 1,625 SQ. FT.
GARAGE — 455 SQ. FT.

TOTAL LIVING AREA:
1,625 SQ. FT.

Main Floor

Alternate Foundation Plan

ZIP QUOTE
HOME COST CALCULATOR
see order pages for details

PLAN NO. 92544

Brick Detail with Arches
PRICE CODE: D

- This plan features:
  — Four bedrooms
  — Two full and one half baths
- Front and back Porches expand the living space and provide inviting access to the open layout
- Spacious Den with a fireplace flanked by built-in shelves and double access to the rear Porch
- Formal Dining Room with an arched window and direct access to the Kitchen
- Efficient, U-shaped Kitchen with a snackbar counter, a bright Breakfast Area and an adjoining Laundry and Garage
- Secluded Master Bedroom Suite with a walk-in closet and a double vanity Bath
- Three additional Bedrooms with walk-in closets, share one and half Baths
- An optional slab or crawl space foundation — please specify when ordering

MAIN FLOOR — 1,987 SQ. FT.
GARAGE/STORAGE — 515 SQ. FT.

TOTAL LIVING AREA:
1,987 SQ. FT.

MAIN FLOOR

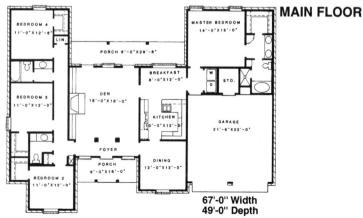

67'-0" Width
49'-0" Depth

To order your Blueprints, call 1-800-235-5700

Informal Family Living

Price Code: C

- This plan features:
  — Three bedrooms
  — Two full and one half baths
- Country styled front Porch sheltering front entrance
- Two-story Foyer gives an open and airy first impression
- Spacious Family Room highlighted by a focal point fireplace
- Kitchen/Dining area separated by an extended counter/snack bar
- First floor Master Suite enhanced by a walk-in closet, and a five piece Bath
- No materials list is available with this plan

FIRST FLOOR — 1,241 SQ. FT.
SECOND FLOOR — 633 SQ. FT.
BASEMENT — 1,241 SQ. FT.
GARAGE — 528 SQ. FT.

TOTAL LIVING AREA:
1,874 SQ. FT.

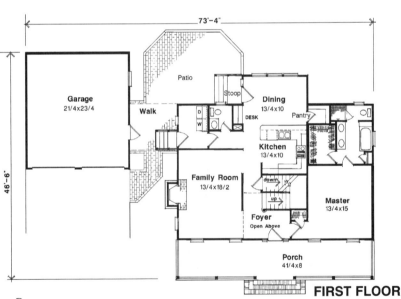

An EXCLUSIVE DESIGN *By Greg Marquis*

FIRST FLOOR No. 93433

SECOND FLOOR

Large Front Window Provides Natural Light

Price Code: B

- ■ This plan features:
- — Three bedrooms
- — Two full and one half baths
- ■ An outstanding, two-story Great Room with an unusual floor-to-ceiling, corner front window and cozy, hearth fireplace
- ■ A formal Dining Room opening from the Great Room
- ■ An efficient Kitchen with a work island and pantry, opens to the Great Room, and a bright eating Nook
- ■ A quiet Master Suite with a vaulted ceiling and a plush Bath with a walk-in closet
- ■ Two more bedrooms share a full hall bath and a Bonus area for multiple uses

FIRST FLOOR — 1,230 SQ. FT.
SECOND FLOOR — 477 SQ. FT.
BONUS ROOM — 195 SQ. FT.

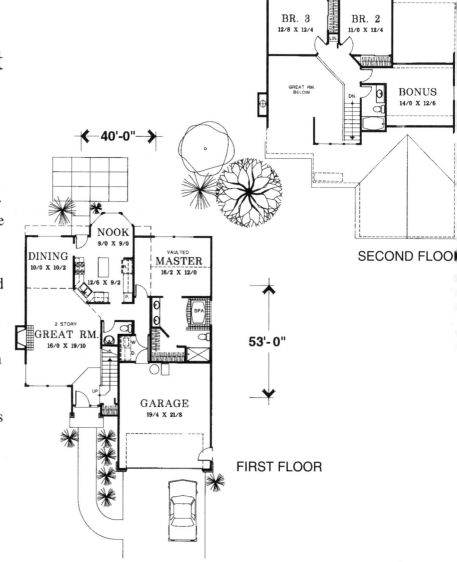

SECOND FLOOR

FIRST FLOOR

TOTAL LIVING AREA:
1,707 SQ. FT.

To order your Blueprints, call 1-800-235-5700

Style and Convenience
PRICE CODE: B

This plan features:
- Three bedrooms
- Two full baths
- A sheltered Porch leads into an easy-care tile Entry
- Spacious Living Room offers a cozy fireplace, triple window and access to Patio
- An efficient Kitchen with a skylight, work island, Dining area, walk-in Pantry and Utility/Garage entry
- Secluded Master Bedroom highlighted by a vaulted ceiling, access to Patio and a lavish Bath
- Two additional Bedrooms, one with a cathedral ceiling, share a full Bath
- No materials list is available for this plan

MAIN FLOOR — 1,653 SQ. FT.
GARAGE — 420 SQ. FT.

TOTAL LIVING AREA:
1,653 SQ. FT.

MAIN FLOOR

Country Charm and Modern Convenience
PRICE CODE: E

- This plan features:
- Three bedrooms
- Two full and one half baths
- Great Room crowned in a cathedral ceiling and accented by a cozy fireplace with built-ins
- Centrally located Kitchen with nearby Pantry serving Breakfast Area and Dining Room with ease
- Master Suite elegantly appointed by a walk-in closet and a lavish Bath
- A Sitting Room with bay window off the Master Suite
- Two secondary Bedrooms sharing a full Bath

FIRST FLOOR — 1,778 SQ. FT.
SECOND FLOOR — 592 SQ. FT.
GARAGE & STORAGE — 622 SQ. FT.
BONUS ROOM — 404 SQ. FT.

TOTAL LIVING AREA:
2,370 SQ. FT.

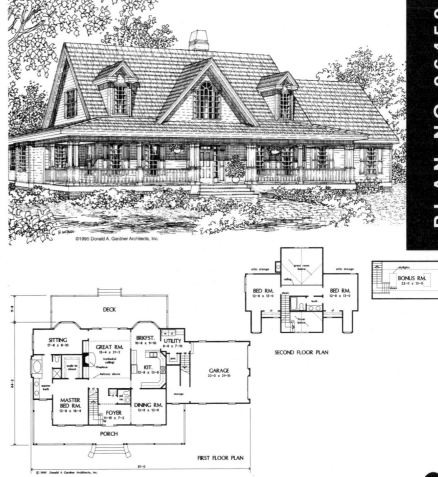

©1995 Donald A. Gardner Architects, Inc.

Warm and Charming Showplace

PRICE CODE: F

■ This plan features:
— Four bedrooms
— Three full and one half baths
■ An imposing stone and brick exterior hides a warm and charming interior
■ The Dining Room is beautified by a double soffit ceiling treatment
■ The uniquely shaped Library is away from high traffic areas
■ The Great Room has a warm fireplace and a rear wall of illuminating windows
■ Casual areas of the home include the Breakfast Bay, and the Hearth Room
■ The Kitchen has a convenient center island
■ What is there to say about the Master Suite except that it is huge
■ Upstairs are the other Bedrooms and Baths
■ A three-car garage with extra storage space finished off the plan
■ No materials list is available for this plan

FIRST FLOOR — 2,479 SQ. FT.
SECOND FLOOR — 956 SQ. FT.
BASEMENT — 2,479 SQ. FT.

TOTAL LIVING AREA:
3,435 SQ. FT.

FIRST FLOOR

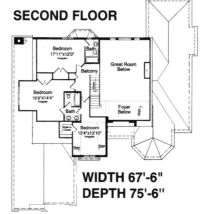

SECOND FLOOR

WIDTH 67'-6"
DEPTH 75'-6"

Perfect Compact Ranch

PRICE CODE: B

■ This plan features:
— Two bedrooms
— Two full baths
■ A large, sunken Great Room, centralized with a cozy fireplace
■ A Master Bedroom with an unforgettable Bathroom including a skylight
■ A huge three-car Garage, including a Work Area for the family carpenter
■ The Kitchen includes a Breakfast Nook for family gatherings

MAIN FLOOR — 1,738 SQ. FT.
BASEMENT — 1,083 SQ. FT.
GARAGE — 796 SQ. FT.

TOTAL LIVING AREA:
1,738 SQ. FT.

ZIP QUOTE
HOME COST CALCULATOR
see order pages for details

MAIN FLOOR

To order your Blueprints, call 1-800-235-5700

Country Victorian

Price Code: C

- This plan features:
  — Three bedrooms
  — Two full and one half baths
- Covered entry leads into an open Foyer
- Formal Living and Dining Rooms offer views on three sides
- Efficient Kitchen with a work island, built-in Pantry and Dining Area
- Expansive Family Room with a cathedral ceiling over a hearth fireplace
- Private Master Bedroom enhanced by a large walk-in closet and whirlpool tub
- Two additional Bedrooms with large closets, share a full Bath
- No materials list is available for this plan

FIRST FLOOR — 1,228 SQ. FT.
SECOND FLOOR — 952 SQ. FT.
GARAGE — 479 SQ. FT.
BASEMENT — 1,228 SQ. FT.

TOTAL LIVING AREA:
2,180 SQ. FT.

SECOND FLOOR

MBR 16' x 13'8
MBATH
WI Closet
BATH 2
BR3 12'4 x 10'
Balcony
Foyer Below
BR2 12'4 x 12'6
36'
31'4

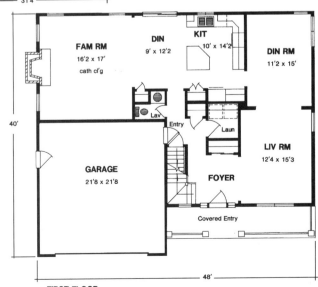

FIRST FLOOR

FAM RM 16'2 x 17' cath cl'g
DIN 9' x 12'2
KIT 10' x 14'2
DIN RM 11'2 x 15'
Lav
Entry
Laun
LIV RM 12'4 x 15'3
GARAGE 21'8 x 21'8
FOYER
Covered Entry
40'
48'

Country Influence

Price Code: B

- This plan features:
  — Three bedrooms
  — Two full and one half baths
- Front Porch entry into unique Sun Room with half-bath and coat closet
- Open Living Room enhanced by palladium window, focal point fireplace and atrium door to Deck
- Bay window brightens formal Dining Room conveniently located between the Living Room and Kitchen
- Efficient L-shaped Kitchen with bay window eating area, laundry closet and handy Garage entrance
- Plush Master Bedroom offers a bay window and double vanity bath
- Two additional bedrooms with arched windows, share a full bath

FIRST FLOOR — 806 SQ. FT.
SECOND FLOOR — 748 SQ. FT.
GARAGE — 467 SQ. FT.

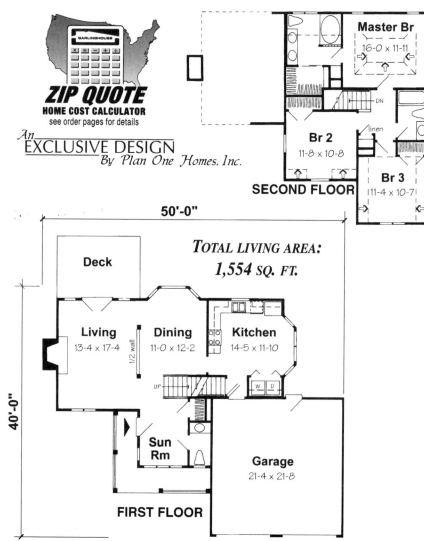

ZIP QUOTE
HOME COST CALCULATOR
see order pages for details

An
EXCLUSIVE DESIGN
By Plan One Homes, Inc.

SECOND FLOOR

Master Br
16-0 x 11-11

Br 2
11-8 x 10-8

linen

Br 3
11-4 x 10-7

DN

50'-0"

40'-0"

TOTAL LIVING AREA:
1,554 SQ. FT.

Deck

Living
13-4 x 17-4

1/2 wall

Dining
11-0 x 12-2

Kitchen
14-5 x 11-10

UP

W D

Sun
Rm

Garage
21-4 x 21-8

FIRST FLOOR

Bathed in Natural Light
PRICE CODE: B

■ This plan features:
– Three bedrooms
– Two full and one half baths
■ A high arched window illuminates the Foyer and adds style to the exterior of the home
■ Vaulted ceilings in the formal Dining Room, Breakfast Room and Great Room create volume
■ The Master Suite is crowned with a decorative tray ceiling
■ The Master Bath has a double vanity, oval tub, separate shower and a walk-in closet
■ The Loft, with the option of becoming a fourth Bedroom, highlights the second floor
■ An optional basement or crawl space foundation — please specify when ordering

FIRST FLOOR — 1,133 SQ. FT.
SECOND FLOOR — 486 SQ. FT.
BASEMENT — 1,133 SQ. FT.
BONUS — 134 SQ. FT.
GARAGE — 406 SQ. FT.

TOTAL LIVING AREA:
1,619 SQ. FT.

© Frank Betz Associates

Multiple Roof Lines
Add to Charm
PRICE CODE: F

■ This plan features:
– Four bedrooms
– Three full baths
■ Entry opens to Gallery, formal Dining and Living rooms with decorative ceilings
■ Spacious Kitchen with a work island opens to Dining alcove, Family Room and Patio beyond
■ Comfortable Family Room offers vaulted ceiling above fireplace and a wetbar
■ Corner Master Bedroom suite enhanced by a vaulted ceiling, double vanity Bath and huge walk-in closet
■ Three additional Bedrooms with walk-in closets have access to full Baths
■ No materials list is available for this plan

MAIN FLOOR — 3,292 SQ. FT.
GARAGE — 670 SQ. FT.

TOTAL LIVING AREA:
3,292 SQ. FT.

WIDTH 101'-1"
DEPTH 73'-10"

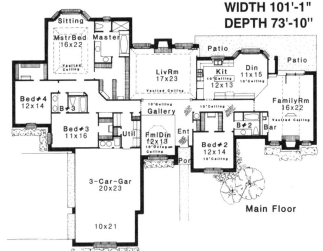

Main Floor

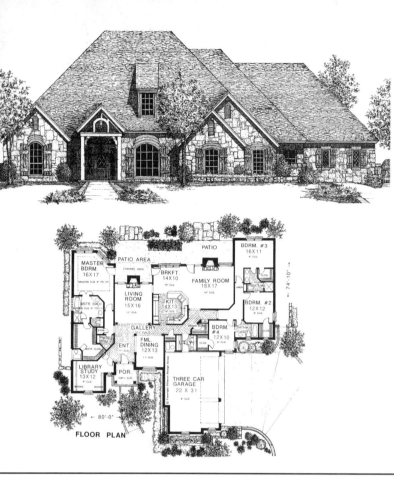

FLOOR PLAN

Roomy and Rustic
Fieldstone

PRICE CODE: E

- This plan features:
  - Four bedrooms
  - Three full and one half baths
- Cathedral Porch leads into easy-care Entry and formal Living Room with fieldstone fireplace
- Hub Kitchen with curved peninsula serving counter convenient to Breakfast Area, Covered Patio, Family Room, Utility/Garage entry and Dining Room
- Corner Master Bedroom enhanced by vaulted ceiling, plush Bath and a huge walk-in closet
- Three additional Bedrooms with walk-in closets and private access to a full Bath
- No materials list is available for this plan

MAIN FLOOR — 3,079 SQ. FT.
GARAGE — 630 SQ. FT.

TOTAL LIVING AREA:
3,079 SQ. FT.

Fan-lights Highlight Facade

PRICE CODE: A

- This plan features:
  - Three bedrooms
  - Two full baths
- Front Porch entry leads into an open Living Room, accented by a hearth fireplace below a sloped ceiling
- Efficient Kitchen with a peninsula counter convenient to the Laundry, Garage, Dining Area and Deck
- Master Bedroom accented by a decorative ceiling, a double closet and a private Bath
- Two additional Bedrooms with decorative windows and ample closets share a full Bath

MAIN FLOOR — 1,312 SQ. FT.
GARAGE — 459 SQ. FT.
BASEMENT — 1,293 SQ. FT.

TOTAL LIVING AREA:
1,312 SQ. FT.

ZIP QUOTE
HOME COST CALCULATOR
see order pages for details

MAIN FLOOR

To order your Blueprints, call 1-800-235-5700

ZIP QUOTE
HOME COST CALCULATOR
see order pages for details

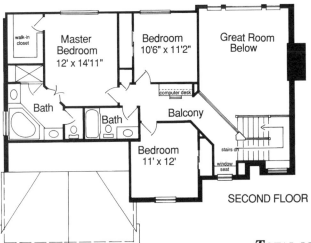

walk-in closet

Master Bedroom
12' x 14'11"

Bedroom
10'6" x 11'2"

Great Room
Below

Bath

computer desk

Bath

Balcony

Bedroom
11' x 12'

stairs dn

window seat

SECOND FLOOR

TOTAL LIVING AREA:
1,897 SQ. FT.

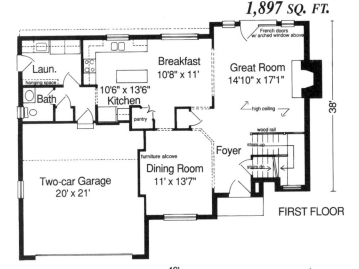

Laun.

hanging space

Bath

Breakfast
10'8" x 11'

10'6" x 13'6"
Kitchen

pantry

French doors
w/ arched window above

Great Room
14'10" x 17'1"

high ceiling

38'

wood rail

Foyer

stairs up

Two-car Garage
20' x 21'

furniture alcove

Dining Room
11' x 13'7"

stairs dn

FIRST FLOOR

48'

Refined and Distinctive

Price Code: C

■ This plan features:

— Three bedrooms

— Two full and one half baths

■ Impressive pilaster entry into open Foyer with landing staircase highlighted by decorative window

■ Great Room accented by hearth fireplace and French doors with arched window

■ Formal Dining Room enhanced by furniture alcove and decorative window

■ Efficient, L-shaped Kitchen with work island, walk-in pantry, bright Breakfast area, and adjoining Garage entry

■ Quiet Master Bedroom offers a walk-in closet, and plush bath with whirlpool tub

■ Two additional bedrooms share a full bath and computer desk

■ A materials list is not available with plan

FIRST FLOOR — 1,036 SQ. FT.
SECOND FLOOR — 861 SQ. FT.
GARAGE — 420 SQ. FT.

© 1995 Donald A Gardner Architects, Inc.

Classic Country Farmhouse

Price Code: D

■ This plan features:

— Three bedrooms

— Two full baths

■ Dormers, arched windows and multiple columns give this home country charm

■ Foyer, expanded by vaulted ceiling, accesses Dining Room, Bedroom/Study and Great Room

■ Expansive Great Room, with hearth fireplace topped by cathedral ceiling, opens to rear Porch and efficient kitchen

■ Tray ceiling adds volume to private Master Bedroom with plush Bath and walk-in closet

■ Extra room for growth offered by bonus room with skylight

MAIN FLOOR — 1,832 SQ. FT.
BONUS ROOM — 425 SQ. FT.
GARAGE & STORAGE — 562 SQ. FT.

ZIP QUOTE
HOME COST CALCULATOR
see order pages for details

TOTAL LIVING AREA:
1,832 SQ. FT.

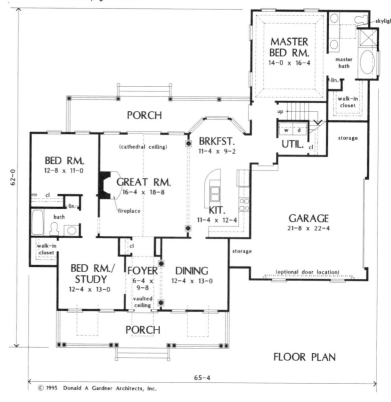

FLOOR PLAN

© 1995 Donald A Gardner Architects, Inc.

Charming Brick Ranch

PRICE CODE: B

This plan features:

- Three bedrooms
- Two full baths
- Sheltered entrance leads into open Foyer and Dining Room defined by columns
- Vaulted ceiling spans Foyer, Dining Room, and Great Room with corner fireplace and atrium door to rear year
- Central Kitchen with separate Laundry and Pantry easily serves Dining Room, Breakfast Area and Screened Porch
- Luxurious Master Bedroom offers tray ceiling and French doors to double vanity, walk-in closet and whirlpool tub
- Two additional Bedrooms, one that can easily convert to a Study, share a full Bath
- No materials list is available for this plan

MAIN FLOOR — 1,782 SQ. FT.
BASEMENT — 1,735 SQ. FT.
GARAGE — 406 SQ. FT.

TOTAL LIVING AREA:
1,782 SQ. FT.

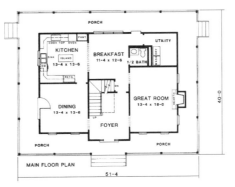

ZIP QUOTE
HOME COST CALCULATOR
see order pages for details

Two-Story Farmhouse

PRICE CODE: D

This plan features:

- Three bedrooms
- Two full and one half baths
- The wrap-around Porch gives a nostalgic appeal to this home
- The Great Room with fireplace is accessed directly from the Foyer
- The formal Dining Room has direct access to the efficient Kitchen
- An island, double sink, plenty of counter/cabinet space and a built-in Pantry complete the Kitchen
- The second floor Master Suite has a five-piece, private Bath and a walk-in closet
- Two other Bedrooms have walk-in closets and share a full Bath
- An optional basement or crawl space foundation — please specify when ordering

FIRST FLOOR — 1,125 SQ. FT.
SECOND FLOOR — 1,138 SQ. FT.
BASEMENT — 1,125 SQ. FT.

TOTAL LIVING AREA:
2,263 SQ. FT.

PLAN NO. 94307

Easy Maintenance
PRICE CODE: A

■ This plan features:
— Two bedroom
— Two three-quarter baths
■ Abundant glass and a wrap-around Deck to enjoy the outdoors
■ A tiled entrance into a large Great Room with a field-stone fireplace and dining area below a sloped ceiling
■ A compact tiled Kitchen open to a Great Room and adjacent to the Utility area
■ Two bedrooms, one with a private bath, offer ample closet space
■ No materials list is available for this plan

MAIN AREA — 786 SQ. FT.

TOTAL LIVING AREA:
786 SQ. FT.

PLAN NO. 20161

Delightful Doll House
PRICE CODE: A

■ This plan features:
— Three bedrooms
— Two full baths
■ A sloped ceiling in the Living Room which also has a focal point fireplace
■ An efficient Kitchen with a peninsula counter and a built-in Pantry
■ A decorative ceiling and sliding glass doors to the Deck in the Dining Room
■ A Master Suite with a decorative ceiling, ample closet space and a private full Bath
■ Two additional Bedrooms that share a full hall Bath

MAIN AREA — 1,307 SQ. FT.
GARAGE — 462 SQ. FT.
BASEMENT — 1,298 SQ. FT.

TOTAL LIVING AREA:
1,307 SQ. FT.

ZIP QUOTE
HOME COST CALCULATOR
see order pages for details

MAIN AREA

An
EXCLUSIVE DESIGN
By Karl Kreeger

To order your Blueprints, call 1-800-235-5700

Ranch Has Many Modern Features

Price Code: D

■ This plan features:

— Three bedrooms

— Three full baths

■ A vaulted-ceiling Great Room with sky-lights and a fireplace

■ A double L-shaped Kitchen with an eating bar opening to a bayed Breakfast Room

■ A Master Suite with a walk-in closet, corner garden tub, separate vanities and a linen closet

■ Two additional bedrooms each with a walk-in closet and built-in desk, sharing a full hall bath

■ A loft that overlooks the Great Room which includes a vaulted ceiling and open rail balcony

■ A basement or crawl space foundation — please specify when ordering

FIRST FLOOR — 1,996 SQ. FT.
LOFT — 305 SQ. FT.

TOTAL LIVING AREA:
2,301 SQ. FT.

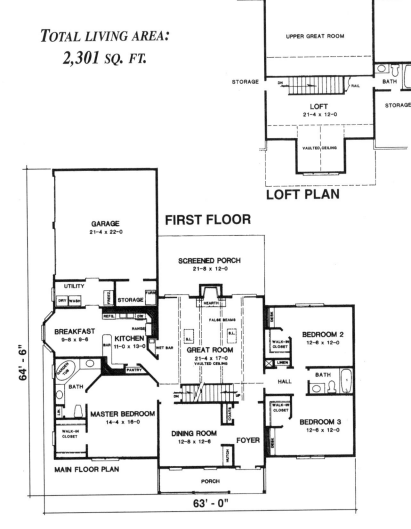

LOFT PLAN

FIRST FLOOR

MAIN FLOOR PLAN

Classic Style and Comfort

Price Code: B

- ■ This plan features:
- — Three bedrooms
- — Two full and one half baths
- ■ Covered Entry into two-story Foyer with a dramatic landing staircase
- ■ Spacious Living/Dining Room combination with hearth fireplace and decorative windows
- ■ Hub Kitchen with built-in pantry and informal Dining area with sliding glass door to rear yard
- ■ First floor Master Bedroom offers a walk-in closet, dressing area and full bath
- ■ Two additional bedrooms on second floor share a full bath
- ■ No materials list available

FIRST FLOOR — 1,281 SQ. FT.
SECOND FLOOR —511 SQ. FT.
GARAGE — 467 SQ. FT.

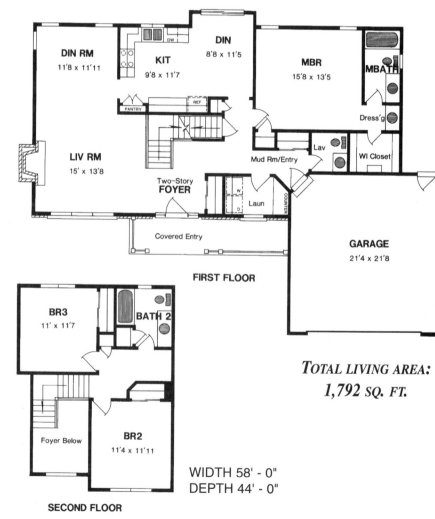

DIN RM
11'8 x 11'11

KIT
9'8 x 11'7

DIN
8'8 x 11'5

MBR
15'8 x 13'5

MBATH

PANTRY

REF

DW

Dress'g

LIV RM
15' x 13'8

Lav

Mud Rm/Entry

WI Closet

Two-Story
FOYER

Laun

COUNTER

Covered Entry

GARAGE
21'4 x 21'8

FIRST FLOOR

BR3
11' x 11'7

BATH 2

Foyer Below

BR2
11'4 x 11'11

SECOND FLOOR

TOTAL LIVING AREA:
1,792 SQ. FT.

WIDTH 58' - 0"
DEPTH 44' - 0"

Country Classic
PRICE CODE: D

This plan features:
- Three bedrooms
- Two full and one half baths
- Casually elegant exterior with dormers, gables and a charming front Porch
- U-shaped Kitchen easily serves both adjacent eating areas
- Nine foot ceilings amplify the first floor
- Master Suite highlighted by a vaulted ceiling and dormer
- Garden tub with a double window are focus of the Master Bath
- Two Bedrooms with walk-in closets sharing a hall Bath, while back stairs lead to a spacious bonus room

FIRST FLOOR — 1,313 SQ. FT.
SECOND FLOOR — 525 SQ. FT.
BONUS ROOM — 367 SQ. FT.
GARAGE — 513 SQ. FT.

TOTAL LIVING AREA:
1,838 SQ. FT.

Four Bedroom Charmer
PRICE CODE: C

This plan features:
- Four bedrooms
- Two full baths
- A vaulted ceiling in the naturally lighted entry
- A Living Room with a masonry fireplace, large windowed bay and vaulted ceiling
- A coffered ceiling and built-in china cabinet in the Dining Room
- A large Family Room with a wood stove alcove
- An island cooktop, built-in Pantry and a telephone desk in the efficient Kitchen
- A luxurious Master Bedroom with whirlpool garden tub, walk-in closet and double sink vanity
- Two additional Bedrooms sharing a full Bath
- A Study with a window seat and built-in bookshelves

MAIN FLOOR — 2,185 SQ. FT.

TOTAL LIVING AREA:
2,185 SQ. FT.

MAIN FLOOR

PLAN NO.20164

Easy Living
PRICE CODE: A

- This plan features:
  — Three bedrooms
  — Two full baths
- A dramatic sloped ceiling and a massive fireplace in the Living Room
- A Dining Room crowned by a sloping ceiling and a plant shelf also having sliding doors to the Deck
- A U-shaped Kitchen with abundant cabinets, a window over the sink and a walk-in Pantry
- A Master Suite with a private full bath, decorative ceiling and walk-in closet
- Two additional Bedrooms that share a full Bath

MAIN FLOOR — 1,456 SQ. FT.
BASEMENT — 1,448 SQ. FT.
GARAGE — 452 SQ. FT.

TOTAL LIVING AREA:
1,456 SQ. FT.

An
EXCLUSIVE DESIGN
By Karl Kreeger

ZIP QUOTE
HOME COST CALCULATOR
see order pages for details

PLAN NO.97715

Exciting Two-Story
PRICE CODE: E

- This plan features:
  — Four bedrooms
  — Three full and one half baths
- This exciting two-story home offers beauty, convenience and luxury
- The large Dining Room has a front wall box bay window
- The Library is located in the quiet front corner of the home
- The two-story Great Room has a corner fireplace
- The U-shaped Kitchen shares a serving bar with the Breakfast Nook
- The Master Bedroom is on the first floor and has a Bath with a Dressing Area
- Upstairs are three secondary Bedrooms and two accompanying Baths
- A three-car Garage rounds out this exciting home
- No materials list is available for this plan

FIRST FLOOR — 1,836 SQ. FT.
SECOND FLOOR — 767 SQ. FT.
BASEMENT — 1,836 SQ. FT.

TOTAL LIVING AREA:
2,603 SQ. FT.

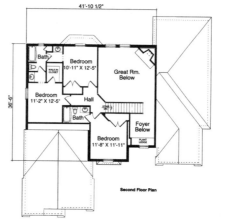

ZIP·QUOTE
HOME COST CALCULATOR
see order pages for details

Home With Many Views

Price Code: B

■ This plan features:

— Three bedrooms

— Two full baths

■ Large Decks and windows taking full advantage of the view

■ A fireplace that divides the Living Room from the Dining Room

■ A Kitchen flowing into the Dining Room

■ A Master Bedroom with full Master Bath

■ A Recreation Room sporting a whirlpool tub and a bar

MAIN FLOOR — 728 SQ. FT.
UPPER FLOOR — 573 SQ. FT.
LOWER FLOOR — 409 SQ. FT.
GARAGE — 244 SQ. FT.

TOTAL LIVING AREA:
1,710 SQ. FT.

Main Floor

28'-0"

Broom
Ref
Linen
DN
Kitchen
11-1 X 7-7
Flue
Brkfst Bar
Dining
11-11 X 8-7
DN
Br 1
12-0 X 11-3
Loft Above
Railing
UP
Fireplace
Living
15-1 X 14-10
DN
Deck

Lower Floor

Util Rm
10-11 X 5-9
Wet Bar
W F
Garage
11-8 X 19-0
Storage
Rec Rm
11-1 X 20-2
Step
UP
Optional Hot Tub

Upper Floor

DN
Loft/ Br 3
11-7 X 16-6
Clg @ 9'-6"
Whirlpool Tub
DN
Mbr
11-8 X 14-0
Railing
Open to Below
Clerestory Windows Above
Roof
Balcony

An
EXCLUSIVE DESIGN
By Marshall Associates

Luxury on One Level

Price Code: C

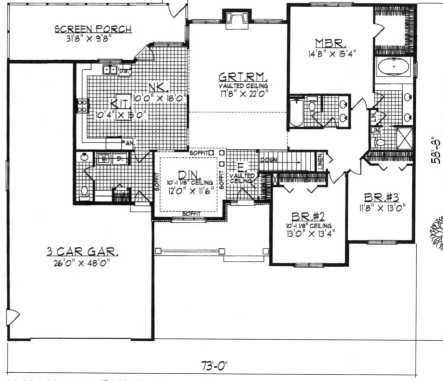

ZIP QUOTE
HOME COST CALCULATOR
see order pages for details

■ This plan features:

— Three bedrooms

— Two full and one half baths

■ Covered front Porch leads into Entry and Great Room with vaulted ceilings

■ Huge Great Room perfect for entertaining or family gatherings with cozy fireplace

■ Country-size Kitchen with a Pantry, work island, bright, Eating Nook with Screen Porch beyond, and nearby Laundry/Garage entry

■ Corner Master Bedroom offers a large walk-in closet and a luxurious Bath with a double vanity and spa tub

■ Two additional Bedrooms, with over-sized closets, share a full Bath

■ No materials list is available for this plan

MAIN FLOOR — 2,196 SQ. FT.
BASEMENT — 2,196 SQ. FT.

TOTAL LIVING AREA:
2,196 SQ. FT.

MAIN FLOOR PLAN

To order your Blueprints, call 1-800-235-5700

Split-Bedroom Ranch

PRICE CODE: C

This plan features:

- Three bedrooms
- Two full baths

The formal Foyer opens into the Great Room which features a vaulted ceiling and a hearth fireplace

The U-shaped Kitchen is located between the Dining Room and the Breakfast Nook

The secluded Master Bedroom is spacious and includes amenities such as walk-in closets and a full Bath

Two secondary Bedrooms have ample closet space and share a full Bath

The covered front Porch and rear Deck provide additional space for entertaining

An optional basement, slab or a crawl space foundation — please specify when ordering

MAIN FLOOR — 1,804 SQ. FT.

BASEMENT — 1,804 SQ. FT.

GARAGE — 506 SQ. FT.

TOTAL LIVING AREA: 1,804 SQ. FT.

MAIN AREA

A Home for Today and Tomorrow

PRICE CODE: B

This plan features:

- Three bedrooms
- Two full baths

An intriguing Breakfast Nook off the Kitchen

A wide open, fireplaced Living Room with glass sliders to an optional Deck

A step-saving Kitchen with a Pantry

A handsome Master Bedroom with skylit compartmentalized Bath

MAIN AREA — 1,583 SQ. FT.

BASEMENT — 1,573 SQ. FT.

GARAGE — 484 SQ. FT.

TOTAL LIVING AREA: 1,583 SQ. FT.

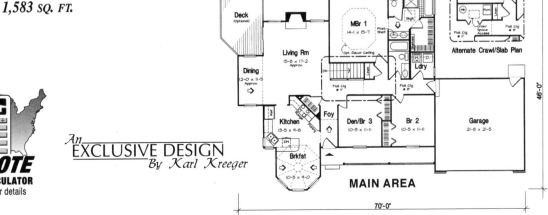

An EXCLUSIVE DESIGN *By Karl Kreeger*

MAIN AREA

ZIP QUOTE
HOME COST CALCULATOR
see order pages for details

Family Room at the Heart of the Home

PRICE CODE: C

- ■ This plan features:
- — Three bedrooms
- — Two full and one half baths
- ■ Formal Foyer opening into the formal Dining Room with grand front window and direct access the Kitchen
- ■ Family Room to the rear of the home
- ■ A vaulted ceiling and a fireplace accent this room
- ■ Kitchen/Breakfast Area has been laid out for ultimate efficiency
- ■ First floor Master Suite is topped by a vaulted ceiling and pampered by a five-piece private Bath
- ■ Three additional Bedrooms, each with ample closet space, are on the second floor
- ■ Full Bath in the hall in proximity to the secondary Bedrooms
- ■ No materials list is available for this plan

FIRST FLOOR — 1,520 SQ. FT.
SECOND FLOOR — 489 SQ. FT.
BONUS — 332 SQ. FT.
BASEMENT — 1,520 SQ. FT.
GARAGE — 541 SQ. FT.

TOTAL LIVING AREA:
2,009 SQ. FT.

SECOND FLOOR

WIDTH 57'-0"
DEPTH 61'-6"

FIRST FLOOR

An
EXCLUSIVE DESIGN
By Greg Marquis

Turret Adds Appeal

PRICE CODE: D

- ■ This plan features:
- — Three bedrooms
- — Two full baths
- ■ A garden entry with double door leading into an open Foyer and Great Room
- ■ Vaulted ceilings above a decorative window in the Dining Area and sliding glass doors to the Veranda in the Great Room
- ■ A private Study with double door and turret windows
- ■ A large, efficient Kitchen featuring a walk-in Pantry and glassed Nook, with skylights, near the Laundry Area and Garage
- ■ A Master Suite with a vaulted ceiling, two huge, walk-in closets, a luxurious Bath and sliding glass doors to the Veranda
- ■ Two additional Bedrooms with over-sized closets sharing a full Bath
- ■ No materials list is available for this plan

MAIN AREA — 2,214 SQ. FT.
GARAGE — 652 SQ. FT.

TOTAL LIVING AREA:
2,214 SQ. FT.

MAIN FLOOR

To order your Blueprints, call 1-800-235-5700

©1995 Donald A. Gardner Architects, Inc.

B. NATHAN.

DECK

MASTER BED RM.
14-8 x 13-4
(cathedral ceiling)

BRKFST.
11-0 x 9-5

fireplace

(cathedral ceiling)

GREAT RM.
16-0 x 19-0

KIT.
11-4 x
10-7

GARAGE
21-0 x 23-4

master bath

walk-in closet

balcony above
up

w d
UTIL.

cl

DINING
11-0 x 12-4

bath

lin.

FOYER
7-4 x
5-8

cl

cl

BED RM.
12-0 x 11-0

BED RM./ STUDY
11-0 x 12-0
(cathedral ceiling)

PORCH

55-4

65-4

© 1995 Donald A Gardner Architects, Inc.

FIRST FLOOR
No. 96463

great room below

(unfinished)
BONUS
14-8 x 17-0

down

railing

(unfinished)
BONUS
11-0 x 12-4

balcony (optional)

attic storage

SECOND FLOOR

Your Family Will Grow In Style

Price Code: D

- This plan features:
— Three bedrooms
— Two full baths
- Open Great Room and Kitchen enlarged by a cathedral ceiling
- Wooden rear Deck expand entertaining to the outdoors
- Cathedral ceiling adding volume and drama to the Master Suite
- Flexible Bedroom/Study includes a cathedral ceiling and an arched double window
- Second floor bonus space may be finished with two more Bedrooms

FIRST FLOOR — 1,633 SQ. FT.
GARAGE & STORAGE — 512 SQ. FT.
SECOND FLOOR BONUS SPACE — 595 SQ. FT.

TOTAL LIVING AREA:
1,633 SQ. FT.

Stately Manor

Price Code: D

■ This plan features:

— Three bedrooms

— Two full and one half baths

■ A porch serving as a grand entrance

■ A very spacious Foyer with an open staircase and lots of angles

■ A great Kitchen equipped with a cook top island and a full bay window wall that includes a roomy Breakfast Nook

■ A Living Room with a vaulted ceiling that flows into the formal Dining Room for ease in entertaining

■ A Master Suite equipped with a walk-in closet and five-piece private bath

FIRST FLOOR — 1,383 SQ. FT.
SECOND FLOOR — 997 SQ. FT.
BASEMENT — 1,374 SQ. FT.
GARAGE — 420 SQ. FT.
WIDTH — 54'-0"
DEPTH — 47'-0"

TOTAL LIVING AREA:
2,380 SQ. FT.

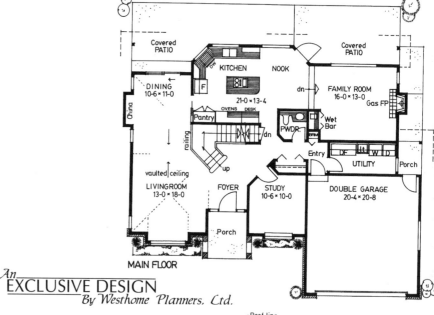

MAIN FLOOR

An
EXCLUSIVE DESIGN
By Westhome Planners, Ltd.

SECOND FLOOR

To order your Blueprints, call 1-800-235-5700

Secluded Master Suite

PRICE CODE: C

■ This plan features:
— Three bedrooms
— Two full baths
■ A convenient one-level design with an open floor plan between the Kitchen, Breakfast Area and Great Room
■ A vaulted ceiling and a cozy fireplace in the spacious Great Room
■ A well-equipped Kitchen using a peninsula counter as an eating bar
■ A Master Suite with a luxurious Master Bath
■ Two additional Bedrooms having use of a full hall Bath
■ An optional crawl space or slab foundation—please specify when ordering

MAIN AREA — 1,680 SQ. FT.
GARAGE — 538 SQ. FT.

TOTAL LIVING AREA:
1,680 SQ. FT.

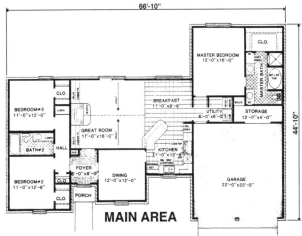

MAIN AREA

A Grand Entrance

PRICE CODE: E

■ This plan features:
— Five bedrooms
— Three full baths
■ The arched window above the front door provides a grand entrance
■ Inside the two-story Foyer find the first of two open rail staircases in this home
■ The formal Living and Dining rooms are only separated by a set of boxed columns
■ The U-shaped Kitchen has a walk-in Pantry and a wall oven
■ A serving bar services the Breakfast Nook
■ The Family Room has a fireplace as well as a vaulted ceiling
■ Rounding out the first floor is a Den/Bedroom with a Bath located off of it
■ Upstairs find the family sleeping quarters and Baths
■ An optional basement or crawl space foundation — please specify when ordering

FIRST FLOOR — 1,424 SQ. FT.
SECOND FLOOR — 1,256 SQ. FT.
BASEMENT — 1,424 SQ. FT.
GARAGE — 494 SQ. FT.

TOTAL LIVING AREA:
2,680 SQ. FT.

FIRST FLOOR

SECOND FLOOR

© Frank Betz Associates

PLAN NO. 90990

MAIN FLOOR

Comfort and Style

PRICE CODE: A

- ■ This plan features:
- — Two or three bedrooms
- — One full and one three-quarter baths
- ■ An unfinished daylight basement, providing possible space for family recreation
- ■ A Master Suite complete with private Bath and skylight
- ■ A large Kitchen including an Eating Nook
- ■ A Sundeck that is easily accessible from the Master Suite, Nook and the Living/Dining Area

MAIN FLOOR — 1,423 SQ. FT.
BASEMENT — 1,423 SQ. FT.
GARAGE — 399 SQ. FT.
WIDTH — 46'-0"
DEPTH — 52'-0"

TOTAL LIVING AREA:
1,423 SQ. FT.

An
EXCLUSIVE DESIGN
By Westhome Planners, Ltd.

PLAN NO. 99208

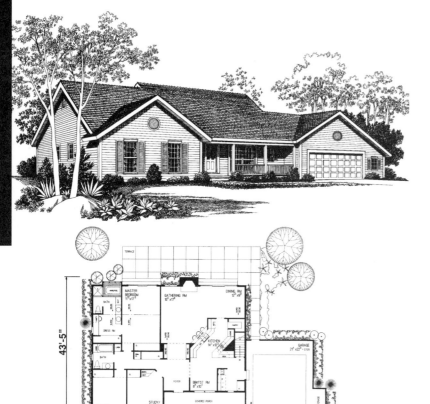

MAIN FLOOR

Cozy Traditional with Style

PRICE CODE: C

- ■ This plan features:
- — Three bedrooms
- — Two full baths
- ■ A convenient one-level design
- ■ A galley-style Kitchen that shares a snack bar with the spacious Gathering Room
- ■ A focal point fireplace making the Gathering Room warm and inviting
- ■ An ample Master Suite with a luxury Bath which includes a whirlpool tub and separate Dressing Room
- ■ Two additional Bedrooms, one that could double as a Study, located at the front of the house

MAIN FLOOR — 1,830 SQ. FT.
BASEMENT — 1,830 SQ. FT.

TOTAL LIVING AREA:
1,830 SQ. FT.

To order your Blueprints, call 1-800-235-5700

FIRST FLOOR

DINING RM
11/0 x 13/0

KITCHEN
11/0 x 13/0

NOOK
9/0 x 9/0

FAMILY ROOM
15/0 x 12/0

UTIL

PANTRY

PWDR

LIVING RM
17/6 x 13/8

GARAGE
21/4 x 24/8

UP

UP

35' - 0"

59' - 6"

SECOND FLOOR

BEDRM • 2
13/10 x 10/0

BEDRM • 3
13/10 x 10/0

LINEN

MASTER BEDROOM
15/0 x 14/0 AVG.

W•I•C

B • 3

DN

SITTING

M • B

FRENCH

36" RAILING

Updated Victorian

Price Code: C

■ This plan features:

— Three bedrooms

— Two full and one half baths

■ A classic Victorian exterior is accented by a turret room and second floor covered Porch

■ A spacious formal Living Room leads into the formal Dining Room

■ Efficient U-shaped Kitchen with loads of counter space and a snackbar

■ The elegant Master Suite has a unique, octagon Sitting Area and a private Porch, an oversized, walk-in closet and private Bath with a double vanity and a window tub

■ Two additional Bedrooms with ample closets share a full hall Bath

FIRST FLOOR — 1,150 SQ. FT.
SECOND FLOOR — 949 SQ. FT.
GARAGE — 484 SQ. FT.

TOTAL LIVING AREA:
2,099 SQ. FT.

Country Living in Any Neighborhood

Price Code: C

- ■ This plan features:
- — Three bedrooms
- — Two full and two half baths
- ■ An expansive Family Room with fireplace
- ■ A Dining Room and Breakfast Nook lit by flowing natural light from bay windows
- ■ A first floor Master Suite with a double vanitied Bath that wraps around his-n-her closets
- ■ An optional basement, slab or crawl space foundation — please specify when ordering

First floor — 1,477 sq. ft.
Second floor — 704 sq. ft.
Basement — 1,374 sq. ft.
Garage — 528 sq. ft.

Total living area: 2,181 sq. ft.

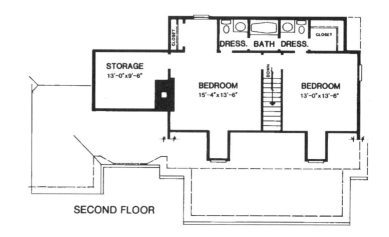

SECOND FLOOR

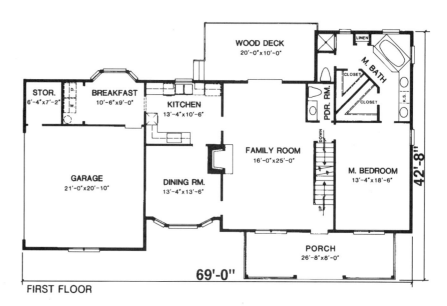

FIRST FLOOR

To order your Blueprints, call 1-800-235-5700

Essence of Style & Grace
PRICE CODE: E

■ This plan features:
— Four bedrooms
— Three full and one half baths
■ French doors introduce Study and columns define the Gallery and formal areas
■ The expansive Family Room with an inviting fireplace and a cathedral ceiling opens to the Kitchen
■ The Kitchen features a cooktop island, butlers Pantry, Breakfast Area and Patio access
■ The First Floor Master Bedroom offers a private Patio, vaulted ceiling, twin vanities and a walk-in closet
■ Three second floor Bedrooms each access a full Bath
■ No materials list is available for this plan
■ An optional basement or slab foundation — please specify when ordering

FIRST FLOOR — 2,036 SQ. FT.
SECOND FLOOR — 866 SQ. FT.
GARAGE — 720 SQ. FT.

TOTAL LIVING AREA:
2,902 SQ. FT.

PLAN NO. 98524

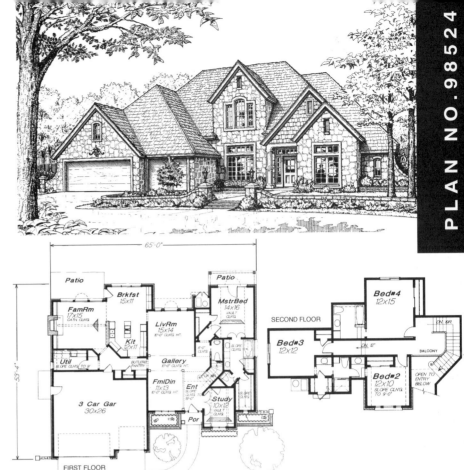

Open Plan Brightens Elegant Traditional
PRICE CODE: C

■ This plan features:
— Three bedrooms
— Three full baths
■ A combination Family Room, Nook and Kitchen Area
■ A well planned Kitchen with an island
■ A bay window in the Nook Area
■ A Butler's Serving Pantry between the Kitchen and the Dining Room that includes a overhead cabinet with glass doors and a lower cabinet
■ A Second Floor Master Suite with a large walk-in closet and private Bath with a whirlpool tub, separate shower and double vanity
■ Two additional Bedrooms share a full Bath

MAIN FLOOR — 1,173 SQ. FT.
UPPER FLOOR — 997 SQ. FT.
BASEMENT — 1,164 SQ. FT.
GARAGE — 574 SQ. FT.

TOTAL LIVING AREA:
2,170 SQ. FT.

An
EXCLUSIVE DESIGN
By Westhome Planners, Ltd.

PLAN NO. 90991

FIRST FLOOR

SECOND FLOOR

To order your Blueprints, call 1-800-235-5700

PLAN NO. 92523

Private Master Suite
PRICE CODE: B

- This plan features:
  — Three bedrooms
  — Two full baths
- A spacious Great Room enhanced by a vaulted ceiling and fireplace
- A well-equipped Kitchen with windowed double sink
- A secluded Master Suite with decorative ceiling, private Master Bath, and walk-in closet
- Two additional Bedrooms sharing hall Bath
- An optional crawl space or slab foundation — please specify when ordering

MAIN AREA — 1,293 SQ. FT.
GARAGE — 433 SQ. FT.

TOTAL LIVING AREA:
1,293 SQ. FT.

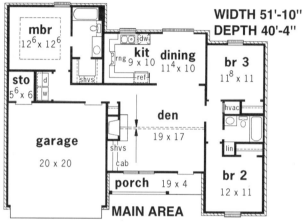

WIDTH 51'-10"
DEPTH 40'-4"

PLAN NO. 93436

Family Room at the Heart of the Home
PRICE CODE: C

- This plan features:
  — Four bedrooms
  — Two full and one half baths
- Formal Foyer opening into the formal Dining Room with grand front window and direct access the Kitchen
- Family Room to the rear of the home
- A vaulted ceiling and a fireplace accent this room
- Kitchen/Breakfast Area has been laid out for ultimate efficiency
- First floor Master Suite is topped by a vaulted ceiling and pampered by a five-piece private bath
- Three additional Bedrooms, each with ample closet space, are on the second floor
- Full Bath in the hall in proximity to the secondary Bedrooms
- No materials list is available for this plan

FIRST FLOOR — 1,441 SQ. FT.
SECOND FLOOR — 632 SQ. FT.
BASEMENT — 1,441 SQ. FT.
GARAGE — 524 SQ. FT.

TOTAL LIVING AREA:
2,073 SQ. FT.

An EXCLUSIVE DESIGN
By Greg Marquis

©1995 Donald A. Gardner Architects, Inc.

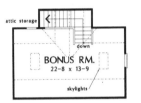

TOTAL LIVING AREA
2,050 SQ. FT.

Dream Home for Contemporary Buyers

Price Code: E

■ This plan features:

— Three bedrooms

— Two full baths

■ Gables, a center front dormer, and a touch of brick combine with desirable amenities and an efficient floor plan

■ Dormer floods the Foyer with sunlight and intrigue, while a cathedral ceiling enlarges the Great Room

■ The Kitchen and Breakfast Area, located next to the Great Room, is punctuated by interior columns

■ Tray ceilings and arched picture windows are featured in the Dining Room and the Living Room

■ Two family Bedrooms share a large full Bath with a double vanity in one wing, while the luxurious Master Suite enjoys privacy in the rear

MAIN FLOOR — 2,050 SQ. FT.
BONUS — 377 SQ. FT.
GARAGE — 503 SQ. FT.

© 1995 Donald A Gardner Architects, Inc.

MAIN FLOOR
No. 96465

Photography Supplied by The Meredith Corporation

Prairie Style Retreat

Price Code: C

- ■ This plan features:
- — Three bedrooms
- — Two full and one half baths
- ■ Shingle siding, tall expanses of glass and wrapping decks accent the exterior
- ■ The octagonal shaped Living Room has a two-story ceiling and French doors
- ■ The Kitchen is enhanced by a cooktop island
- ■ The main level Master Suite offers a private Bath
- ■ Two additional, second floor Bedrooms share the full Bath in the hall
- ■ No materials list is available for this plan

FIRST FLOOR — 1,213 SQ. FT.
SECOND FLOOR — 825 SQ. FT.
BASEMENT — 1,213 SQ. FT.

TOTAL LIVING AREA: 2,038 SQ. FT.

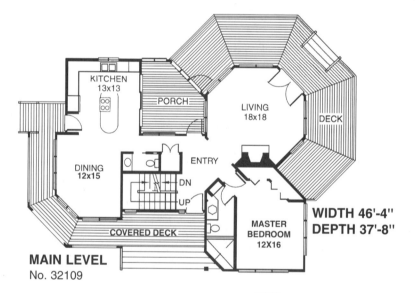

KITCHEN 13x13
PORCH
LIVING 18x18
DECK
DINING 12x15
ENTRY
DN
UP
COVERED DECK
MASTER BEDROOM 12X16

WIDTH 46'-4"
DEPTH 37'-8"

MAIN LEVEL
No. 32109

ZIP QUOTE
HOME COST CALCULATOR
see order pages for details

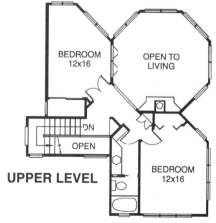

BEDROOM 12x16
OPEN TO LIVING
DN
OPEN
BEDROOM 12x16

UPPER LEVEL

To order your Blueprints, call 1-800-235-5700

One-Floor Living
PRICE CODE: C

This plan features:
- Three bedrooms
- Two full and one half baths

Angular windows and recessed ceilings separating the two dining areas from the adjoining island Kitchen

A window wall flanking the fireplace in the soaring, sky-lit Living Room

A Master Suite with a bump-out window and a double-vanity Bath

Main floor — 2,020 sq. ft.
Basement — 2,020 sq. ft.
Garage — 534 sq. ft.

TOTAL LIVING AREA:
2,020 SQ. FT.

An
EXCLUSIVE DESIGN
By Karl Kreeger

ZIP QUOTE
HOME COST CALCULATOR
see order pages for details

MAIN FLOOR

An Open Concept Floor Plan
PRICE CODE: D

This plan features:
- Four bedrooms
- Two full and one half baths

The Kitchen, Breakfast Room and the Family Room are adjacent to one another and open to one another, perfect for family gatherings

A well-appointed Kitchen with ample cabinet space, a peninsula counter, and in close proximity to both the Dining Room and the Breakfast Room/Family Room

A stupendous fireplace on the center of the rear wall between the Family Room and the Breakfast Room

An expansive Living Room that flows into the Breakfast Room/Family Room

A private Master Suite with a large Master Bath

An oval tub, separate shower, compartmented toilet, double vanity and his-n-her walk-in closets in the Master Bath

Two additional Bedrooms with walk-in closets and a full hall bath in close proximity

No materials list is available for this plan

Main floor — 2,511 sq. ft.
Garage — 469 sq. ft.

TOTAL LIVING AREA:
2,511 SQ. FT.

© Larry E. Belk

MAIN FLOOR

To order your Blueprints, call 1-800-235-5700

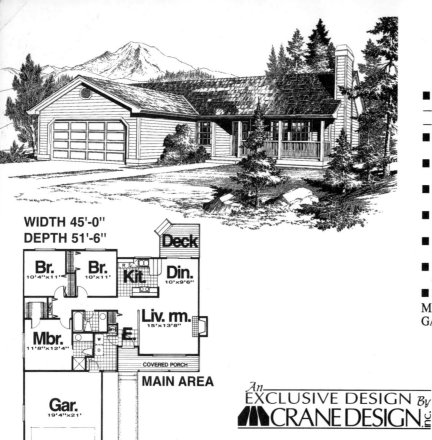

Charming Country Porch Entry
PRICE CODE: A

- This plan features:
— Three bedrooms
— One full and one three-quarter baths
- Attractive front Porch leads into tiled entry and open Living/Dining Room for ease in entertaining
- An inviting fireplace, double window and sliding glass door to Deck enhance open space
- Efficient Kitchen with a peninsula counter/snackbar, easily serves Dining Area and Deck beyond
- Roomy Master Bedroom features a walk-in closet and private Bath
- Two additional Bedrooms with ample closets, share a full Bath
- Laundry facilities conveniently located near Garage and entry
- No materials list is available for this plan

MAIN FLOOR — 1,220 SQ. FT.
GARAGE — 440 SQ. FT.

TOTAL LIVING AREA:
1,220 SQ. FT.

WIDTH 45'-0"
DEPTH 51'-6"

Deck

Br. 10'4"x11'
Br. 10'x11'
Kit.
Din. 10'9"x6"
Liv. rm. 15'x13'8"
Mbr. 11'8"x12'4"
COVERED PORCH
MAIN AREA
Gar. 19'4"x21'

An EXCLUSIVE DESIGN *By* CRANE DESIGN inc.

Stucco & Stone
PRICE CODE: E

- This plan features:
— Three bedrooms
— Two full and one half baths
- Vaulted Great Room is highlighted by a fireplace and French doors to the rear yard
- Decorative columns define the Dining Room
- A built-in Pantry and a radius window above the double sink in the Kitchen
- The Breakfast Bay is crowned by a vaulted ceiling
- A tray ceiling over the Master Bedroom and Sitting Area and a vaulted ceiling crowns the Master Bath
- Two additional Bedrooms, each with a walk-in closet, share the full, double vanity Bath in the hall
- An optional basement, crawl space or slab foundation — please specify when ordering
- No material list is available for this plan

FIRST FLOOR — 1,796 SQ. FT.
SECOND FLOOR — 629 SQ. FT.
BONUS ROOM — 208 SQ. FT.
BASEMENT — 1,796 SQ. FT.
GARAGE — 588 SQ. FT.

TOTAL LIVING AREA:
2,425 SQ. FT.

WIDTH 54'-0"
DEPTH 53'-10"

Family Room Below
Bedroom 2 13'0" x 11'4"
Storage
OVERLOOK
W.i.c.
Bath
LINEN
Bedroom 3 12'8" x 14'0"
W.i.c.
Foyer Below
Optional Bonus Room 10'5" x 18'7"
SECOND FLOOR

Sitting Area
FPL
FPL
FRENCH DOOR
Vaulted Breakfast
Master Suite 13'0" x 19'9"
TRAY CLG.
Vaulted Great Room 15'0" x 17'3"
Kitchen
RADIUS WDW.
Vaulted M. Bath
REF
RANGE
PANTRY
NICHE
W.i.c.
PLANT SHELF ABOVE
DECORATIVE COLUMNS
LINEN
Laundry
Dining Room 12'8" x 14'0"
Pdr.
Living Room 11' x 13'
Two Story Foyer
Garage 20'5" x 21'0"
FIRST FLOOR

© Frank Betz Associates

To order your Blueprints, call 1-800-235-5700

© 1997 Donald A. Gardner Architects, Inc.

B. NATHAN.

TOTAL LIVING AREA:
2,250 SQ. FT.

SECOND FLOOR PLAN

Second floor labels: BED RM. 12-0 x 12-8, great room below, walk-in closet, bath, bath, linen, down, walk-in closet, down, down, storage, BED RM. 12-4 x 12-8, foyer below, skylights, BONUS RM. 15-6 x 21-8

First floor labels: SCREEN PORCH 12-0 x 11-0, PORCH, GREAT RM. 17-4 x 17-9, BRKFST. 12-0 x 11-0, master bath, fireplace, walk-in closet, walk-in closet, KITCHEN 12-4 x 13-11, pan., MASTER BED RM. 13-0 x 14-0, up, pd. rm., cl, DINING 12-4 x 12-8, w d, UTILITY 10-6 x 6-10, up, storage, FOYER 11-4 x 6-5, PORCH, GARAGE 22-4 x 21-8, 67-4, 61-7

FIRST FLOOR PLAN

© 1997 Donald A Gardner Architects, Inc.

Traditional Two-Story Home

Price Code: E

- This plan features:
- — Three bedrooms
- — Two full and two half baths
- Facade handsomely accented by multiple gables, keystone arches and transom windows
- Arched clerestory window lights two-story Foyer for dramatic entrance
- Two-story Great Room exciting with inviting fireplace, wall of windows and back Porch access
- Cooks will enjoy open Kitchen and easy access to screen Porch and Dining Room
- Private Master Bedroom Suite offers two walk-in closets and deluxe Bath

FIRST FLOOR — 1,644 SQ. FT.
SECOND FLOOR — 606 SQ. FT.
BONUS ROOM — 548 SQ. FT.
GARAGE & STORAGE — 657 SQ. FT.

The Ultimate Kitchen

Price Code: C

- This plan features:
- — Three bedrooms
- — Two full and one half baths
- Front Porch invites visiting and leads into an open entry with an angled staircase
- Living Room with a wall of windows and an island fireplace, opens to Dining Room with a bright, bay window
- Large and efficient Kitchen with a work island, walk-in Pantry, garden window over sink, skylit Nook and nearby Deck
- Corner Master Suite enhanced by Deck access, vaulted ceiling, a large walk-in closet and Spa Bath
- Guest/Utility Room offers a pullman bed and Laundry
- Two second floor Bedrooms with large closets, share a full Bath

FIRST FLOOR — 1,472 SQ. FT.
SECOND FLOOR — 478 SQ. FT.
GARAGE — 558 SQ. FT.

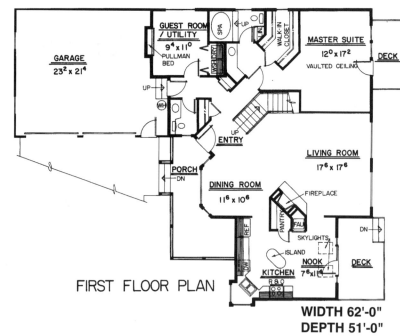

FIRST FLOOR PLAN

WIDTH 62'-0"
DEPTH 51'-0"

TOTAL LIVING AREA:
1,950 SQ. FT.

SECOND FLOOR PLAN

To order your Blueprints, call 1-800-235-5700

Especially Unique

PRICE CODE: E

This plan features:
- Four bedrooms
- Three full and one half baths
- An arch covered entry and arched windows add a unique flair to this home
- From the 11-foot entry turn left into the Study/Media Room
- The formal Dining Room is open to the Gallery, and the Living Room beyond
- The Family Room has a built in entertainment center, a fireplace and access to the rear patio
- The Master Bedroom is isolated, and has a fireplace, a private bath, and a walk-in closet
- Three additional bedrooms are on the opposite side of the home share two full baths
- A three-car garage
- No materials list is available for this plan

MAIN FLOOR — 2,748 SQ. FT.
GARAGE — 660 SQ. FT.

TOTAL LIVING AREA:
2,748 SQ. FT.

ZIP QUOTE
HOME COST CALCULATOR
see order pages for details

MAIN FLOOR

WIDTH 75'-0"
DEPTH 64'-5"

Convenient Country Kitchen

PRICE CODE: C

This plan features:
- Three bedrooms
- Two full baths
- Easy-care, tiled Foyer opens to formal Dining and Living Rooms defined by column and a decorative ceiling
- Efficient, U-shaped Country Kitchen with a work island, eating Nook with sliding glass door to rear yard, a cozy fireplace and nearby Laundry/Garage entry
- Beautiful bay window, a pampering Bath and a walk-in closet highlight the Master Bedroom
- Two additional Bedrooms with over-sized closets, share a full Bath
- No materials list is available for this plan

MAIN FLOOR — 1,821 SQ. FT.
BASEMENT — 1,821 SQ. FT.
GARAGE — 568 SQ. FT.

TOTAL LIVING AREA:
1,821 SQ. FT.

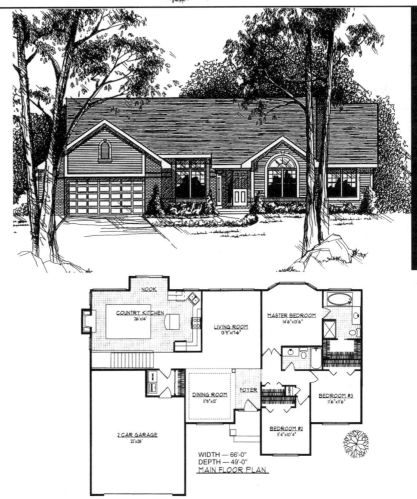

To order your Blueprints, call 1-800-235-5700

Compact and Efficient
PRICE CODE: A

- This plan features:
  — Three bedrooms
  — Two full baths
- A covered Porch entrance
- A skylight over the Dining Room, that illuminates naturally
- A vaulted ceiling and a cozy fireplace in the Living Room
- An efficient and convenient Kitchen with an abundance of cabinets and counter space
- A private Master Suite that includes a walk-in closet and a Master Bath
- Two secondary Bedrooms that share a full hall Bath
- No materials list is available for this plan

FIRST FLOOR — 1,390 SQ. FT.
GARAGE — 440 SQ. FT.

TOTAL LIVING AREA:
1,390 SQ. FT.

MAIN FLOOR

Character and Charm
PRICE CODE: C

- This plan features:
  — Three bedrooms
  — Two full and one half baths
- Dining Room with direct access to the Kitchen, yet can be made private by the pocket door
- Kitchen made efficient by a cooktop island, an abundance of counter space and a built-in Pantry
- Sun room adjoining Kitchen and the Family Room
- Fireplace and a fourteen foot ceiling highlighting the Family Room.
- Master Suite with a five-piece Bath and a walk-in closet
- No materials list is available for this plan

FIRST FLOOR — 1,626 SQ. FT.
SECOND FLOOR — 522 SQ. FT.
BASEMENT — 336 SQ. FT.
GARAGE — 522 SQ. FT.

TOTAL LIVING AREA:
2,148 SQ. FT.

An
EXCLUSIVE DESIGN
By Greg Marquis

84

To order your Blueprints, call 1-800-235-5700

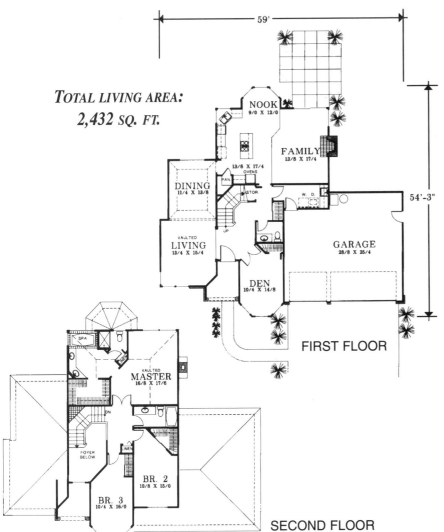

**TOTAL LIVING AREA:
2,432 SQ. FT.**

FIRST FLOOR

SECOND FLOOR

Designed for Today's Busy Lifestyle
Price Code: D

■ This plan features:

— Three bedrooms

— Two full and one half baths

■ Open lay-out between the Kitchen, Family Room and Eating Nook giving a feeling of spaciousness

■ A fireplace in both the Family Room and the Living Room

■ An efficient Kitchen that easily accesses the Eating Nook as well as the Formal Dining Room

■ A large triple window provides view of the front yard from the Den

■ A Master Suite with decorative ceiling, large walk-in closet and private Master Bath

■ Two additional bedrooms share a full hall bath

FIRST FLOOR — 1,408 SQ. FT.
SECOND FLOOR — 1,024 SQ. FT.
FOUNDATION — BASEMENT OR CRAWLSPACE

Traditional Elements Combine in Friendly Colonial

Price Code: C

■ This plan features:

— Four bedrooms

— Two full and one half baths

■ A beautiful circular stair ascending from the central foyer and flanked by the formal Living Room and Dining Room

■ Exposed beams, wood paneling, and a brick fireplace wall in the Family Room

■ A separate dinette opening to an efficient Kitchen

FIRST FLOOR — 1,099 SQ. FT.
SECOND FLOOR — 932 SQ. FT.
BASEMENT — 1,023 SQ. FT.
GARAGE — 476 SQ. FT.

TOTAL LIVING AREA:
2,031 SQ. FT.

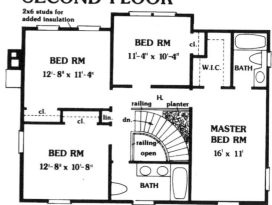

SECOND FLOOR

2x6 studs for added insulation

BED RM
12'-8" x 11'-4"

BED RM
11'-4" x 10'-4"

cl.

W.I.C.

BATH

cl.

cl.

lin.

dn.

railing

H. planter

MASTER BED RM
16' x 11'

BED RM
12'-8" x 10'-8"

railing open

BATH

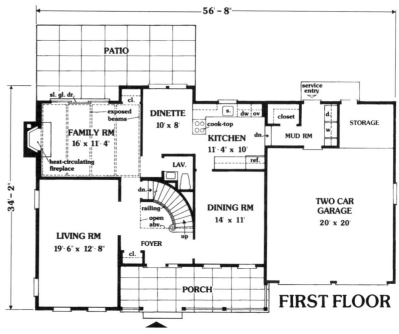

FIRST FLOOR

56'-8"

34'-2"

PATIO

sl. gl. dr.

cl.

exposed beams

FAMILY RM
16' x 11'-4"

heat-circulating fireplace

DINETTE
10' x 8'

s.

dw ov

cook-top

KITCHEN
11'-4" x 10'

ref.

service entry

closet

dn.

MUD RM

d.
w.

STORAGE

LAV.

dn.

railing

open abv.

up

LIVING RM
19'-6" x 12'-8"

FOYER

cl.

DINING RM
14' x 11'

TWO CAR GARAGE
20' x 20'

PORCH

Simplicity at it's Finest

PRICE CODE: B

■ This plan features:
— Three bedrooms
— Two full and one half baths
■ A covered Porch gives the home a nostalgic feel
■ The volume Great Room offers a fireplace with transom windows on either side
■ A built-in planning desk and Pantry in the Breakfast Area
■ A snack bar for informal meals highlights the Kitchen
■ The formal Dining Room overlooks the Porch, which has easy access to the Kitchen
■ An isolated Master Suite has a five-piece Bath and a walk-in closet

FIRST FLOOR — 1,298 SQ. FT.
SECOND FLOOR — 396 SQ. FT.
BASEMENT — 1,298 SQ. FT.
GARAGE — 513 SQ. FT.

TOTAL LIVING AREA:
1,694 SQ. FT.

© design basics, inc.

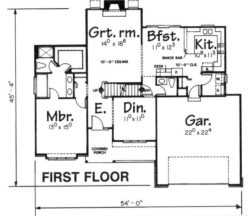

FIRST FLOOR

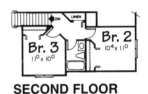

SECOND FLOOR

Easy Living Plan

PRICE CODE: D

■ This plan features:
— Three bedrooms
— Two full baths
■ Sunlit Foyer flows easily into the generous Great Room
■ Great Room crowned in a cathedral ceiling and accented by a fireplace
■ Accent columns define the open Kitchen and Breakfast Bay
■ Master Bedroom topped by a tray ceiling and highlighted by a well-appointed Master Bath
■ Two additional Bedrooms, sharing a skylit Bath in the hall, create the children's wing

FIRST FLOOR—1,864 SQ. FT.
BONUS ROOM—319 SQ. FT.
GARAGE—503 SQ. FT.

TOTAL LIVING AREA:
1,864 SQ. FT.

©1996 Donald A. Gardner Architects, Inc.

© 1996 Donald A Gardner Architects, Inc.

FLOOR PLAN

B. NATHAN

European Richness
PRICE CODE: F

■ This plan features:
— Four bedrooms
— Three full and one half baths
■ The exterior of this home is graced by dual box bay windows and curved stairs
■ A grand Foyer leading to the Gallery greets your guests
■ The Dining Room and the Library each take advantage of light from their front windows
■ The immense Master Suite includes a huge walk-in closet and Bath
■ The formal Great Room is located at the center of the home and includes a fireplace
■ Informal gathering can be held in the warm Hearth Room or the Breakfast Nook
■ The secondary Bedrooms are located on the second floor and all have walk-in closets
■ A rear Terrace is perfect for entertaining in warm weather
■ A three-car Garage completes this luxurious home
■ No material list is available for this plan

FIRST FLOOR — 3,392 SQ. FT.
SECOND FLOOR — 1,197 SQ. FT.
BASEMENT — 3,392 SQ. FT.

TOTAL LIVING AREA:
4,589 SQ. FT.

Covered Porch Entry
PRICE CODE: A

■ This plan features:
— Three bedrooms
— Two full and one half baths
■ There is a convenient pass-through from the Kitchen into the Family Room
■ An easy flow into the Dining Room enhances the interaction of the living spaces on the first floor
■ A fireplace highlights the spacious Family Room
■ The Kitchen opens to the Breakfast Room which has a French door that accesses the rear yard
■ Decorative Ceiling treatment highlights the Master Bedroom while a vaulted ceiling tops the Master Bath
■ Two additional Bedrooms share the use of the full Bath in the hall
■ An optional basement or crawl space foundation — please specify when ordering

FIRST FLOOR — 719 SQ. FT.
SECOND FLOOR — 717 SQ. FT.
BASEMENT — 719 SQ. FT.
GARAGE — 480 SQ. FT.

© Frank Betz Associates

TOTAL LIVING AREA:
1,436 SQ. FT.

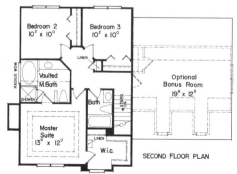

To order your Blueprints, call 1-800-235-5700

B. NATHAN

Beautiful From Front to Back

Price Code: D

- This plan features:
  — Three bedrooms
  — Two full baths
- Porches front and back, gables and dormers providing special charm
- Central Great Room with a cathedral ceiling, fireplace, and a clerestory window which bringing natural light
- Columns dividing the open Great Room from the Kitchen and the Breakfast Bay
- A tray ceiling and columns dressing up the formal Dining Room
- Skylit Master Bath with shower, whirlpool tub, dual vanity and spacious walk-in closet

MAIN FLOOR — 1,632 SQ. FT.
GARAGE & STORAGE — 561 SQ. FT.

TOTAL LIVING AREA:
1,632 SQ. FT.

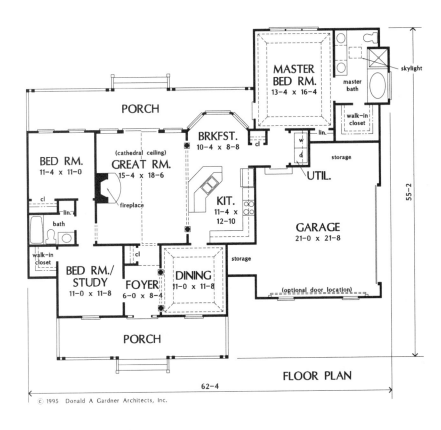

FLOOR PLAN

Create a Dramatic Impression

Price Code: C

- This plan features:
- — Three bedrooms
- — Two full baths
- A two-story Entry
- A cooktop island and breakfast bar in the efficient Kitchen
- A vaulted ceiling and wood stove in the Great Room
- A built-in desk in each of the first floor Bedrooms
- A luxurious Master Suite with an adjoining skylit Bath and a Dressing Room
- An optional basement, crawl space or slab foundation — please specify when ordering

FIRST FLOOR — 1,450 SQ. FT.
SECOND FLOOR — 650 SQ. FT.
BASEMENT — 1,450 SQ. FT.
GARAGE — 558 SQ. FT.

FIRST FLOOR
No. 91400

TOTAL LIVING AREA:
2,100 SQ. FT.

SECOND FLOOR

To order your Blueprints, call 1-800-235-5700

French Country Styling

PRICE CODE: D

This plan features:
- Four bedrooms
- Two full, one half, and one three-quarter baths
- A bay window with a copper roof, a large eyebrow dormer and an arched covered Entry add to the country flavor of this home
- The large Great Room includes a brick fireplace and a built-in entertainment center
- An elegant formal Dining Room and angled Study are located to each side of the Entry
- The convenient Kitchen has its own Dining Area for informal occasions
- The Master Suite is located on the First Floor and has a large Bath
- Three Bedrooms and a future room are located on the Second Floor

FIRST FLOOR — 1,765 SQ. FT.
SECOND FLOOR — 802 SQ. FT.
BONUS ROOM — 275 SQ. FT.
GARAGE — 462 SQ. FT.

TOTAL LIVING AREA:
2,567 SQ. FT.

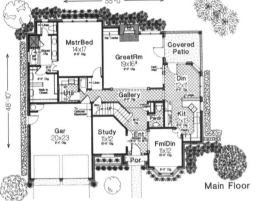

Main Floor

Upper Floor

PLAN NO. 96471

Easy Living

PRICE CODE: A

This plan features:
- Three bedrooms
- Two full baths
- A covered front Porch shelters the Entry to this home
- The Family Room is enlarged by a vaulted ceiling and also has a fireplace
- The Kitchen is L-shaped and includes a center island
- The Dining Room is open to the Kitchen for maximum convenience
- A covered walkway leads to the two car Garage
- The Master Bedroom has a private Bath, which has two building options
- Both of the secondary Bedrooms have walk-in closets
- No material list is available for this plan

MAIN FLOOR — 1,474 SQ. FT.
GARAGE — 454 SQ. FT.

TOTAL LIVING AREA:
1,474 SQ. FT.

An
EXCLUSIVE DESIGN
By Greg Marquis

MAIN FLOOR

PLAN NO. 93447

B. N ATHAN

© 1996 Donald A. Gardner Architects, Inc.

Polished & Poised
PRICE CODE: E

- This plan features:
  - Three bedrooms
  - Two full and one half baths
- Hip roof, gables and brick accents add poise and polish to this traditional home
- Curved transom window and sidelights illuminate the gracious Foyer
- A curved balcony overlooks the Great Room which has cathedral ceiling, fireplace and a wall of windows overlooking the Patio
- Hub Kitchen easily serves the Dining Room, Breakfast Area and the Patio beyond
- Master Bedroom wing is enhanced by a tray ceiling, walk-in closet and a deluxe Bath

FIRST FLOOR — 1,577 SQ. FT.
SECOND FLOOR — 613 SQ. FT.
BONUS ROOM — 360 SQ. FT.
GARAGE & STORAGE — 634 SQ. FT

TOTAL LIVING AREA:
2,190 SQ. FT.

FIRST FLOOR PLAN

© 1996 Donald A Gardner Architects, Inc.

SECOND FLOOR PLAN

Classic Home
PRICE CODE: F

- This plan features:
  - Four bedrooms
  - Three full and one half baths
- Space and light connect the Entry, Gallery, Dining Room, and Living Room
- A Butler's Pantry connects the Kitchen to the Dining Room
- The Master Suite encompasses a whole wing on the first floor
- Up the curved staircase find three Bedrooms all with walk in closets
- Also upstairs is a Game Room with built in cabinets
- A three car Garage completes this home
- An optional basement and a slab foundation — please specify when ordering
- No materials list is available for this plan

FIRST FLOOR — 2,688 SQ. FT.
SECOND FLOOR — 1,540 SQ. FT.
BASEMENT — 2,688 SQ. FT.
GARAGE — 635 SQ. FT.

TOTAL LIVING AREA:
4,228 SQ. FT.

Optional Basement Access

© Carmichael & Dame

Second floor

First floor

To order your Blueprints, call 1-800-235-5700

© 1996 Donald A. Gardner Architects, Inc.

For a Narrow Lot

Price Code: C

- ■ This plan features:
- — Three bedrooms
- — Two full baths
- ■ A Great Room topped by a cathedral ceiling and accented by a fireplace
- ■ A convenient pass-through opening from the Kitchen
- ■ The Master Suite is loaded with luxuries, including a walk-in closet and a private Bath with a separate shower and garden tub
- ■ Two additional Bedrooms share a full Bath

MAIN FLOOR — 1,350 SQ. FT.
GARAGE & STORAGE — 309 SQ. FT.

TOTAL LIVING AREA:
1,350 SQ. FT.

Floor Plan Labels

MASTER BED RM.
14-0 x 12-0
(cathedral ceiling)

walk-in closet

BED RM.
11-0 x 10-4

master bath

walk-in closet

bath

DINING
11-0 x 11-4

KITCHEN
11-4 x 7-8

pan.

BED RM.
11-0 x 10-0

7' wall

cl

cl

storage

GREAT RM.
15-0 x 16-4
(cathedral ceiling)

fireplace

GARAGE
13-8 x 20-8

PORCH

FLOOR PLAN
No. 99868

41-0

51-8

c 1996 Donald A Gardner Architects, Inc.

Distinctive Splendor

Price Code: E

■ This plan features:

— Four bedrooms

— Two full and one half baths

■ An expansive Kitchen with a cooktop island/eating bar and corner double sinks

■ A spacious Family Room equipped with a built-in wetbar and a cozy fireplace

■ A formal Living Room with a second fireplace

■ A bay window adding elegance to the formal Dining Room

■ A pampering Master Bath adding to the privacy of the Master Suite

■ Three additional bedrooms that share a full hall bath

■ A balcony that overlooks the Foyer and the Family Room

■ No materials list available

FIRST FLOOR — 1,720 SQ. FT.
SECOND FLOOR — 1,305 SQ. FT.
BASEMENT — 1,720 SQ. FT.
GARAGE — 768 SQ. FT.

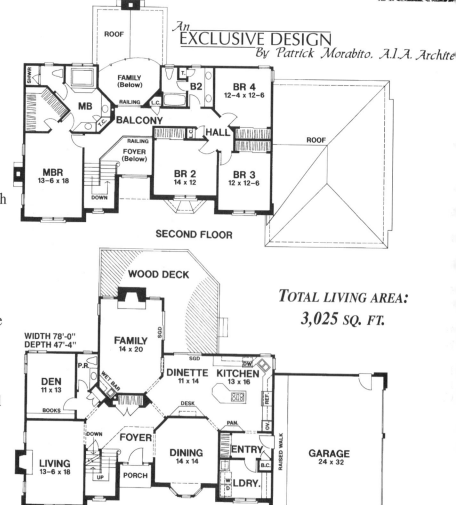

An EXCLUSIVE DESIGN
By Patrick Morabito, A.I.A. Archite

SECOND FLOOR

TOTAL LIVING AREA:
3,025 SQ. FT.

WIDTH 78'-0"
DEPTH 47'-4"

FIRST FLOOR

To order your Blueprints, call 1-800-235-5700

Bonus Loft with Balcony

PRICE CODE: C

This plan features:
- Three bedrooms
- Two full and one half baths
- Exterior details and decorative windows surround sheltered Entry
- Central Great Room with an inviting fireplace, vaulted, two-story ceiling, entertainment wall and Deck access
- Open Kitchen efficiently serves bright Eating Area and Deck with cooktop work island and peninsula counter
- Utility/Mud Room with Loft stairs and Garage entry
- Corner Master Bedroom offers backyard view, large walk-in closet and double vanity Bath with window tub
- Two additional Bedrooms with decorative windows and ample closets share a full Bath
- Loft/Bonus opens to Balcony and Great Room below
- An optional basement or crawl space foundation — please specify when ordering
- No materials list is available for this plan

MAIN FLOOR — 1,941 SQ. FT.
BONUS ROOM — 200 SQ. FT.
BASEMENT — 1,592 SQ. FT.
GARAGE — 720 SQ. FT.

TOTAL LIVING AREA:
1,941 SQ. FT.

MAIN AREA

Keystones and Arched Windows

PRICE CODE: B

© Frank Betz Associates

This plan features:
- Three bedrooms
- Two full baths
- A large arched window in the Dining Room offers eye-catching appeal
- A decorative column helps to define the Dining Room from the Great Room
- A fireplace and French door to the rear yard can be found in the Great Room
- An efficient Kitchen includes a serving bar, Pantry and pass-through to the Great Room
- A vaulted ceiling over the Breakfast Room
- A plush Master Suite includes a private Bath and a walk-in closet
- Two additional Bedrooms share a full Bath in the hall
- An optional basement, slab or crawl space foundation — please specify when ordering

MAIN FLOOR — 1,671 SQ. FT.
BASEMENT — 1,685 SQ. FT.
GARAGE — 240 SQ. FT.

TOTAL LIVING AREA:
1,671 SQ. FT.

WIDTH 50'-0"
DEPTH 51'-0"

MAIN FLOOR

PLAN NO. 93192

Perfect for Your Corner Lot

PRICE CODE: C

- This plan features:
— Three bedrooms
— Two full and one half baths
- Pillars and decorative windows highlight front entrance into Foyer with cathedral ceiling and a large closet
- Spacious Living Room enhanced by a central fireplace and decorative window
- Convenient Kitchen with a work island, Dining Area with outdoor access, and nearby Laundry/Garage entry
- Corner Master Suite offers direct access to backyard, a large walk-in closet and a pampering Bath
- Two additional Bedrooms with ample closet space and easy access to a full Bath
- No materials list is available for this plan

MAIN FLOOR — 1,868 SQ. FT.
BASEMENT — 1,868 SQ. FT.

TOTAL LIVING AREA:
1,868 SQ. FT.

MAIN FLOOR PLAN

PLAN NO. 93193

Wonderful One-Level Living

PRICE CODE: C

- This plan features:
— Three bedrooms
— Two full and one half baths
- Charming front porch accesses easy-care Entry with archway to Dining Room
- Central Great Room enhanced by a cathedral ceiling over a cozy fireplace set in a wall of windows
- Large and convenient Kitchen with work island/snack-bar, eating Nook with sliding glass door to backyard, and nearby Laundry/Garage entry
- Corner Master Bedroom features a walk-in closet and plush bath with a double vanity and spa tub
- Two additional Bedrooms with ample closets and double windows, share a full B0ath
- No materials list is available for this plan

MAIN FLOOR — 1,802 SQ. FT.
BASEMENT — 1,802 SQ. FT.

TOTAL LIVING AREA:
1,802 SQ. FT.

MAIN FLOOR PLAN

96

To order your Blueprints, call 1-800-235-5700

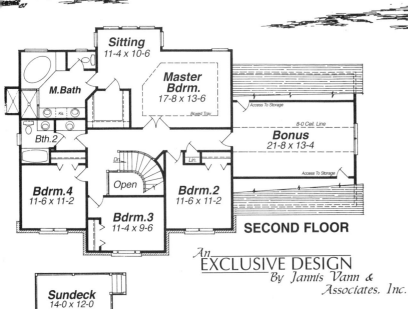

Sitting
11-4 x 10-6

Master Bdrm.
17-8 x 13-6
Boxed Tray

M.Bath

Access To Storage

8-0 Ceil. Line

Bth.2

Bonus
21-8 x 13-4

Access To Storage

Dn.

Bdrm.4
11-6 x 11-2

Open

Lin.

Bdrm.2
11-6 x 11-2

Bdrm.3
11-4 x 9-6

SECOND FLOOR

An
EXCLUSIVE DESIGN
*By Jannis Vann &
Associates, Inc.*

Sundeck
14-0 x 12-0

Brkfst.
11-4 x 15-6

Dw.

Kit.
12-0 x 11-6

Family Rm.
13-6 x 17-6

Desk   Pant.   Ref.

Ov.

40-0

Lav.

Lnd.

W. D.

Cts.

Double Garage
21-8 x 23-4

Living
11-6 x 13-6

Dn.

Open

Dining
11-6 x 13-6

Foyer
13-8 x 15-2

Cts.   Cts.

FIRST FLOOR

60-0

Elegant Master Suite

Price Code: E

■ This plan features:

— Four bedrooms

— Two full and one half baths

■ Comfortable Family Room with a fireplace

■ Efficient Kitchen with built-in Pantry and serving counter

■ Master Suite with decorative ceiling, Sitting Room and a plush Bath

■ An optional basement, slab, or crawl space foundation — please specify when ordering

■ No materials list available

FIRST FLOOR — 1,307 SQ. FT.
SECOND FLOOR — 1,333 SQ. FT.
BONUS — 308 SQ. FT.
BASEMENT — 1,307 SQ. FT.
GARAGE — 528 SQ. FT.

GARLINGHOUSE

ZIP QUOTE
HOME COST CALCULATOR
see order pages for details

TOTAL LIVING AREA:
2,640 SQ. FT.

What a First Impression

Price Code: C

- This plan features:
- — Three bedrooms
- — Two full and one half baths
- The Traditionally styled exterior makes a lasting first impression
- Inside the Foyer, find a wood railed staircase that leads to the second floor
- The sunken Great room with fireplace opens to both the Solarium and the Breakfast Nook
- The Kitchen has a dual sided island with an eating bar and counter space
- Upstairs the Master bedroom has a decorative high ceiling
- If you need more space there is a Bonus Room provided over the Garage
- No materials list is available for this plan

FIRST FLOOR —1,060 SQ. FT.
SECOND FLOOR — 927 SQ. FT.
BONUS — 267 SQ. FT.

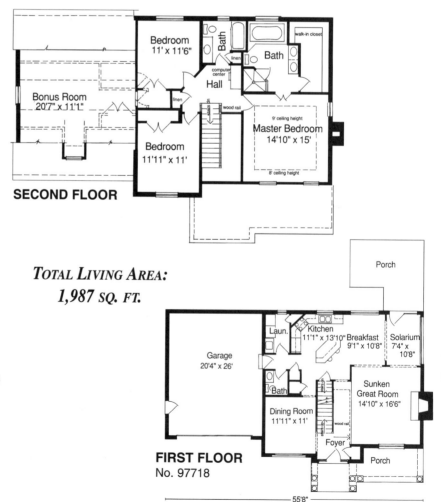

SECOND FLOOR

Bedroom 11' x 11'6"
Bath
Bath
walk-in closet
linen
computer center
Hall
linen
wood rail
Bedroom 11'11" x 11'
9' ceiling height
Master Bedroom 14'10" x 15'
8' ceiling height
Bonus Room 20'7" x 11'1"

TOTAL LIVING AREA:
1,987 SQ. FT.

Porch

Laun.
Kitchen 11'1" x 13'10"
Breakfast 9'1" x 10'8"
Solarium 7'4" x 10'8"
Garage 20'4" x 26'
Bath
Sunken Great Room 14'10" x 16'6"
Dining Room 11'11" x 11'
wood rail
Foyer
Porch

FIRST FLOOR
No. 97718

55'8"

To order your Blueprints, call 1-800-235-5700

Arches Enhance Style
PRICE CODE: F

- This plan features:
  – Four bedrooms
  – Three full and one half baths
- Open layout of rooms separated by arched openings
- Living Room is graced by a fireplace and adjoins the Dining Room
- Family Room has a second fireplace and is open to the Breakfast Nook and Kitchen
- A mid level Study is brightened by a large front window
- This plan has four huge Bedrooms and three full Baths upstairs
- No material list is available for this plan

FIRST FLOOR — 1,786 SQ. FT.
SECOND FLOOR — 1,607 SQ. FT
GARAGE — 682 SQ. FT.

TOTAL LIVING AREA: 3,393 SQ. FT.

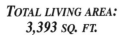

ZIP QUOTE
HOME COST CALCULATOR
see order pages for details

© Carmichael & Dame

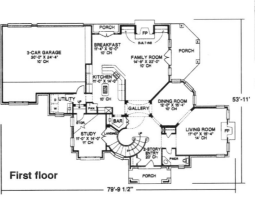

First floor

Second floor

Optional Basement Access

Eye-Catching Glass Turrets
PRICE CODE: D

- This plan features:
  – Three bedrooms
  – Three full baths
- Two-story Foyer with a curved staircase, opens to a unique Living Room with an alcove of windows and inviting fireplace
- Alcove of glass and a vaulted ceiling in the open Dining Area
- Kitchen with built-in Pantry and desk, cooktop island/snackbar and a Nook with double door
- Comfortable Family Room highlighted by another fireplace and wonderful outdoor views
- Vaulted Master Suite offers a plush Dressing Area with walk-in closet and spa tub
- Two additional Bedrooms, one with a glass alcove, share a double vanity Bath
- Bonus room available for future use

FIRST FLOOR — 1,592 SQ. FT.
SECOND FLOOR — 958 SQ. FT.
BONUS ROOM — 194 SQ. FT.
GARAGE — 956 SQ. FT.

TOTAL LIVING AREA: 2,550 SQ. FT.

FIRST FLOOR

SECOND FLOOR

Hip Roof Ranch
PRICE CODE: B

- This plan features:
  - Three bedrooms
  - Two full baths
- Cozy front Porch leads into Entry with vaulted ceiling and sidelights
- Open Living Room enhance by a cathedral ceiling, a wall of windows and corner fireplace
- Large and efficient Kitchen with an extended counter and a bright Dining Area with access to screen Porch
- Convenient Utility Area with access to Garage and Storage Area
- Spacious Master Bedroom with a walk-in closet and private Bath
- Two additional Bedrooms with ample closets, share a full Bath
- No materials list is available for this plan

MAIN AREA — 1,540 SQ. FT.
BASEMENT — 1,540 SQ. FT.

TOTAL LIVING AREA:
1,540 SQ. FT.

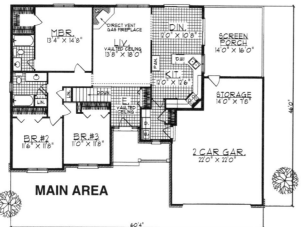

MAIN AREA

© Frank Betz Associates

Small, Yet Lavishly Appointed
PRICE CODE: C

- This plan features:
  - Three bedrooms
  - Two full and one half baths
- The Dining Room, Living Room, Foyer and Master Bath all topped by high ceilings
- Master Bedroom includes a decorative tray ceiling and a walk-in closet
- Kitchen open to the Breakfast Room enhanced by a serving bar and a Pantry
- Living Room with a large fireplace and a French door to the rear yard
- Master Suite located on opposite side from secondary Bedrooms, allowing for privacy
- An optional basement or crawl space foundation — please specify when ordering

MAIN FLOOR — 1,845 SQ. FT.
BONUS — 409 SQ. FT.
BASEMENT — 1,845 SQ. FT.
GARAGE — 529 SQ. FT.

TOTAL LIVING AREA:
1,845 SQ. FT.

To order your Blueprints, call 1-800-235-5700

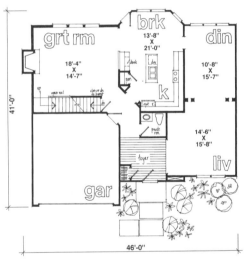

MAIN LEVEL
No. 93602

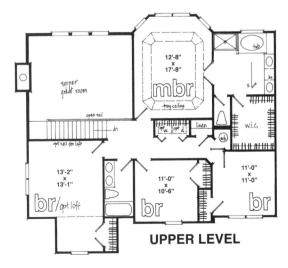

UPPER LEVEL

Thoughtfully Designed

Price Code: D

■ This plan features:

— Four bedrooms

— Two full and one half baths

■ Foyer opens to formal Living and Dining rooms defined with columns

■ Two-story Great Room has an impressive fireplace and a wall of windows

■ Hub Kitchen with cooktop work island, built-in Pantry and desk

■ Elegant Master Bedroom with a tray ceiling, window alcove and plush Bath

■ Three additional bedrooms with ample closets share a full Bath

■ No materials list is available for this plan

MAIN LEVEL — 1,209 SQ. FT.
UPPER LEVEL — 1,202 SQ. FT.
BASEMENT — 1,209 SQ. FT.
GARAGE — 370 SQ. FT.

TOTAL LIVING AREA:
2,411 SQ. FT.

Photography Supplied by The Meredith Corporation

Mansion Mystique

Price Code: F

- ■ This plan features:
- — Four bedrooms
- — Four full and one half baths
- ■ A beautiful exterior includes multiple rooflines and a covered porch
- ■ The Entry includes a curved staircase
- ■ Multi purpose rooms include a Guest Room/Study and an upstairs Office
- ■ Both the Family Room and the Great Room have fireplaces
- ■ The L-shaped Kitchen opens to the Breakfast Nook
- ■ Upstairs find multiple Bedrooms, Baths, and a bonus space
- ■ No materials list is available for this plan

MAIN LEVEL — 2,727 SQ. FT.
UPPER LEVEL — 1,168 SQ. FT.
BONUS — 213 SQ. FT.
BASEMENT — 2,250 SQ. FT.
GARAGE — 984 SQ. FT.

TOTAL LIVING AREA:
3,895 SQ. FT.

ZIP QUOTE
HOME COST CALCULATOR
see order pages for details

WIDTH 73'-8"
DEPTH 72'-2"

To order your Blueprints, call 1-800-235-5700

Functional Contemporary

PRICE CODE: D

■ This plan features:
— Three bedrooms
— Two full and one half baths
■ Exciting contemporary exterior design for an abundance of curb appeal
■ Great Room topped by a vaulted ceiling accessing the Sun Room and Deck through sliding glass doors
■ U-shaped Kitchen with a garden window, breakfast bar, and ample cabinet space
■ Master Suite privately located on the first floor with cathedral ceiling, fireplace and Sun Room access
■ An optional basement or crawl space foundation — please specify when ordering

FIRST FLOOR — 1,338 SQ. FT.
SECOND FLOOR — 545 SQ. FT.
GARAGE & STORAGE — 454 SQ. FT.

TOTAL LIVING AREA:
1,883 SQ. FT.

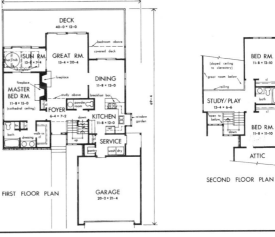

Home Recalls the South

PRICE CODE: D

■ This plan features:
— Three bedrooms
— Two full and one half baths
■ A Master Bedroom Suite with a private Study
■ Fireplaces enhancing the formal Living Room and spacious Family Room
■ A lovely, screened Porch/Patio skirting the Family Room and the Kitchen
■ A Utility Room with access into the Storage and Garage Areas

MAIN AREA — 2,466 SQ. FT.
BASEMENT — 1,447 SQ. FT.
GARAGE — 664 SQ. FT.

TOTAL LIVING AREA:
2,466 SQ. FT.

ZIP QUOTE
HOME COST CALCULATOR
see order pages for details

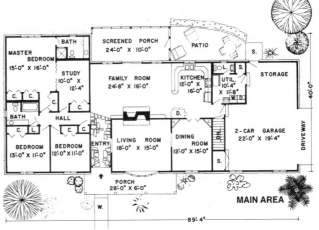

PLAN NO. 20204

Abundance of Closet Space

PRICE CODE: B

- This plan features:
- — Three bedrooms
- — Two full baths
- Roomy walk-in closets in all the bedrooms
- A Master Bedroom with decorative ceiling and a private full Bath
- A fireplaced Living Room with sloped ceilings and sliders to the Deck
- An efficient Kitchen, with plenty of cupboard space and a Pantry

MAIN AREA — 1,532 SQ. FT.
GARAGE — 484 SQ. FT.

TOTAL LIVING AREA:
1,532 SQ. FT.

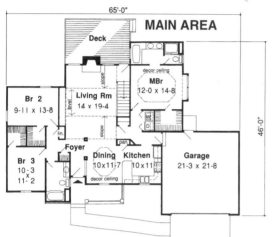

MAIN AREA

65'-0"

Deck

Living Rm
14 x 19-4

Br 2
9-11 x 13-8

MBr
12-0 x 14-8

decor ceiling

Foyer

Br 3
10-3
x
11-2

Dining
10 x 11-7

Kitchen
10 x 11

Garage
21-3 x 21-8

decor ceiling

46'-0"

An
EXCLUSIVE DESIGN
By Karl Kreeger

PLAN NO. 98005

©1997 Donald A. Gardner Architects, Inc.

Arched Windows Make Wonderful Accents

PRICE CODE: D

- This plan features
- — Three bedrooms
- — Two full baths
- Privacy and openness are balanced in this efficient house designed with expansion in mind
- The combined Great Room and dining area feature a cathedral ceiling, a fireplace, and access to the Deck
- An efficient, U-shaped Kitchen is convenient to Dining and Utility areas
- Crowned with a tray ceiling, the master bedroom includes a walk-in closet and fully appointed Bath.
- Two secondary Bedrooms, one an optional Study with a tray ceiling, share the second full Bath

MAIN FLOOR — 1,542 SQ. FT.
BONUS — 352 SQ. FT.
GARAGE — 487 SQ. FT.

TOTAL LIVING AREA :
1,542 SQ. FT.

DECK

UTIL.
6-0 x 8-4

DINING
10-0 x 10-11

GREAT RM.
15-0 x 19-6

(cathedral ceiling)

fireplace

master bath

MASTER BED RM.
14-8 x 13-0

KIT.
12-0 x 11-0

bath

walk-in closet

storage

FOYER
10-0 x 5-4

BED RM.
11-0 x 11-0

GARAGE
21-0 x 20-8

PORCH

BED RM./
STUDY
12-0 x 11-0

attic storage

down

attic storage

BONUS RM.
13-8 x 20-8

FLOOR PLAN

9-6

45-0

55-8

© 1997 Donald A. Gardner Architects, Inc.

To order your Blueprints, call 1-800-235-5700

Luxurious Touches

Price Code: D

WIDTH 42'-0"
DEPTH 53'-4"

FIRST FLOOR
No. 91526

NOOK
7/4 X 10/0

DINING
10/0 X 13/0

FAMILY
16/0 X 15/8
(9' CLG.)

LIVING
13/8 X 15/4
(12' CLG.)

DEN
12/0 X 10/6

GARAGE
19/4 X 21/2

UP

SECOND FLOOR

SPA

MASTER
16/8 X 14/8
(9'-3" CLG.)

BR. 2
11/10 X 11/0

BR. 3
11/10 X 10/0

BR. 4
11/4 X 11/0

LINEN

DN.

- This plan features:
— Four bedrooms
— Two full and one half baths

- An elegant fireplace and a twelve-foot ceiling in the Living Room

- A well-appointed and efficient Kitchen equipped with a range-top island, built-in Pantry and double sink

- A casual Breakfast Nook for informal dining

- A formal Dining Room to accommo-date formal entertaining

- A comfortable Family Room with a second fireplace

- A Master Suite that includes a spa tub, a double vanity and a walk-in closet

- Three additional Bedrooms that share a full hall Bath

FIRST FLOOR — 1,321 SQ. FT.
SECOND FLOOR — 1,155 SQ. FT.
GARAGE — 420 SQ. FT.

TOTAL LIVING AREA:
2,476 SQ. FT.

Comfortable Contemporary

Price Code: B

■ This plan features:

— Three bedrooms

— Two full and one half baths

■ Covered Porch entrance into convenient Foyer with closet and Powder Room

■ High ceiling accenting arched window in Living Room opens to Dining Room with sliding glass door to Patio

■ Efficient U-shaped Kitchen with serving counter, Dinette Area and indispensable Mudroom

■ Private Master Bedroom with two closets and Bath with whirlpool tub

■ Two additional Bedrooms with ample closets share a full Bath

FIRST FLOOR — 810 SQ. FT.
SECOND FLOOR — 781 SQ. FT.
BASEMENT — 746 SQ. FT.
GARAGE /STORAGE — 513 SQ. FT.

TOTAL LIVING AREA:
1,591 SQ. FT.

SECOND FLOOR PLAN

FIRST FLOOR PLAN

Graceful Home
PRICE CODE: B

This plan features:
- Three bedrooms
- Two full baths
- Open and airy central living areas
- Split bedroom plan assuring the utmost privacy to the Master Suite
- Drive under Garage with capacity for three vehicles
- An optional Loft above the Kitchen Area
- No materials list is available for this plan

MAIN FLOOR — 1,656 SQ. FT.
BASEMENT — 728 SQ. FT.
GARAGE — 784 SQ. FT.
DECK — 270 SQ. FT.

TOTAL LIVING AREA:
1,656 SQ. FT

An EXCLUSIVE DESIGN *By Garrell Associates Inc.*

MAIN FLOOR

Stately Colonial Home
PRICE CODE: E

This plan features:
- Four bedrooms
- Three full and one half baths
- Stately columns and arched windows project luxury and quality that is evident throughout this home
- The entry is highlighted by a palladian window, a plant shelf and an angled staircase
- The formal Living and Dining Rooms located off the entry for ease in entertaining
- The comfortable Great Room has an inviting fireplace and opens to Kitchen/Breakfast Area and the Patio
- The Master Bedroom wing offers Patio access, a luxurious Bath and a walk-in closet
- No materials list is available for this plan

FIRST FLOOR — 1,848 SQ. FT.
SECOND FLOOR — 1,111 SQ. FT.
GARAGE & SHOP — 722 SQ. FT.

TOTAL LIVING AREA:
2,959 SQ. FT.

ZIP QUOTE
HOME COST CALCULATOR
see order pages for details

FIRST FLOOR

SECOND FLOOR

To order your Blueprints, call 1-800-235-5700

PLAN NO. 98427

© Frank Betz Associates

Split Bedroom Plan
PRICE CODE: C

■ This plan features:
— Three bedrooms
— Two full baths
■ Dining Room is crowned by a tray ceiling
■ Living Room/Den privatized by double doors at its entrance, and is enhanced by a bay window
■ The Kitchen includes a walk-in Pantry and a corner double sink
■ The vaulted Breakfast Room flows naturally from the Kitchen
■ The Master Suite is topped by a tray ceiling, and contains a compartmental Bath plus two walk-in closets
■ Two roomy additional Bedrooms share a full Bath in the hall
■ An optional basement or crawl space foundation — please specify when ordering

MAIN FLOOR — 2,051 SQ. FT.
BASEMENT — 2,051 SQ. FT.
GARAGE — 441 SQ. FT.

TOTAL LIVING AREA:
2,051 SQ. FT.

PLAN NO. 96476

© 1994 Donald A. Gardner Architects, Inc.

FIRST FLOOR PLAN

SECOND FLOOR PLAN

Sunny Two-Story Foyer
PRICE CODE: D

■ This plan features:
— Three bedrooms
— Two full and one half baths
■ The two-story Foyer off the formal Dining Room sets an elegant mood in this one-and-a-half story, dormered home
■ The Great Room and Breakfast Area are both topped by a vaulted ceiling
■ The screened Porch has a relaxing atmosphere
■ The Master Suite on the first floor includes a cathedral ceiling and an elegant Bath with whirlpool tub and separate shower
■ There is plenty of Attic and Garage/Storage space available

FIRST FLOOR — 1,335 SQ. FT.
SECOND FLOOR — 488 SQ. FT.
GARAGE & STORAGE — 465 SQ. FT.

TOTAL LIVING AREA:
1,823 SQ. FT.

To order your Blueprints, call 1-800-235-5700

Great Starter or Empty Nester

Price Code: A

- This plan features:
  — Two bedrooms
  — Two full baths
- A formal Living Room or a cozy Den, the front room to the right of the Entry Hall adapts to your lifestyle
- An efficient Kitchen with ample counter and storage space
- A formal Dining Room situated next to the Kitchen and flowing from the Great Room
- A corner fireplace highlighting the Great Room
- A walk-in closet and a private double vanity Bath in the Master Suite
- An additional Bedroom that easily accesses the full hall Bath
- This home cannot be built in Clark County, Washington

MAIN AREA — 1,420 SQ. FT.

TOTAL LIVING AREA:
1,420 SQ. FT.

◀ 40' ▶

MASTER
13/8 X 12/4 +/-

DINING
10/0 X 11/0

GREAT RM.
14/4 X 15/0 +/-

BR. 2
11/0 X 11/0

13/0 X 13/0

58'

LINEN

PAN. REF.

LR./DEN
13/0 X 11/8 +/-

GARAGE
19/4 X 21/8

OPTIONAL
BUILT-IN
OR CLOSET

PORCH

MAIN AREA
No. 91545

© 1997 Donald A. Gardner Architects, Inc.

B. NATHAN

Relaxed Country Living

Price Code: E

■ This plan features:

— Three bedrooms

— Two full baths

■ Comfortable Country home with deluxe Master Suite, front and back Porches and dual-sided fireplace

■ Vaulted Great Room brightened by two clerestory dormers and fireplace shared with Breakfast Bay

■ Dining Room and front Bedroom/Study dressed up with tray ceilings

■ Master Bedroom features vaulted ceiling, back Porch access, and luxurious Bath with over-sized, walk-in closet

■ Skylit bonus room over Garage provides extra room for family needs

MAIN FLOOR — 2,027 SQ. FT.
BONUS ROOM — 340 SQ. FT.
GARAGE & STORAGE — 532 SQ. FT.

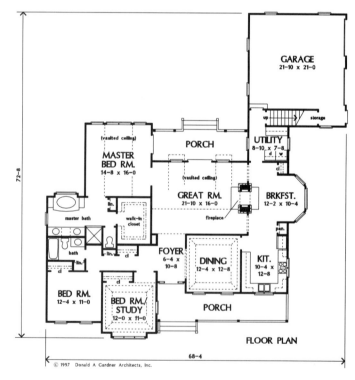

FLOOR PLAN

© 1997 Donald A Gardner Architects, Inc.

TOTAL LIVING AREA:
2,027 SQ. FT.

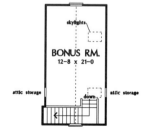

To order your Blueprints, call 1-800-235-5700

Fashionable Country Style
PRICE CODE: E

▪ This plan features:
- Four bedrooms
- Two full, one three-quarter and one half baths
▪ The large covered front Porch adds old fashioned appeal to this modern floor plan
▪ The Dining Room features a decorative ceiling and a built in hutch
▪ The Kitchen has a center island and is adjacent to the gazebo shaped Nook
▪ The Great Room is accented by transom windows and a fireplace with bookcases on either side of it
▪ The Master Bedroom has a cathedral ceiling, a door to the front Porch, and a large Bath with a whirlpool tub
▪ Upstairs are three additional Bedrooms and two full Baths
▪ An optional basement or crawl space foundation — please specify when ordering

First Floor — 1,881 sq. ft.
Second Floor — 814 sq. ft.
Garage — 534 sq. ft.
Basement — 1,020 sq. ft.

Total Living Area:
2,695 sq. ft.

© design basics, inc.

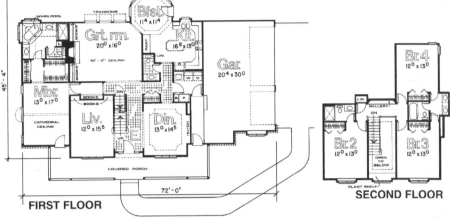

FIRST FLOOR

SECOND FLOOR

Glass Dining Alcove
PRICE CODE: C

▪ This plan features:
- Four bedrooms
- Two full and one half baths
▪ Covered Entry opens to two-story Foyer accented by a medallion window
▪ Formal Living and Dining rooms convenient for entertaining
▪ A large fireplace and a wall of windows enhance Family Room
▪ An efficient Kitchen with snack bar/serving counter, built-in Pantry and desk, Dining Area and nearby Laundry and Garage entry
▪ Corner Master Bedroom enhanced by a walk-in closet, dressing area and full Bath
▪ Three additional Bedrooms with ample closets, share a full Bath

First Floor — 1,100 sq. ft.
Second Floor — 892 sq. ft.
Garage — 458 sq. ft.
Basement — 1,100 sq. ft.

Total Living Area:
1,992 sq. ft.

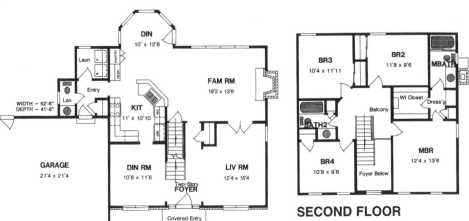

FIRST FLOOR

SECOND FLOOR

PLAN NO. 94103

To order your Blueprints, call 1-800-235-5700

111

PLAN NO. 99450

An Exciting Mixture
PRICE CODE: E

■ This plan features:
— Four bedrooms
— Two full and one half baths
■ The exterior is an exciting mixture of brick, and siding
■ The Dining Room has five windows that view the wrapping front Porch
■ A fireplace with built-ins set between it adds character the Great Room
■ The U-shaped Kitchen is the ultimate for cooking convenience
■ There is a rear-covered Porch and a breezeway that lead to the Garage
■ The walk-in closet in the Master Bedroom is a delight
■ Lovely windows brighten all of the secondary Bedroom
■ There is a bonus room over the Garage awaiting your finishing touches

MAIN FLOOR — 2,273 SQ. FT.
BONUS — 342 SQ. FT.
GARAGE — 528 SQ. FT.

TOTAL LIVING AREA:
2,273 SQ. FT.

PLAN NO. 98535

Tremendous Appeal
PRICE CODE: F

■ This plan features:
— Four bedrooms
— Two full and one half baths
■ A European Country exterior with a modern American interior
■ The circular stairway highlights the entry
■ The formal Dining Room has a bay window and easy access to the Kitchen
■ A private Study with a double door entry
■ Formal Living Room has a fireplace and elegant columns
■ The large Family Room boasts a large brick fireplace and a built-in TV cabinet
■ An angled Kitchen contains all the conveniences that the cook demands, including a built-in Pantry and ovens
■ A large informal Dining Area that is adjacent to the Kitchen
■ The Master Suite occupies one wing of the house with a Bath and a huge walk-in closet
■ No material list is available for this plan

MAIN FLOOR — 2,658 SQ. FT.
UPPER FLOOR — 854 SQ. FT.
GARAGE — 660 SQ. FT.

TOTAL LIVING AREA:
3,512 SQ. FT.

Small, But Not Lacking

Price Code: C

■ This plan features:

— Three bedrooms

— One full and one three-quarter baths

■ Great Room adjoining the Dining Room for ease in entertaining

■ Kitchen highlighted by a peninsula counter/snack bar extending work space and offering convenience in serving informal meals or snacks

■ Split-bedroom plan allowing for privacy for the Master Bedroom with a private Bath and a walk-in closet

■ Two additional Bedrooms share the full family Bath in the hall

■ Garage entry convenient to the kitchen

MAIN FLOOR — 1,546 SQ. FT.
BASEMENT — 1,530 SQ. FT.
GARAGE — 440 SQ. FT.

TOTAL LIVING AREA:
1,546 SQ. FT.

MAIN FLOOR
No. 94116

Floor plan labels:
BR2 10'6 x 12'
WI Closet
GREAT RM 13'10 x 14'6
DIN 11'2 x 10'2
MBATH
MBR 14' x 14'10
SNACK BAR
WI Closet
FOYER
KIT 11'2 x 13'2
Entry
Laun
DIN RM 10'4 x 12'8
BR3 10'11 x 10'8
Covered Entry
GARAGE
43'
60'

Warm and Inviting

Price Code: D

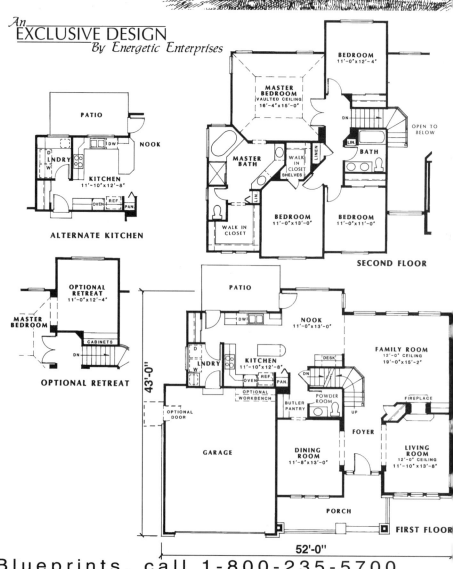

■ This plan features:

— Four bedrooms

— Two full and one half baths

■ A see-through fireplace between the Living Room and the Family Room

■ A gourmet Kitchen with work island, built-in pantry, and double sink

■ A Master Bedroom with a vaulted ceiling

■ A Master Bath with a large double vanity, linen closet, a corner tub, a separate shower, a compartmented toilet, and huge walk-in closet

■ Three additional bedrooms, one with walk-in closet share full hall Bath

■ No materials list available

FIRST FLOOR — 1,241 SQ. FT.
SECOND FLOOR — 1,170 SQ. FT.

TOTAL LIVING AREA:
2,411 SQ. FT.

An
EXCLUSIVE DESIGN
By Energetic Enterprises

ALTERNATE KITCHEN

OPTIONAL RETREAT

SECOND FLOOR

FIRST FLOOR

To order your Blueprints, call 1-800-235-5700

Distinguished Look

PRICE CODE: C

This plan features:
- Three bedrooms
- Two full and one half baths
- The Family Room, Breakfast Room and the Kitchen are presented in an open layout
- A fireplace in the Family Room provides a warm atmosphere
- The plush Master Suite pampers the owner and features a trapezoid glass above the tub
- Two additional Bedrooms share the use of the double vanity Bath in the hall
- An optional basement, crawl space or slab foundation — please specify when ordering

FIRST FLOOR — 1,028 SQ. FT.
SECOND FLOOR — 878 SQ. FT.
BONUS ROOM — 315 SQ. FT.
GARAGE — 497 SQ. FT.

TOTAL LIVING AREA:
1,906 SQ. FT.

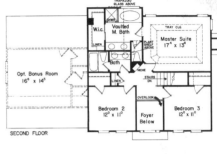

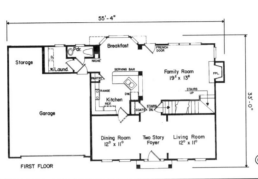

© Frank Betz Associates

Growing Families Take Note

PRICE CODE: D

This plan features:
- Three bedrooms
- Two full baths
- Unlimited options on the second floor bonus area
- Columns accenting the Dining Room, adjacent to the Foyer
- Great Room, open to the Kitchen and Breakfast Room, enlarged by a cathedral ceiling
- Living and entertaining space expands to the Deck
- Master Suite topped by a tray ceiling and including a walk-in closet skylit Bath with garden tub and a double vanity
- Flexible Bedroom/Study share a Bath with another Bedroom

FIRST FLOOR — 1,803 SQ. FT.
SECOND FLOOR — 80 SQ. FT.
GARAGE & STORAGE — 569 SQ. FT.
BONUS SPACE — 918 SQ. FT.

TOTAL LIVING AREA:
1,883 SQ. FT.

© 1995 Donald A. Gardner Architects, Inc.

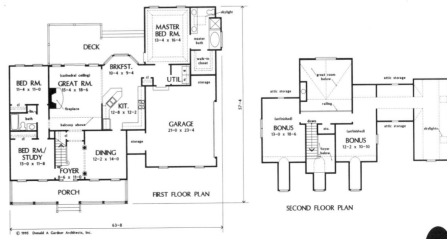

To order your Blueprints, call 1-800-235-5700

PLAN NO. 92405

Perfect for a First Home
PRICE CODE: B

- This plan features:
  — Three bedrooms
  — Two full baths
- A spacious Master Suite including a separate Master Bath with a garden tub and shower
- A Dining Room and Family Room highlighted by vaulted ceilings
- An oversized Patio accessible from the Master Suite, Family Room and Breakfast Room
- A well planned Kitchen measuring 12' x 11'
- No materials list is available for this plan

MAIN AREA — 1,564 SQ. FT.
GARAGE & STORAGE — 476 SQ. FT.

TOTAL LIVING AREA:
1,564 SQ. FT.

MAIN AREA

PLAN NO. 94124

Open Family Living Area
PRICE CODE: E

- This plan features:
  — Four Bedrooms
  — Two full and one half baths
- An immediate spacious feeling created by a two-story Foyer
- Formal Living Room topped by a vaulted ceiling
- Pocket doors between the Family Room and the Living Room
- Open layout between the Family Room, Dinette and Kitchen
- Efficient Kitchen with an island, Pantry and snack bar
- A bayed window enhancing elegant formal Dining Room
- Secluded Master Suite with a double door entry and plush Master Bath
- No materials list is available for this plan

FIRST FLOOR — 1,861 SQ. FT.
SECOND FLOOR — 598 SQ. FT.
BASEMENT — 1,802 SQ. FT.
GARAGE — 523 SQ. FT.

TOTAL LIVING AREA:
2,459 SQ. FT.

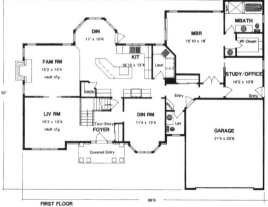

To order your Blueprints, call 1-800-235-5700

© design basics inc.

FIRST FLOOR
No. 99452

SECOND FLOOR

ZIP QUOTE
HOME COST CALCULATOR
see order pages for details

Traditional Home

Price Code: E

■ This plan features:

— Four bedrooms

— Two full, one three-quarter and one half baths

■ Dining Room has a built-in hutch and a bay window

■ Cozy Den and Great Room have high ceilings and transom windows

■ Conveniently arranged Kitchen adjoins the Breakfast Nook

■ The warm Gathering Room features a fireplace and a cathedral ceiling

■ The secluded Master Bedroom is a world away from the busy areas of the home

■ Upstairs are three Bedrooms and two full Baths

FIRST FLOOR — 2,158 SQ. FT.
SECOND FLOOR — 821 SQ. FT.
BASEMENT — 2,158 SQ. FT.
GARAGE — 692 SQ. FT.

TOTAL LIVING AREA:
2,979 SQ. FT.

DUPLEX DESIGN

Country Style

Price Code: G

- This plan features(per unit):
— Two or three bedrooms
— One full and one half baths

- Covered sitting Porch, cedar shingles on gable ends, wood shutters and window boxes add to country flavor

- Tiled entry into spacious Living Area with decorative window, opens to Dining Area

- Efficient, U-shaped Kitchen with a serving counter/snackbar

- First floor Study/Bedroom with closet and access to a half Bath

- Large second floor Bedrooms offer maximum privacy with separating roof

- Rear Bedroom enhanced by two closets and private access to double vanity Bath

MAIN FLOOR — 700 SQ. FT.
SECOND FLOOR — 588 SQ. FT.

TOTAL UNIT LIVING AREA: 1,288 SQ. FT.

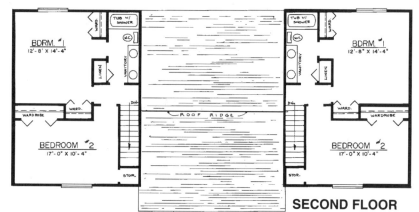

SECOND FLOOR

WIDTH — 66'-0"
DEPTH — 32'-0"

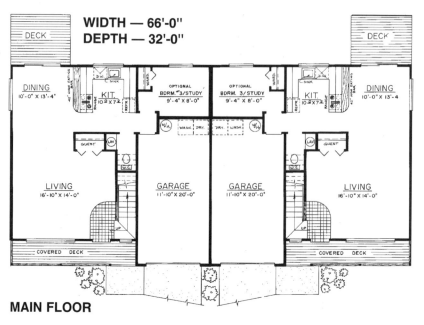

MAIN FLOOR

To order your Blueprints, call 1-800-235-5700

Attractive Roof Lines

PRICE CODE: F

■ This plan features:
— Four bedrooms
— Two full and one half baths

■ Two-story Living Room highlighted by a fireplace and a convenient wetbar

■ Dining Room adjoins the living room topped by an elegant decorative ceiling

■ Kitchen made more efficient by a peninsula counter/snack bar and ample storage space

■ Family enhanced by built-in cabinetry and a corner fireplace

■ Decorative ceiling, spa tub, separate shower and a double vanity pampering the Master Suite

■ No materials list is available for this plan

FIRST FLOOR — 1,894 SQ. FT.
SECOND FLOOR — 1,544 SQ. FT.

TOTAL LIVING AREA:
3,438 SQ. FT.

PLAN NO. 91587

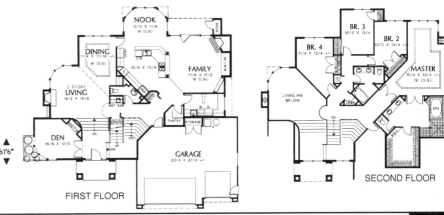

FIRST FLOOR

SECOND FLOOR

Country Cottage Charm

PRICE CODE: F

■ This plan features:
— Four bedrooms
— Two full and one half baths

■ Vaulted Master Bedroom has a private skylight Bath and large walk-in closet with a built in chest of drawers

■ Three more Bedrooms (one possibly a Study) have walk-in closets and share a full Bath

■ A loft and bonus room above the Living Room

■ Family Room has built-in book shelves, a fireplace, and overlooks the covered Verandah in the backyard

■ The huge three car Garage has a separate Shop Area

■ An optional slab or a crawl space foundation — please specify when ordering

FIRST FLOOR — 2,787 SQ. FT.
SECOND FLOOR — 636 SQ. FT.

TOTAL LIVING AREA:
3,423 SQ. FT.

PLAN NO. 98536

ZIP QUOTE
HOME COST CALCULATOR
see order pages for details

Upper Floor

Upper Floor
Optional Bonus Room & Loft

Main Floor

119

PLAN NO. 98430

With All the Amenities
PRICE CODE: C

- This plan features:
  — Three bedrooms
  — Two full and one half baths
- A sixteen foot high over the Foyer
- Arched openings highlight the hallway accessing the Great Room which is further enhanced by a fireplace
- A French door to the rear yard and decorative columns at its arched entrance
- Another vaulted ceiling topping the Dining Room, convenient to both the Living Room and the Kitchen
- An expansive Kitchen features a center work island, a built-in Pantry and a Breakfast Area defined by a tray ceiling
- A Master Suite also has a tray ceiling treatment and includes a lavish private Bath and a huge walk-in closet
- Secondary Bedrooms have private access to a full Bath
- An optional basement, crawl space or slab foundation — please specify when ordering

MAIN FLOOR — 1,884 SQ. FT.
BASEMENT — 1,908 SQ. FT.
GARAGE — 495 SQ. FT.

TOTAL LIVING AREA:
1,884 SQ. FT.

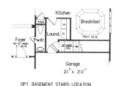

OPT. BASEMENT STAIRS LOCATION

© Frank Betz Associates

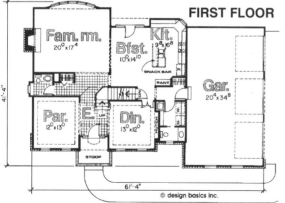 

PLAN NO. 99454

Captivating Colonial
PRICE CODE: D

- This plan features:
  — Four bedrooms
  — Two full and one half baths
- Decorative windows and brick detailing
- Dining room highlighted by decorative ceiling, French doors, and hutch space
- The Family Room has a fireplace and a bow window
- The Breakfast Nook and Kitchen are perfectly set up for meals on the run
- Upstairs find the Master Bedroom and Bath fully complemented
- Three more Bedrooms and a Bath completed the second floor plan
- An optional a basement or slab foundation — please specify when ordering

FIRST FLOOR — 1,362 SQ. FT.
SECOND FLOOR — 1,223 SQ. FT.
GARAGE — 734 SQ. FT.

TOTAL LIVING AREA:
2,585 SQ. FT.

FIRST FLOOR

© design basics inc.

SECOND FLOOR

To order your Blueprints, call 1-800-235-5700

Colonial with Contemporary Flair

Price Code: D

- This plan features:
  - — Four bedrooms
  - — Two full and one half baths
- The Master Bedroom has a walk-in closet and an attached Bath with a skylight
- Upstairs there are three additional Bedrooms and one full Bath
- The Dining Room and Living Room are traditionally placed
- The Family Room and Dinette are laid out with plenty of open space
- The island Kitchen has a useful snack bar
- No materials listIS available for this plan

FIRST FLOOR — 1,108 SQ. FT.
SECOND FLOOR — 942 SQ. FT.
BASEMENT — 1,108 SQ. FT.
GARAGE — 455 SQ. FT.

TOTAL LIVING AREA:
2,050 SQ. FT.

WIDTH 66'-0"
DEPTH 32'-0"

GARAGE
21'4 x 21'4

Laun
W
D

Entry

PANTRY

DIN
9' x 10'

DW

BRICK BAR

KIT
12'6 x 13'8
minus

Lav

FM RM
19'2 x 13'4
minus

DIN RM
12'4 x 11'8

Two-Story
FOYER

LIV RM
13'2 x 11'6

FIRST FLOOR
No. 94141

MBATH

WI Closet

BR 4
10'4 x 10

BR 3
10'6 x 10

Balcony

BATH 2

MBR
12'4 x 17'10

BR 2
13'2 x 11'6

Foyer Below

SECOND FLOOR

Let the Sun Shine In

Price Code: E

■ This plan features:

— Four bedrooms

— Two full and one three-quarter baths

■ Two-story entrance with a second floor window

■ Den with windows on two sides including a corner window

■ Family Room, Nook and Kitchen are open to each other for a spacious feeling

■ Cooktop island/snack bar built-in desk and a pantry highlight the efficient Kitchen

■ Family Room enhanced by a second fireplace

■ Lavish Master Suite with a decorative ceiling in the Bedroom and a private, plush Bath

■ No materials list is available for this plan

FIRST FLOOR — 1,575 SQ. FT.
SECOND FLOOR — 1,338 SQ. FT.
GARAGE — 864 SQ. FT.

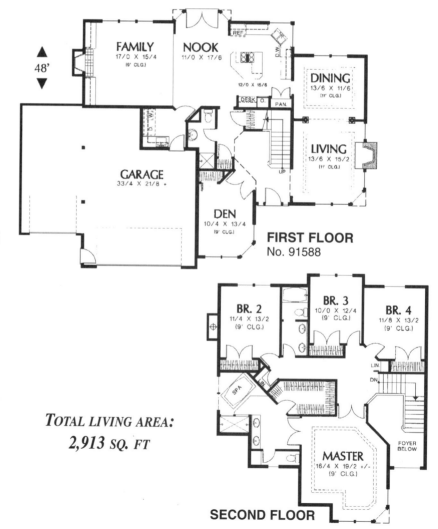

TOTAL LIVING AREA:
2,913 SQ. FT

SECOND FLOOR

To order your Blueprints, call 1-800-235-5700

©1997 Donald A. Gardner Architects, Inc.

Pretty as a Picture

Price Code: D

SCREEN PORCH
16-8 x 7-0

BRKFST.
12-0 x 11-0

GARAGE
23-0 x 21-0

BONUS RM.
16-0 x 21-0

attic storage

down

attic storage

bath

UTIL.

w
d

walk-in closet

master bath

GREAT RM.
17-0 x 19-0

fireplace
(cathedral ceiling)

KIT.
12-0 x 10-8

BED RM./ OFFICE
11-4 x 11-8

BED RM.
11-4 x 11-8

DINING
12-0 x 12-8

FOYER
9-0 x 7-8

MASTER BED RM.
17-2 x 13-4

PORCH

65-10

62-10

MAIN AREA
No. 98008

© 1997 Donald A Gardner Architects, Inc.

MAIN FLOOR — 1,911 sq. ft.
BONUS — 406 sq. ft.
GARAGE — 551 sq. ft.

TOTAL LIVING AREA:
1,911 sq. ft.

■ This plan features:

— Three bedrooms

— Two full baths

■ Picture perfect this Country style plan offers space and flexibility

■ The wrapping front Porch is beautiful and functional at the same time

■ Inside the Great Room has a cathedral ceiling and a fireplace

■ The Dining Room has windows that overlook the front Porch, plus a tray ceiling

■ The Kitchen has a convenient layout with a good work triangle

■ The Master Bedroom is isolated and features a galley Bath that leads into the walk-in closet

■ Two additional bedrooms are located in their own wing with a full Bath

■ The two-car Garage is conveniently located in the rear of the home

■ There is a Bonus Room over the Garage waiting to be finished to suit your needs

To order your Blueprints, call 1-800-235-5700

123

F. NATHAN

© 1995 Donald A. Gardner Architects, Inc.

Comfort and Charm

Price Code: D

■ This plan features:

— Three bedrooms

— Two full and one half baths

■ The Foyer opens into the dormers vaulted ceiling

■ A cathedral ceiling in the Great Room soars up to a palladian window

■ The Kitchen is equipped with an angled island peninsula

■ Bay windows accent the formal Dining Room and Breakfast Nook

■ The Master Suite accesses the Deck and includes a private Bath

■ Upstairs find two Bedrooms and a balcony that overlooks the Great Room

FIRST FLOOR — 1,480 SQ. FT.
SECOND FLOOR — 511 SQ. FT.
BONUS ROOM — 363 SQ. FT.
GARAGE — 621 SQ. FT.

TOTAL LIVING AREA:
1,991 SQ. FT.

FIRST FLOOR
No. 96480

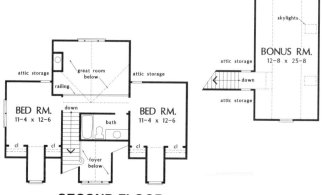

SECOND FLOOR

124

To order your Blueprints, call 1-800-235-5700

Stucco Accents
PRICE CODE: E

This plan features:
- Four bedrooms
- Two full, one three-quarter and one half baths
- Stucco accents and graceful window treatments enhance the front of this home
- Double doors open to the private Den which features brilliant bayed windows
- French doors open to a large screened-in Verandah ideal for outdoor entertaining
- The open Living Room and handsome curved staircase add drama to the entry area
- The gourmet Kitchen, dinette bay and Family Room flow together for easy living
- The elegant Master Bedroom has a ten foot vaulted ceiling
- Two walk-in closets, his-n-her vanities and a whirlpool tub highlight the master Bath
- Three additional Bedrooms have private access to full Baths
- An optional basement or slab foundation — please specify when ordering

FIRST FLOOR — 1,631 SQ. FT.
SECOND FLOOR — 1,426 SQ. FT.
BASEMENT — 1,631 SQ. FT.
GARAGE — 681 SQ. FT.

TOTAL LIVING AREA:
3,057 SQ. FT.

© design basics inc.

SECOND FLOOR   **FIRST FLOOR**

PLAN NO.98431

Exceptional Family Living
PRICE CODE: F

This plan features:
- Four bedrooms
- Three full and one half baths
- A decorative dormer, a bay window and an eyebrow arched window provide for a pleasing Country farmhouse facade
- The cozy Study has its own fireplace and a bay window
- The large formal Living Room has a fireplace and built-in bookcases
- The huge island Kitchen is open to the Breakfast Bay and the Family Room
- The Master Suite includes a large Bath with a unique closet
- Three more Bedrooms located at the other end of the home each have private access to a full Bath

MAIN FLOOR — 4,082 SQ. FT.
GARAGE — 720 SQ. FT.

TOTAL LIVING AREA:
4,082 SQ. FT.

PLAN NO. 98538

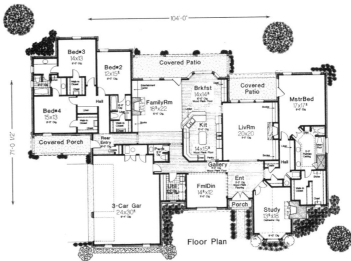

Floor Plan

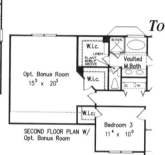

© Frank Betz Associates

With Room to Expand
PRICE CODE: B

■ This plan features:
— Three bedrooms
— Two full and one half baths
■ An impressive two-story Foyer
■ The Kitchen is equipped with ample cabinet and counter space
■ Spacious Family Room flows from the Breakfast Bay and is highlighted by a fireplace and a French door to the rear yard
■ The Master Suite is topped by a tray ceiling and is enhanced by a vaulted, five-piece master Bath
■ Two additional Bedrooms share the full Bath in the hall
■ An optional crawl space or slab foundation — please specify when ordering

FIRST FLOOR — 882 SQ. FT.
SECOND FLOOR — 793 SQ. FT.
BONUS ROOM — 416 SQ. FT.
BASEMENT — 882 SQ. FT.
GARAGE — 510 SQ. FT.

TOTAL LIVING AREA:
1,675 SQ. FT.

FIRST FLOOR PLAN

Garage 19'9 x 25'0
Breakfast
PANTRY
Kitchen
RANGE
DW.
REF.
FPL.
FRENCH DOOR
Family Room 17'6 x 12'0
Dining Room 11'4 x 10'0
Living Room 12'5 x 11'4
Two Story Foyer
Covered Porch
Pwdr.
NICHE
COATS
STAIRS DN
49'-6"
35'-4"

SECOND FLOOR PLAN
BHWR
Vaulted M.Bath
Master Suite 17'0 x 12'0
TRAY CLG.
PLANT SHELF ABOVE
LINEN
W.I.c.
Laund.
Bath
LINEN
Bedroom 3 11'4 x 10'0
Bedroom 2 10'2 x 11'4
Foyer Below
OVERLOOK
STAIRS DOWN
SHELF

SECOND FLOOR PLAN W/ Opt. Bonus Room
Opt. Bonus Room 15'5 x 20'3
Vaulted M.Bath
BHWR
W.I.c.
LINEN
PLANT SHELF ABOVE
W.I.c.
Bedroom 3 11'4 x 10'0

Great Room
With Vaulted Ceiling
PRICE CODE: F

■ This plan features:
— Four bedrooms
— Three full and one half aths
■ Cozy covered porch leading into an impressive two-story foyer
■ Formal dining room accented by a bay window
■ A gas fireplace in the Great Room
■ Kitchen and Dinette topped by a vaulted ceiling, adjoining with only a peninsula counter between them
■ Island Kitchen has an abundance of work and storage space
■ First floor Master Suite affording privacy and luxury
■ No materials list is available for this plan

FIRST FLOOR — 1,845 SQ. FT.
SECOND FLOOR — 876 SQ. FT.
BASEMENT — 1,832 SQ. FT.

TOTAL LIVING AREA:
2,721 SQ. FT.

First floor
GARAGE 21'4 x 21'4
vault cl'g DIN 11' x 9'10 plus
KIT 13' x 16'
vault cl'g GREAT RM 15'4 x 19'8
GAS FIREPLACE
MBATH
Wl Closet
MBR 12'10 x 15'6
Lav
Lav
Entry
Laun
DIN RM 13' x 11'8
Two-Story FOYER
STUDY 13' x 11'8
Covered Entry

Second floor
Din Below
Great Room Below
BR2 10'7 x 9'4
BATH 2
BR3 12' x 11'8
Balcony
Foyer Below
BATH 3
BR4 11'1 x 11'

To order your Blueprints, call 1-800-235-5700

PLAN NO. 99859

© 1990 Donald A. Gardner, Architects, Inc.

TOTAL LIVING AREA:
1,831 SQ. FT.

Flexibility to Expand

Price Code: D

■ This plan features:

— Three bedrooms

— Two full and one half baths

■ Three Bedroom country cottage has lots of room to expand

■ Two-story Foyer contains palladian window in a clerestory dormer

■ Efficient Kitchen opens to Breakfast Area and Deck for outdoor dining

■ Columns separating the Great Room and the Dining Room that have nine foot ceilings

■ Master Bedroom Suite is on the first level and features a skylight above the whirlpool tub

■ An optional basement or crawl space foundation— please specify when ordering

FIRST FLOOR — 1,289 SQ. FT.
SECOND FLOOR — 542 SQ. FT.
BONUS ROOM — 393 SQ. FT.
GARAGE & STORAGE — 521 SQ. FT.

FIRST FLOOR PLAN

- seat
- DECK
- 10-0
- KIT. 9-0 x 11-8 (8' ceiling)
- BRKFST. 9-8 x 9-8
- UTILITY 10-4 x 6-4
- d w cl
- pd. rm.
- up
- storage
- DINING 12-0 x 12-0
- master bath skylight
- GARAGE 21-8 x 20-4
- 40-4
- down
- walk-in closet
- cl
- GREAT RM. 13-4 x 19-4
- fireplace
- MASTER BED RM. 13-4 x 13-0
- up
- PORCH
- 66-4

© 1990 Donald A Gardner Architects, Inc.

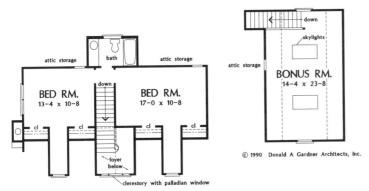

SECOND FLOOR PLAN

- attic storage
- bath
- attic storage
- attic storage
- down
- skylights
- BONUS RM. 14-4 x 23-8
- BED RM. 13-4 x 10-8
- down
- BED RM. 17-0 x 10-8
- cl
- cl
- cl
- cl
- foyer below
- clerestory with palladian window

© 1990 Donald A Gardner Architects, Inc.

© 1996 Donald A Gardner Architects, Inc.

Cathedral Ceiling
Enlarges Great Room

Price Code: D

- This plan features:
  - — Three bedrooms
  - — Two full baths
- Two dormers add volume to the Foyer
- Great Room, topped by a cathedral ceiling, is open to the Kitchen and Breakfast Area
- Accent columns define the Foyer, Great Room, Kitchen, and Breakfast Area
- Private Master Suite crowned in a tray ceiling and highlighted by a skylit Bath
- The front Bedroom is topped by a tray ceiling

MAIN FLOOR — 1,699 SQ. FT.
BONUS — 336 SQ. FT.
GARAGE — 498 SQ. FT.

TOTAL LIVING AREA:
1,699 SQ. FT.

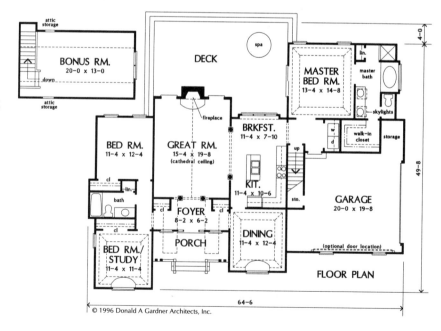

© 1996 Donald A Gardner Architects, Inc.

To order your Blueprints, call 1-800-235-5700

design basics inc.

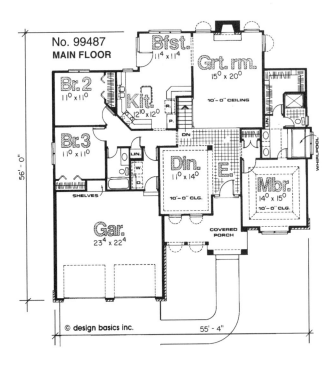

No. 99487
MAIN FLOOR

Br. 2
11⁰ x 11⁰

Br. 3
11⁰ x 11⁰

Kit.
12¹⁰ x 12⁰

Bfst.
11⁴ x 11⁴

Grt. rm.
15⁰ x 20⁰
10'-0" CEILING

Din.
11⁰ x 14⁰
10'-0" CLG.

Mbr.
14⁰ x 15⁰
10'-0" CLG.

Gar.
23⁴ x 22⁴

SHELVES

LIN.

W.
D.

DN

WHIRLPOOL

COVERED PORCH

© design basics inc.

56' - 0"

55' - 4"

Columns and Arched Windows

Price Code: C

■ This plan features:

— Three bedrooms

— Two full baths

■ Ten-foot entry with formal views of the Dining Room and the Great Room

■ A brick fireplace and arched windows in the Great Room

■ Large island Kitchen with an angled range and a built-in Pantry

■ Master Suite with a whirlpool Bath and a sloped ceiling

■ An optional basement or slab foundation — please specify when ordering

MAIN FLOOR — 1,806 SQ. FT.
GARAGE — 548 SQ. FT.

TOTAL LIVING AREA:
1,806 SQ. FT.

S. NATHAN

© 1990 Donald A. Gardner Architects, Inc.

Compact Three Bedroom

Price Code: C

ZIP QUOTE
HOME COST CALCULATOR
see order pages for details

■ This plan features:

— Three bedrooms

— Two full baths

■ Contemporary interior punctuated by elegant columns

■ Dormers above the covered Porch light the Foyer leading to the dramatic Great Room crowned in a cathedral ceiling and enhanced by a fireplace

■ Great Room opens to the island Kitchen with Breakfast Area and access to a spacious rear Deck

■ Tray ceilings adding interest to the Bedroom/Study, Dining Room and the Master Bedroom

■ Luxurious Master Bedroom suite highlighted by a walk-in closet and a Bath with dual vanity, separate shower and a whirlpool tub

MAIN FLOOR — 1,452 SQ. FT.
GARAGE AND STORAGE — 427 SQ. FT.

TOTAL LIVING AREA: 1,452 SQ. FT.

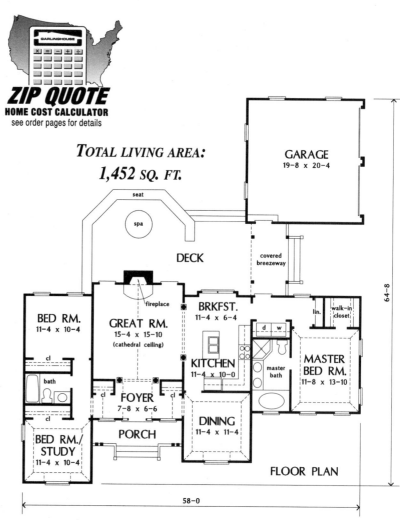

FLOOR PLAN

To order your Blueprints, call 1-800-235-5700

An Estate of Epic Proportion
PRICE CODE: F

- This plan features
  - Four bedrooms
  - Three full and one half baths
- Front door opening into a grand Entry way with a 20′ ceiling and a spiral staircase
- Flanking the Entry way on the right is the Living Room with cathedral ceiling and fireplace, and on the left is the bayed formal Dining Room
- Walk down the Gallery to the Study with a full wall built in bookcase
- The enormous Master Bedroom has a walk in closet, sumptuous Bath and a bayed Sitting Area
- Family Room has a wetbar, a fireplace, and a door which leads outside to the covered Verandah
- Upstairs are three Bedrooms, two full Baths, and a Study Area with a built-in desk
- An optional basement or a slab foundation — please specify when ordering
- No materials list is available for this plan

FIRST FLOOR — 2,751 SQ. FT.
SECOND FLOOR — 1,185 SQ. FT.
BONUS — 343 SQ. FT.
GARAGE — 790 SQ. FT.

TOTAL LIVING AREA:
3,936 SQ. FT.

ZIP QUOTE
HOME COST CALCULATOR
see order pages for details

MAIN FLOOR

UPPER FLOOR

Elegant Palladian Window
PRICE CODE: B

- This plan features:
  - Four bedrooms
  - Two full baths
- Gracious entry with columns framing Living and Breakfast Rooms
- Living Room enhanced by a cathedral ceiling, palladian window and hearth fireplace between bookshelves
- Efficient Kitchen with corner pantry, peninsula counter serving Breakfast Area and Patio beyond, and nearby Utility/Garage entry
- Corner Master Bedroom offers a cozy Sitting Area, Patio access, walk-in closet and lavish Bath
- Three additional Bedrooms with over-sized closets, share a double vanity Bath
- No materials list is available for this plan

MAIN FLOOR — 1,696 SQ. FT.
GARAGE — 389 SQ. FT.

TOTAL LIVING AREA:
1,696 SQ. FT.

Floor Plan

To order your Blueprints, call 1-800-235-5700

Fireplace Center of Circular Living Area

PRICE CODE: B

■ This plan features:
— Three bedrooms
— One full and one three-quarter baths
■ A dramatically positioned fireplace as a focal point for the main living area
■ The Kitchen, Dining and Living Rooms form a circle that allows work areas to flow into living areas
■ Sliding glass doors accessible to wood a Deck
■ A convenient Laundry Room located off the Kitchen
■ A double Garage providing excellent storage

MAIN AREA— 1,783 SQ. FT.
GARAGE — 576 SQ. FT.

TOTAL LIVING AREA:
1,783 SQ. FT.

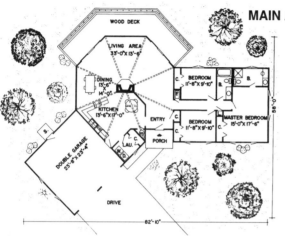

MAIN AREA

Coastal Delight

PRICE CODE: F

■ This plan features:
— Three bedrooms
— Two full baths
■ Living area above the Garage and Storage/Bonus areas offering a "piling" design for coastal, waterfront or low-lying terrain
■ Double-door Entry into an open Foyer with landing staircase leads into the Great Room
■ Three sets of double doors below a vaulted ceiling in the Great Room offer lots of air, light and easy access to both the Sun Deck and Veranda
■ A Dining Room convenient to the Great Room and Kitchen featuring vaulted ceilings and decorative windows
■ A glassed-in Nook adjacent to the efficient Kitchen with an island work center
■ Two secondary Bedrooms, a full Bath and a Utility Room on the first floor
■ A second floor Master Suite with a vaulted ceiling, double door to a private Deck, his-n-her closets and a plush Bath

FIRST FLOOR — 1,736 SQ. FT.
SECOND FLOOR — 640 SQ. FT.
CARPORT — 840 SQ. FT.
BONUS ROOM — 253 SQ. FT.

TOTAL LIVING AREA:
2,376 SQ. FT.

CARPORT

SECOND FLOOR

FIRST FLOOR

To order your Blueprints, call 1-800-235-5700

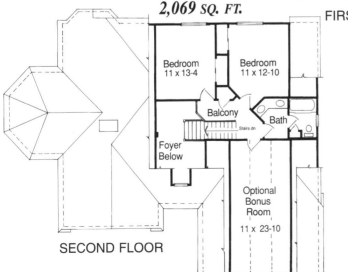

ZIP QUOTE
HOME COST CALCULATOR
see order pages for details

Breakfast 9-6 x 14-8

Kitchen 10 x 16-4

1/2 Circle window above

Bath

Master Bedroom 15 x 13

Lin.

Dining Room 14 x 13-2

Pass thru

Pantry

Ent. Ctr.

Hall

Laun.

Walk-in closet

Stairs up

WIDTH 57'-6"
DEPTH 45'-0"

Sunken Great Room 16-4 x 16-4

Slope ceiling   Slope ceiling

Foyer

Two-car Garage 20 x 20

TOTAL LIVING AREA:
2,069 SQ. FT.

FIRST FLOOR

Bedroom 11 x 13-4

Bedroom 11 x 12-10

Balcony

Bath

Stairs dn

Foyer Below

Optional Bonus Room 11 x 23-10

SECOND FLOOR

Great for Empty-Nesters or Families with Teens

Price Code: C

■ This plan features:

— Three bedrooms

— Two full and one half baths

■ Decorative brick, arched windows and unique hip roof, a two-story Foyer with an open staircase, and balcony

■ A grand sunken Great Room with a cathedral ceiling, built-in entertainment center and a stone fireplace

■ Kitchen with a central work island, built-in Pantry, a pass-thru to Dining Room, a bay windowed Breakfast Area

■ A first floor Master Suite with walk-in closet, and a plush Bath

■ Three second floor Bedrooms sharing a full hall Bath and a bonus room

■ No materials list is available for this plan

FIRST FLOOR — 1,557 SQ. FT.
SECOND FLOOR — 512 SQ. FT.
BONUS — 280 SQ. FT.

© 1997 Donald A. Gardner Architects, Inc.

B. NATHAN

Casual Country Charmer

Price Code: D

- This plan features:
- — Three bedrooms
- — Two full baths
- Columns and arches frame the front Porch
- The open floor plan combines the Great Room, Kitchen and Dining Room
- The Kitchen offers a convenient breakfast bar for meals on the run
- The Master Suite features a private Bath oasis
- Secondary Bedrooms share a full Bath with a dual vanity

MAIN FLOOR — 1,770 SQ. FT.
BONUS — 401 SQ. FT.
GARAGE — 630 SQ. FT.

TOTAL LIVING AREA:
1,770 SQ. FT.

MAIN FLOOR
No. 96493

NOOK
11/0 X 16/0 +/-
(9' CLG.)

WIDTH 50'-0"
DEPTH 60'-6"

VAULTED
FAMILY
17/0 X 14/2

13/6 X 17/0 +/-

O. REF.

PAN.

UP

10/8 X 19/4

GARAGE
19/8 X 21/8

DINING
13/0 X 11/0
(9' CLG.)

LIVING
13/0 X 15/4 +/-
(9' CLG.)

FIRST FLOOR
No. 91589

DECK

SPA

MASTER
13/0 X 16/0 +/-
(9'-4" CLG.)
(8' CLG.)

FAMILY
BELOW

BR. 2
11/2 X 12/2

DN.

NICHE

LIN.

BR. 3
11/6 X 12/8 +/-

FOYER
BELOW

DEN
9/6 X 11/0

BR. 4
13/0 X 11/0

SECOND FLOOR

Impressive Entrance

Price Code: D

■ This plan features:

— Four bedrooms

— Two full and one half baths

■ Two-story entrance with a large window above the entry door

■ Living Room enhanced by a fireplace and a bay window

■ Kitchen, Nook and Family Room laid out in an open format

■ A vaulted ceiling and a corner fireplace in the Family Room

■ Nook includes a bay window for a cheerful and bright living space

■ Spacious Master Suite with a decorative ceiling treatment and large Master Bath

■ No materials list is available for this plan

FIRST FLOOR — 1,466 SQ. FT.
SECOND FLOOR — 1,369 SQ. FT.
GARAGE — 640 SQ. FT.

TOTAL LIVING AREA:
2,835 SQ. FT.

Smart Stucco

Price Code: C

■ This plan features:

— Three bedrooms

— Two full baths

■ A large Living Area with a fireplace

■ A formal Dining Room convenient to Kitchen

■ A double sink, ample cabinet and counter area, a built-in pantry and direct access to a Sun deck in the Kitchen/Breakfast Room

■ Private Master Suite with a luxurious bath and walk-in closet

■ Two additional bedrooms that share a full hall bath

■ A Loft Area with three skylights that will become a special area, customized for the family's needs

■ No materials list available

FIRST FLOOR — 1,678 SQ. FT.
SECOND FLOOR — 282 SQ. FT.
BASEMENT — 836 SQ. FT.
GARAGE — 784 SQ. FT.
DECK — 288 SQ. FT.

SECOND FLOOR

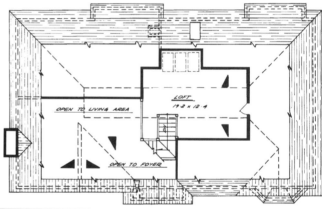

An
EXCLUSIVE DESIGN
By Jannis Vann & Associates, Inc.

TOTAL LIVING AREA:
1,960 SQ. FT.

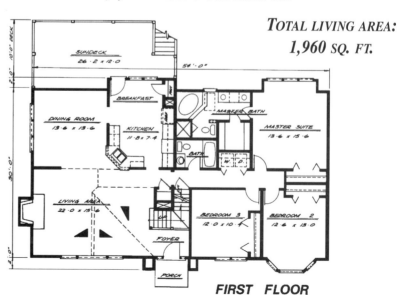

FIRST FLOOR

To order your Blueprints, call 1-800-235-5700

Keystones, Arches and Gables

PRICE CODE: B

■ This plan features:
- Three bedrooms
- Two full and one half baths
■ Tiled entry opens to Living Room with focal point fireplace
■ U-shaped Kitchen with a built-in Pantry, eating bar and nearby Laundry/Garage entry
■ Comfortable Dining Room with bay window and French doors to screen Porch expanding living area outdoors
■ Corner Master Bedroom offers a great walk-in closet and private Bath
■ Two additional Bedrooms with ample closets and double windows, share a full Bath
■ No materials list is available for this plan

MAIN FLOOR — 1,642 SQ. FT.
BASEMENT — 1,642 SQ. FT.

TOTAL LIVING AREA:
1,642 SQ. FT.

MAIN FLOOR PLAN

Keystones and Arched Windows

PRICE CODE: B

■ This plan features:
— Three bedrooms
— Two full baths
■ A large arched window in the Dining Room offers eye-catching appeal
■ A decorative column helps to define the Dining Room from the Great Room
■ A fireplace and French door to the rear yard can be found in the Great Room
■ An efficient Kitchen includes a serving bar, Pantry and pass through to the Great Room
■ A vaulted ceiling over the Breakfast Room
■ A plush Master Suite includes a private Bath and a walk-in closet
■ Two additional Bedrooms share a full Bath in the hall
■ An optional basement, slab or crawl space foundation — please specify when ordering

MAIN FLOOR — 1,670 SQ. FT.
GARAGE — 240 SQ. FT.

TOTAL LIVING AREA:
1,670 SQ. FT.

© Frank Betz Associates

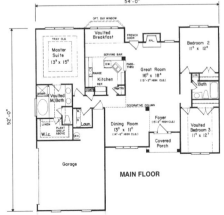

MAIN FLOOR

Stunning Southwestern Style

PRICE CODE: D

- This plan features:
  — Four bedrooms
  — Two full and one half baths
- Large circle top windows, stucco, and a tile roof add style to this home
- The common space of the home is impressive with 12′ ceilings and columns
- The Kitchen is partially enclosed by 8′ high walls
- A screen Porch in the rear is perfect for entertaining guests
- The Master Bedroom has a tray ceiling and a private Bath
- A versatile room, the Study/Bedroom has a bay in the front of it
- Two additional Bedrooms with ample closet space share a hall Bath
- An optional slab or a crawl space foundation — please specify when ordering

MAIN FLOOR — 1,954 SQ. FT.

TOTAL LIVING AREA:
1,954 SQ. FT.

Cozy Country Ranch

PRICE CODE: B

- This plan features:
  — Three bedrooms
  — Two full baths
- Front Porch shelters outdoor visiting and entrance into Living Room
- Expansive Living Room highlighted by a boxed window and hearth fireplace between built-ins
- Columns frame entrance to Dining Room with access to backyard
- Efficient, U-shaped Kitchen with direct access to the screened Porch and the Dining Room
- Master Bedroom wing enhanced by a large walk-in closet and a double vanity Bath with a whirlpool tub
- Two additional Bedrooms with large closets share a double vanity Bath with Laundry Center

MAIN FLOOR — 1,576 SQ. FT.
BASEMENT — 1,454 SQ. FT.
GARAGE — 576 SQ. FT.

TOTAL LIVING AREA:
1,576 SQ. FT.

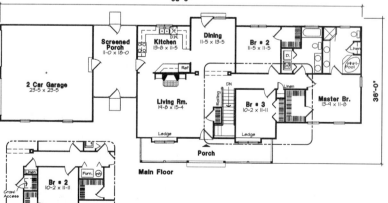

ZIP QUOTE
HOME COST CALCULATOR
see order pages for details

To order your Blueprints, call 1-800-235-5700

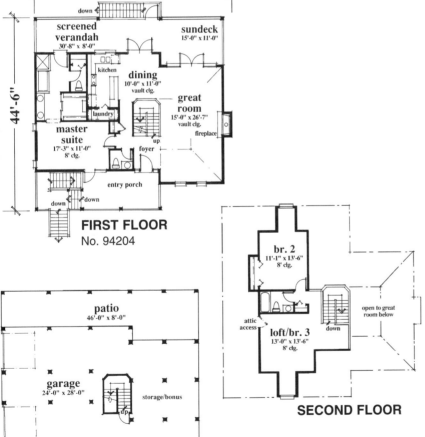

FIRST FLOOR
No. 94204

- 46'-0"
- 44'-6"

down

screened verandah
30'-8" x 8'-0"

sundeck
15'-0" x 11'-0"

kitchen

dining
10'-0" x 11'-0"
vault clg.

great room
15'-0" x 26'-7"
vault clg.

fireplace

laundry

up

master suite
17'-3" x 11'-0"
8' clg.

foyer

entry porch

down   down

GARAGE PLAN

patio
46'-0" x 8'-0"

garage
24'-0" x 28'-0"

storage/bonus

up

SECOND FLOOR

br. 2
11'-1" x 13'-6"
8' clg.

attic access

loft/br. 3
13'-0" x 13'-6"
8' clg.

open to great room below

down

Year Round Living

Price Code: B

- ■ This plan features:
- — Three bedrooms
- — Two full baths
- ■ An Entry Porch leads into the expansive Great Room with a hearth fireplace and a vaulted ceiling
- ■ An inviting Dining Area with a vaulted ceiling and and access to the screened Veranda and Sun Deck
- ■ An efficient Kitchen with a peninsula counter and adjacent Laundry
- ■ An airy Master Suite with a walk-in closet and outdoor access
- ■ Another Bedroom and a Bedroom/loft area on the second floor share a full Bath
- ■ No materials list is available with this plan

FIRST FLOOR — 1,189 SQ. FT.
SECOND FLOOR — 575 SQ. FT.
BONUS ROOM — 581 SQ. FT.
GARAGE — 658 SQ. FT

TOTAL LIVING AREA:
1,764 SQ. FT.

©1997 Donald A. Gardner Architects, Inc.

B·NATHAN

Style and Versatility

Price Code: E

■ This plan features:

— Four Bedrooms

— Three full baths

■ Traditional hip roof arched and picture windows, and a barrel vaulted entrance

■ Stunning Great Room with magnificent cathedral ceiling

■ Cozy fireplace with space saving built-ins shields the Great Room from Kitchen noise

■ Secluded Master Suite with twin walk-in closets and a stately tray ceiling in the Bedroom

■ Cathedral ceiling enhances both Bedrooms on the second floor

■ First floor Study/Bedroom providing ample flexibility

FIRST FLOOR — 1,687 SQ. FT.
SECOND FLOOR — 514 SQ. FT.
BONUS — 336 SQ. FT.
GARAGE — 489 SQ. FT.

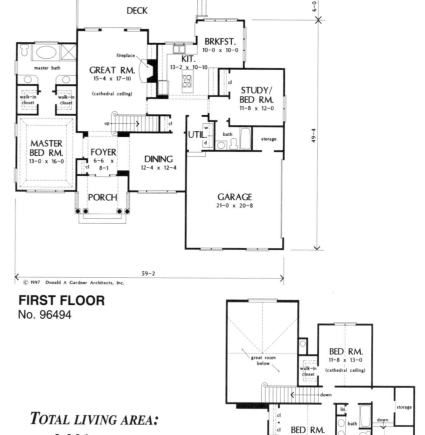

FIRST FLOOR
No. 96494

© 1997 Donald A Gardner Architects, Inc.

TOTAL LIVING AREA:
2,201 SQ. FT.

SECOND FLOOR

To order your Blueprints, call 1-800-235-5700

SECOND FLOOR

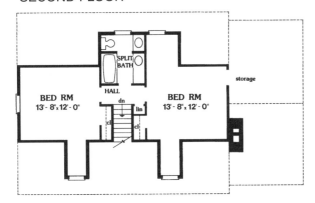

Adapt this Colonial to Your Lifestyle

Price Code: B

- ■ This plan features:
- — Four bedrooms
- — Two full baths
- ■ A Living Room with a beam ceiling and a fireplace
- ■ An eat-in Kitchen efficiently serving the formal Dining Room
- ■ A Master Bedroom with his and her closets
- ■ Two upstairs bedrooms sharing a split bath

FIRST FLOOR — 1,056 SQ. FT.
SECOND FLOOR — 531 SQ. FT.

TOTAL LIVING AREA:
1,587 SQ. FT.

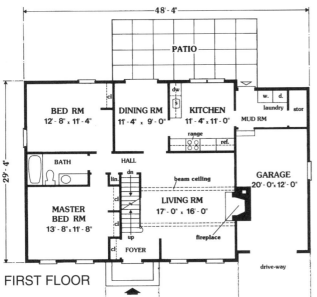

FIRST FLOOR

© 1994 Donald A. Gardner Architects, Inc.

B. NATHAN

Elegance And A Relaxed Lifestyle

Price Code: E

- This plan features:
  - Four bedrooms
  - Three full baths
- This family home has combined elegance with a relaxed lifestyle in an open plan full of surprises
- Open two-level Foyer has a palladian window which visually ties in the formal Dining area to the expansive Great Room
- Windows all around, including bays in Master Bedroom Suite and Breakfast Area provide natural light, while nine foot ceilings create volume
- Master Bedroom suite features a whirlpool tub, separate shower and his-n-her vanities

FIRST FLOOR — 1,841 SQ. FT.
SECOND FLOOR — 594 SQ. FT.
BONUS ROOM — 411 SQ. FT.
GARAGE & STORAGE — 596 SQ. FT.

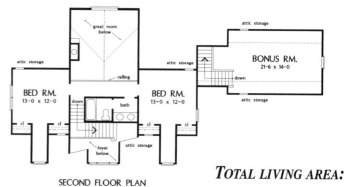

SECOND FLOOR PLAN

TOTAL LIVING AREA:
2,435 SQ. FT.

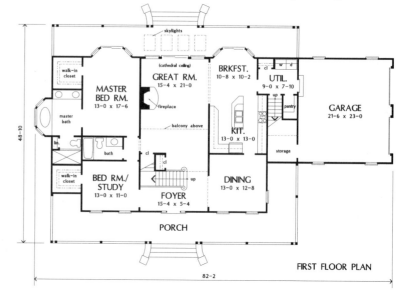

FIRST FLOOR PLAN

English Tudor Styling

PRICE CODE: E

This plan features:
- Four bedrooms
- Three full and one half baths
- This Tudor styled gem has a unique mix of exterior materials
- Inside the Entry either turn left to the Living room or right into the Dining room
- At the end of the Gallery is the Master bedroom, which has dual walk in closets
- The Family room has a sloped ceiling and a rear wall fireplace
- The Kitchen has a center island and opens to the Breakfast area
- A skylight brightens the staircase to the second floor
- Upstairs find three large bedrooms and two full baths
- Also upstairs access the future bonus room that is located over the garage
- No materials list is available for this plan

FIRST FLOOR — 2,082 SQ. FT.
SECOND FLOOR — 904 SQ. FT.
BONUS — 408 SQ. FT.
GARAGE — 605 SQ. FT.

TOTAL LIVING AREA:
2,986 SQ. FT.

FIRST FLOOR

SECOND FLOOR

PLAN NO. 94993

Arches are Appealing

PRICE CODE: B

- This plan features:
- Three bedrooms
- Two full baths
- Welcoming front Porch enhanced by graceful columns and curved windows
- Parlor and Dining Room frame entry hall
- Expansive Great Room accented by a corner fireplace and outdoor access
- Open and convenient Kitchen with a work island, angled, peninsula counter/eating bar, and nearby Laundry and Garage entry
- Secluded Master Bedroom with a large walk-in closet and luxurious Bath with a dressing table
- Two additional Bedrooms with ample closets, share a double vanity Bath
- No materials list is available for this plan

MAIN FLOOR — 1,642 SQ. FT.
BASEMENT — 1,642 SQ. FT.
GARAGE — 430 SQ. FT.

TOTAL LIVING AREA:
1,642 SQ. FT.

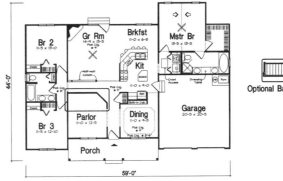

MAIN FLOOR

PLAN NO. 24717

ZIP QUOTE
HOME COST CALCULATOR
see order pages for details

Delightful Decorative Windows
PRICE CODE: E

■ This plan features:
— Four bedrooms
— Two full, one three-quarter and one half baths
■ Arched transom window highlights two-story Entry
■ Formal Dining Room enhanced by hutch space and a bowed window
■ Living Room features a volume ceiling and see through fireplace
■ Spacious Family Room with a dual entertainment center and transom windows
■ Octagon Breakfast Bay, a walk-in Pantry, work island and planning desk compliment Kitchen
■ Secluded Master Bedroom offers a decorative ceiling, double walk-in closet, and lavish Bath
■ Three additional Bedrooms with private access to a full Bath

FIRST FLOOR — 1,860 SQ. FT.
SECOND FLOOR — 848 SQ. FT.
GARAGE — 629 SQ. FT.
BASEMENT — 1,860 SQ. FT.

TOTAL LIVING AREA:
2,708 SQ. FT.

FIRST FLOOR

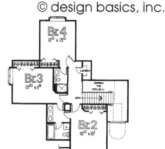

© design basics, inc.

SECOND FLOOR

A Streamlined Design
PRICE CODE: F

■ This plan features:
— Three bedrooms
— One full, one three quarter and two half baths
■ Recessed, glass arched entrance leads into unique Entry and Living Room beyond with alcove access to covered Porch
■ Formal Dining Room with triple arch window, adjoins Living Room for ease in entertaining
■ Ideal Kitchen with a walk-in Pantry, work island, extended serving bar, Porch access, Breakfast bay and nearby Utility Area
■ Open Family Room with a cozy fireplace and lots of windows
■ Master Bedroom wing offers an alcove of windows, two walk-in closets and a luxurious Bath
■ Two additional Bedrooms with walk-in closets and private Bath access
■ No materials list is available for this plan

MAIN FLOOR — 3,312 SQ. FT.
GARAGE — 752 SQ. FT.

TOTAL LIVING AREA:
3,312 SQ. FT.

© Carmichael & Dame

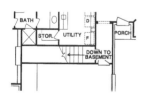

MAIN FLOOR

To order your Blueprints, call 1-800-235-5700

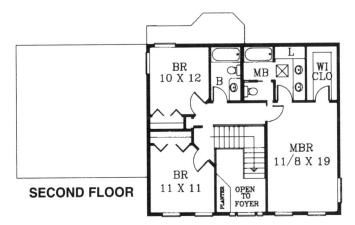

SECOND FLOOR

BR 10 X 12

B

MB

WI CLO

L

MBR 11/8 X 19

BR 11 X 11

OPEN TO FOYER

PLANTER

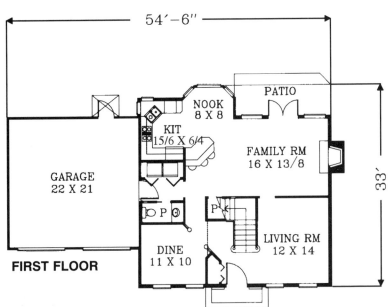

FIRST FLOOR

54'-6"

33'

NOOK 8 X 8

PATIO

KIT 15/6 X 6/4

FAMILY RM 16 X 13/8

GARAGE 22 X 21

P

P

DINE 11 X 10

LIVING RM 12 X 14

Compact Classic

Price Code: B

- This plan features:
  - Three bedrooms
  - Two full and one half baths
- A spacious Family Room with a cozy fireplace and direct access to the patio
- A well-appointed Kitchen with an eating bar peninsula, double sink and sunny eating Nook
- A formal Living Room and Dining Room located at the front of the house
- A Master Suite equipped with a walk-in closet, a double vanity and a full Master Bath
- An optional basement, slab or crawl space foundation — please specify when ordering

FIRST FLOOR — 963 SQ. FT.
SECOND FLOOR — 774 SQ. FT.

TOTAL LIVING AREA:
1,737 SQ. FT.

Two–Sink Baths Ease Rush

Price Code: C

- This plan features:
- — Four bedrooms
- — Two full and one half baths
- A wood beam ceiling in the spacious Family Room
- An efficient Kitchen with a sunny bay window dinette
- A formal Living Room with a heat-circulating fireplace
- A large Master Suite with a walk-in closet and a private Master Bath
- Three additional bedrooms sharing a full hall bath

FIRST FLOOR — 983 SQ. FT.
SECOND FLOOR — 1,013 SQ. FT.
MUDROOM — 99 SQ. FT.
GARAGE — 481 SQ. FT.

**TOTAL LIVING AREA:
2,095 SQ. FT.**

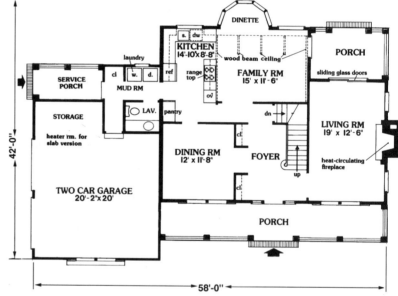

FIRST FLOOR PLAN

SECOND FLOOR PLAN

To order your Blueprints, call 1-800-235-5700

1995 Donald A. Gardner Architects, Inc.

B. NATHAN.

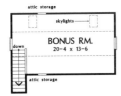

attic storage

skylights

BONUS RM.
20-4 x 13-6

down

attic storage

SECOND FLOOR PLAN

skylight

cl

bath

BED RM.
11-8 x 12-0

BED RM.
12-0 x 13-0

railing

down

walk-in closet

attic storage

great room below

master bedroom below

foyer below

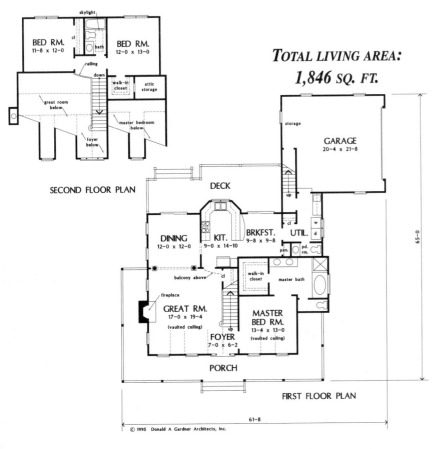

FIRST FLOOR PLAN

TOTAL LIVING AREA:
1,846 SQ. FT.

storage

GARAGE
20-4 x 21-8

up

DECK

DINING
12-0 x 12-0

KIT.
9-0 x 14-10

BRKFST.
9-8 x 9-8

UTIL.

w d

cl

pan.

pd. rm.

balcony above

cl

walk-in closet

master bath

fireplace

GREAT RM.
17-0 x 19-4
(vaulted ceiling)

MASTER BED RM.
13-4 x 13-0
(vaulted ceiling)

FOYER
7-0 x 6-2

up

PORCH

61-8

65-0

© 1995 Donald A Gardner Architects, Inc.

Farmhouse Charm

Price Code: D

■ This plan features:

— Three bedrooms

— Two full and one half baths

■ Nine foot ceilings and vaulted ceilings in Great Room and Master Bedroom add spaciousness

■ Dining Room accented by columns and accesses Deck for outdoor living

■ Efficient Kitchen features peninsula counter with serving bar for Breakfast Area

■ Master Bedroom Suite includes luxurious Bath with walk-in closet, garden tub, shower and double vanity

■ Two upstairs Bedrooms, one with walk-in closet, share full Bath with skylight

FIRST FLOOR — 1,380 SQ. FT.
SECOND FLOOR — 466 SQ. FT.
BONUS ROOM — 326 SQ. FT.
GARAGE — 523 SQ. FT.

Friendly Front Porch

Price Code: D

- This plan features:
- — Four bedrooms
- — Two full and one half baths
- Central Foyer with a graceful staircase
- Inviting fireplace and front to back windows highlight the Great Room
- L-shaped Kitchen with work island/snackbar and Butler's Pantry
- Nearby Laundry Room, walk-in closet and Garage entry add to Kitchen efficiency
- Corner Master Bedroom accented by a slope ceiling, Dressing Area and walk-in closet
- Three additional Bedrooms with ample closets, share a full Bath
- No materials list is available for this plan

FIRST FLOOR — 1,199 SQ. FT.
SECOND FLOOR — 1,060 SQ. FT.

TOTAL LIVING AREA:
2,259 SQ. FT.

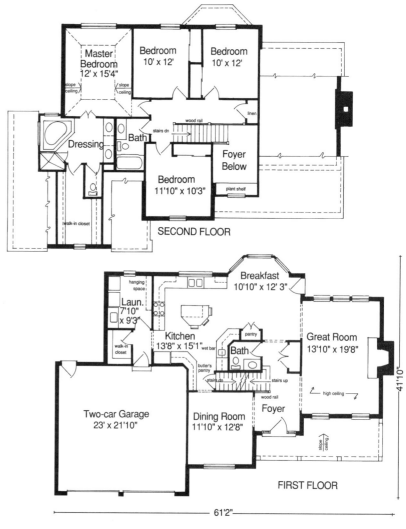

148

To order your Blueprints, call 1-800-235-5700

Simply Cozy

PRICE CODE: A

■ This plan features:
— Three bedrooms
— Two full baths
■ Quaint front Porch sheltering Entry into the Living Area showcased by a massive fireplace and built-ins below a vaulted ceiling
■ Formal Dining Room accented by a bay of glass with Sun Deck access
■ Efficient, galley Kitchen with Breakfast Area, Laundry facilities and outdoor access
■ Secluded Master Bedroom offers a roomy walk-in closet and plush Bath with dual vanity and a garden window tub
■ Two additional Bedrooms with ample closets, share a full Bath with a skylight

MAIN FLOOR — 1,345 SQ. FT.
BASEMENT — 556 SQ. FT.
GARAGE — 724 SQ. FT.

TOTAL LIVING AREA:
1,345 SQ. FT.

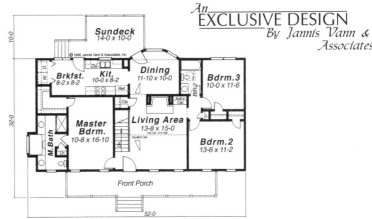

An EXCLUSIVE DESIGN
By Jannis Vann & Associates, Inc.

Sundeck 14-0 x 10-0
Brkfst. 8-2 x 8-2
Kit. 10-0 x 8-2
Dining 11-10 x 10-0
Bdrm.3 10-0 x 11-6
Master Bdrm. 10-8 x 16-10
M.Bath
Living Area 13-8 x 15-0
Bdrm.2 13-6 x 11-2
Front Porch
52-0

Grand Design Highlighted by Turrets

PRICE CODE: F

■ This plan features:
— Four bedrooms
— Three full and one half baths
■ Triple arches at entry lead into Grand Foyer and Gallery with arched entries to all areas
■ Triple French doors catch the breeze and access to rear grounds in Living and Leisure Rooms
■ Spacious Kitchen with large walk-in Pantry, cooktop/work island and angled serving counter/snack-bar, glass Nook, Utility Room and Garage entry
■ Master Suite wing offers Veranda access, two closets and vanities, and a garden window tub
■ Three second floor Bedrooms with walk-in closets, balcony and full Bath access
■ No materials list is available for this plan

FIRST FLOOR — 3,546 SQ. FT.
SECOND FLOOR — 1,213 SQ. FT.
GARAGE — 822 SQ. FT.

TOTAL LIVING AREA:
4,759 SQ. FT.

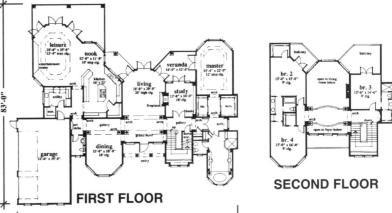

leisure
nook
veranda
master
living
study
garage
dining
grand foyer
entry
FIRST FLOOR
95'-4"
83'-0"

balcony
br. 2
br. 3
open to living room below
br. 4
open to foyer below
SECOND FLOOR

PLAN NO. 94136

Unique Dining Area
PRICE CODE: E

- This plan features:
  — Four bedrooms
  — Two full and one half baths
- Covered entry in central Foyer between formal Living and Dining rooms
- Corner Study with double door entry for many activities
- Open Great Room with fireplace between built-ins and backyard access
- Convenient Kitchen with cooktop island, octagon Dinette, built-in Pantry, and nearby Laundry and Garage entry
- Corner Master Bedroom with a walk-in closet and two options for ceiling treatment and skylight Bath
- Three additional Bedrooms share a double vanity Bath and Storage Area
- No materials list is available for this plan

FIRST FLOOR — 1,458 SQ. FT.
SECOND FLOOR — 1,135 SQ. FT.
BASEMENT — 1,458 SQ. FT.
GARAGE — 476 SQ. FT.

TOTAL LIVING AREA:
2,593 SQ. FT.

PLAN NO. 91591

Beautiful Front Windows
PRICE CODE: D

- This plan features:
  — Three bedrooms
  — Two full baths
- Living Room enhanced by a see-through fireplace shared with the Den
- Formal Dining Room located in close proximity to the kitchen for easy serving
- Family Room accented with a second fireplace
- Spacious Kitchen made more efficient by a cooktop island/snack bar
- Decorative ceiling tops Master Bedroom
- No materials list is available for this plan

MAIN FLOOR — 2,225 SQ. FT.
GARAGE — 420 SQ. FT.

TOTAL LIVING AREA:
2,225 SQ. FT.

To order your Blueprints, call 1-800-235-5700

An
EXCLUSIVE DESIGN
By Patrick Morabito, A.I.A. Architect

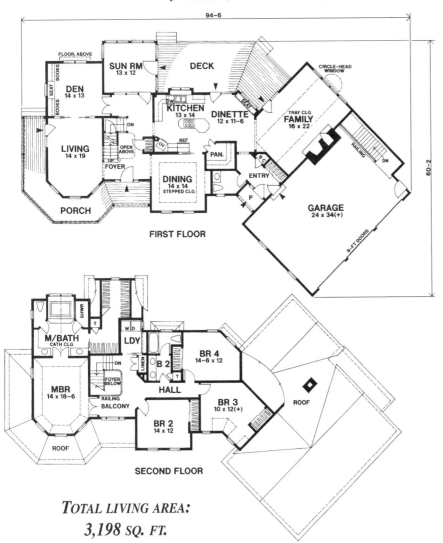

FIRST FLOOR

94-6

60-2

- FLOOR, ABOVE
- BOOKS
- SEAT
- DEN 14 x 13
- BOOKS
- SUN RM 13 x 12
- DECK
- CIRCLE-HEAD WINDOW
- KITCHEN 13 x 14
- DINETTE 12 x 11-6
- TRAY CLG
- FAMILY 16 x 22
- DW
- DN
- LIVING 14 x 19
- OPEN ABOVE
- UP
- FOYER
- DV
- REF
- PAN.
- DINING 14 x 14 STEPPED CLG
- ENTRY
- P
- RAILING
- DN
- GARAGE 24 x 34(+)
- 9-FT DOORS

SECOND FLOOR

- M/BATH CATH CLG
- LDY
- W/D
- BR 4 14-6 x 12
- B 2
- LINEN
- MBR 14 x 18-6
- FOYER BELOW
- DN
- HALL
- RAILING
- BALCONY
- BR 3 10 x 12(+)
- ROOF
- BR 2 14 x 12
- ROOF

TOTAL LIVING AREA:
3,198 SQ. FT.

A Whisper of Victorian

Price Code: E

■ This plan features:

— Four bedrooms

— Two full and one half baths

■ A formal Living Room with wrap-around windows and access to the cozy Den

■ An elegant, formal Dining Room accented by a stepped ceiling

■ An efficient Kitchen equipped with a cooktop island/eating bar, a huge walk-in pantry and a Dinette with a window seat and a Deck access

■ An all-purpose glass-walled Sun Room

■ A fireplaced Family Room, with a tray ceiling topping a circle-head window

■ A Master Suite with a decorative ceiling and a Bath with a raised, atrium tub, and two vanities

■ Three additional bedrooms sharing a full bath with a double vanity

■ No materials list available

FIRST FLOOR — 1,743 SQ. FT.
SECOND FLOOR — 1,455 SQ. FT.

Colonial Charmer

Price Code: C

■ This plan features:

— Four bedrooms

— Two full and one half baths

■ An oversized Family Room that opens into the Kitchen/Nook area creating a feeling of space

■ A large fireplace and access to the Patio in the Family Room

■ A peninsula counter and double sinks as well as an abundance of counter and cupboard space in the Kitchen

■ A formal Living Room and Dining Room for entertaining

■ A Master Suite that includes two closets, a jacuzzi and double vanity

■ Three additional Bedrooms, one with a walk-in closet, that share a full hall Bath

FIRST FLOOR — 970 SQ. FT.
SECOND FLOOR — 950 SQ. FT.
BASEMENT — 970 SQ. FT.
GARAGE — 462 SQ. FT.

TOTAL LIVING AREA:
1,920 SQ. FT.

OPTIONAL
BASEMENT

SECOND FLOOR

FIRST FLOOR

To order your Blueprints, call 1-800-235-5700

© 1997 Donald A. Gardner Architects, Inc.

B. NATHAN

Victorian Charm

Price Code: D

■ This plan features:

— Four bedrooms

— Two full baths

■ This home combines Victorian charm with today's lifestyle needs

■ Ceilings vaulted in Great Room and ten feet height in Foyer, Dining Room, Kitchen/Breakfast bay and Bedroom/Study

■ Secluded Master Bedroom suite features tray ceiling, walk-in closet and private, skylit bath

■ Two additional bedrooms, located in separate wing, share a full bath

■ Front and rear Porches extend living area outdoors

MAIN FLOOR — 1,903 SQ. FT.
GARAGE & STORAGE — 531 SQ. FT.

TOTAL LIVING AREA:
1,903 SQ. FT.

Floor Plan

master bath
skylight
lin.
MASTER BED RM.
13-4 x 16-0
(10' ceiling)

walk-in closet

storage

UTILITY
8-0 x 5-6
d. w.

BRKFST.
9-0 x 11-0
(10' ceiling)

PORCH

fireplace

BED RM.
12-0 x 11-0

KIT.
11-4 x 11-10

GREAT RM.
18-8 x 16-2
(vaulted ceiling)

lin.
bath
cl

GARAGE
22-0 x 21-10

DINING
11-4 x 12-4
(10' ceiling)

FOYER
7-0 x 9-4
(10' ceiling)

BED RM./STUDY
11-4 x 12-0
(10' ceiling)

optional closet

BED RM.
12-0 x 11-0

PORCH

55-7

65-8

FLOOR PLAN

© 1997 Donald A. Gardner Architects, Inc.

Country-Style Home

Price Code: D

- This plan features:
- — Four bedrooms
- — Two full and two half baths
- A typical farmhouse front porch sheltering the double door entrance
- A sunken formal living room, enhanced by a focal point fireplace and a large windowed bay and a stepped ceiling
- An elegant formal Dining Room angled to form an octagon
- A large Kitchen with a central island
- A fireplaced Family Room
- Master Bedroom suite, with sitting bay, dressing area, three closets, and a deluxe bath
- Three additional bedrooms sharing the full double vanity bath in the hall
- Studio area above the garage includes a half-bath

FIRST FLOOR — 1,217 SQ. FT.
SECOND FLOOR — 1,249 SQ. FT.
BASEMENT — 1,217 SQ. FT.
GARAGE — 431 SQ. FT.

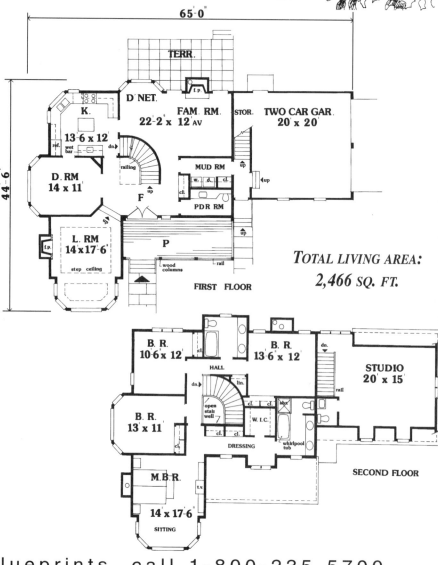

TERR.

D´NET.

K. 13´6 x 12

FAM. RM. 22´-2 x 12´ AV

STOR.

TWO CAR GAR. 20´ x 20´

wet bar

D. RM 14 x 11

railing

MUD RM

up

up

F

up

PDR RM

L. RM 14 x 17´6

step ceiling

P

wood columns

rail

up

FIRST FLOOR

65´-0˝

44´-6˝

TOTAL LIVING AREA: *2,466 SQ. FT.*

B. R. 10´6 x 12´

HALL

B. R. 13´6 x 12´

dn.

STUDIO 20´ x 15´

dn.

open stair well

lin.

cl.

cl.

W. I. C.

rail

B. R. 13 x 11

cl.

cl.

DRESSING

whirlpool tub

M. B. R. 14 x 17´6

t.v.

SITTING

SECOND FLOOR

To order your Blueprints, call 1-800-235-5700

Rambling Farmhouse

PRICE CODE: E

This plan features:
- Three bedrooms
- Two full and one half baths
- Front and back dormers and wrapping Porches
- An unconventional rear staircase in the Great Room capped by an impressive second story balcony
- Master Suite privately situated downstairs with his-n-her walk-in closets, a linen closet, dual vanity and a separate tub and shower
- Dormer alcoves and walk-in closets in each second story Bedroom

FIRST FLOOR — 1,471 SQ. FT.
SECOND FLOOR — 577 SQ. FT.
BONUS — 368 SQ. FT.
GARAGE — 505 SQ. FT.

TOTAL LIVING AREA: 2,048 SQ. FT.

© Donald A. Gardner Architects, Inc.

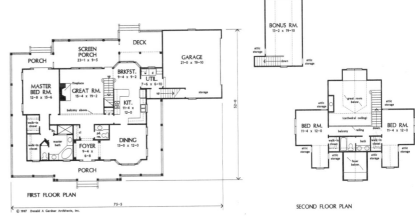

FIRST FLOOR PLAN

© 1997 Donald A Gardner Architects, Inc.

SECOND FLOOR PLAN

Champagne Style on a Soda-Pop Budget

PRICE CODE: A

This plan features:
- Three bedrooms
- One full and one three-quarter baths
- Multiple gables, circle-top windows, and a unique exterior setting this delightful Ranch apart in any neighborhood
- Living and Dining Rooms flowing together to create a very roomy feeling
- Sliding doors leading from the Dining Room to a covered Patio
- A Master Bedroom with a private Bath

MAIN FLOOR — 988 SQ. FT.
BASEMENT — 988 SQ. FT.
GARAGE — 280 SQ. FT
OPTIONAL 2-CAR GARAGE — 384 SQ. FT.

TOTAL LIVING AREA: 988 SQ. FT.

An EXCLUSIVE DESIGN
By Marshall Associates

Optional Basement Plan

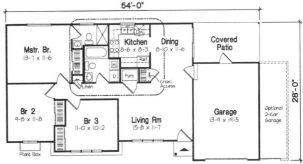

Main Floor

ZIP QUOTE
HOME COST CALCULATOR
see order pages for details

To order your Blueprints, call 1-800-235-5700

Impressive Elevation
PRICE CODE: E

■ This plan features:
— Three bedrooms
— Three full baths
■ Glass arch entrance into Foyer and Grand Room accented by fireplace between built-ins and multiple French doors leading to Veranda
■ Decorative windows highlight Study and formal Dining Room
■ Spacious Kitchen with walk-in Pantry and peninsula serving counter easily serves Nook, Veranda and Dining Room
■ Luxurious Master Suite with step ceiling, Sitting Area, his-n-hers closets and pampering Bath
■ Two additional Bedrooms, one with a private Deck, have bay windows and walk-in closets
■ No material list is available for this plan

FIRST FLOOR — 2,181 SQ. FT.
SECOND FLOOR — 710 SQ. FT.
GARAGE — 658 SQ. FT.

TOTAL LIVING AREA:
2,891 SQ. FT.

FIRST FLOOR

SECOND FLOOR

© 1997 Donald A. Gardner Architects, Inc.

Always in Style
PRICE CODE: H

■ This plan features:
— Four bedrooms
— Four full and two half baths
■ Brick, gables and a traditional hip roof always seem to be in style
■ Inside find dramatic spaces that include the Dining room and the Great Room both with 14' ceilings
■ The Study features a wall of built in bookshelves
■ The Kitchen has a center island with a cooktop
■ The Sun Room and the Breakfast Nook share a counter with the Kitchen
■ The Master Bedroom is opulent with dual Baths and closets
■ Storage space abounds with a walk-in Pantry, numerous closets, and storage space in the Garage

MAIN FLOOR — 4,523 SQ. FT.
GARAGE — 1,029 SQ. FT.

TOTAL LIVING AREA:
4,523 SQ. FT.

This plan is not to be built in Greenville County, SC, sold as reproducible only.

MAIN FLOOR

© 1998 Donald A Gardner Architects, Inc.

WIDTH 43'-0''
DEPTH 69'-0''

GARAGE
21/4 X 20/0

NOOK
10/6 X 13/0
(9' CLG.)

REF.

FAMILY
15/0 X 16/4 +/-
(9' CLG.)

DESK

DINING
12/0 X 10/0
(9' CLG.)

FOYER

LIVING
14/0 X 11/0 +/-
(9' CLG.)

DEN
14/0 X 10/0 +
(9' CLG.)

FIRST FLOOR
No. 91592

BR. 3
10/6 X 13/0

PLANT SHELF

FAMILY BELOW

BR. 2
12/4 X 11/0

DN

VAULTED MASTER
12/0 X 15/0

SECOND FLOOR

Cozy Accommodations

Price Code: E

■ This plan features:

— Three bedrooms

— Two full and one half baths

■ A quaint, wrapping porch sheltering the entrance

■ Foyer giving access to the combined Living and Dining rooms, and the secluded Den or Family Room

■ A terrific, two-sided fireplace accentuating the Den and Family Room

■ Second floor Master Suite with a vaulted ceiling

FIRST FLOOR — 1,371 SQ. FT.
SECOND FLOOR — 916 SQ. FT.

TOTAL LIVING AREA:
2,287 SQ. FT.

Rich Classic Lines

Price Code: D

■ This plan features:

— Four bedrooms

— Three full and one half baths

■ A two story Foyer flooded by light through a half-round transom

■ A vaulted ceiling in the Great Room that continues into the Master Suite

■ A corner fireplace in the Great Room with French doors to the Breakfast/Kitchen area

■ A center island in the Kitchen with a built-in desk and pantry

■ A tray ceiling and recessed hutch area in the formal Dining Room

■ A Master Suite with a walk-in closet, a whirlpool tub, and a double sink vanity

■ A materials list is not available with this plan

FIRST FLOOR — 1,496 SQ. FT.
SECOND FLOOR — 716 SQ. FT.
BASEMENT — 1,420 SQ. FT.
GARAGE — 460 SQ. FT.

TOTAL LIVING AREA:
2,212 SQ. FT.

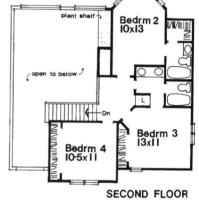

SECOND FLOOR

Bedrm 2 10x13
plant shelf
open to below
Dn
Bedrm 3 13x11
Bedrm 4 10·5x11

58'

46'

Patio

Patio

Master Suite 13·4x15·4 vaulted

Greatrm 20x17·5 vaulted

Brk 10x8·6

desk

Pan

Util. D W

whirlpool

Entry

Dining 13x11 tray ceiling

Dn

Garage 22x22

FIRST FLOOR

To order your Blueprints, call 1-800-235-5700

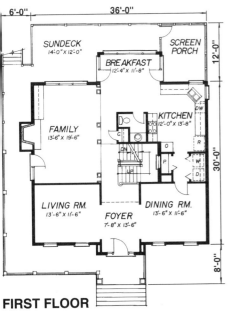

FIRST FLOOR

- SUNDECK 14'-0" X 12'-0"
- SCREEN PORCH
- BREAKFAST 12'-4" X 11'-8"
- KITCHEN 12'-0" X 13'-8"
- FAMILY 13'-6" X 19'-6"
- LIVING RM. 13'-6" X 11'-6"
- FOYER 7'-8" X 13'-6"
- DINING RM. 13'-6" X 11'-6"

6'-0"   36'-0"   12'-0"   30'-0"   8'-0"

An EXCLUSIVE DESIGN *By Jannis Vann & Associates, Inc.*

ZIP QUOTE
HOME COST CALCULATOR
see order pages for details

TOTAL LIVING AREA:
2,464 SQ. FT.

SECOND FLOOR

- DECK
- BEDROOM·4 13'-6" X 11'-6"
- MASTER BR. 12'-4" X 17'-6"
- M. BATH
- BATH·2
- BEDROOM·3 13'-6" X 11'-6"
- OPEN TO FOYER
- BEDROOM·2 13'-6" X 11'-6"

Wrap-Around Porch Adds to Classic Styling

Price Code: D

■ This plan features:

— Four bedrooms

— Two full and one half baths

■ A wrap-around Porch adds a cozy touch

■ A two-story Foyer area is open to the formal Dining and Living rooms

■ The Family Room is accentuated by columns and a fireplace

■ The sunny Breakfast Area has direct access to the Sun Deck, Screen Porch and the Kitchen

■ The Kitchen is situated between the formal Dining Room and Breakfast Area

■ A private Deck highlights the Master Suite which includes a luxurious Bath

FIRST FLOOR — 1,250 SQ. FT.
SECOND FLOOR — 1,166 SQ. FT.
FINISHED STAIRS — 48 SQ. FT.
BASEMENT — 448 SQ. FT.
GARAGE — 706 SQ. FT.

Balconies Offer Style

Price Code: F

- ■ This plan features:
- — Three bedrooms
- — Two full and one half baths
- ■ Cascading steps lead to the entrance and the formal Dining and Living rooms
- ■ Vaulted Living Room is enhanced by French doors to the balcony
- ■ An elegant ceiling tops a decorative window in the Dining Room
- ■ Spacious and convenient Kitchen with a cooktop island/snack bar
- ■ Corner fireplace and a triple window accent the Family Room
- ■ Corner Master Bedroom offers a private balcony, decorative ceiling and deluxe Dressing Area
- ■ Two additional Bedrooms have walk-in closets
- ■ No materials list is available for this plan

MAIN LEVEL — 1,989 SQ. FT.
UPPER LEVEL — 1,349 SQ. FT.
LOWER LEVEL — 105 SQ. FT.
BONUS ROOM — 487 SQ. FT.

TOTAL LIVING AREA:
3,443 SQ. FT.

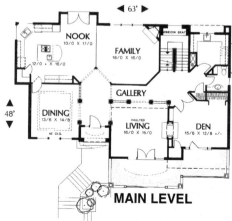

To order your Blueprints, call 1-800-235-5700

Expansive Living Room
PRICE CODE: A

This plan features:
- Three bedrooms
- Two full baths
- Vaulted ceiling crowns spacious Living Room highlighted by a fireplace
- Built-in Pantry and direct access from the Garage adding to the conveniences of the Kitchen
- Walk-in closet and a private five-piece Bath topped by a vaulted ceiling in the Master Bedroom Suite
- Proximity to the full Bath in the hall from the secondary Bedrooms
- An optional basement, slab or crawl space — please specify when ordering

MAIN FLOOR — 1,346 SQ. FT.
BASEMENT — 1,358 SQ. FT.
GARAGE — 385 SQ. FT.

TOTAL LIVING AREA:
1,346 SQ. FT.

© Frank Betz Associates

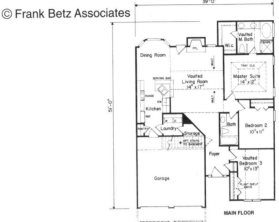

MAIN FLOOR

A Comfortable Informal Design
PRICE CODE: B

This plan features:
- Three bedrooms
- Two full baths
- Warm, country front Porch with wood details
- Spacious Activity Room enhanced by a pre-fab fireplace
- Open and efficient Kitchen/Dining area highlighted by bay window, adjacent to Laundry and Garage entry
- Corner Master Bedroom offers a pampering Bath with a garden tub and double vanity topped by a vaulted ceiling
- Two additional Bedrooms with ample closets, share a full Bath
- An optional slab or crawl space foundation — please specify when ordering

MAIN FLOOR — 1,300 SQ. FT.
GARAGE — 576 SQ. FT.

TOTAL LIVING AREA:
1,300 SQ. FT.

MAIN FLOOR

To order your Blueprints, call 1-800-235-5700

PLAN N 98434

© 1998 Donald A. Gardner, Inc.

Stately Arched Entry
PRICE CODE: E

- This plan features:
 — Three bedrooms
 — Two full and one half baths
- The stately arched entry Porch is supported by columns
- The Dining Room has a tray ceiling and is defined by columns
- The Great Room has a fireplace and accessed the rear Porch/Deck
- The Kitchen is full of cabinet and counter space
- The Master Bedroom has a rear wall bay window and a tray ceiling
- The Master Bath features dual vanities and walk-in closets
- There are two secondary Bedrooms, one of which could be used as a Study
- A bonus room is located over the two-car Garage

MAIN FLOOR — 2,024 SQ. FT.
BONUS — 423 SQ. FT.
GARAGE — 623 SQ. FT.

TOTAL LIVING AREA:
2,024 SQ. FT.

© 1998 Donald A. Gardner, Inc.

PLAN NO. 96500

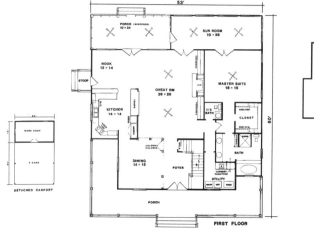

Friendly Front Porch
PRICE CODE: E

- This plan features:
 — Three bedrooms
 — Two full and one half baths
- Wrap-around front Porch and double French doors are an inviting sight
- Central Foyer with a lovely landing staircase opens to the Dining and Great Rooms
- The fireplace is framed by a built-in credenza in the Great Room
- Kitchen boasts a buffet, Pantry and a peninsula counter/snack bar
- Master Bedroom offers direct access to the Sun Room, a walk-in closet and a luxurious Bath

FIRST FLOOR — 2,361 SQ. FT.
SECOND FLOOR — 650 SQ. FT.
DETACHED CARPORT/WORK SHOP — 864 SQ. FT.

TOTAL LIVING AREA:
3,011 SQ. FT.

To order your Blueprints, call 1-800-235-5700

TOTAL LIVING AREA:
4,106 SQ. FT.

Spectacular Stucco and Stone

Price Code: F

■ This plan features:

— Four bedrooms

— One full, two three-quarter and one half baths

■ Arches and columns accent formal spaces

■ Open Living Room with fireplace and multiple doors to rear grounds

■ Formal Dining Room has a bay window conveniently located

■ Angled Kitchen with walk-in Pantry and peninsula counter

■ Master wing offers a step ceiling, two walk-in closets and a lavish Bath

■ Two additional Bedrooms and a Guest Suite share second floor and Decks

■ No materials list is available with this plan

FIRST FLOOR — 3,027 SQ. FT.
SECOND FLOOR — 1,079 SQ. FT.
BASEMENT — 3,027 SQ. FT.
GARAGE — 802 SQ. FT.

SECOND FLOOR

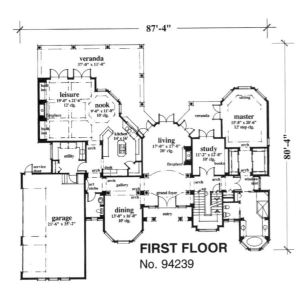

FIRST FLOOR
No. 94239

Photography Supplied by The Meredith Corporation

Outdoor Oriented

Price Code: F

■ This plan features:

—Three bedrooms

■ Two full, two three-quarter and one half baths

■ This home offers comfortable outdoor oriented living and year round practicality

■ Special features of this home include the Office, Den, and Sunroom all on the main level

■ On the lower level find a Game Room with a bar and a Family Room with a fireplace

■ A screened Porch and multiple Decks add to the living space outdoors

■ The Master Bedroom is located next to a secondary Bedroom on the main level

■ On the upper level find an additional Bedroom, a loft and a full Bath

■ The Kitchen is well planned and appointed

■ No materials list is available for this plan

UPPER LEVEL

OPEN
BEDROOM 11x12
LOFT 21x12
DN
OPEN

MAIN LEVEL
No. 32042

DECK
DECK
SCREENED PORCH 30x10
SUN-ROOM 12x10
DINING/GREAT-ROOM 29x20
MASTER BEDROOM 14x18
BATH
DEN 12x11
KITCHEN 13x14
CLOSET
OFFICE 12x10
DN UP
ENTRY
BEDROOM 14x11
CLOS
PORCH
UTILITY 14x6
W D
GARAGE 24x25

WIDTH 70'-0"
DEPTH 66'-0"

ZIP QUOTE
HOME COST CALCULATOR
see order pages for details

LOWER LEVEL

HOT TUB
LOWER PATIO
UP
GAMES 11x19
FAMILY 29x20
BAR
UP
SHOP 11x12
STORAGE 22x6

MAIN FLOOR — 2,072 SQ. FT.
UPPER FLOOR — 522 SQ. FT.
LOWER FLOOR —1,275 SQ. FT.

TOTAL LIVING AREA:
3,869 SQ. FT.

© 1994 Donald A. Gardner Architects, Inc.

ZIP QUOTE
HOME COST CALCULATOR
see order pages for details

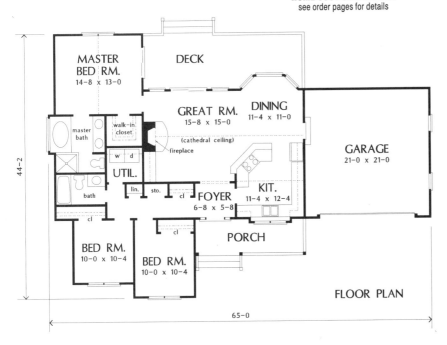

MASTER BED RM.
14-8 x 13-0

DECK

GREAT RM.
15-8 x 15-0

DINING
11-4 x 11-0

GARAGE
21-0 x 21-0

walk-in closet

master bath

(cathedral ceiling)

fireplace

w d

UTIL.

lin. sto. cl

bath

FOYER
6-8 x 5-8

KIT.
11-4 x 12-4

cl

BED RM.
10-0 x 10-4

cl

BED RM.
10-0 x 10-4

PORCH

FLOOR PLAN

44-2

65-0

Perfect for Family Gatherings

Price Code: C

■ This plan features:

— Three bedrooms

— Two full baths

■ An open layout between the Great Room, Kitchen, and Breakfast Bay sharing a cathedral ceiling and a fireplace

■ Master Suite with a soaring cathedral ceiling, direct access to the Deck and a well appointed Bath with a large walk-in closet

■ Additional bedrooms sharing a full Bath in the hall

■ Centrally located Utility and Storage spaces

MAIN FLOOR — 1,346 SQ. FT.
GARAGE AND STORAGE — 462 SQ. FT.

TOTAL LIVING AREA:
1,346 SQ. FT.

Master Suite Is Home Away From Home

Price Code: D

■ This plan features:

— Three bedrooms

— Two full and one half baths

■ A secluded, second floor Master Suite with sky-lit Master Bath, laundry chute, private study and a corner fireplace

■ A pre-fabricated Solarium, doubling the size of the bright Kitchen/Family Room

■ An elegant Living Room with a corner fireplace and large front windows

■ A formal Dining Room conveniently located next to the Kitchen

■ Two additional bedrooms that are served by a full hall bath

FIRST FLOOR — 1,856 SQ. FT.
SECOND FLOOR — 618 SQ. FT.
GARAGE — 704 SQ. FT.

TOTAL LIVING AREA:
2,474 SQ. FT.

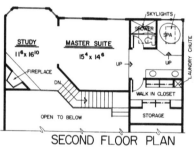

SECOND FLOOR PLAN

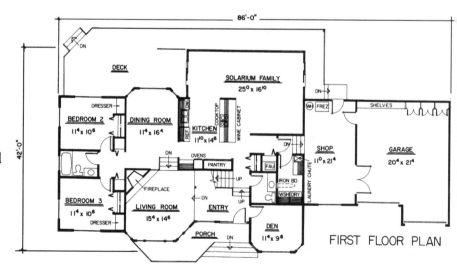

FIRST FLOOR PLAN

To order your Blueprints, call 1-800-235-5700

Packed with Options

PRICE CODE: C

- This plan features:
  - Three bedrooms
  - Three full baths
- This home has a tiled entry and Gallery that connects the living space
- The Great Room has a rear wall fireplace that is set between windows
- Both Dining Areas are located steps away from the Kitchen
- The Study has a sloped ceiling and a front bay of windows
- The Master Bedroom has a private Bath and a galley-like walk- in closet
- Two secondary Bedrooms are on the opposite side of the home
- No materials list is available for this plan

MAIN FLOOR — 2,081 SQ. F.T
GARAGE — 422 SQ. F.T

TOTAL LIVING AREA:
2,081 SQ. FT.

ZIP QUOTE
HOME COST CALCULATOR
see order pages for details

MAIN FLOOR

Carefree Convenience

PRICE CODE: B

- This plan features:
  - Three bedrooms
  - Two full baths
- A galley Kitchen, centrally-located between the Dining, Breakfast and Living Room Areas
- A huge Family Room which exits onto the Patio
- A Master Suite with double closets and vanity with two additional Bedrooms share a full half Bsath

MAIN AREA — 1,600 SQ. FT.
GARAGE — 465 SQ. FT.

TOTAL LIVING AREA:
1,600 SQ. FT.

ZIP QUOTE
HOME COST CALCULATOR
see order pages for details

MAIN AREA

To order your Blueprints, call 1-800-235-5700

Formal Balance
PRICE CODE: A

- This plan features:
  — Three bedrooms
  — Two full baths
- A cathedral ceiling in the Living Room with a heat-circulating fireplace as the focal point
- A bow window in the Dining Room that adds elegance as well as natural light
- A well-equipped Kitchen that serves both the Dinette and the formal Dining Room efficiently
- A Master Bedroom with three closets and a private Master Bath with sliding glass doors to the Master Deck with a hot tub

FIRST FLOOR — 1,374 SQ. FT.
MUDROOM/LAUNDRY — 102 SQ. FT.
BASEMENT — 1,361 SQ. FT.
GARAGE — 548 SQ. FT.

TOTAL LIVING AREA:
1,476 SQ. FT.

MAIN FLOOR

Country Ranch
PRICE CODE: A

- This plan features:
  — Three bedrooms
  — Two full baths
- A railed and covered wrap-around porch, adding charm to this country-styled home
- A high vaulted ceiling in the Living Room
- A smaller Kitchen with ample cupboard and counter space, that is augmented by a large pantry
- An informal Family Room with access to the wood deck
- A private Master Suite with a spa tub and a walk-in closet
- Two family bedrooms that share a full hall bath
- A shop and storage area in the two-car garage

MAIN FLOOR — 1,485 SQ. FT.
GARAGE — 701 SQ. FT.

TOTAL LIVING AREA:
1,485 SQ. FT.

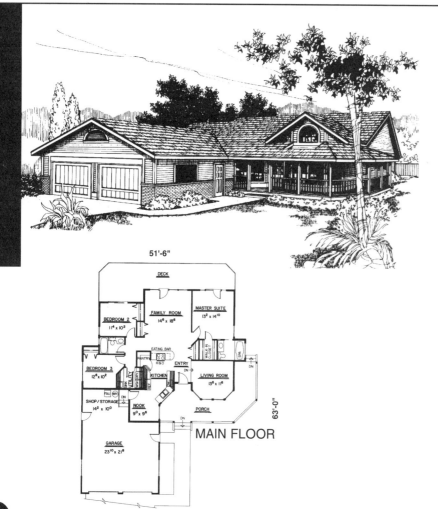

MAIN FLOOR

To order your Blueprints, call 1-800-235-5700

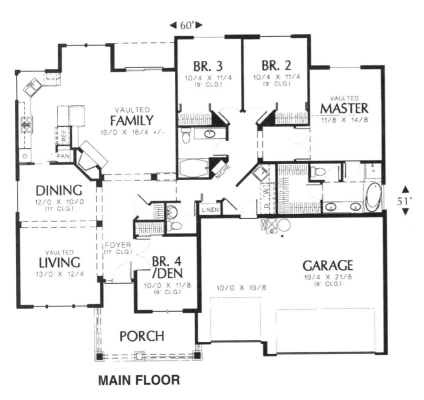

◀ 60' ▶

BR. 3
10/4 X 11/4
(9' CLG.)

BR. 2
10/4 X 11/4
(9' CLG.)

VAULTED
MASTER
11/8 X 14/8

VAULTED
FAMILY
16/0 X 16/4 +/-

REF.

PAN.

DINING
12/0 X 10/0
(11' CLG.)

NICHE

LINEN

51'

LIVING
VAULTED
13/0 X 12/4

FOYER
(11' CLG.)

**BR. 4
/DEN**
10/0 X 11/8
(9' CLG.)

10/0 X 19/8

GARAGE
19/4 X 21/8
(8' CLG.)

PORCH

MAIN FLOOR

One Floor Convenience

Price Code: C

- ■ This plan features:
- — Three bedrooms
- — Two full and one half baths
- ■ A quaint front Porch adding style to this Ranch styled home.
- ■ Living Room and Dining Room adjoining with a pocket door between the Dining Room and the Kitchen
- ■ Family Room opens to the Breakfast Nook highlighted by a corner fireplace.
- ■ Three Bedrooms are situated in a private wing of the home
- ■ Master Suite crowned in a vaulted ceiling with a five-piece Bath and walk-in closet

MAIN FLOOR — 1,997 SQ. FT.

TOTAL LIVING AREA:
1,997 SQ. FT.

Columned Keystone Arched Entry

Price Code: D

- ■ This plan features:
- — Three bedrooms
- — Two full baths
- ■ Keystone arches and arched transoms above the windows
- ■ Formal Dining Room and Study flank the Foyer
- ■ Fireplace in Great Room
- ■ Efficient Kitchen with a peninsula counter and bayed Nook
- ■ A step ceiling in the Master Suite and interesting Master Bath with a triangular area for the oval bath tub
- ■ The secondary Bedrooms share a full Bath in the hall

MAIN FLOOR — 2,256 SQ. FT.
GARAGE — 514 SQ. FT.

TOTAL LIVING AREA:
2,256 SQ. FT.

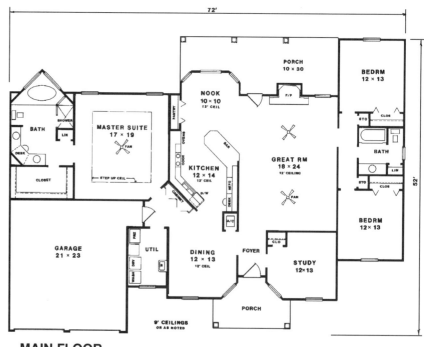

MAIN FLOOR
No. 96503

To order your Blueprints, call 1-800-235-5700

© 1996 Donald A Gardner Architects, Inc.

Unique and Desirable

Price Code: D

■ This plan features:

— Three bedrooms

— Two full baths

■ Private Master Bedroom has a walk-in closet and a skylight Bath

■ Two additional Bedrooms, one with a possible use as a Study, share a full Bath

■ From the Foyer pass through two columns into the Great Room with a cathedral ceiling and a fireplace

■ In the rear of the home is a skylight screen Porch and a Deck that features built in seats and a Spa

■ The Kitchen is conveniently located between the Dining Room and the skylight Breakfast Area

■ An optional basement or crawl space foundation—please specify when ordering

MAIN FLOOR — 1,977 SQ. FT.
BONUS ROOM — 430 SQ. FT
GARAGE & STORAGE — 610 SQ. FT.

TOTAL LIVING AREA:
1,977 SQ. FT.

ZIP QUOTE
HOME COST CALCULATOR
see order pages for details

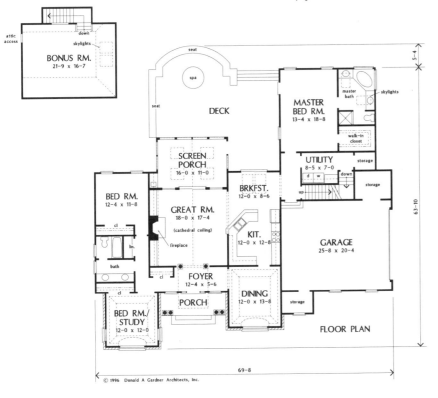

attic access

down

skylights

BONUS RM.
21-9 x 16-7

seat

spa

seat

DECK

MASTER
BED RM.
13-4 x 18-8

master bath

skylights

walk-in closet

SCREEN
PORCH
16-0 x 11-0

UTILITY
8-5 x 7-0

d   w

up   down

storage

storage

BRKFST.
12-0 x 8-6

BED RM.
12-4 x 11-8

GREAT RM.
18-0 x 17-4

(cathedral ceiling)

fireplace

cl

lin.

bath

KIT.
12-0 x 12-8

GARAGE
25-8 x 20-4

cl

FOYER
12-4 x 5-6

cl

BED RM./
STUDY
12-0 x 12-0

PORCH

DINING
12-0 x 13-8

storage

FLOOR PLAN

5-4

63-10

69-8

© 1996 Donald A Gardner Architects, Inc.

Separate Guest Quarters

Price Code: F

- ■ This plan features:
- — Four bedrooms
- — Three full and one half baths
- ■ Portico Entry way opens up to a unique courtyard
- ■ Octagon-shaped Grand Salon overlooks Lanai
- ■ An efficient Kitchen with a walk-in Pantry
- ■ Open Leisure Room has a high ceiling
- ■ Master wing has a large bedroom with a stepped ceiling, a bayed Sitting Area, glass doors to a Lanai, built-ins and a lavish Bath area
- ■ Two upstairs Bedrooms with private Decks, share a double vanity Bath
- ■ Private Guest House offers luxurious accommodations
- ■ No materials list is available for this plan

FIRST FLOOR — 2,853 SQ. FT.
SECOND FLOOR — 627 SQ. FT.
GUEST HOUSE — 312 SQ. FT.
GARAGE — 777 SQ. FT.

TOTAL LIVING AREA:
3,792 SQ. FT.

SECOND FLOOR

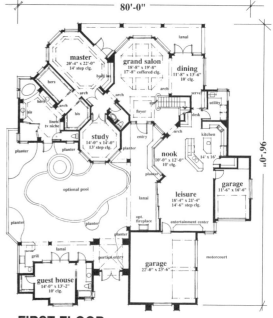

FIRST FLOOR
No. 94246

Outstanding Four Bedroom

PRICE CODE: C

This plan features:
- Four bedrooms
- Two full baths
- Radius window highlighting the exterior and the formal Dining Room
- High ceiling topping the Foyer for a grand first impression
- Vaulted ceiling enhances the Great Room accented by a fireplace framed by windows to either side
- Arched opening to the Kitchen from the Great Room
- Breakfast Room topped by a vaulted ceiling and enhanced by elegant French door to the rear yard
- Tray ceiling and a five piece compartmental Bath gives luxurious presence to the Master Suite
- Three additional Bedrooms share a full, double vanity Bath in the hall
- An optional slab or basement foundation — please specify when ordering

MAIN FLOOR — 1,945 SQ. FT.

TOTAL LIVING AREA:
1,945 SQ. FT.

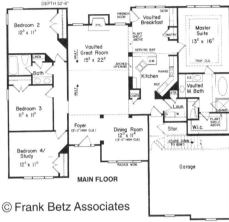

© Frank Betz Associates

Classic Cottage

PRICE CODE: D

- This plan features:
- Three bedrooms
- Two full and one half baths
- An economic design for a narrow lot width
- Twin dormers and a gabled Garage provide substantial curb appeal
- Dramatic Great Room enhanced by two clerestory dormers and a balcony overlooking
- Crowned in an elegant tray ceiling, the first floor Master Suite has a private Bath and a walk-in closet

FIRST FLOOR — 1,336 SQ. FT.
SECOND FLOOR — 523 SQ. FT.
GARAGE & STORAGE — 492 SQ. FT.
BONUS ROOM — 225 SQ. FT.

TOTAL LIVING AREA:
1,859 SQ. FT.

© 1998 Donald A. Gardner, Inc.

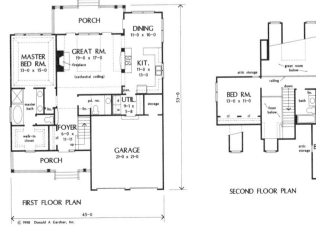

To order your Blueprints, call 1-800-235-5700

173

© 1995 Donald A Gardner Architects, Inc.

Tremendous Curb Appeal
PRICE CODE: C

- This plan features:
  — Three bedrooms
  — Two full baths
- Great Room topped by a cathedral ceiling and enhanced by a fireplace
- Great Room, Dining Room and Kitchen open to each other for a feeling of spaciousness
- Pantry, skylight and peninsula counter add to the comfort and efficiency of the Kitchen
- Cathedral ceiling crowns the Master Suite and has these amenities; walk-in and linen closet, a luxurious private Bath
- Swing Room, Bedroom or Study, topped by a cathedral ceiling
- Skylight over full hall Bath naturally illuminates the room

MAIN FLOOR — 1,246 SQ. FT.
GARAGE — 420 SQ. FT.

TOTAL LIVING AREA:
1,246 SQ. FT.

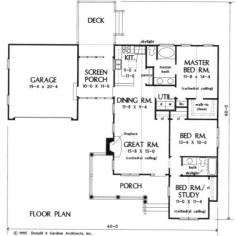

© 1995 Donald A Gardner Architects, Inc.

Cathedral Ceiling in Living Room and Master Suite
PRICE CODE: A

- This plan features:
  — Three bedrooms
  — Two full baths
- A spacious Living Room with a cathedral ceiling and elegant fireplace
- A Dining Room that adjoins both the Living Room and the Kitchen
- An efficient Kitchen, with double sinks, ample cabinet space and peninsula counter that doubles as an eating bar
- A convenient hallway Laundry Center
- A Master Suite with a cathedral ceiling and a private Master Bath

MAIN AREA — 1,346 SQ. FT.
GARAGE — 449 SQ. FT.

TOTAL LIVING AREA:
1,346 SQ. FT.

MAIN AREA

ZIP QUOTE
HOME COST CALCULATOR
see order pages for details

An
EXCLUSIVE DESIGN
By Upright Design

To order your Blueprints, call 1-800-235-5700

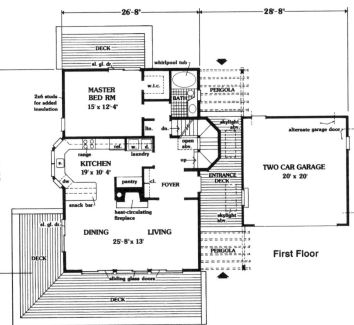

DECK

sl. gl. dr.

whirlpool tub

w.i.c.

MASTER BED RM 15' x 12'-4"

BATH

PERGOLA

2x6 studs for added insulation

lin.

dn.

skylight abv.

open abv.

alternate garage door

ref. w. d.

range

laundry

up

KITCHEN 19' x 10' 4"

TWO CAR GARAGE 20' x 20'

s.

dw

pantry

cl.

FOYER

ENTRANCE DECK

snack bar

heat-circulating fireplace

skylight abv.

sl. gl. dr.

DINING

LIVING 25'-8" x 13'

DECK

PERGOLA

First Floor

sliding glass doors

DECK

26'-8"   28'-8"

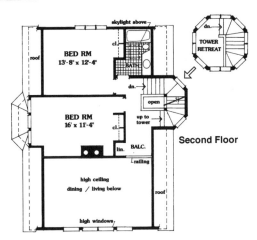

skylight above

BED RM 13'-8" x 12'-4"

cl.

TOWER RETREAT

roof

dn.

BATH

dn.

open

BED RM 16' x 11'-4"

cl.

up to tower

lin.

BALC.

railing

high ceiling dining / living below

roof

Second Floor

high windows

Farmhouse Flavor

Price Code: B

■ This plan features:

— Three bedrooms

— Two full baths

■ An octagonal stair tower

■ A Foyer opening to a Living and Dining Room combination, enhanced by a striking glass wall

■ A heat circulating fireplace adding welcome warmth

■ A galley-style Kitchen including a large pantry, snack bar, and laundry area

■ A Master Suite with a private deck overlooking the backyard

FIRST FLOOR — 1,073 SQ. FT.
SECOND FLOOR — 604 SQ. FT.
RETREAT TOWER — 93 SQ. FT.
GARAGE — 428 SQ. FT.

TOTAL LIVING AREA: **1,770** SQ. FT.

To order your Blueprints, call 1-800-235-5700

© 1993 Donald A. Gardner Architects, Inc.

Economical Three Bedroom

Price Code: C

- This plan features:
- — Three bedrooms
- — Two full baths
- Dormers above the covered Porch casting light into the Foyer
- Columns punctuating the entrance to the open Great Room/Dining Room Area with a shared cathedral ceiling and a bank of operable skylights
- Kitchen with a breakfast counter, open to the Dining Area
- Private Master Bedroom suite with a tray ceiling and luxurious Bath featuring a double vanity, separate shower, and skylights over the whirlpool tub

MAIN FLOOR — 1,322 SQ. FT.
GARAGE & STORAGE — 413 SQ. FT.

TOTAL LIVING AREA: 1,322 SQ. FT.

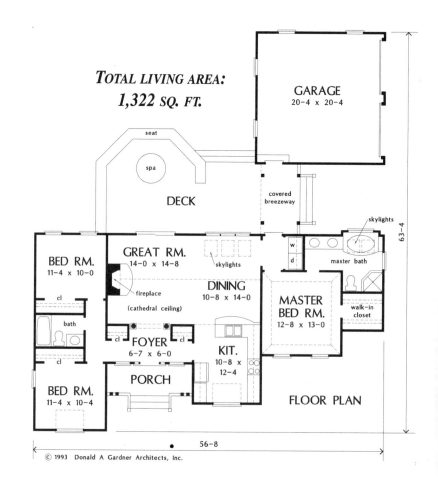

© 1993 Donald A Gardner Architects, Inc.

To order your Blueprints, call 1-800-235-5700

An <u>EXCLUSIVE DESIGN</u>
By Britt J. Willis

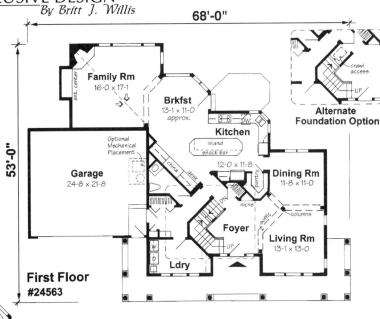

68'-0"

53'-0"

First Floor
#24563

- Family Rm 16-0 x 17-1
- ent. center
- Brkfst 13-1 x 11-0 approx.
- Kitchen
- island snack bar
- 12-0 x 11-8
- Optional Mechanical Placement
- Garage 24-8 x 21-8
- china desk
- Dining Rm 11-8 x 11-0
- pantry
- DN
- niche
- soffit
- columns
- Foyer
- Living Rm 13-1 x 13-0
- UP
- W D
- Ldry

crawl access
UP
Alternate Foundation Option

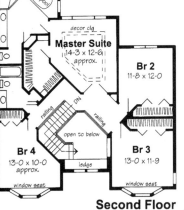

Master Suite 14-3 x 12-6 approx.
decor clg
whirlpool
Br 2 11-8 x 12-0
DN
railing
open to below
railing
Br 4 13-0 x 10-0 approx.
ledge
Br 3 13-0 x 11-9
window seat
window seat

Second Floor

TOTAL LIVING AREA:
2,861 SQ. FT.

ZIP QUOTE
HOME COST CALCULATOR
see order pages for details

Classic Front Porch

Price Code: E

■ This plan features:

— Four bedrooms

— Two full and one half baths

■ Stone and columns accenting the wrap-around front Porch

■ A formal Living Room and Dining Room adjoining with columns at their entrances

■ An island Kitchen with a double sink, plenty of cabinet and counter space and a walk-in Pantry

■ A Breakfast Room flowing into the Family Room and the Kitchen

■ A corner fireplace and a built-in entertainment center in the Family Room

■ A lavish Master Suite topped by a decorative ceiling and an ultra Bath

■ Three roomy, additional Bedrooms sharing a full hall Bath

FIRST FLOOR — 1,584 SQ. FT.
SECOND FLOOR — 1,277 SQ. FT.
GARAGE — 550 SQ. FT.
BASEMENT — 1,584 SQ. FT.

Master Suite with Private Sun Deck

Price Code: C

■ This plan features:

— Four bedrooms

— Two full and one half baths

■ A sunken Living Room, formal Dining Room, and convenient Kitchen enjoying an expansive view of the Patio and backyard

■ A fireplaced Living Room keeping the house toasty after the sun goes down

■ Skylights brightening the Balcony and Master Bath

■ An optional basement, slab, or crawl space foundation — please specify when ordering

FIRST FLOOR — 1,249 SQ. FT.
SECOND FLOOR — 890 SQ. FT.
GARAGE — 462 SQ. FT.

TOTAL LIVING AREA:
2,139 SQ. FT.

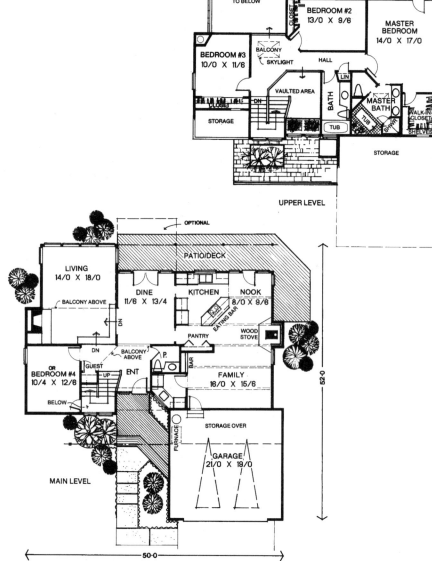

UPPER LEVEL

MAIN LEVEL

Inviting Wrap-Around Porch

PRICE CODE: B

This plan features:

Three bedrooms

Two full baths

A warm and inviting welcome, achieved by a wrap-around Porch

A skylight illuminating the entry

A corner gas fireplace and two skylights highlighted in the Great Room

Flowing from the Great Room, the Dining Room naturally lighted by the sliding glass doors to a rear deck and a skylight above

A well-appointed, U-shaped Kitchen separated from the Dining Room by a breakfast bar and including another skylight

A luxurious Master Bedroom equipped with a plush Bath and access to a private Deck

Two additional Bedrooms sharing the full Bath in the hall and receiving light from the dormers

No materials list is available for this plan

MAIN FLOOR — 1,716 SQ. FT.

BASEMENT — 1,716 SQ. FT.

TOTAL LIVING AREA:
1,716 SQ. FT.

An EXCLUSIVE DESIGN By Independent Designs

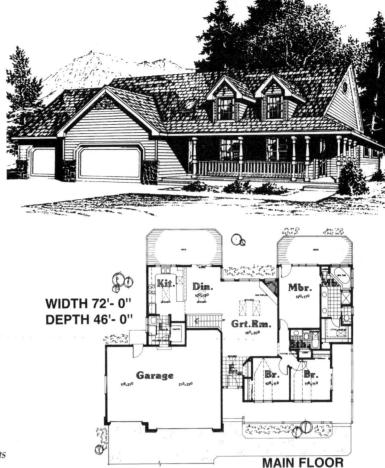

WIDTH 72'- 0"
DEPTH 46'- 0"

MAIN FLOOR

Today's Lifestyle

PRICE CODE: D

This plan features:

— Four bedrooms

— Two full and one half baths

A large Family Room with a fireplace and access to the Patio

A Breakfast Area that flows directly into the Family Room

A well-appointed Kitchen equipped with an eating bar, double sinks, built-in Pantry and an abundance of counter and cabinet space

A Master Suite with a decorative ceiling and a private Bath

Three additional Bedrooms that share a full Bath

MAIN AREA — 2,542 SQ. FT.

GARAGE — 510 SQ. FT.

TOTAL LIVING AREA:
2,542 SQ. FT.

An EXCLUSIVE DESIGN By Jannis Vann & Associates, Inc.

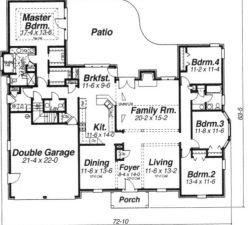

Private Master Suite
PRICE CODE: D

- This plan features:
— Three bedrooms
— Two full and one half baths
- Secluded Master Bedroom Suite tucked into the rear le[ft] corner of the home with a five-piece bath and two walk[-]in closets
- Two additional Bedrooms at the opposite side of the home sharing the full Bath in the hall
- Expansive Living Room highlighted by a corner fireplace and access to the rear Porch
- Kitchen is located between the bright, bayed Nook and the formal Dining Room providing ease in serving

MAIN FLOOR — 2,069 SQ. FT.
GARAGE — 481 SQ. FT.

TOTAL LIVING AREA:
2,069 SQ. FT.

MAIN FLOOR

Relax on the Veranda
PRICE CODE: E

- This plan features:
— Four bedrooms
— Three full and one half baths
- A wrap-around Veranda
- A sky-lit Master Suite with elevated custom spa, twin basins, a walk-in closet, and an additional vanity outside the Bathroom
- A vaulted ceiling in the Den
- A fireplace in both the Family Room and the formal Living Room
- An efficient Kitchen with a peninsula counter and a double sink
- Two additional Bedrooms with walk-in closets, served by a compartmentalized Bath
- A Guest Suite with a private Bath

MAIN AREA — 3,051 SQ. FT.
GARAGE — 646 SQ. FT.

TOTAL LIVING AREA:
3,051 SQ. FT.

MAIN FLOOR

To order your Blueprints, call 1-800-235-5700

WIDTH 46'-0"
DEPTH 30'-0"

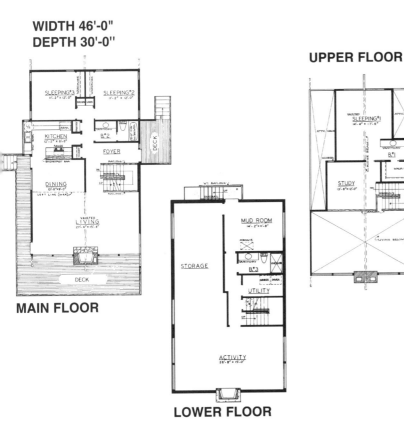

UPPER FLOOR

MAIN FLOOR

LOWER FLOOR

All Seasons

Price Code: E

■ This plan features:

— Three bedrooms

— One full, one three-quarter and one half baths

■ A wall of windows taking full advantage of the front view

■ An open stairway to the upstairs Study and the Master Bedroom

■ A Master Bedroom with a private master Bath and a walk-in wardrobe

■ An efficient Kitchen including a breakfast bar that opens into the Dining Area

■ A formal Living Room with a vaulted ceiling and a stone fireplace

MAIN FLOOR — 1,306 SQ. FT.
UPPER FLOOR — 598 SQ. FT.
LOWER FLOOR — 1,288 SQ. FT.

TOTAL LIVING AREA:
3,192 SQ. FT.

Luxurious One-Floor Living

Price Code: F

■ This plan features:

— Four bedrooms

— Three full baths

■ Decorative windows enhance the facade

■ Formal Living Room accented by fireplace

■ Formal Dining Room highlighted by decorative window

■ Breakfast bar, work island, and an abundance of storage and counter space featured in Kitchen

■ Bright alcove for informal Dining and Family rooms

■ Spacious Master Bedroom has access to covered Patio, and huge a walk-in closet

■ Three additional bedrooms have large closets

■ No materials list is available for this plan

MAIN FLOOR — 3,254 SQ. FT.
GARAGE — 588 SQ. FT.

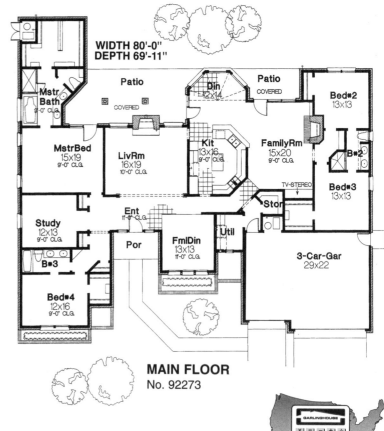

WIDTH 80'-0"
DEPTH 69'-11"

MAIN FLOOR
No. 92273

TOTAL LIVING AREA:
3,254 SQ. FT.

ZIP QUOTE
HOME COST CALCULATOR
see order pages for details

PLAN NO. 93212

An
EXCLUSIVE DESIGN
By Jannis Vann & Associates, Inc.

SECOND FLOOR

STUDY
11·2 x 11·1

BEDROOM 2
13·6 x 13·4

BEDROOM 3
12·0 x 13·4

BATH

BONUS ROOM
11·8 x 21·10

TOTAL LIVING AREA:
2,091 SQ. FT.

FIRST FLOOR — 1,362 SQ. FT.
SECOND FLOOR — 729 SQ. FT.
BONUS ROOM — 384 SQ. FT.
GARAGE — 559 SQ. FT.

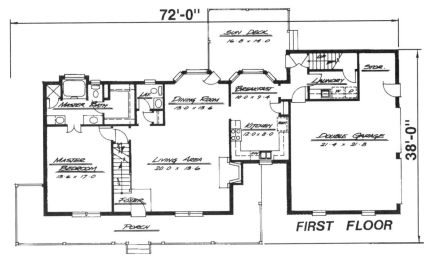

72'-0"

38'-0"

SUN DECK
16·8 x 14·0

MASTER BATH

DINING ROOM
13·0 x 13·6

BREAKFAST
10·0 x 9·4

LAUNDRY

STOR.

KITCHEN
12·0 x 8·0

MASTER BEDROOM
13·6 x 17·0

LIVING AREA
20·0 x 13·6

DOUBLE GARAGE
21·4 x 21·8

FOYER

PORCH

FIRST FLOOR

An Old-Fashioned Country Feeling

Price Code: C

■ This plan features:

— Three bedrooms

— Two and a half baths

■ A large Living Room with a cozy fireplace opens to the Dining Room for easy entertaining

■ A formal Dining Room with a bay window and direct access to the Sun Deck

■ A U-shaped Kitchen, efficiently arranged with ample work space and a pantry

■ A first floor Master Bedroom with an elegant bath complete with jacuzzi, two vanities, and a walk-in closet

■ Two additional bedrooms, with ample closets, share a full bath and study

■ Please specify a basement, slab, or crawl space foundation when ordering

© 1993 Donald A Gardner Architects, Inc.

Traditional Beauty

Price Code: D

- This plan features:
  — Three bedrooms
  — Two full baths

- Traditional beauty with large arched windows, round columns, covered Porch and a brick veneer

- Clerestory dormers above covered Porch lighting the Foyer

- Cathedral ceiling enhancing the Great Room along with a cozy fireplace

- Island Kitchen with Breakfast Area accessing the large Deck with an optional spa

- Columns defining spaces

- Tray ceiling over the Master Bedroom, Dining Room and Bedroom/Study

- Dual vanity, separate shower, and whirlpool tub in the Master Bath

MAIN FLOOR — 1,576 SQ. FT.
GARAGE — 465 SQ. FT.

TOTAL LIVING AREA:
1,576 SQ. FT.

ZIP QUOTE
HOME COST CALCULATOR
see order pages for details

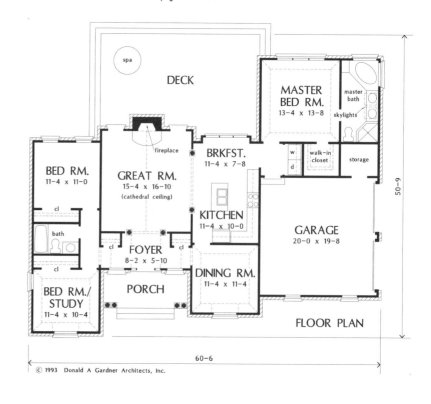

© 1993 Donald A Gardner Architects, Inc.

To order your Blueprints, call 1-800-235-5700

Varied Roof Heights Create Interesting Lines

PRICE CODE: B

This plan features:
- Three bedrooms
- Two full and one half baths
- A spacious Family Room with a heat-circulating fireplace, which is visible from the Foyer
- A large Kitchen with a cooktop island, opening into the Dinette bay
- A Master Suite with his-n-her closets and a private Master Bath
- Two additional Bedrooms which share a full hall Bath
- Formal Dining and Living Rooms, flowing into each other for easy entertaining

MAIN AREA — 1,613 SQ. FT.
BASEMENT — 1,060 SQ. FT.
GARAGE — 461 SQ. FT.

TOTAL LIVING AREA:
1,613 SQ. FT.

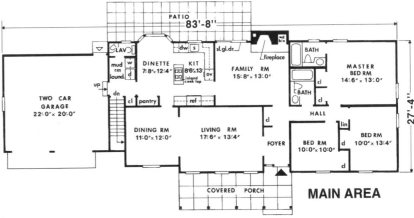

MAIN AREA

Windows Distinguish Design

PRICE CODE: F

This plan features:
- Five bedrooms
- Four full and one half baths
- Light shines into the Dining Room and the Living Room through their respective elegant windows
- A hall through the butler's Pantry leads the way into the Breakfast Nook
- The two-story Family Room has a fireplace with built in bookcases on either side
- The upstairs Master Suite has a Sitting Room and a French door that leads into the Master Bath
- There are three additional Bedrooms upstairs
- An optional basement or crawl space foundation — please specify when ordering

FIRST FLOOR — 1,786 SQ. FT.
SECOND FLOOR — 1,739 SQ. FT.
BASEMENT — 1,786 SQ. FT.
GARAGE — 704 SQ. FT.

TOTAL LIVING AREA:
3,525 SQ. FT.

© Frank Betz Associates

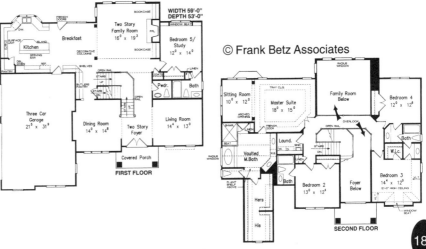

185

PLAN NO. 96506

Attractive Ceiling Treatments and Open Layout
PRICE CODE: B

■ This plan features:
— Three bedrooms
— Two full and one half baths
■ Great Room and Master Suite with step-up ceiling treatments
■ A cozy fireplace providing warm focal point in the Great Room
■ Open layout between Kitchen, Dining and Great Room lending a more spacious feeling
■ Five-piece, private Bath and walk-in closet pampering Master Suite

MAIN FLOOR — 1,654 SQ. FT.
GARAGE — 480 SQ. FT.

TOTAL LIVING AREA
1,654 SQ. FT.

MAIN FLOOR

PLAN NO. 94247

© The Sater Group, Inc.

Designed for Entertaining
PRICE CODE: E

■ This plan features:
— Three bedrooms
— Three full and one half baths
■ Large, open floor plan with an array of amenities for successful gatherings
■ Grand Room and Dining Area separated by a 3-sided fireplace and wetbar both access screened Verandah
■ Spacious Kitchen with a cooktop island, eating Nook and ready access to Verandah and Dining Room
■ Secluded Master Suite enhanced by a private Spa Deck, huge walk-in closet and whirlpool tub
■ Study and two additional Bedrooms have private access to full Baths
■ No material list is available for this plan

FIRST FLOOR — 2,066 SQ. FT.
SECOND FLOOR — 809 SQ. FT.
GARAGE — 798 SQ. FT.

TOTAL LIVING AREA:
2,875 SQ. FT.

FIRST FLOOR

SECOND FLOOR

LOWER FLOOR

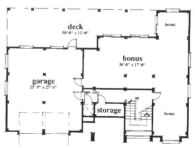

To order your Blueprints, call 1-800-235-5700

Traditional Energy Saver

Price Code: E

■ This plan features:

— Four bedrooms

— Two full, one three-quarter and one half baths

■ A heat storing floor in the Sun Room adjoining the Living Room and Breakfast Room

■ A Living Room with French doors and a massive fireplace

■ A balcony overlooking the soaring two-story Foyer and Living Room

■ An island Kitchen centrally-located between the formal and informal Dining Rooms

FIRST FLOOR — 2,186 SQ. FT.
SECOND FLOOR — 983 SQ. FT.
BASEMENT — 2,186 SQ. FT.
GARAGE — 704 SQ. FT.

TOTAL LIVING AREA:
3,169 SQ. FT.

An
EXCLUSIVE DESIGN
By Karl Kreeger

European Style

Price Code: F

TOTAL LIVING AREA:
2,727 SQ. FT.

■ This plan features:

— Four bedrooms

— Three full and one half baths

■ Central Foyer between spacious Living and Dining rooms with arched windows

■ Hub Kitchen with extended counter and nearby Utility/Garage entry, easily serves Breakfast area and Dining Room

■ Spacious Den with a hearth fireplace between built-ins and sliding glass doors to Porch

■ Master Bedroom wing with decorative ceiling, plush Bath with two walk-in closets

■ Three additional Bedrooms have ample closets and private access to a full Bath

■ An optional basement or crawl space foundation — please specify when ordering

MAIN AREA — 2,727 SQ.
GARAGE — 569 SQ. FT.

WIDTH 70'-10"
DEPTH 64'-5"

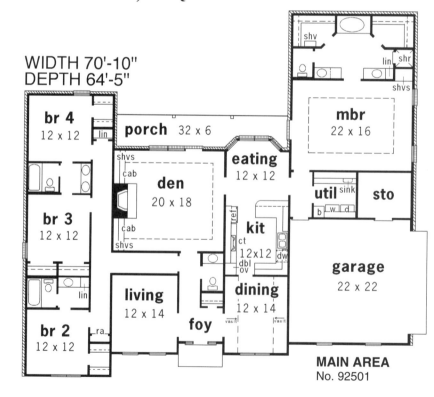

MAIN AREA
No. 92501

second floor plan

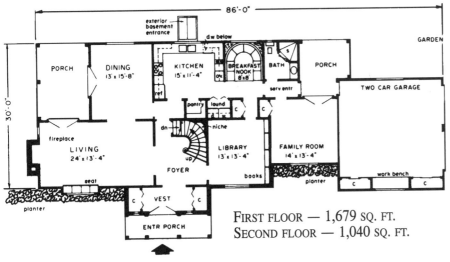

first floor plan

FIRST FLOOR — 1,679 SQ. FT.
SECOND FLOOR — 1,040 SQ. FT.

TOTAL LIVING AREA:
2,719 SQ. FT.

Stately Tudor
Price Code: E

■ This plan features:

— Three bedrooms

— Three full baths

■ Eye-catching tower, soaring above main roof, houses a dramatic, curved staircase

■ Carved double doors framed by side lights accesses vestibule and Foyer

■ Impressive Living Room with a nine foot ceiling, full window with built-in seat, a huge fireplace, and French doors to covered Porch

■ Comfortable Library with built-in shelves and Family Room with French doors to another Porch

■ U-shaped Kitchen easily serves formal Dining Room and informal Breakfast alcove

■ Master Bedroom Suite enhanced by a walk-in closet, cedar closet and plush bath

■ Two additional bedrooms with double closets, share a full bath

To order your Blueprints, call 1-800-235-5700

© 1998 Donald A. Gardner Architects, Inc. B. NATHAN.

Porches Front and Rear

Price Code: D

■ This plan features:

— Three bedrooms

— Two full and one half baths

■ A covered front Porch wraps the front and side of the home while a screen Porch spans the rear

■ The Foyer has a two-story ceiling and is separated from the Dining Room by columns

■ The Kitchen has a well-planned work triangle for added convenience

■ The Great Room and the Breakfast Nook both have a bay of windows that overlooks the rear Porch

■ The Master Bedroom encompasses one whole side of the home

■ Upstairs find two identical Bedrooms that share a full Bath

FIRST FLOOR — 1,271 SQ. FT.
SECOND FLOOR — 490 SQ. FT.
GARAGE — 543 SQ. FT.

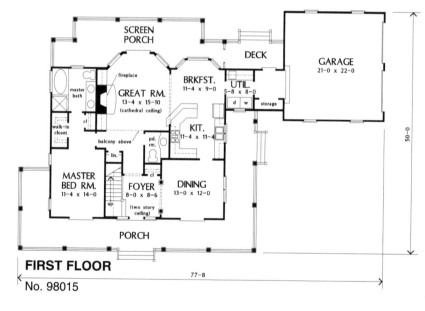

SCREEN PORCH
DECK
GARAGE 21-0 x 22-0
master bath
BRKFST. 11-4 x 9-0
UTIL. 5-8 x 8-0
d w
storage
GREAT RM. 13-4 x 15-10 (cathedral ceiling)
walk-in closet
cl
KIT. 11-4 x 11-4
balcony above
pd. rm.
lin.
MASTER BED RM. 11-4 x 14-0
FOYER 8-0 x 8-6
cl
DINING 13-0 x 12-0
up
(two story ceiling)
PORCH

FIRST FLOOR
No. 98015

50-0

77-8

TOTAL LIVING AREA:
1,761 SQ. FT.

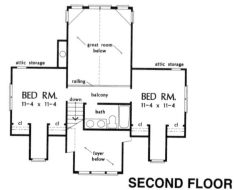

great room below
attic storage
attic storage
railing
BED RM. 11-4 x 11-4
down
balcony
BED RM. 11-4 x 11-4
cl
bath
cl
cl
cl
foyer below

SECOND FLOOR

To order your Blueprints, call 1-800-235-5700

Easy Everyday Living and Entertaining

PRICE CODE: B

This plan features:

- Three bedrooms
- Two full baths
- Front entrance accented by segmented arches, sidelight and transom windows
- Open Living Room with focal point fireplace, wetbar and access to Patio
- Dining Area open to both the Living Room and Kitchen
- Efficient Kitchen with a cooktop island, walk-in Pantry and Utility area with a Garage entry
- Large walk-in closet, double vanity Bath and access to Patio featured in the Master Bedroom
- Two additional Bedrooms share a double vanity Bath
- No materials list is available for this plan

MAIN FLOOR — 1,664 SQ. FT.
BASEMENT — 1,600 SQ. FT.
GARAGE — 440 SQ. FT

TOTAL LIVING AREA:
1,664 SQ. FT.

ZIP QUOTE
HOME COST CALCULATOR
see order pages for details

Lavish Appointments

PRICE CODE: F

This plan features:

- Four bedrooms
- Four full and one half baths
- Highly glassed two-story entry and brick detailing
- The staircase to the second floor accents the marble Entry Hall
- A sloped ceiling and a fireplace enhance the Living Room
- The Dining Room has a rear wall of windows
- The Kitchen has a center island with a cooktop
- The Study has a fireplace and a huge front wall window
- The lavish Master Bedroom includes a Sitting Area and an Exercise Area
- Two Baths service three Bedrooms upstairs
- No materials list is available for this plan

MAIN FLOOR — 3,145 SQ. FT.
UPPER FLOOR — 1,181 SQ. FT.
GARAGE — 792 SQ. FT.

TOTAL LIVING AREA:
4,326 SQ. FT.

WIDTH 134'-2"
DEPTH 45'-10"

To order your Blueprints, call 1-800-235-5700

191

Affordable Energy-Saver
PRICE CODE: A

- This plan features:
  — Three bedrooms
  — Two full baths
- A covered Porch leading into an open Foyer and Living/Dining Room with skylights and front to back exposure
- An efficient Kitchen with a bay window Dinette Area, walk-in Pantry and adjacent to the Mud Room, Garage Area
- A private Master Bedroom with a luxurious Master Bath leading to a private Deck complete with a hot tub
- Two additional Bedrooms with access to a full hall Bath

MAIN FLOOR — 1,393 SQ. FT.
BASEMENT — 1,393 SQ. FT.
GARAGE — 542 SQ. FT.

TOTAL LIVING AREA:
1,393 SQ. FT.

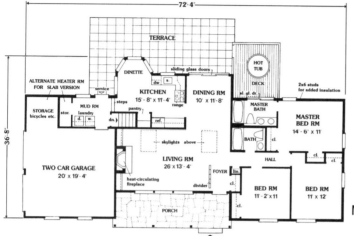

MAIN FLOOR

Inviting Porch Has Dual Function
PRICE CODE: A

- This plan features:
  — Three bedrooms
  — One full and one three-quarter baths
- An inviting, wrap-around porch entry with sliding glass doors leading right into a bayed Dining Room
- A Living Room with a cozy feeling, enhanced by the fireplace
- An efficient Kitchen opening to both Dining and Living Rooms
- A Master Suite with a walk-in closet and private Master Bath
- An optional basement, slab or crawl space foundation — please specify when ordering

MAIN FLOOR — 1,295 SQ. FT.
GARAGE — 400 SQ. FT.

TOTAL LIVING AREA:
1,295 SQ. FT.

MAIN FLOOR

To order your Blueprints, call 1-800-235-5700

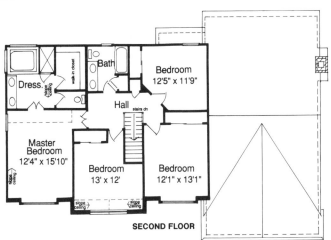

SECOND FLOOR

WIDTH 59' - 6"
DEPTH 40' - 0"

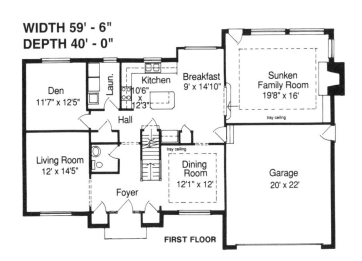

FIRST FLOOR

Distinguished Four Bedroom

Price Code: E

■ This plan features:

— Four bedrooms

— Two full and one half baths

■ Efficient, L-shaped Kitchen with work island/snack bar, Breakfast Area and access to Laundry, Den, Family Room, Dining Room and Garage

■ Sunken Family Room with a cozy fireplace and access to rear yard

■ Master Bedroom wing offers a plush Bath with double vanity and whirlpool tub

■ Three additional Bedrooms with ample closets share a double vanity Bath

■ No materials list is available for this plan

FIRST FLOOR — 1,516 SQ. FT.
SECOND FLOOR — 1,148 SQ. FT.
BASEMENT — 1,127 SQ. FT.
GARAGE — 440 SQ. FT.

TOTAL LIVING AREA:
2,664 SQ. FT.

© 1997 Donald A Gardner Architects, Inc.

Dressed to Impress

Price Code: E

■ This plan features:

— Three bedrooms

— Two full and one half baths

■ A stone and stucco exterior plus a dramatic entry with square columns provide impressive curb appeal

■ The Great Room has a cathedral ceiling and adjoins the Breakfast Area

■ The Kitchen is enhanced by an angled counter with stove top, a Pantry and easy access to the formal Dining Room

■ A separate Utility Room with built-in cabinets and a counter top with a Laundry sink add efficiency

■ Double doors lead into the Master Suite with a box bay window, two walk-in closets and a lavish Bath

■ Two more Bedrooms are located upstairs along with a full Bath, a linen closet and a skylit Bonus Room

First floor — 1,572 sq. ft.

Second floor — 549 sq. ft.

Bonus — 384 sq. ft.

Garage & storage — 540 sq. ft.

FIRST FLOOR
No. 99824

© 1997 Donald A Gardner Architects, Inc.

TOTAL LIVING AREA:
2,121 SQ. FT.

SECOND FLOOR

194

To order your Blueprints, call 1-800-235-5700

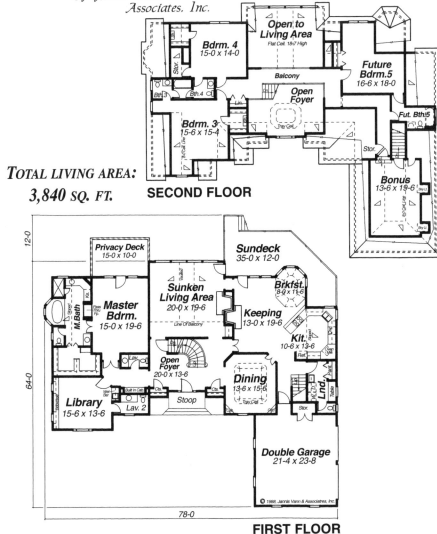

**TOTAL LIVING AREA:
3,840 SQ. FT.**

SECOND FLOOR

FIRST FLOOR

Impressive Residence

Price Code: F

- This plan features:
  - Three bedrooms
  - Two full and four half baths
- Grand entrance with two-story Foyer, curved staircase and Balcony
- Spacious Living Room with a vaulted ceiling above a wall of windows, Sundeck access and an inviting fireplace
- Ideal Kitchen with extended cooktop serving counter, octagon glass Breakfast Area, Keeping Room with a cozy fireplace, and nearby Laundry and Garage entry
- Palatial Master Bedroom suite with a fireplace, private Deck, a double walk-in closet and spectacular Bath
- No materials list is available for this plan

FIRST FLOOR — 2,656 SQ. FT.
SECOND FLOOR — 1,184 SQ. FT.
BONUS — 508 SQ. FT.
BASEMENT — 2,642 SQ. FT.
GARAGE — 528 SQ. FT.

Curb Appeal

Price Code: F

- This plan features:
— Four bedrooms
— Three full baths

- A private Master Bedroom with a raised ceiling and attached Bath with a spa tub

- A wing of three Bedrooms that share two full Baths on the right side of the home

- An efficient Kitchen is straddled by an Eeating Nook and a Dining Room

- A cozy Den with a raised ceiling and a fireplace that is the focal point of the home

- A two-car Garage has a storage area

- An optional crawl space or slab foundation — please specify when ordering

MAIN FLOOR — 2,735 SQ. FT.
GARAGE — 561 SQ. FT.

TOTAL LIVING AREA:
2,735 SQ. FT.

WIDTH 68'-10"
DEPTH 67'-4"

mbr
15 x 21⁴
raised clg

porch
8 x 30⁸

br 4
14 x 12

sto
8⁶ x 8

util 8⁶ x 9

eating
13 x 11

den
18 x 24

raised clg

garage
21 x 22

kit
13 x 13

br 3
14 x 12

ledge

pan

dining
14 x 12

foy

porch

br 2
14 x 12

MAIN FLOOR
No. 92550

Country Charmer

PRICE CODE: A

This plan features:
- Three bedrooms
- Two full baths

■ Quaint front Porch is perfect for sitting and relaxing
■ Great Room opening into Dining Area and Kitchen
■ Corner Deck in rear of home accessed from Kitchen and Master Suite
■ Master Suite with a private Bath, walk-in closet and built-in shelves
■ Two large secondary Bedrooms in the front of the home share a hall Bath
■ Two car Garage located in the rear of the home

MAIN FLOOR — 1,438 SQ. FT.
GARAGE — 486 SQ. FT.

TOTAL LIVING AREA:
1,438 SQ. FT.

MAIN FLOOR

Delightful Home

PRICE CODE: C

■ This plan features:
- Three bedrooms
- Two full baths

■ Grand Room with a fireplace, vaulted ceiling and double French doors to the rear Deck
■ Kitchen and Dining Room open to continue the overall feel of spaciousness
■ Kitchen has a large walk-in Pantry, island with a sink and dishwasher creating a perfect triangular workspace
■ Dining Room with doors to both Decks, has expanses of glass looking out to the rear yard
■ Master Bedroom features a double door entry, private bath
■ No material list is available for this plan

FIRST FLOOR — 1,342 SQ. FT.
SECOND FLOOR — 511 SQ. FT.

TOTAL LIVING AREA:
1,853 SQ. FT.

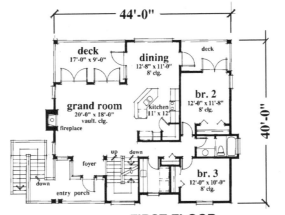

FIRST FLOOR

SECOND FLOOR

© Frank Betz Associates

High Ceilings and Arched Windows

PRICE CODE: B

■ This plan features:
— Three bedrooms
— Two full baths

■ Natural illumination streaming into the Dining Room and Sitting Area of the Master Suite through large arched windows

■ Kitchen with convenient pass through to the Great Room and a serving bar for the Breakfast Room

■ Great Room topped by a vaulted ceiling accented by a fireplace and a French door

■ Decorative columns accenting the entrance of the Dining Room

■ Tray ceiling over the Master Suite and a vaulted ceiling over the Sitting Room and the Master Bath

■ An optional basement or crawl space foundation — please specify when ordering

■ No materials list is available for this plan

MAIN FLOOR — 1,502 SQ. FT.
GARAGE — 448 SQ. FT.
BASEMENT — 1,555 SQ. FT.

TOTAL LIVING AREA: 1,502 SQ. FT.

OPT. BASEMENT STAIR LOCATION

FLOOR PLAN

© 1998 Donald A. Gardner, Inc.

Stunning Stucco

PRICE CODE: E

■ This plan features:
— Three bedrooms
— Two full and one half baths

■ A lovely courtyard greets your entry into this stunning stucco home

■ The Dining Room boasts a dramatic eleven-foot ceiling and a curved window wall

■ The Great Room includes a fireplace and a cathedral ceiling

■ The U-shaped Kitchen has a center island and is open to the Breakfast Bay

■ A rear Deck and Porch add living space in the warmer months

■ A private Bath and dual walk in closets compliment the Master Suite

■ Two secondary Bedrooms share a full Bath located between them

■ A two-car Garage completes this plan

MAIN FLOOR — 2,027 SQ. FT.
GARAGE — 565 SQ. FT.

TOTAL LIVING AREA: 2,027 SQ. FT.

FLOOR PLAN
© 1998 Donald A. Gardner, Inc.

To order your Blueprints, call 1-800-235-5700

© 1997 Donald A. Gardner Architects, Inc.

Illusion of Spaciousness

Price Code: C

DECK

skylight

SCREEN PORCH
10-0 x 12-0

KIT.
10-0 x 11-0

walk-in closet

MASTER BED RM.
14-0 x 11-8
(cathedral ceiling)

GARAGE
19-4 x 20-4

DINING
12-4 x 9-4
(cathedral ceiling)

UTIL.
d w

master bath

cl

BED RM.
13-4 x 10-0

GREAT RM.
15-8 x 15-0
fireplace

PORCH

bath

BED RM./ STUDY
11-0 x 11-4
(cathedral ceiling)

FLOOR PLAN

10-0

48-0

60-0

© 1997 Donald A Gardner Architects, Inc.

■ This plan features:

— Three bedrooms

— Two full baths

■ Open living spaces and vaulted ceilings creating an illusion of spaciousness

■ Cathedral ceilings maximize space in Great Room and Dining Room

■ Kitchen features skylight and breakfast bar

■ Well equipped Master Suite in rear for privacy

■ Two additional Bedrooms in front share a full Bath

MAIN FLOOR — 1,246 SQ. FT.
GARAGE — 420 SQ. FT.

TOTAL LIVING AREA:
1,246 SQ. FT.

National Treasure

Price Code: C

- This plan features:
- — Three bedrooms
- — Two full and one half baths
- A wrap-around covered Porch
- Decorative vaulted ceilings in the fireplaced Living Room
- A large Kitchen with central island/breakfast bar
- A sun-lit Sitting Area

FIRST FLOOR — 1,034 SQ. FT.
SECOND FLOOR — 944 SQ. FT.
BASEMENT — 944 SQ. FT.
GARAGE — 675 SQ. FT.

TOTAL LIVING AREA:
1,978 SQ. FT.

ZIP QUOTE
HOME COST CALCULATOR
see order pages for details

An
EXCLUSIVE DESIGN
By Upright Design

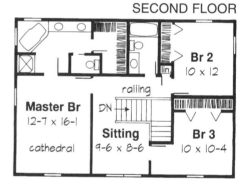

SECOND FLOOR

Master Br
12-7 x 16-1
cathedral

Br 2
10 x 12

railing

DN

Sitting
9-6 x 8-6

Br 3
10 x 10-4

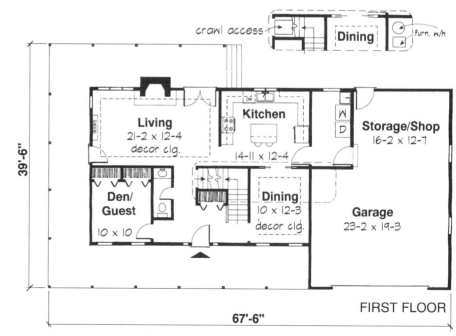

crawl access

Dining

furn. w/h

Living
21-2 x 12-4
decor clg.

Kitchen
14-11 x 12-4

Storage/Shop
16-2 x 12-7

Den/
Guest
10 x 10

Dining
10 x 12-3
decor clg.

Garage
23-2 x 19-3

39'-6"

67'-6"

FIRST FLOOR

To order your Blueprints, call 1-800-235-5700

© 1993 Donald A. Gardner Architects, Inc.

PLAN NO. 96404

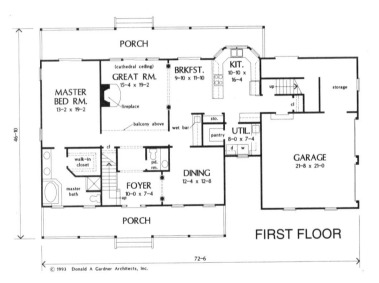

PORCH

(cathedral ceiling)
GREAT RM.
15–4 x 19–2

BRKFST.
9–10 x 11–10

KIT.
10–10 x
16–4

MASTER
BED RM.
13–2 x 19–2

fireplace

storage

up

cl

balcony above

wet bar

sto.

pantry

UTIL.
8–0 x 7–4

d   w

GARAGE
21–8 x 21–0

walk-in
closet

cl

pd.
rm.

master
bath

FOYER
10–0 x 7–4

up

DINING
12–4 x 12–8

46–10

PORCH

FIRST FLOOR

72–6

© 1993 Donald A Gardner Architects, Inc.

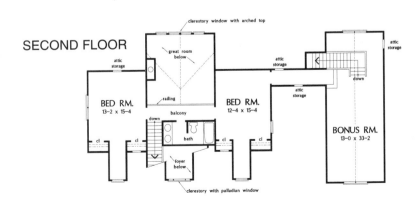

SECOND FLOOR

clerestory window with arched top

great room
below

attic
storage

attic
storage

attic
storage

attic
storage

down

railing

BED RM.
13–2 x 15–4

BED RM.
12–4 x 15–4

BONUS RM.
13–0 x 33–2

cl

cl

down

balcony

bath

cl

cl

foyer
below

clerestory with palladian window

Covered Porches Front and Back

Price Code: E

■ This plan features:
— Three bedrooms
— Two full and one half baths

■ Two-story Foyer with palladian, clerestory window and balcony overlooking Great Room

■ Great Room with cozy fireplace provides perfect gathering place

■ Columns visually separate Great Room from Breakfast Area and smart, U-shaped Kitchen

■ Privately located Master Bedroom accesses Porch and luxurious Master Bath with separate shower and double vanity

FIRST FLOOR — 1,632 SQ. FT.
SECOND FLOOR — 669 SQ. FT.
BONUS ROOM — 528 SQ. FT.
GARAGE & STORAGE — 707 SQ. FT.

TOTAL LIVING AREA:
2,301 SQ. FT.

201

Distinctive Design

Price Code: C

■ This plan features:

— Three bedrooms

— Two full and one half baths

■ Living Room is distinguished by a bay window and French doors leading to Family Room

■ Built-in curio cabinet and hutch adds interest to formal Dining Room

■ Well-appointed Kitchen with island cooktop, Breakfast Area, adjoining Laundry and Garage entry

■ Family Room with focal point fireplace

■ Spacious Master Bedroom Suite with vaulted ceiling and plush Dressing Area

■ Secondary Bedrooms share a double vanity Bath

FIRST FLOOR — 1,093 SQ. FT.
SECOND FLOOR — 905 SQ. FT.
GARAGE — 527 SQ. FT.
BASEMENT — 1,093 SQ. FT.

TOTAL LIVING AREA:
1,998 SQ. FT.

SECOND FLOOR

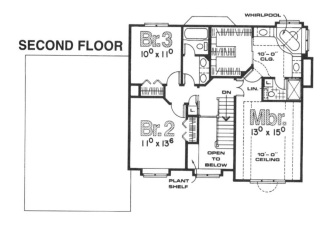

© design basics, inc.

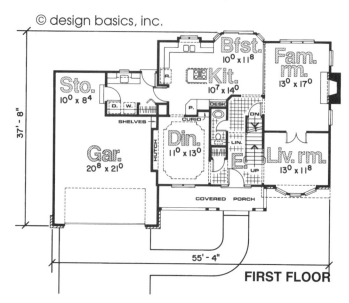

FIRST FLOOR

To order your Blueprints, call 1-800-235-5700

Elegant Row House
PRICE CODE: C

PLAN NO. 94259

■ This plan features:
– Three bedrooms
– Two full and one half baths
■ Arched columns define the formal and casual spaces
■ Wrap-around Porticos on two levels provide views to the living areas
■ Four sets of French doors let the outside in to the Great Room
■ The Master Suite features a private Bath designed for two people
■ Generous bonus space awaits your ideas for completion
■ The Guest Bedroom leads to a Gallery hallway with Deck access
■ No materials list is available for this plan

MAIN FLOOR — 1,305 SQ. FT.
UPPER FLOOR — 1,215 SQ. FT.
BONUS — 935 SQ. FT.
GARAGE — 480 SQ. FT.

TOTAL LIVING AREA:
2,520 SQ. FT.

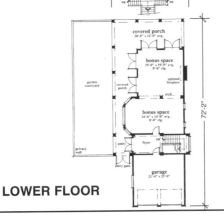

LOWER FLOOR　　**FIRST FLOOR**　　**SECOND FLOOR**

L-Shaped Front Porch
PRICE CODE: A

PLAN NO. 98747

■ This plan features:
– Three bedrooms
– Two full baths
■ Attractive wood siding and a large L-shaped covered Porch
■ Front entry leading to generous Living Room with a vaulted ceiling
■ Large two-car Garage with access through Utility Room
■ Roomy secondary Bedrooms share the full Bath in the hall
■ Kitchen highlighted by a built-in Pantry and a garden window
■ Vaulted ceiling adds volume to the Dining Room
■ Master Suite in an isolated location enhanced by abundant closet space, separate vanity, and linen storage

MAIN FLOOR — 1,280 SQ. FT.

TOTAL LIVING AREA:
1,280 SQ. FT.

To order your Blueprints, call 1-800-235-5700

203

PLAN NO. 98443

One Floor Convenience
PRICE CODE: A

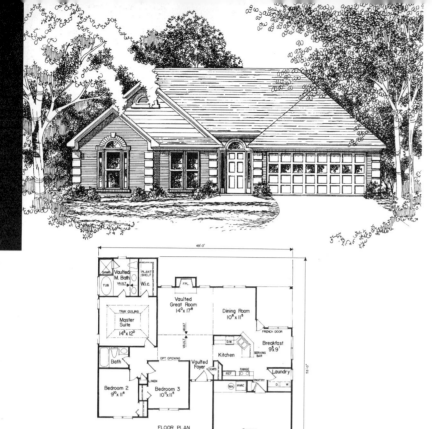

© Frank Betz Associates

- This plan features:
  — Three bedrooms
  — Two full baths
- Vaulted Foyer blending with the vaulted Great Room giving a larger feeling to the home
- Formal Dining Room opening into the Great Room allowing for a terrific living area in which to entertain
- Kitchen including a serving bar and easy flow into the Breakfast Room
- Master Suite topped by a decorative tray ceiling and a vaulted ceiling in the Master Bath
- Two additional Bedrooms sharing the full Bath in the hall
- No materials list is available for this plan
- An optional crawl space or slab foundation — please specify when ordering

MAIN FLOOR — 1,359 SQ. FT.
GARAGE — 439 SQ. FT.

TOTAL LIVING AREA:
1,359 SQ. FT.

PLAN NO. 99825

Luxuriant Living
PRICE CODE: F

© 1997 Donald A Gardner Architects, Inc.

- This plan features:
  — Four bedrooms
  — Three full and one half baths
- French doors, windows, and a high gabled Entry make a dramatic entrance to this home
- Formal Living Room features a box bay window and a fireplace
- Dining Room is illuminated by a bank of windows
- Large Family Room has a two-story ceiling, a fireplace and accessed the rear Patio
- Kitchen and Nook adjoin handy home Office that has a full Bath
- The Master Suite features a private Bath and a Sitting Area
- Upstairs find two Bedrooms each with a walk-in closet, a full Bath and a Bonus Room

FIRST FLOOR — 2,249 SQ. FT.
SECOND FLOOR — 620 SQ. FT.
BONUS — 308 SQ. FT.
GARAGE — 642 SQ. FT.

TOTAL LIVING AREA:
2,869 SQ. FT.

© 1997 Donald A Gardner Architects, Inc.

To order your Blueprints, call 1-800-235-5700

© 1994 Donald A. Gardner Architects, Inc.

PLAN NO. 99844

TOTAL LIVING AREA:
1,737 SQ. FT.

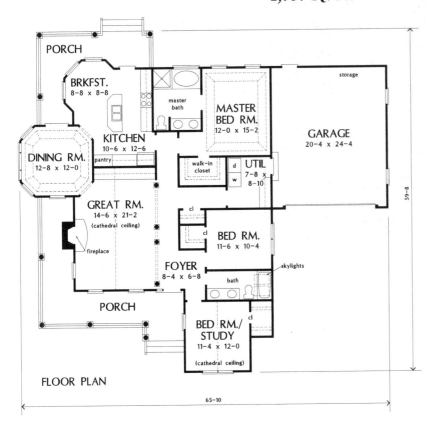

FLOOR PLAN

Clever Use of Interior Space

Price Code: D

- This plan features:
  — Three bedrooms
  — Two full baths

- Efficient interior with cathedral and tray ceilings create feeling of space

- Great Room boosts cathedral ceiling above cozy fireplace, built-in shelves and columns

- Octagon Dining Room and Breakfast Alcove bathed in light and easily access Porch

- Open Kitchen features island counter sink and Pantry

- Master Bedroom suite enhance by tray ceiling and plush Bath

MAIN FLOOR — 1,737 SQ. FT.
GARAGE & STORAGE — 517 SQ. FT.

To order your Blueprints, call 1-800-235-5700

205

One Floor Living

Price Code: A

■ This plan features:

— Three bedrooms

— Two full baths

■ A covered front Porch is supported by columns and accented by balusters

■ The Living Room features a cozy fireplace and a ceiling fan

■ The Kitchen is distinguished by an angled serving bar

■ The Dining Room is convenient to the Kitchen and accessed the rear Porch

■ Two secondary Bedrooms share a Bath in the hall

■ The Master Bedroom has a walk in closet and a private Bath

■ A two-car Garage with storage space is located in the rear of the home

MAIN FLOOR —1,247 SQ. FT.
GARAGE — 512 SQ. FT.

TOTAL LIVING AREA:
1,247 SQ. FT.

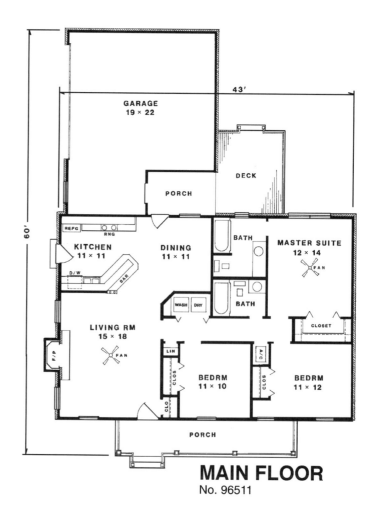

MAIN FLOOR
No. 96511

To order your Blueprints, call 1-800-235-5700

European Styling with a Georgian Flair

Price Code: D

■ This plan features:

— Four bedrooms

— Two full baths

■ Arched windows, quoins and shutters create an eye-catching home

■ Formal Foyer accesses the Dining Room and Den

■ Kitchen flows into the informal Eating Area and is separated from the Den by an angled extended counter eating bar

■ Split Bedroom plan, Master Suite is privately place to the rear

■ Three additional Bedrooms share a full Bath in the hall

■ An optional crawl space or slab foundation — please specify when ordering

MAIN FLOOR — 1,873 SQ. FT.
BONUS — 145 SQ. FT.
GARAGE — 613 SQ. FT.

TOTAL LIVING AREA:
1,873 SQ. FT.

WIDTH 72'-10"
DEPTH 54'-5"

bonus rm
12 x 15

mbr
15 x 14

util 6 x 8
d W

eating
8 x 10   por   4 x 7

br 4
11 x 12

garage
24 x 22

kit
12x12
ref
rng
dw

den
17 x 16

lin

sto

dining
11 x 12

foy

br 2
11 x 11

br 3
11 x 12

11x9

porch

MAIN FLOOR
No. 92552

Poetic Symmetry

Price Code: E

■ This plan features:

— Three bedrooms

— Three full and one half baths

■ The open Living and Dining areas are defined by French doors with windows above

■ A cozy fireplace is framed by built-ins

■ The Kitchen has a center island and loads of cabinets

■ The Master Suite is located for maximum in privacy

■ Upstairs find two Guest Rooms each with a private Bath and Sun Deck

■ Also upstairs is a Gallery Loft and a Computer Loft, which overlooks the Grand Room

■ The ground level features a two-car Garage and plenty of storage space

■ No materials list is available for this plan

MAIN FLOOR — 1,642 SQ. FT.
UPPER FLOOR — 1,165 SQ. FT.

TOTAL LIVING AREA:
2,807 SQ. FT.

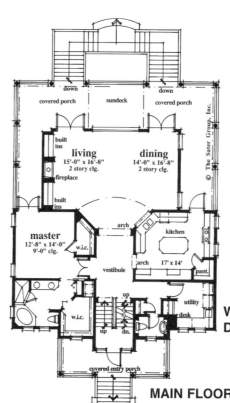

MAIN FLOOR
No. 94261

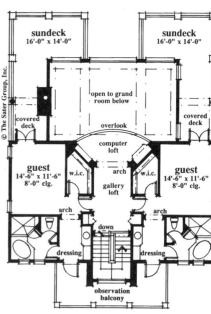

UPPER FLOOR

WIDTH 44'-6"
DEPTH 62'-0"

To order your Blueprints, call 1-800-235-5700

Impressive Entry

PRICE CODE: C

- This plan features:
  - Three bedrooms
  - Two full and one half baths
- High arched Entry as a prelude to impressive floor plan
- Living Room topped by a vaulted ceiling and enhanced by a gas fireplace
- Dining Room topped by a vaulted ceiling adjoins the Living Room to create a large living space
- Pocket doors opening to the Kitchen/Nook Area from the Dining Room
- A work island and a walk-in Pantry add to the convenience and efficiency of the Kitchen
- An attractive French door accesses the covered Patio from Nook Area
- Family Room contains another gas fireplace
- Master Suite includes a whirlpool Bath and a separate shower
- Two additional Bedrooms share the full Bath in the hall

FIRST FLOOR — 1,212 SQ. FT.
SECOND FLOOR — 922 SQ. FT.
BASEMENT — 1,199 SQ. FT.
GARAGE — 464 SQ. FT.

TOTAL LIVING AREA:
2,134 SQ. FT.

FIRST FLOOR

SECOND FLOOR

Style and Practicality

PRICE CODE: D

© 1998 Donald A. Gardner, Inc.

B. NATHAN

- This plan features:
  - Three bedrooms
  - Two full baths
- Slightly wrapping front and side Porches
- Plan easily fits on a narrow lot
- A cathedral ceiling enhancing the Great Room with fireplace and built-ins
- An optional Loft/Study above the Kitchen overlooking the Great Room
- Columns framing Entry to the formal Dining Room top by a tray ceiling
- Complete Master Suite with tray ceiling, bay window, side porch access, dual walk-in closets, and Bath with garden tub and separate shower

MAIN FLOOR — 1,795 SQ. FT.
BONUS ROOM — 368 SQ. FT.
GARAGE — 520 SQ. FT.

TOTAL LIVING AREA:
1,795 SQ. FT.

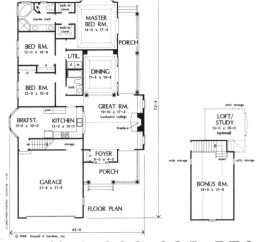

© 1998 Donald A. Gardner, Inc.

Beautiful Stucco & Stone
PRICE CODE: C

- This plan features:
  — Three bedrooms
  — Two full and one half baths
- This home is accented by keystone arches and a turret styled roof
- The two story Foyer includes a half Bath
- The vaulted Family Room is highlighted by a fireplace and French doors to the rear yard
- The Dining Room adjoins the Family Room which has access to the covered Porch and the Kitchen
- The Master Bedroom is crowned by a tray ceiling, while Master Bath has a vaulted ceiling
- Two additional Bedrooms share a full double vanity Bath
- A Balcony overlooks the Family Room and Foyer below
- An optional basement, slab or a crawl space foundation — please specify when ordering
- No materials list is available for this plan

FIRST FLOOR — 1,398 SQ. FT.
SECOND FLOOR — 515 SQ. FT.
BASEMENT — 1,398 SQ. FT.
GARAGE — 421 SQ. FT.

TOTAL LIVING AREA:
1,913 SQ. FT.

FIRST FLOOR PLAN

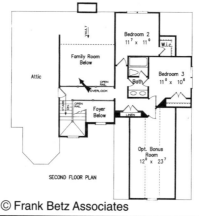

SECOND FLOOR PLAN

© Frank Betz Associates

Elegant Brick Exterior
PRICE CODE: B

- This plan features:
  — Three bedrooms
  — Two full baths
- Detailing and accenting columns highlighting the covered front Porch
- Den is enhanced by a corner fireplace and adjoining with Dining Room
- Efficient Kitchen well-appointed and with easy access to the Utility/Laundry Room
- Master Bedroom topped by a vaulted ceiling and pampered by a private Bath and a walk-in closet
- Two secondary Bedrooms are located at the opposite end of home sharing a full Bath located between the two rooms
- An optional slab or crawl space foundation — please specify when ordering

MAIN FLOOR — 1,390 SQ. FT.
GARAGE — 590 SQ. FT.

TOTAL LIVING AREA:
1,390 SQ. FT.

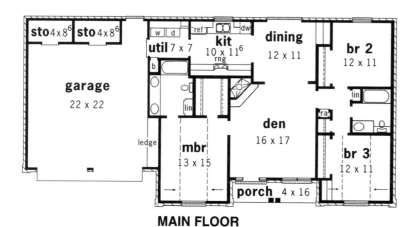

MAIN FLOOR

To order your Blueprints, call 1-800-235-5700

An
EXCLUSIVE DESIGN
By Energetic Enterprises

BEDROOM
11'-0"x12'-4"

MASTER BEDROOM
(vaulted ceiling)
16'-4"x15'-0"

DN

OPEN TO BELOW

LIN

LIN

BATH

MASTER BATH

WALK IN CLOSET SHELVES

WALK IN CLOSET

BEDROOM
11'-0"x13'-0"

BEDROOM
11'-0"x11'-0"

SECOND FLOOR

OPTIONAL RETREAT
11'-0"x12'-4"

MASTER BEDROOM

CABINETS

DN

OPTIONAL RETREAT

PATIO

D **LNDRY** **W** **DW** **NOOK**

KITCHEN
11'-10"x12'-8"

OVEN **REF** **PAN**

ALTERNATE KITCHEN

PATIO

D **DW** **LNDRY** **W**

NOOK
11'-0"x13'-0"

KITCHEN
11'-10"x12'-8"

OVEN **REF** **PAN**

OPTIONAL WORKBENCH

DESK

DN

FAMILY ROOM
12'-0" CEILING
19'-0"x15'-2"

POWDER ROOM

BUTLER PANTRY

FIREPLACE

OPTIONAL DOOR

UP

FOYER

GARAGE

DINING ROOM
11'-8"x13'-0"

LIVING ROOM
12'-0" CEILING
11'-10"x13'-8"

PORCH

FIRST FLOOR

43'-0"

52'-0"

Attractive Hip and Valley Style Roof

Price Code: D

■ This plan features:

— Four bedrooms

— Two full and one half baths

■ A see-through fireplace between the Living Room and the Family Room

■ A gourmet Kitchen with an extended serving counter, built-in Pantry, and nearby Laundry

■ A Master Bedroom with a vaulted ceiling, double vanity Bath, and walk-in closet

■ Three additional Bedrooms, one with walk-in closet share a full hall Bath

FIRST FLOOR — 1,241 SQ. FT.
SECOND FLOOR — 1,170 SQ. FT.
GARAGE — 500 SQ. FT.

TOTAL LIVING AREA:
2,411 SQ. FT.

A Modern Slant On A Country Theme

Price Code: B

■ This plan features:

— Three bedrooms

— Two full and one half baths

■ Country styled front Porch highlighting exterior enhanced by dormer windows

■ Modern open floor plan for a more spacious feeling

■ Great Room accented by a quaint, corner fireplace and a ceiling fan

■ Dining Room flowing from the Great Room for easy entertaining

■ Kitchen graced by natural light from attractive bay window and a convenient snack bar for meals on the go

■ Master Suite secluded in separate wing for total privacy

■ Two additional Bedrooms sharing full Bath in the hall

MAIN FLOOR — 1,648 SQ. FT.
GARAGE — 479 SQ. FT.

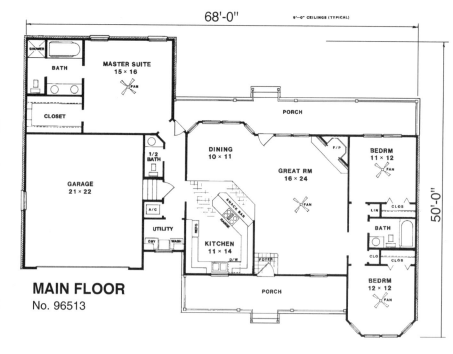

MAIN FLOOR
No. 96513

TOTAL LIVING AREA
1,648 SQ. FT.

To order your Blueprints, call 1-800-235-5700

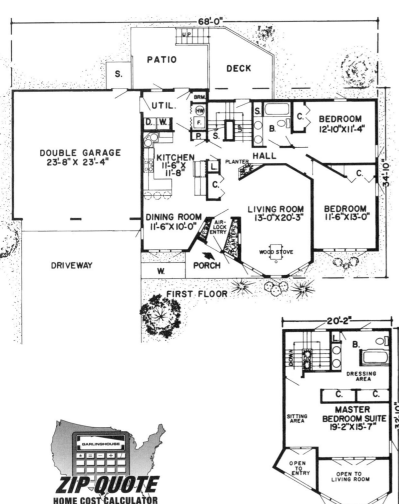

Master Suite Crowns Plan

Price Code: B

■ This plan features:

— Three bedrooms

— Two full baths

■ A Master Bedroom which occupies the entire second level

■ A passive solar design

■ A Living Room which rises two stories in the front

■ Skylights in the sloping ceilings of the Kitchen and Master Bath

FIRST FLOOR — 1,306 SQ. FT.
SECOND FLOOR — 472 SQ. FT.
GARAGE — 576 SQ. FT.

TOTAL LIVING AREA:
1,778 SQ. FT.

ZIP QUOTE
HOME COST CALCULATOR
see order pages for details

To order your Blueprints, call 1-800-235-5700

Attention to Detail

Price Code: E

■ This plan features:

— Four bedrooms

— Three full and one half bath

■ A two story Foyer

■ A formal Living Room and Dining Room perfect for entertaining

■ A two story Grand Room with a focal point fireplace that can be seen from the Foyer

■ A gourmet Kitchen with a work island, walk-in pantry, built-in planning desk, double sink and more than ample cabinet and counter space

■ A first floor Master Suite with a decorative ceiling and a luxurious Master Bath

■ Three upstairs bedrooms, two have direct access to a full bath

■ A materials list is not available for this plan

FIRST FLOOR — 2,115 SQ. FT.
SECOND FLOOR — 914 SQ. FT.
BASEMENT — 2,115 SQ. FT.
GARAGE — 448 SQ. FT.

TOTAL LIVING AREA:
3,029 SQ. FT.

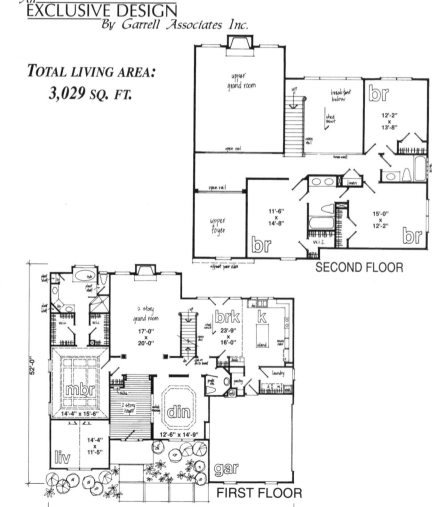

SECOND FLOOR

FIRST FLOOR

To order your Blueprints, call 1-800-235-5700

Exciting Ceilings And Open Spaces

PRICE CODE: C

■ This plan features:
— Three bedrooms
— Two full baths
■ Double gables and a covered Porch adding charm to the exterior
■ Common living areas in an open format topped by a cathedral ceiling
■ Front Bedroom, doubling as a Study, topped by a cathedral ceiling and accented by a picture window with circle top.
■ Master Bedroom crowned in a cathedral ceiling pampered by a lavish Bath

Main floor — 1,298 sq. ft.

Total Living Area:
1,298 sq. ft.

PLAN

FLOOR PLAN

Tidewater Comfort

PRICE CODE: A

PLAN NO. 94263

■ This plan features:
— Two bedrooms
— Two full baths
■ A hooded pediment and a sunburst transom announce a glass-paneled entry
■ The Foyer is separated from the Dining Room by a half wall
■ The Kitchen has ample counter space and shares an eating bar with the Great Room
■ The Dining Room accesses the covered Porch through French doors
■ The Great Room also accesses the covered Porch through French doors
■ The Master Suite encompasses one side of the home
■ The other Bedroom has a distinctive front window
■ No materials list is available for this plan

Main Floor — 1,288 sq. ft.

Total Living Area:
1,288 sq. ft.

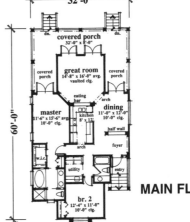

MAIN FLOOR

Details, Details, Details
PRICE CODE: C

- This plan features:
  — Three bedrooms
  — Two full and one half baths
- This elevation is highlighted by stucco, stone and detailing around the arched windows
- The two-story Foyer allows access to the Dining Room and the Great Room
- A vaulted ceiling and a fireplace can be found in the Great Room
- The Breakfast Room has a vaulted ceiling and flows into the Kitchen and the Keeping Room
- Two secondary Bedrooms, each with a walk-in closet, share a full hall Bath
- The Master Suite has a tray ceiling a huge walk-in closet and a compartmental Bath

FIRST FLOOR — 1,628 SQ. FT.
SECOND FLOOR — 527 SQ. FT.
BONUS ROOM — 207 SQ. FT.
BASEMENT — 1,628 SQ. FT.
GARAGE — 440 SQ. FT.

TOTAL LIVING AREA:
2,155 SQ. FT.

© Frank Betz Associates

A Stately Manor
PRICE CODE: D

- This plan features:
  — Four bedrooms
  — Two full and one half baths
- This stately home boasts a Foyer with a lovely staircase to the second floor
- The front Parlor has a front wall of windows with transoms above them
- Enter the Dining Hall from the Parlor through an arched opening
- A center wall fireplace warms the Family Room
- Informal meals are served in the casual Morning Room just off the Kitchen
- The Master Suite has a decorative ceiling and a huge walk-in closet
- Three more Bedrooms share a full Bath in the hall
- An optional basement or a crawl space foundation — please specify when ordering
- No materials list is available for this plan

FIRST FLOOR — 1,290 SQ. FT.
SECOND FLOOR — 1,241 SQ. FT.
BASEMENT — 1,290 SQ. FT.
GARAGE — 501 SQ. FT.

TOTAL LIVING AREA:
2,531 SQ. FT.

To order your Blueprints, call 1-800-235-5700

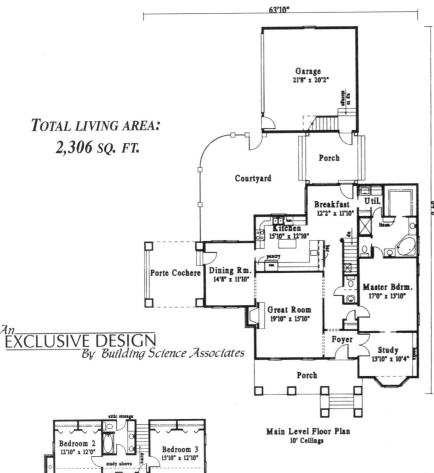

TOTAL LIVING AREA: 2,306 SQ. FT.

Garage
21'8" x 20'2"

Porch

Courtyard

Breakfast
12'2" x 11'10"

Util.

Kitchen
15'10" x 12'10"

linen

Dining Rm.
14'8" x 11'10"

pantry

Master Bdrm.
17'0" x 13'10"

Porte Cochere

Great Room
19'10" x 15'10"

Foyer

Study
13'10" x 10'4"

Porch

An
EXCLUSIVE DESIGN
By Building Science Associates

Main Level Floor Plan
10' Ceilings

attic storage

Bedroom 2
12'10" x 12'0"

study alcove

Bedroom 3
13'10" x 12'10"

Upper Level Floor Plan
8' Ceilings

Yesterday's Style for Today's Lifestyle

Price Code: D

■ This plan features:

— Three bedrooms

— Two full and one half baths

■ Front Porch shelters entrance into Foyer, Great Room and Study

■ Great Room with inviting fireplace opens to formal Dining Room

■ Spacious Kitchen with work island, built-in pantry and serving/snackbar for Breakfast area and Porch

■ Master Bedroom adjoins Study, pampering bath and Utility area

■ Two second floor bedrooms with double closets, share a double vanity bath and study alcove

■ No materials list available

FIRST FLOOR — 1,748 SQ. FT.
SECOND FLOOR — 558 SQ. FT.
GARAGE — 440 SQ. FT.
FOUNDATION —SLAB OR CRAWL SPACE

Stunning Home

Price Code: F

- This plan features:
- — Three bedrooms
- — Three full baths and one half baths
- Twin arched covered entry leading through double doors into a grand Foyer
- Side by side formal Living and Dining rooms
- Arches and niche space highlighting the gallery hallways
- Nook with curved glass to the rear yard views
- Master Suite with bayed Sitting Room, French doors to the covered Lanai, and a step ceiling
- No materials list is available for this plan

MAIN FLOOR — 3,250 SQ. FT.

TOTAL LIVING AREA:
3,250 SQ. FT.

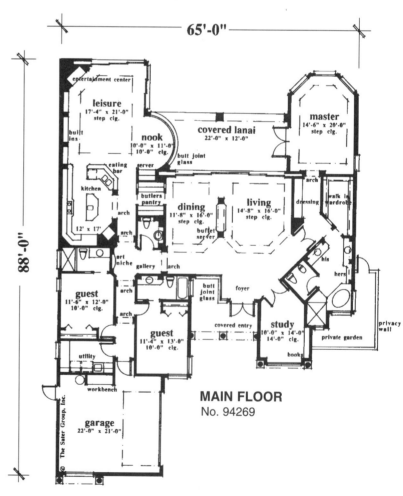

MAIN FLOOR
No. 94269

To order your Blueprints, call 1-800-235-5700

Covered Front and Rear Porches

Price Code: C

- This plan features:
  —Three bedrooms
  —Two full baths
- Traditional Country styling with front and rear covered Porches
- Peninsula counter/eating bar in Kitchen for meals on the go
- Informal Breakfast Area and formal Dining Room with built-in cabinet
- Vaulted ceiling and cozy fireplace highlighting Den
- Master Bedroom in private corner pampered by a five-piece bath
- Split Bedroom plan with additional bedrooms at the opposite of home sharing full Bath
- An optional slab or crawl space foundation — please specify when ordering

MAIN FLOOR — 1,660 SQ. FT.
GARAGE — 544 SQ. FT.

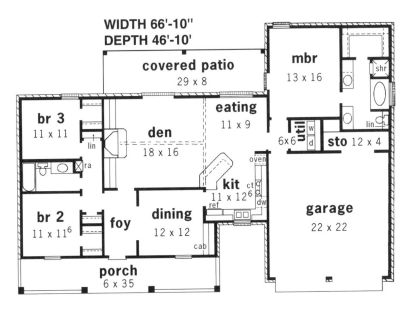

WIDTH 66'-10"
DEPTH 46'-10'

covered patio 29 x 8

mbr 13 x 16

shr

eating 11 x 9

br 3 11 x 11

den 18 x 16

lin

util 6x6 w/d lin

sto 12 x 4

ra

oven

kit 11 x 12⁶

ct

br 2 11 x 11⁶

foy

dining 12 x 12

ref

dw

garage 22 x 22

cab

porch 6 x 35

MAIN FLOOR
No. 92560

TOTAL LIVING AREA:
1,660 SQ. FT.

Sprawling Country Porch

Price Code: E

- ■ This plan features:
  - — Five bedrooms
  - — Four full baths
- ■ Welcoming Porch leads into an open, two-story Foyer with a landing staircase
- ■ Vaulted Living Area has a cozy fireplace, is open to formal Dining Room and accesses the Deck
- ■ Efficient Kitchen with a bright Breakfast Area and nearby Laundry
- ■ Private Master Bedroom is enhanced by a hearth fireplace and a bay window
- ■ Double door leads into a quiet Library/ Bedroom
- ■ Three second floor Bedrooms share two full Baths
- ■ No materials list is available for this plan

FIRST FLOOR — 2,047 SQ. FT.
SECOND FLOOR — 1,011 SQ. FT.
FINISHED STAIRCASE — 64 SQ. FT.
BASEMENT — 1,954 SQ. FT.

FIRST FLOOR
No. 98910

An
EXCLUSIVE DESIGN
By Jannis Vann & Associates, Inc.

TOTAL LIVING AREA:
3,122 SQ. FT.

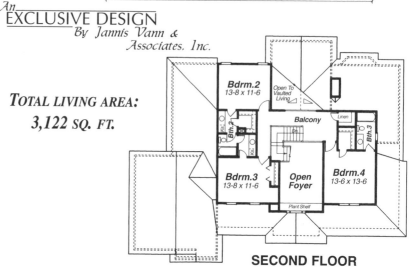

SECOND FLOOR

To order your Blueprints, call 1-800-235-5700

Distinctive Detailing
PRICE CODE: D

This plan features:
- Three bedrooms
- Two full and one half baths
- Interior columns distinguishing the inviting two-story Foyer from the Dining Room
- Spacious Great Room set off by two story windows and opening to the Kitchen and Breakfast Bay
- Nine foot ceilings adding volume and drama to the first floor
- Secluded Master Suite topped by a space amplifying tray ceiling and enhanced by a plush Bath
- Two generous additional Bedrooms with ample closet and storage space
- Skylit bonus room enjoying second floor access

FIRST FLOOR — 1,436 SQ. FT.
SECOND FLOOR — 536 SQ. FT.
GARAGE & STORAGE — 520 SQ. FT.
BONUS ROOM — 296 SQ. FT.

TOTAL LIVING AREA:
1,972 SQ. FT.

PLAN NO. 99829

SECOND FLOOR PLAN

FIRST FLOOR PLAN

© 1995 Donald A Gardner Architects, Inc.

Split Bedroom
Floor Plan
PRICE CODE: A

This plan features:
- Three bedrooms
- Two full baths
- A split Bedroom floor plan gives the Master Bedroom ultimate privacy
- The Great Room is highlighted by a fireplace and a vaulted ten foot ceiling
- A snack bar peninsula counter is one of the many conveniences of the Kitchen
- The Patio is accessed from the Dining Room and expands dining to the outdoors
- Two additional Bedrooms share the full Bath in the hall
- An optional crawl space or a slab foundation — please specify when ordering this plan
- No materials list is available for this plan

MAIN FLOOR — 1,234 SQ. FT.
GARAGE — 523 SQ. FT.

TOTAL LIVING AREA:
1,243 SQ. FT.

PLAN NO. 96519

MAIN FLOOR

To order your Blueprints, call 1-800-235-5700

Striking Facade of Stone and Wood

PRICE CODE: D

■ This plan features:
— Four bedrooms
— Two full baths
■ Recessed entrance leads into the tiled Foyer, and bright, expansive Living Room with a skylight and a double fireplace below a sloped ceiling
■ The Library/Den features a Study Alcove, a storage space, a decorative window and a fireplace between built-in bookshelves
■ Ideal Kitchen with a work island, a cooktop snackbar, a walk-in Pantry and a tiled Dining Area
■ Master Suite with a corner fireplace, a walk-in closet and a plush Bath with two vanities and a raised, tiled tub below a skylight

MAIN FLOOR — 2,450 SQ. FT.
BASEMENT — 2,450 SQ. FT.
GARAGE — 739 SQ. FT.

TOTAL LIVING AREA: 2,450 SQ. FT.

MAIN FLOOR

ZIP QUOTE
HOME COST CALCULATOR
see order pages for details

An EXCLUSIVE DESIGN
By Karl Kreeger

European Sophistication

PRICE CODE: D

■ This plan features:
— Three bedrooms
— Two full baths
■ Keystone arches, gables and stucco give the exterior European sophistication
■ Large Great Room with fireplace, and U-shaped Kitchen and a large Utility Room nearby
■ Octagonal tray ceiling dresses up the Dining Room
■ Special ceiling treatments include a cathedral ceiling in the Great Room and tray ceilings in the Master and front Bedrooms
■ Indulgent Master Bath with a separate toilet area, a garden tub, shower and twin vanities
■ Bonus Room over the Garage adds flexibility

MAIN FLOOR — 1,699 SQ. FT.
BONUS — 386 SQ. FT.
GARAGE — 637 SQ. FT.

TOTAL LIVING AREA: 1,699 SQ. FT.

© 1996 Donald A Gardner Architects, Inc.

FLOOR PLAN

Charming One-Story
Price Code: D

■ This plan features:

— Three bedrooms

— Two full baths

■ High-pitched roof lines and a stone facade achieve a look of elegance

■ Great Room plan provides flexibility in a layout that can be ideal for entertaining or basic family living

■ A wall with built-ins and a fireplace create an exciting focal point in the Great Room

■ Large sliding glass doors open the Living Room to the covered Lanai

■ Formal Dining Room detailed by arches and columns

■ Oversized Kitchen with a walk-in Pantry, an eating bar and an island cooktop

■ Owner's wing has a Study with built-ins

■ No materials list is available for this plan

MAIN FLOOR — 2,312 SQ. FT.
GARAGE — 608 SQ. FT.

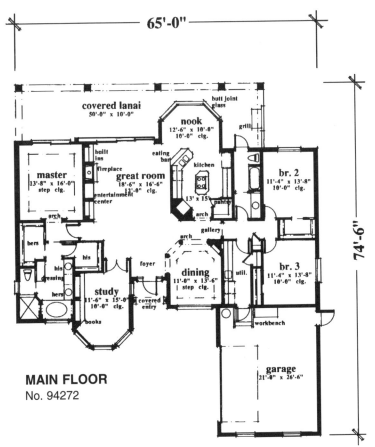

MAIN FLOOR
No. 94272

TOTAL LIVING AREA:
2,312 SQ. FT.

Family-Sized Accommodations

Price Code: C

■ This plan features:
— Four bedrooms
— Two full and one half baths

■ A spacious feeling is created by a vaulted ceiling in Foyer

■ A fireplace is nestled by an alcove of windows in Family Room which invites cozy gatherings

■ An angled Kitchen with a work island and a pantry easily serves the Breakfast Area and the Dining Room

■ The Master Bedroom is accented by a tray ceiling, a lavish Bath and a walk-in closet

■ An optional basement or crawl space foundation — please specify when ordering this plan

FIRST FLOOR — 1,320 SQ. FT.
SECOND FLOOR — 554 SQ. FT.
BONUS ROOM — 155 SQ. FT.
GARAGE — 406 SQ. FT.

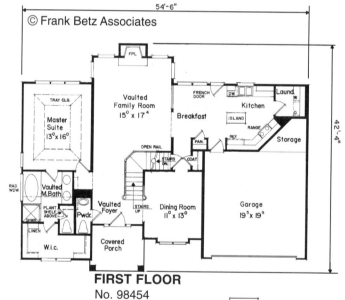

FIRST FLOOR
No. 98454

TOTAL LIVING AREA:
1,874 SQ. FT.

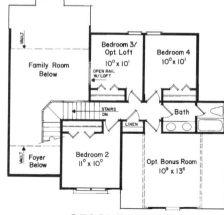

SECOND FLOOR

To order your Blueprints, call 1-800-235-5700

ZIP QUOTE
HOME COST CALCULATOR
see order pages for details

Br 2
13-11 x 11-1

Master Br
13-10 x 17-0

Sitting
11-1 x 9-7

Br 3
10-6 x 13-0

Second Floor

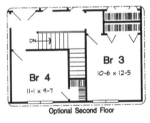

Br 4
11-1 x 9-7

Br 3
10-6 x 12-5

Optional Second Floor

An
EXCLUSIVE DESIGN
By Upright Design

Family
Dining
8-10 x 14-1

Kit.
10-0 x 14-1

desk

Optional Kitchen

Workshop
14-5 x 14-5

Crawl Space / Slab Option

Yesteryear Flavor

Price Code: D

- ■ This plan features:
- — Three or four bedrooms
- — Three full baths
- ■ Wrap-around Porch invites access into gracious Foyer with landing staircase
- ■ Formal Living Room/Guest Room
- ■ Family Room with a decorative ceiling, cozy fireplace, book shelves and Porch
- ■ Country-size Kitchen with island snackbar, built-in desk and nearby Dining Room, Laundry/Workshop and Garage access
- ■ Master Bedroom with a walk-in closet and plush Bath with a whirlpool tub
- ■ Two Bedrooms with walk-in closets, share a full Bath and Sitting Area

FIRST FLOOR — 1,236 SQ. FT.
SECOND FLOOR — 1,120 SQ. FT.

TOTAL LIVING AREA:
2,356 SQ. FT.

68'-8 1/2"

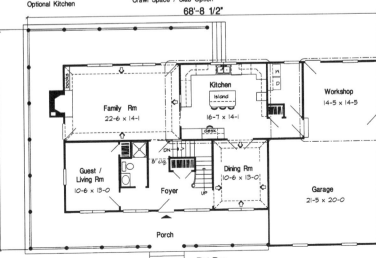

42'-0"

Family Rm
22-6 x 14-1

Kitchen
16-7 x 14-1
island
desk

Workshop
14-5 x 14-5

Guest /
Living Rm
10-6 x 13-0

Foyer

Dining Rm
10-6 x 13-0

Garage
21-5 x 20-0

Porch

First Floor

Unique Traditional

Price Code: E

■ This plan features:

— Three bedrooms

— Two full and one half baths

■ A raised entry with a double-gable roof line

■ Slump arched windows in the Foyer and in the Study

■ Formal Living and Dining rooms are side by side and access the rear yard through three pairs of French doors

■ Two Guest Suites share a full bath are separated from the owner's wing

■ The master suite has glass doors to the lanai and tray ceiling

■ Master Bath is highlighted by a dressing area and a make-up space

■ No materials list is available for this plan

MAIN FLOOR — 2,850 SQ. FT.
GARAGE — 588 SQ. FT.

TOTAL LIVING AREA:
2,850 SQ. FT.

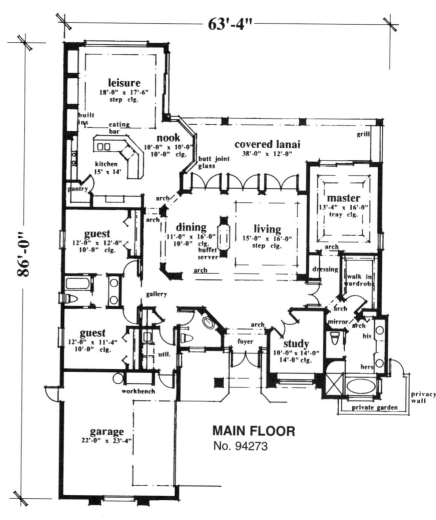

MAIN FLOOR
No. 94273

Cozy Three Bedroom
PRICE CODE: B

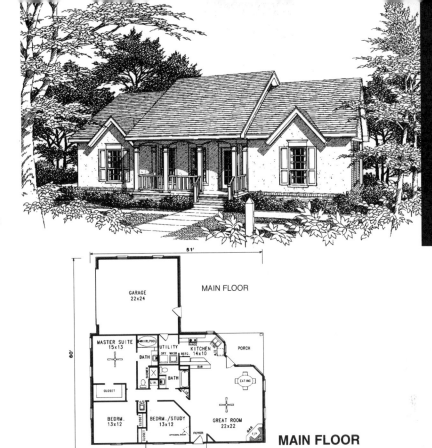

This plan features:
- Three bedrooms
- Two full baths
- The triple arched front Porch adds to the curb appeal of the home
- The expansive Great Room is accented by a cozy gas fireplace
- The efficient Kitchen includes an eating bar that separates it from the Great Room
- The Master Bedroom is highlighted by a walk-in closet and a whirlpool Bath
- Two secondary bedrooms share use of the full hall Bath
- The rear Porch extends dining to the outdoors
- An optional crawl space or slab foundation — please specify when ordering

MAIN FLOOR — 1,515 SQ. FT.
GARAGE — 528 SQ. FT.

TOTAL LIVING AREA:
1,515 SQ. FT.

MAIN FLOOR

Sophisticated Southern Styling
PRICE CODE: E

- This plan features:
- Five bedrooms
- Three full and one half baths
- Covered front and rear Porches expanding the living space to the outdoors
- A Den with a large fireplace and built-in cabinets and shelves
- A cooktop island, built-in desk, and eating bar complete the Kitchen
- The Master Suite has two walk-in closets and a luxurious Bath
- Four additional bedrooms, two on the first floor and two on the second floor, all have easy access to a full Bath
- An optional slab or crawl space foundation — please specify when ordering

FIRST FLOOR — 2,256 SQ. FT.
SECOND FLOOR — 602 SQ. FT.
BONUS — 264 SQ. FT.
GARAGE — 484 SQ. FT.

TOTAL LIVING AREA:
2,858 SQ. FT.

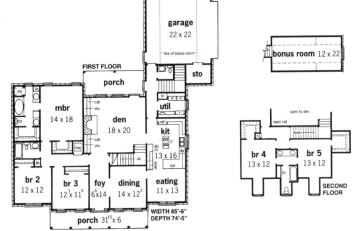

To order your Blueprints, call 1-800-235-5700

227

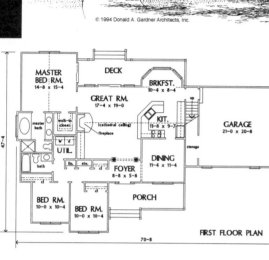

© 1994 Donald A. Gardner Architects, Inc.

Didn't Waste An Inch
PRICE CODE: D

■ This plan features:
— Three bedrooms
— Two full baths
■ Great Room with fireplace and built-in cabinets sharing a cathedral ceiling with angled Kitchen
■ Separate Dining Room allows for more formal entertaining
■ Master Bedroom topped by a cathedral ceiling, walk-in closet, and well-appointed Bath
■ Front and rear covered Porches encourage relaxation
■ Skylit bonus room makes a great Recreation Room or Office in the future

FIRST FLOOR — 1,575 SQ. FT.
BONUS — 276 SQ. FT.
GARAGE — 536 SQ. FT.

TOTAL LIVING AREA:
1,575 SQ. FT.

FIRST FLOOR PLAN

- MASTER BED. RM. 14-8 x 15-4
- DECK
- BRKFST. 10-4 x 8-4
- GREAT RM. 17-4 x 19-0
- KIT. 11-8 x 9-7
- GARAGE 21-0 x 20-8
- DINING 11-4 x 11-4
- FOYER 8-8 x 5-8
- BED RM. 10-0 x 10-4
- BED RM. 10-0 x 10-4
- PORCH
- BONUS RM. 24-8 x 11-8

47-4
70-8

Luxurious Lodgings
PRICE CODE: E

■ This plan features:
— Four bedrooms
— Three full and one half baths
■ This luxurious home features a two-story Grand Room with a corner fireplace
■ The large Dining Room is perfect for dinner parties or holiday celebrations
■ The U-shaped Kitchen has a center island and is adjacent to the informal Nook
■ The cozy Library has a fireplace and built-in book shelves
■ The first floor Master Suite has a tray ceiling and a huge walk-in closet
■ Upstairs find three more Bedrooms all with walk-in closets
■ An optional basement or slab foundation — please specify when ordering
■ No materials list is available for this plan

FIRST FLOOR — 2,113 SQ. FT.
SECOND FLOOR — 1,061 SQ. FT.
BASEMENT — 2,113 SQ. FT.
GARAGE — 574 SQ. FT.

TOTAL LIVING AREA:
3,174 SQ. FT.

WIDTH 62'-0"
DEPTH 67'-0"
FIRST FLOOR

SECOND FLOOR

To order your Blueprints, call 1-800-235-5700

© 1990 Donald A. Gardner Architects, Inc.

B. NATHAN

French Influenced One-Story

Price Code: E

■ This plan features:

— Three bedrooms

— Two full baths

■ Elegant details including arched windows, round columns and brick veneer

■ Arched clerestory window in the Foyer introduces natural light to a large Great Room with cathedral ceiling and built-in cabinets

■ Sky lighted Sun Room with a wetbar opens onto a spacious Deck

■ Kitchen with cooking island has access to a large Pantry and Utility Room

■ Large Master Bedroom opening to the Deck and featuring a garden tub, separate shower, and dual sink vanity

■ An optional basement or crawl space foundation—please specify when ordering

MAIN FLOOR — 2,045 SQ. FT.
GARAGE & STORAGE — 563 SQ. FT.

Main Floor Plan

72-6

53-10

seat

DECK
25-2 × 10-0

MASTER BED RM.
13-4 × 17-8

master bath

walk-in closet

storage

skylights

SUN RM.
16-0 × 7-6

wet bar

BRKFST.
8-6 × 10-10

skylights

pantry

BED RM.
11-4 × 11-8

cl

fireplace

GREAT RM.
18-0 × 16-2
(cathedral ceiling)

KIT.
12-0 × 10-0

cl

UTIL.

GARAGE
21-0 × 19-6

bath

lin

cl

FOYER
12-4 × 5-6

vaulted clerestory

storage

cl

DINING
12-0 × 12-0

PORCH
15-2 × 4-9

BED RM.
12-0 × 12-0

MAIN FLOOR

TOTAL LIVING AREA:
2,045 SQ. FT.

Alternate Plan for Basement

pantry

cl

down

kitchen

garage

storage

ALTERNATE PLAN
FOR BASEMENT

Stately Stucco and Brick

Price Code: B

■ This plan features:

— Three bedrooms

— Two full and one half baths

■ Stucco, brick, and a covered front Porch highlight the exterior

■ Drama is added to the two-story Foyer by an angled staircase

■ The formal Dining Room features a bank of windows at its front

■ The Kitchen features plenty of counter space as well as a walk in Pantry

■ The Living Room has a fireplace and access to the rear Sun Deck

■ Upstairs find the Master Bedroom, which has a Bath and a walk in closet

■ Also upstairs are two identical secondary Bedrooms with a Bath set between them

FIRST FLOOR — 797 SQ. FT.
SECOND FLOOR — 886 SQ. FT.
BASEMENT — 797 SQ. FT.
GARAGE — 440 SQ. FT.

TOTAL LIVING AREA:
1,683 SQ. FT.

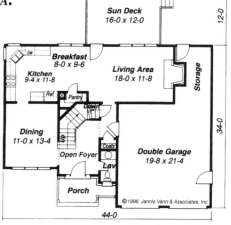

FIRST FLOOR
No. 98923

An EXCLUSIVE DESIGN
By Jannis Vann &
Associates, Inc.

SECOND FLOOR

To order your Blueprints, call 1-800-235-5700

SECOND FLOOR

Deck

Sunken
Family Room
18 x 15-4

Breakfast
9-10 x 13-3

Kitchen
8-10
x
11-11

WIDTH 61'-0"
DEPTH 37'-6"

Two-car Garage
22-4 x 22

stairs up

stairs dn

Laun.

Bath

Hall

Living Room
14-8 x 12-7

Foyer

Dining Room
14-8 x 12-7

Porch

TOTAL LIVING AREA:
2,653 SQ. FT.

Bath

Bedroom
12-5 x 10-11

Bedroom
10-10 x 10-11

walk-in
closet

walk-in
closet

shelves

stairs dn

Bath
sky-light

laun.
chute

Balcony

Master
Bedroom
14-8 x
16-2

Foyer
Below

Bedroom
12-3 x 12-7

plant shelf

FIRST FLOOR

Luxury Personified

Price Code: E

■ This plan features:

— Four bedrooms

— Two full and one-half baths

■ A tray ceiling in the formal Living Room and Dining Room with corner columns

■ Convenient Kitchen with a corner sink with windows to either side flooding the counter with natural light

■ A sunken Family Room with a cozy fireplace

■ A luxurious Master Suite with double walk-in closets, sloped ceiling and private Master Bath

■ Three additional Bedrooms share a skylit full Bath with a laundry chute

■ A balcony overlooking the Foyer with a plant shelf, arched window and skylight

■ No materials list is available for this plan

FIRST FLOOR — 1,365 SQ. FT.
SECOND FLOOR — 1,288 SQ. FT.
BASEMENT — 1,217 SQ. FT.
GARAGE — 491 SQ. FT.

Every Luxurious Feature One Could Want

Price Code: F

■ This plan features:

— Four bedrooms

— Two full and one half baths

■ An open staircase leading to the bedrooms and dividing the space between the vaulted Living and Dining Rooms

■ A wide family area including the Kitchen, Dinette and Family Room complete with built-in bar, bookcases, and fireplace

■ A Master Bedroom with a vaulted ceiling, spacious closets and Jacuzzi

FIRST FLOOR — 1,786 SQ. FT.
SECOND FLOOR — 1,490 SQ. FT.
BASEMENT — 1,773 SQ. FT.
GARAGE — 579 SQ. FT.

TOTAL LIVING AREA: 3,276 SQ. FT.

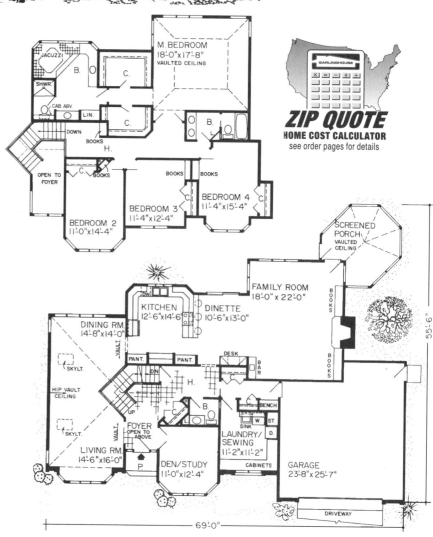

Unique Floor Plan

PRICE CODE: F

■ This plan features:
— Three bedrooms
— Three full and one half baths
■ Curved bay windows at the Dining Room and Study giving the front of this stucco house a custom design look
■ Arches and a raised ceiling defining the formal spaces
■ Living Room enhanced by an abundance of glass looking toward the atrium and rear yard views
■ Kitchen with a walk-in Pantry, island eating and prep bar, a cook top center and a desk space
■ Family nook has mitered glass and glass corner sliding doors that pocket back giving the Leisure Room an open feel with the covered Lanai
■ Owners' wing with a Study, Master Suite and sumptuous vault
■ Two secondary guest's suites privately located away from the master side
■ No materials list is available for this plan

MAIN FLOOR — 3,244-SQ. FT.
GARAGE — 810 SQ. FT.

TOTAL LIVING AREA:
3,244 SQ. FT.

MAIN FLOOR

Spacious Elegance

PRICE CODE: D

■ This plan features:
— Four bedrooms
— Three full baths
■ This appealing home has gables a hip roof, and keystone window accents
■ The two-story Foyer with palladian window illuminates a lovely staircase and the Dining Room
■ The Family Room has a vaulted ceiling and an inviting fireplace
■ Vaulted ceiling and a radius window highlight the Breakfast Area and the efficient Kitchen
■ The Master Bedroom boasts a tray ceiling, luxurious Bath and a walk-in closet
■ An optional basement or crawl space foundation — please specify when ordering

FIRST FLOOR — 1,761 SQ. FT.
SECOND FLOOR — 588 SQ. FT.
BONUS ROOM — 267 SQ. FT.
GARAGE — 435 SQ. FT.

TOTAL LIVING AREA:
2,349 SQ. FT.

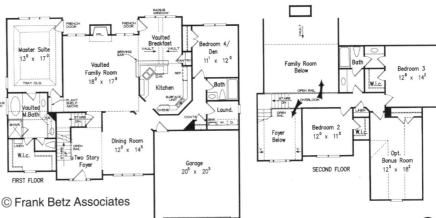

© Frank Betz Associates

© 1997 Donald A. Gardner Architects, Inc.

Private Master Suite

PRICE CODE: D

■ This plan features:
— Three bedrooms
— Two full baths
■ Working at the Kitchen island focuses your view to the Great Room with its vaulted ceiling and a fireplace
■ Clerestory dormers emanate light into the Great Room
■ Both the Dining Room and Master Bedroom are enhanced by tray ceilings
■ Skylights floods natural light into the bonus space
■ The private Master Suite has its own Bath and an expansive walk-in closet

MAIN FLOOR — 1,515 SQ. FT.
BONUS — 288 SQ. FT.
GARAGE — 476 SQ. FT.

TOTAL LIVING AREA:
1,515 SQ. FT.

FLOOR PLAN

© 1997 Donald A Gardner Architects, Inc.

Decorative Ceilings
Add Accents

PRICE CODE: B

■ This plan features:
— Three bedrooms
— Two full baths
■ The cozy front Porch leads into the formal Foyer
■ A secluded Study is to the right of the Foyer
■ Colonial columns and a half wall separate the Dining area from the Foyer
■ The Great Room is accented by a fireplace and a tray ceiling
■ The Kitchen is laid out in an efficient U-shape and features an extended counter/eating bar
■ The Master Suite is tucked into the left rear corner of the home
■ A tray ceiling highlights the Bedroom Area of the Master Suite
■ Two additional Bedrooms, located on the opposite side of the home share a full Bath in the hall

MAIN FLOOR — 1,771 SQ. FT.
GARAGE — 480 SQ. FT.

TOTAL LIVING AREA:
1,771 SQ. FT.

MAIN FLOOR

To order your Blueprints, call 1-800-235-5700

© 1991 Donald A. Gardner Architects, Inc.

Country Farmhouse

Price Code: D

■ This plan features:

— Three bedrooms

— Two full and one half baths

■ Ready, set, grow with this lovely country home enhanced by wrap-around Porch and rear Deck

■ Palladian window in clerestory dormer bathes two-story Foyer in natural light

■ Private Master Bedroom suite offers everything: walk-in closet, whirlpool tub, shower, and double vanity

■ Two upstairs Bedrooms with dormers and storage access, share a full Bath

■ Keep growing with skylit bonus room over Garage and optional basement

■ An optional basement or crawl space foundation—please specify when ordering

FIRST FLOOR — 1,356 SQ. FT.
SECOND FLOOR — 542 SQ. FT.
BONUS ROOM — 393 SQ. FT.
GARAGE & STORAGE — 543 SQ. FT.

ZIP QUOTE
HOME COST CALCULATOR
see order pages for details

storage

GARAGE
20-4 x 21-8

seat   seat

DECK

up

DINING
13-0 x 12-0

KIT.
10-4 x 12-0

BRKFST.
10-8 x 9-8

pd. rm.

UTIL.
d   w

cl

walk-in
closet

master bath

GREAT RM.
13-4 x 19-4

down

cl

fireplace

up

FOYER

MASTER
BED RM.
13-4 x 13-0

64-4

PORCH

FIRST FLOOR PLAN

59-0

c 1991 Donald A Gardner Architects, Inc.

skylights

BONUS RM.
23-8 x 14-4

TOTAL LIVING AREA:
1,898 SQ. FT.

attic storage   bath   attic storage

BED RM.
13-4 x 10-8

down

BED RM.
17-0 x 10-8

cl   cl   cl   cl

foyer
below

clerestory with palladian window

© 1991 Donald A Gardner Architects, Inc.
SECOND FLOOR PLAN

To order your Blueprints, call 1-800-235-5700

235

© 1997 Donald A. Gardner Architects, Inc.

Perfect Home

Price Code: D

■ This plan features:

— Three bedrooms

— Two full and one half baths

■ Wraparound Porch and two-car Garage features unusual for narrow lot floor plan

■ Alcove of windows and columns add distinction to Dining Room

■ Cathedral ceiling above inviting fireplace accent spacious Great Room

■ Efficient Kitchen with peninsula counter accesses side Porch and Deck

■ Master suite on first floor and two additional Bedrooms and bonus room on second floor

FIRST FLOOR — 1,219 SQ. FT.
SECOND FLOOR — 450 SQ. FT.
BONUS ROOM — 406 SQ. FT.
GARAGE — 473 SQ. FT.

TOTAL LIVING AREA:
1,669 SQ. FT.

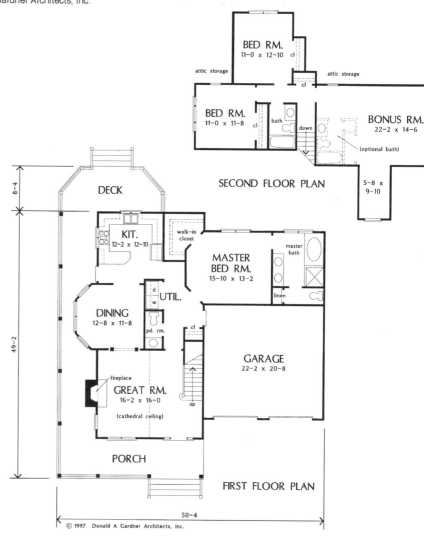

© 1997 Donald A Gardner Architects, Inc.

To order your Blueprints, call 1-800-235-5700

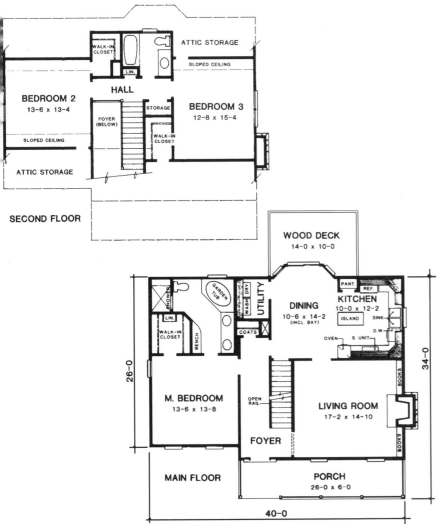

WALK-IN CLOSET

ATTIC STORAGE

SLOPED CEILING

LIN.

HALL

BEDROOM 2
13-6 x 13-4

FOYER (BELOW)

STORAGE

BEDROOM 3
12-8 x 15-4

SLOPED CEILING

WALK-IN CLOSET

ATTIC STORAGE

SECOND FLOOR

WOOD DECK
14-0 x 10-0

SHOWER

GARDEN TUB

WASH **DRY**

UTILITY

DINING
10-6 x 14-2
(INCL. BAY)

PANT.

REF.

KITCHEN
10-0 x 12-2

ISLAND

SINK

D.W.

LIN.

WALK-IN CLOSET

BENCH

COATS

OVEN

S. UNIT

26-0

34-0

M. BEDROOM
13-6 x 13-8

OPEN RAIL

LIVING ROOM
17-2 x 14-10

BOOKS

BOOKS

FOYER

MAIN FLOOR

PORCH
26-0 x 6-0

40-0

Rustic Warmth

Price Code: B

■ This plan features:
— Three bedrooms

— Two full baths

■ A fireplaced Living Room with built-in bookshelves

■ A fully-equipped Kitchen with an island

■ A sunny Dining Room with glass sliders to a wood deck

■ A first floor Master Suite with walk-in closet and lavish Master Bath

■ An optional basement or crawl space foundation — please specify when ordering

FIRST FLOOR — 1,100 SQ. FT.
SECOND FLOOR — 664 SQ. FT.
BASEMENT — 1,100 SQ. FT.

TOTAL LIVING AREA:
1,764 SQ. FT.

PLAN NO. 10785

Farmhouse Flavor

Price Code: C

- This plan features:
- — Three bedrooms
- — Two full and one half baths
- A inviting wrap-around Porch with old-fashioned charm
- Two-story Foyer
- A wood stove in the Living Room that warms the entire house
- A modern Kitchen flowing easily into the bayed Dining Room
- A first floor Master Bedroom with private Master Bath
- Two additional Bedrooms with walk-in closets and cozy gable sitting nooks

FIRST FLOOR — 1,269 SQ. FT.
SECOND FLOOR — 638 SQ. FT.
BASEMENT — 1,269 SQ. FT.

TOTAL LIVING AREA:
1,907 SQ. FT.

An
EXCLUSIVE DESIGN
By Karl Kreeger

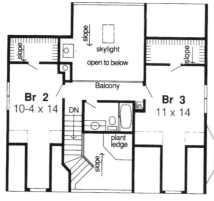

SECOND FLOOR

Br 2
10-4 x 14

Br 3
11 x 14

slope
skylight
open to below
Balcony
DN
plant ledge
slope

ZIP QUOTE
HOME COST CALCULATOR
see order pages for details

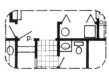

Slab/Crawl Space Option

FIRST FLOOR

Optional Deck

Living Rm
13 x 19-6

MBr 1
13-6 x 14

wood stove

Ldry

Kitchen
11 x 12

Dining Rm
12-10 x 13-6

Foyer

DN

39'-0"

47'-0"

Fit for a Family
PRICE CODE: C

This plan features:
- Three bedrooms
- Two full and one half baths
- Inviting Porch leads into central Foyer and banister staircase
- Formal Living and Dining Rooms enhanced by decorative windows
- Expansive Family Room with cozy fireplace and bright bay window
- L-shaped Kitchen with work island and Breakfast Area with sliding glass door to rear yard
- Handy half Bath, Laundry and Garage entry off Kitchen
- Private Master Bedroom with plush Bath and walk-in closet
- Two additional Bedrooms with ample closets share a full Bath
- Optional fourth Bedroom for future needs
- No materials list is available for this plan

FIRST FLOOR — 1,113 SQ. FT.
SECOND FLOOR — 835 SQ. FT.
OPTIONAL BEDROOM — 245 SQ. FT.

TOTAL LIVING AREA:
1,948 SQ. FT.

Classic Columns
PRICE CODE: D

This plan features:
- Three bedrooms
- Two full and one half baths
- Entrance framed by columns accesses Entry, Dining and Living rooms
- Expansive Living Room with two-way fireplace and access to covered Porch
- Formal Dining Room highlighted by a lovely arched window
- Convenient Kitchen with work island, eating bar and nearby Breakfast Area and Utility Room
- Master Bedroom wing offers a huge, walk-in closet and a pampering Bath
- Two additional Bedrooms with ample closets, share a full Bath
- No materials list available for this plan

MAIN FLOOR — 2,329 SQ. FT.
GARAGE — 582 SQ. FT.

TOTAL LIVING AREA:
2,329 SQ. FT.

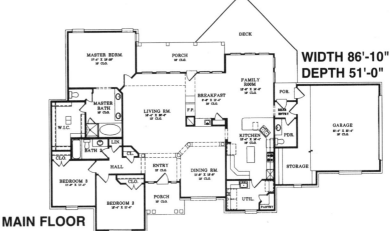

WIDTH 86'-10"
DEPTH 51'-0"

MAIN FLOOR

High Ceilings Add Volume
PRICE CODE: B

- This plan features:
  — Three bedrooms
  — Two full baths
- A covered entry gives way to a 14-foot high ceiling in the Foyer
- An arched opening greets you in the Great Room that also has a vaulted ceiling and a fireplace
- The Dining Room is brightened by triple windows with transoms above
- The Kitchen is a gourmet's delight and is open to the Breakfast Nook
- The Master Suite is sweet with a tray ceiling, vaulted Sitting Area and private Bath
- Two Bedrooms on the opposite side of the home share Bath in the hall
- An optional basement, slab or crawl space foundation – please specify when ordering

MAIN FLOOR — 1,715 SQ. FT.
BASEMENT — 1,715 SQ. FT.
GARAGE — 450 SQ. FT.

TOTAL LIVING AREA:
1,715 SQ. FT.

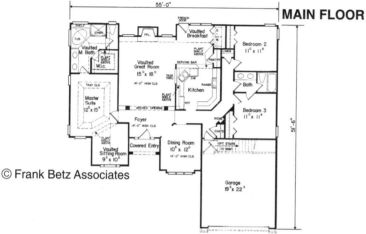

MAIN FLOOR

© Frank Betz Associates

Ideal Ranch
PRICE CODE: B

- This plan features:
  — Three bedrooms
  — Two full baths
- A spacious Living Room with a vaulted ceiling that catches your eye as you enter
- An open floor plan, making the rooms seem more spacious
- A private Master Suite with a walk-in closet and terrific Master Bath
- Two additional Bedrooms with ample closet space that share a full Bath
- Stairs off the Foyer that lead to a basement, where there is plenty of room for future expansion
- No materials list is available for this plan

FIRST FLOOR — 1,508 SQ. FT.
BASEMENT — 1,508 SQ. FT.
GARAGE — 400 SQ. FT.

TOTAL LIVING AREA:
1,508 SQ. FT.

MAIN FLOOR PLAN

To order your Blueprints, call 1-800-235-5700

© 1997 Donald A. Gardner Architects, Inc.

PLAN NO. 96407

FIRST FLOOR

- GARAGE 21-8 x 23-8
- storage
- PORCH
- BRKFST. 15-8 x 10-6
- UTIL. 14-2 x 6-8
- storage
- storage
- (vaulted ceiling)
- fireplace
- MASTER BED RM. 15-4 x 15-4
- GREAT RM. 18-8 x 20-8
- KITCHEN 15-8 x 14-6
- sto.
- walk-in closet
- balcony above
- pd. rm.
- master bath
- DINING 13-8 x 12-8
- FOYER 8-8 x 7-2
- PORCH
- 82-0
- 64-2

© 1997 Donald A Gardner Architects, Inc.

SECOND FLOOR

- BED RM. 12-4 x 13-0
- great room below
- BED RM. 12-8 x 13-0
- BONUS RM. 14-2 x 23-8
- railing
- down
- attic storage
- BED RM. 11-4 x 11-6
- foyer below
- bath
- bath
- attic storage
- attic storage
- down

1997 Donald A Gardner Architects, Inc.

Perfect for Entertaining

Price Code: F

■ This plan features:
— Four bedrooms
— Three full and one half baths

■ With front dormers and a wrap-around Porch, the home offers formal entertaining and casual living

■ Dramatic Great Room boasts cathedral ceiling and fireplace nestled between built-in shelves

■ French doors expand living space to full length rear Porch

■ Center island and peninsula counter create an efficient Kitchen/Breakfast Area

■ First floor Master Bedroom Suite features walk-in closet and spacious Master Bath

FIRST FLOOR — 1,831 SQ. FT.
SECOND FLOOR — 941 SQ. FT.
BONUS ROOM — 539 SQ. FT.
GARAGE & STORAGE — 684 SQ. FT.

TOTAL LIVING AREA:
2,772 SQ. FT.

To order your Blueprints, call 1-800-235-5700

241

© 1995 Donald A. Gardner Architects, Inc.

Appealing Design

Price Code: D

■ This plan features:

— Three bedrooms

— Two full and one half baths

■ Comfortable farmhouse features an easy to build floor plan with all the extras

■ Active families will enjoy the Great Room which is open to the Kitchen and Breakfast Bay, as well as expanded living space provided by the full back Porch

■ For narrower lot restrictions, the Garage can be modified to open in front

■ Second floor Master Bedroom suite contains a walk-in closet and a private Bath with a garden tub and separate shower

■ Two more Bedrooms on the second floor, one with a walk-in closet, share a full Bath

FIRST FLOOR — 959 SQ. F.T
SECOND FLOOR — 833 SQ. FT.
BONUS ROOM — 344 SQ. FT.
GARAGE & STORAGE — 500 SQ. FT.

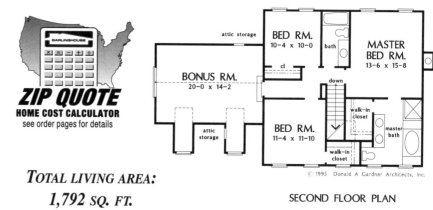

ZIP QUOTE
HOME COST CALCULATOR
see order pages for details

TOTAL LIVING AREA:
1,792 SQ. FT.

SECOND FLOOR PLAN

attic storage

BED RM.
10-4 x 10-0

bath

MASTER
BED RM.
13-6 x 15-8

BONUS RM.
20-0 x 14-2

cl

down

walk-in
closet

attic
storage

BED RM.
11-4 x 11-10

walk-in
closet

master
bath

© 1995 Donald A Gardner Architects, Inc.

FIRST FLOOR PLAN

PORCH

storage

UTIL.
7-0 x
6-0

d
w

BRKFST.
9-8 x 9-2

GREAT RM.
14-4 x 20-0

KIT.
11-4 x 11-4

fireplace

GARAGE
20-0 x 20-0

pan.

DINING
11-4 x 14-4

up

FOYER
10-6 x 7-8

pd.
rm.

cl

(optional door location)

PORCH

52-6

42-8

© 1995 Donald A Gardner Architects, Inc.

To order your Blueprints, call 1-800-235-5700

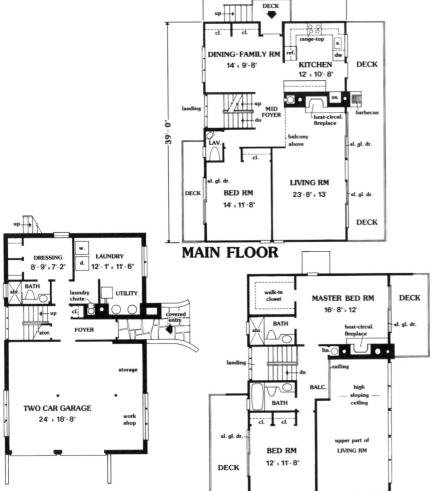

MAIN FLOOR

25'-8"

39'-0"

DECK

up

cl. cl.

DINING-FAMILY RM
14' x 9'-8"

range-top

ref.

s.

dw

KITCHEN
12' x 10'-8"

DECK

landing

up

dn

MID
FOYER

heat-circul.
fireplace

barbecue

LAV.

balcony
above

cl.

sl. gl. dr.

sl. gl. dr.

DECK

BED RM
14' x 11'-8"

LIVING RM
23'-8" x 13'

sl. gl. dr.

DECK

LOWER FLOOR

up

DRESSING
8'-9" x 7'-2"

w.
d.

LAUNDRY
12'-1" x 11'-6"

BATH

shr.

laundry
chute

cl.

UTILITY

FOYER

covered
entry

up

stor.

storage

TWO CAR GARAGE
24' x 18'-8"

work
shop

UPPER FLOOR

walk-in
closet

MASTER BED RM
16'-8" x 12'

DECK

BATH

shr.

heat-circul.
fireplace

sl. gl. dr.

lin.

landing

dn

railing

BALC.

high
sloping
ceiling

BATH

cl. cl.

sl. gl. dr.

BED RM
12' x 11'-8"

upper part of
LIVING RM

DECK

A Home For All Seasons

Price Code: C

- This plan features:
- — Three bedrooms
- — Three full and one half baths
- All rooms with outdoor decks
- A Living Room with a heat-circulating fireplace
- A Kitchen with ample counter and cabinet space and easy access to the Dining Room and outdoor dining area
- A Master Bedroom with a heat-circulating fireplace, plush Master Bath and a walk-in closet

MAIN FLOOR — 1,001 SQ. FT.
UPPER FLOOR — 712 SQ. FT.
LOWER FLOOR — 463 SQ. FT.

TOTAL LIVING AREA:
2,176 SQ. FT.

Elegant Elevation

Price Code: D

- This plan features:
  — Three bedrooms
  — Two full baths

- Brick trim, sidelights and a transom window give a warm welcome to this home

- High ceilings continue from Foyer into Great Room which counts among its amenities a fireplace and entertainment center

- The Kitchen serves the formal and informal dining areas with ease

- The Master Suite is positioned for privacy on the first floor

- The second floor has loads of possibilities with a Bonus space and a Study

- Two Bedrooms each with walk-in closets share a full Bath

- No materials list is available for this plan

FIRST FLOOR — 1,542 SQ. FT.
SECOND FLOOR — 667 SQ. FT.
BONUS — 236 SQ. FT.
BASEMENT — 1,367 SQ. FT.
GARAGE — 420 SQ. FT

TOTAL LIVING AREA:
2,209 SQ. FT.

FIRST FLOOR
No. 92662

SECOND FLOOR

ZIP QUOTE
HOME COST CALCULATOR
see order pages for details

Gracious Living
PRICE CODE: D

This plan features:
- Three bedrooms
- Two full and one half baths

Arched Portico enhances entry into Gallery and spacious Living Room, with focal point fireplace surrounded by glass

Cathedral ceilings top Family Room and formal Dining Room

An efficient Kitchen with breakfast area opens to Family Room, Utility Room with convenient Garage entry

Corner Master Bedroom suite with access to covered Patio and private bath with a double vanity and garden window tub

Two additional bedrooms with walk-in closets share a full bath

No materials list is available for this plan

MAIN FLOOR — 2,470 SQ. FT.
GARAGE — 483 SQ. FT.
FOUNDATION — SLAB OR CRAWL SPACE

TOTAL LIVING AREA:
2,470 SQ. FT.

Main Floor

Elegant Entertaining Indoors and Out
PRICE CODE: C

This plan features:
— Four bedrooms
— Two full and one half baths

Gracious double doors lead into the Reception Foyer with a unique bridge over a moat to the Living Room

Huge, stone fireplace with a barbeque and a wood storage on the Terrace side, a concealed bar and French doors enhance this Living Room

Gracious Dining Room equipped with an open grill

Efficient Kitchen with an eating bar as part of the Family Room, highlighted by a corner fireplace

Sunken Master Bedroom suite with a decorative window topped by a cathedral ceiling, three closets and a private bath with a Roman tub

Three large bedrooms with ample closet space share a full bath

MAIN FLOOR — 2,177 SQ. FT.
FOUNDATION — BASEMENT OR CRAWLSPACE

TOTAL LIVING AREA:
2,177 SQ. FT.

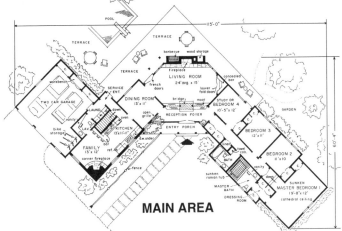

MAIN AREA

To order your Blueprints, call 1-800-235-5700

Dormers and Front Porch Create a Cozy Exterior
PRICE CODE: C

■ This plan features:
— Three bedrooms
— Two full and one half baths
■ A decorative ceiling treatment and a corner fireplace achieving a wonderful first impression
■ The Dining Room is open to the Great Room and the Kitchen creating the illusion of more space
■ Secondary Bedrooms located to the right of the home are situated with a full Bath between them
■ The Master Suite is topped by a decorative ceiling treatment, and highlighted by a five-piece bath and two walk-in closets
■ An optional crawl space or a slab foundation — please specify when ordering

MAIN FLOOR — 1,843 SQ. FT.
GARAGE — 531 SQ. FT.

TOTAL LIVING AREA:
1,843 SQ. FT.

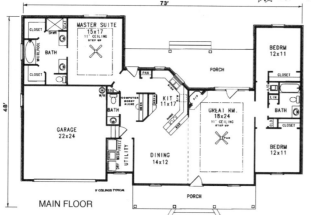

MAIN FLOOR

Country Style Split Level
PRICE CODE: B

■ This plan features:
— Three bedrooms
— Two full baths
■ A large front Porch greets you
■ Step into the huge Living Room, which features a cathedral ceiling and fireplace
■ The efficient Kitchen is open to the Breakfast Nook
■ The formal Dining Room overlooks the rear Sun Deck
■ The Master Bedroom has two walk in closets as well as a private Bath
■ There are two equally sized secondary Bedrooms with bright front windows
■ A two-car Garage as well as bonus space is featured on the lower level
■ No material list is available for this plan

MAIN FLOOR — 1,617 SQ. FT.
GARAGE — 524 SQ. FT.

TOTAL LIVING AREA:
1,617 SQ. FT.

An
EXCLUSIVE DESIGN
By Jannis Vann & Associates, Inc.

MAIN FLOOR

To order your Blueprints, call 1-800-235-5700

An
EXCLUSIVE DESIGN
By Karl Kreeger

TOTAL LIVING AREA:
2,149 SQ. FT.

Second

ledge

Br 2
12 x 14-4

Br 3
12 x 12

DN
lin.
slope

66'-0"

50'-0"

Deck

Kitchen
11 x 13-4

pan.

Hearth Rm
18-4 x 11-6

slope

decor. ceiling

Dining Rm
12 x 14-2

DN   UP

Garage
21-8 x 21-8

D W L

lin.

Foy

MBr 1
15-8 x 13-4

Living Rm
16-10 x 17

First Floor

Stone and Stucco Family Home

Price Code: C

■ This plan features:

— Three bedrooms

— Two full and one half baths

■ A formal Living Room that is enhanced by a large front window

■ A distinctive formal Dining Room with a decorative ceiling

■ A sloped ceiling and a stunning fireplace in the Hearth Room

■ A range-top island Kitchen having a corner double sink, built-in pantry, ample counter space and a sunny bay window Breakfast nook

■ A first-floor Master Suite equipped with a luxury bath with double vanities, a walk-in closet, and a dressing area

■ Two additional bedrooms that share a full hall bath

FIRST FLOOR — 1,606 SQ. FT.
SECOND FLOOR — 543 SQ. FT.
BASEMENT — 1,606 SQ. FT.
GARAGE — 484 SQ. FT.

Eye–Catching Elevation

Price Code: A

■ This plan features:

— Two bedrooms

— Two three-quarter baths

■ An entrance to the Spa Deck is a few steps down to the open Living Area with a cozy fireplace

■ An efficient Kitchen with a peninsula counter/eating bar opens to Living area

■ A first floor Bedroom next to the full bath and Utility area

■ A second floor Master Bedroom with an over-sized and private Bath

■ No materials list is available for this plan

FIRST FLOOR — 680 SQ. FT.
SECOND FLOOR — 345 SQ. FT.
GARAGE — 357 SQ. FT.

TOTAL LIVING AREA:
1,025 SQ. FT.

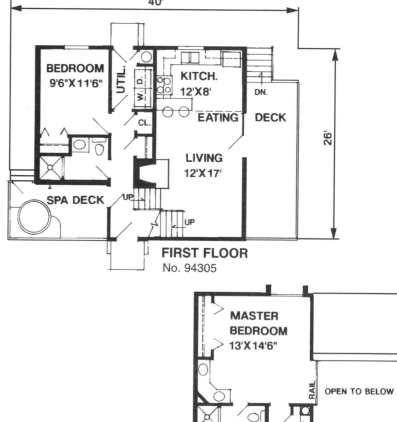

FIRST FLOOR
No. 94305

An EXCLUSIVE DESIGN
By Marshall Associates

SECOND FLOOR

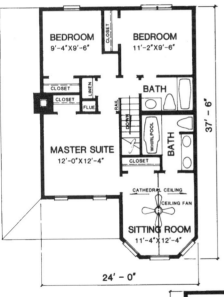

Compact Victorian Ideal for Narrow Lot

Price Code: B

- This plan features:
  — Three bedrooms
  — Three full baths

- A large, front Parlor with a raised hearth fireplace

- A Dining Room with a sunny bay window

- An efficient galley Kitchen serving the formal Dining Room and informal Breakfast Room

- A beautiful Master Suite with two closets, an oversized tub and double vanity, plus a private sitting room with a bayed window and vaulted ceiling

- An optional basement, slab or crawl space foundation — please specify when ordering

FIRST FLOOR — 954 SQ. FT.
SECOND FLOOR — 783 SQ. FT.

TOTAL LIVING AREA:
1,737 SQ. FT.

PLAN NO. 99805

© 1994 Donald A Gardner Architects, Inc.

Exciting Three Bedroom

Price Code: D

- This plan features:
- — Three bedrooms
- — Two full baths

- A Great Room enhanced by a fireplace, cathedral ceiling, and built-in book-shelves

- A Kitchen designed for efficiency with a food preparation island and a Pantry

- A Master Suite topped by a cathedral ceiling and pampered by a luxurious Bath and a walk-in closet

- Two additional Bedrooms, one with a cathedral ceiling and a walk-in closet, sharing a sky lit Bath

- A second floor bonus room, perfect for a Study or a Play Area

- An optional basement or crawl space foundation available—please specify when ordering

TOTAL LIVING AREA:
1,787 SQ. FT.

ZIP QUOTE
HOME COST CALCULATOR
see order pages for details

FLOOR PLAN

© 1994 Donald A Gardner Architects, Inc.

BONUS RM.
14-2 x 17-10

MAIN FLOOR — 1,787 SQ. FT.
GARAGE & STORAGE — 521 SQ. FT.
BONUS ROOM — 326 SQ. FT.

250 To order your Blueprints, call 1-800-235-5700

A Noble Dwelling

PRICE CODE: E

This plan features:
- Four bedrooms
- Four full baths

- Inside the Foyer is an elegant curved staircase to the second floor
- The Dining Hall overlooks the sunken Grand Room
- A Guest Room/Office is located behind the three-car Garage
- The Family Room has a fireplace and overlooks the rear Terrace
- The Kitchen is incredible and a delight to work in with it's spacious amenities
- Upstairs the Master Suite encompasses an entire side of the home
- Three more Bedrooms and two Baths complete the second floor
- The Laundry Room is conveniently located upstairs
- An optional basement and a slab foundation — please specify when ordering
- No materials list is available for this plan

FIRST FLOOR — 1,593 SQ. FT.
SECOND FLOOR — 1,559 SQ. FT.
BASEMENT — 1,593 SQ. FT.
GARAGE — 513 SQ. FT.

TOTAL LIVING AREA:
3,152 SQ. FT.

PLAN NO. 98206

FIRST FLOOR

SECOND FLOOR

Double Gables and Exciting Entry

PRICE CODE: D

This plan features:
- Four bedrooms
- Two full and one half baths

- Impressive exterior features double gables and arched window
- Spacious Foyer separates the formal Dining Room and Living Room
- Roomy Kitchen and Breakfast Bay are adjacent to the large Family Room which has a fireplace and accesses the rear Deck
- Spacious Master Bedroom features private Bath with dual vanity, shower stall and whirlpool tub
- Three additional Bedrooms share a full hall Bath
- No materials list is available for this plan

FIRST FLOOR — 1,207 SQ. FT.
SECOND FLOOR — 1,181 SQ. FT.
BASEMENT — 1,207 SQ. FT.

TOTAL LIVING AREA:
2,388 SQ. FT.

PLAN NO. 92692

ZIP QUOTE
HOME COST CALCULATOR
see order pages for details

251

To order your Blueprints, call 1-800-235-5700

PLAN NO. 92281

Small Yet Sophisticated
PRICE CODE: A

- This plan features:
  — Three bedrooms
  — Two full baths
- Spacious Great Room highlighted by a fireplace and built-in shelving
- Efficient, U-shaped Kitchen with ample work and storage space, sliding glass door to Covered Patio and a Dining area with a window seat
- Spacious Master Bedroom suite enhanced by window seats, vaulted ceiling, a lavish Bath and large walk-in closet
- Two additional Bedrooms share a full Bath
- Convenient Utility Area and Garage entry
- No materials list is available for this plan

MAIN FLOOR — 1,360 SQ. FT.
GARAGE — 380 SQ. FT.

TOTAL LIVING AREA:
1,360 SQ. FT.

MAIN FLOOR

PLAN NO. 99321

Nostalgia Returns
PRICE CODE: A

- This plan features:
  — Three bedrooms
  — Two full baths
- A half-round transom window with quarter-round detail and a vaulted ceiling in the Great Room
- A cozy corner fireplace which brings warmth to the Great Room
- A vaulted ceiling in the Kitchen/Breakfast Area
- A Master Suite with a walk-in closet and a private Master Bath
- Two additional Bedrooms which share a full hall Bath

MAIN FLOOR — 1,368 SQ. FT.
BASEMENT — 1,368 SQ. FT.
GARAGE — 412 SQ. FT.

TOTAL LIVING AREA:
1,368 SQ. FT.

Floor Plan

To order your Blueprints, call 1-800-235-5700

Great Room Center of Attention

Price Code: C

■ This plan features:

— Three bedrooms

— Two full baths

■ Foyer with vaulted ceiling to the dormer

■ The Great Room has a rear wall fireplace, and opens to the rear Porch

■ The Kitchen features an eating bar and opens into the Dining bay

■ The Master suite has a tray ceiling and a whirlpool Bath

■ Two secondary Bedrooms and a Study round out this plan

MAIN FLOOR — 1,972 SQ. FT.
GARAGE — 462 SQ. FT.

TOTAL LIVING AREA:
1,972 SQ. FT.

MAIN FLOOR
No. 96527

Modern Luxury

Price Code: E

■ This plan features:

— Four bedrooms

— Three full and one half baths

■ A feeling of spaciousness is created by the two-story Foyer and volume ceilings

■ Arched openings and decorative windows enhance the Dining and Living rooms

■ The efficient Kitchen has a work island, a Pantry and a Breakfast Area open to the Family Room

■ The plush Master Suite features a tray ceiling above and an alcove of windows

■ Three secondary Bedrooms on the second floor have walk-in closets

■ An optional basement or crawl space foundaion — please specify when ordering

FIRST FLOOR — 1,883 SQ. FT.
SECOND FLOOR — 803 SQ. FT.
BASEMENT — 1,883 SQ. FT.
GARAGE — 495 SQ. FT.

TOTAL LIVING AREA:
2,686 SQ. FT.

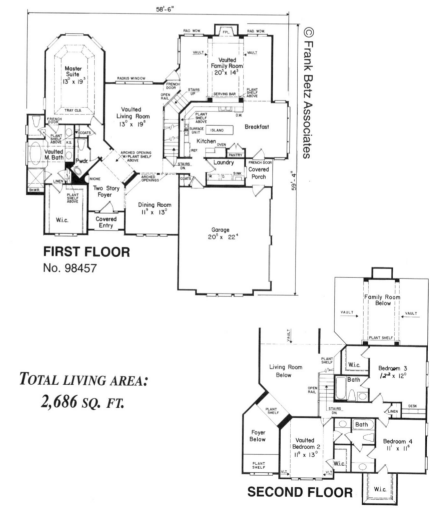

© Frank Betz Associates

FIRST FLOOR
No. 98457

SECOND FLOOR

To order your Blueprints, call 1-800-235-5700

PLAN NO. 92653

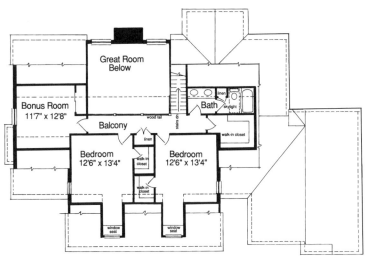

Great Room Below

Bonus Room
11'7" x 12'8"

Balcony

Bath

linen
skylight

walk-in closet

linen

Bedroom
12'6" x 13'4"

walk-in closet

Bedroom
12'6" x 13'4"

walk-in closet

window seat

window seat

wood rail

stairs dn

SECOND FLOOR

TOTAL LIVING AREA:
2,443 SQ. FT.

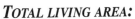

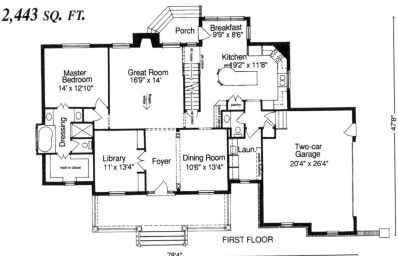

Porch

Breakfast
9'9" x 8'6"

Kitchen
9'2" x 11'8"

Master Bedroom
14' x 12'10"

Great Room
16'9" x 14'

slope ceiling

pantry

Dressing

walk-in closet

Library
11' x 13'4"

Foyer

Dining Room
10'6" x 13'4"

Laun.

Two-car Garage
20'4" x 26'4"

FIRST FLOOR

78'4"

47'8"

Country Brick

Price Code: D

■ This plan features:

— Three or four bedrooms

— Two full and one half baths

■ Front Porch leads into a gracious open Foyer and Great Room beyond

■ Secluded Library offers built-in shelves

■ Great Room enhanced by focal point fireplace topped by sloped ceiling

■ Country-size Kitchen with island snack-bar, bright Breakfast Area, Pantry and nearby Laundry/Garage entry

■ Private Master Bedroom offers a deluxe Bath and spacious walk-in closet

■ Two additional Bedrooms with walk-in closets and window seats, share a double vanity Bath, and Bonus Room

■ No materials list is available for this plan

FIRST FLOOR — 1,710 SQ. FT.
SECOND FLOOR — 733 SQ. FT.
BONUS — 181 SQ. FT.
BASEMENT — 1,697 SQ. FT.
GARAGE — 499 SQ. FT.

Grand Country Porch

Price Code: E

- This plan features:
- — Four bedrooms
- — Three full baths

- Large front Porch provides shade and Southern hospitality

- Spacious Living Room with access to Covered Porch and Patio, and a cozy fireplace between built-in shelves

- Country Kitchen with a cooktop island, bright Breakfast bay, Utility Room, Garage entry

- Corner Master Bedroom with a walk-in closet and private bath

- First floor Bedroom with private access to a full bath

- Two additional second floor bedrooms with dormers, walk-in closets and vanities, share a full bath

- An optional crawl space or slab foundation — please specify when ordering

- No materials list is available for this plan

FIRST FLOOR — 1,916 SQ. FT.
SECOND FLOOR — 749 SQ. FT.
GARAGE — 479 SQ. FT.

TOTAL LIVING AREA:
2,665 SQ. FT.

WIDTH 62'-0"
DEPTH 63'-8 1/2"

SECOND FLOOR

FIRST FLOOR

256

Stylish Brick Ranch
PRICE CODE: F

This plan features:
- Three bedrooms
- Two full and one half baths
- This brick design is accented by the turret effect of the dining bay
- A dormer above it lights the two-story Entry
- The Family room has a corner fireplace and a decorative ceiling treatment
- The Kitchen has ample counter space as well as a center island
- The Master Bedroom has a separate Sitting Area and a private Deck
- This home features a formal Living Room and Dining Room
- Upstairs find two large Bedrooms serviced by a full Bath
- No materials list is available for this plan

FIRST FLOOR — 2,372 SQ. FT.
SECOND FLOOR — 752 SQ. FT.
FINISHED STAIRCASE — 144 SQ. FT.
BASEMENT — 2,207 SQ. FT.
GARAGE — 508 SQ. FT.

TOTAL LIVING AREA:
3,268 SQ. FT.

An
EXCLUSIVE DESIGN
By Jannis Vann & Associates, Inc.

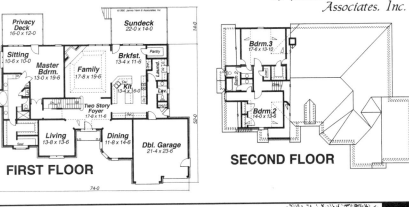

FIRST FLOOR

SECOND FLOOR

Attractive Combination of Brick and Siding
PRICE CODE: C

This plan features:
- Two or three Bedrooms
- Two full Baths
- A Great Room sunny bayed area, fireplace and built-in entertainment center
- A private Master Bedroom with luxurious Master Bath and walk-in closet
- Dining Room has a butler's Pantry
- Two additional Bedrooms have use of hall full Bath

MAIN LEVEL — 2,010 SQ. FT.
BASEMENT — 2,010 SQ. FT.

TOTAL LIVING AREA:
2,010 SQ. FT.

An

EXCLUSIVE DESIGN
By Energetic Enterprises

MAIN LEVEL

To order your Blueprints, call 1-800-235-5700

PLAN NO. 94622

Multiple Porches Provide Added Interest

PRICE CODE: E

■ This plan features:
— Four bedrooms
— Three full and one half baths
■ Two-story central Foyer flanked by Living and Dining rooms
■ Spacious Great Room with large fireplace between french doors to Porch and Deck
■ Country-size Kitchen with cooktop work island, walk-in pantry and Breakfast Area with Porch access
■ Pampering Master Bedroom offers a decorative ceiling, Sitting Area, Porch and Deck access, a huge walk-in closet and lavish Bath
■ Three second floor Bedrooms with walk-in closets, have private access to a full Bath
■ An optional crawl space or slab foundation — please specify when ordering
■ No materials list is available for this plan

FIRST FLOOR — 2,033 SQ. FT.
SECOND FLOOR — 1,116 SQ. FT.

TOTAL LIVING AREA: 3,149 SQ. FT.

SECOND FLOOR

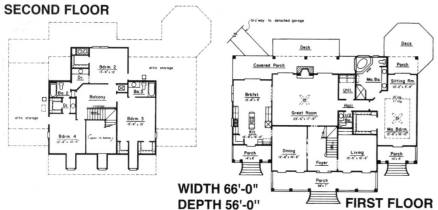

WIDTH 66'-0"
DEPTH 56'-0"

FIRST FLOOR

PLAN NO. 20104

Easy One-Level Living

PRICE CODE: B

■ This plan features:
— Three bedrooms
— Two full baths
■ A sky-lit Kitchen
■ Ample closet space
■ Built-in storage areas in the Kitchen
■ A Master bath with dual vanity, a raised tub, and a walk-in shower

MAIN AREA — 1,686 SQ. FT.
BASEMENT — 1,677 SQ. FT.
GARAGE — 475 SQ. FT.

TOTAL LIVING AREA: 1,686 SQ. FT.

An
EXCLUSIVE DESIGN
By Karl Kreeger

MAIN AREA

To order your Blueprints, call 1-800-235-5700

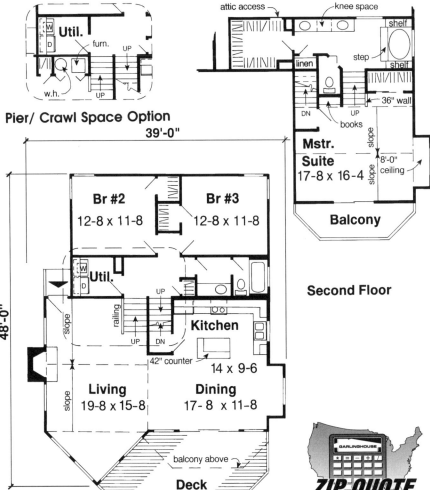

Pier/ Crawl Space Option

Util.
furn.
UP
w.h.
UP
W
D

39'-0"

48'-0"

Br #2
12-8 x 11-8

Br #3
12-8 x 11-8

Util.
W
D

slope

railing

UP

UP

DN

Kitchen
42" counter
14 x 9-6

slope

Living
19-8 x 15-8

Dining
17-8 x 11-8

slope

balcony above

Deck

First Floor

attic access

knee space

shelf

linen

step

shelf

DN

UP

books

36" wall

slope

slope

Mstr. Suite
17-8 x 16-4

8'-0" ceiling

Balcony

Second Floor

Home on a Hill

Price Code: C

■ This plan features:
— Three bedrooms
— Two full baths

■ Window walls combining with sliders to unite active areas with a huge outdoor deck

■ Interior spaces flowing together for an open feeling, that is accentuated by the sloping ceilings and towering fireplace in the Living Room

■ An island Kitchen with easy access to the Dining Room

■ A Master Suite complete with a garden spa, abundant closet space, and a balcony

FIRST FLOOR — 1,316 SQ. FT.
SECOND FLOOR — 592 SQ. FT.

TOTAL LIVING AREA:
1,908 SQ. FT.

To order your Blueprints, call 1-800-235-5700

Solar Room More Than Just a Greenhouse

Price Code: B

■ This plan features:

— Three bedrooms

— Two full baths

■ A passive design that will save on heating costs

■ A heat-circulating fireplace in the Living Room adding atmosphere as well as warmth

■ A Master Suite, with lofty views of the Living Area

■ Two additional Bedrooms with ample closet space and a shared full hall Bath

FIRST FLOOR — 1,242 SQ. FT.
SECOND FLOOR — 490 SQ. FT.

TOTAL LIVING AREA: *1,732 SQ. FT.*

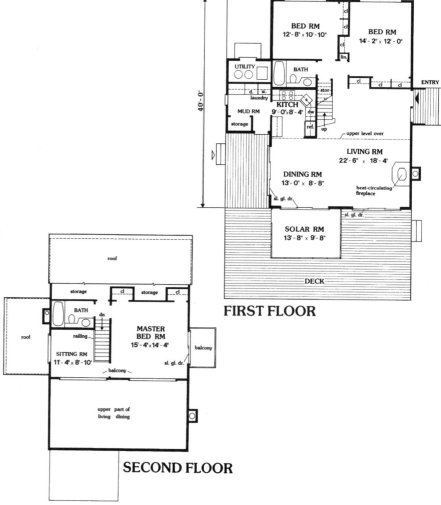

FIRST FLOOR

SECOND FLOOR

To order your Blueprints, call 1-800-235-5700

© 1993 Donald A. Gardner Architects, Inc.

B. NATHAN

PORCH

GREAT RM.
15-4 x 14-8

BRKFST.
11-0 x 9-0

w | d

UTIL.
6-2 x
cl 5-10

MASTER
BED RM.
12-0 x 15-0

fireplace

balcony above

KIT.
11-0 x
12-0

cl

walk-in
closet

cl

pd.
rm.

master
bath

DINING
13-4 x 12-8

FOYER
9-10 x 8-6

up

PORCH

45-4

49-5

FIRST FLOOR PLAN

clerestory with palladian window

bath

walk-in
closet

great room
below

BED RM.
11-0 x 12-0

cl

railing

cl

lin.

walk-in
closet

down

bath

BED RM.
11-0 x 17-8

foyer
below

BED RM.
11-0 x 12-8

clerestory with palladian window

SECOND FLOOR PLAN

Whimsical Two-story Farmhouse

Price Code: E

- This plan features:
— Four bedrooms
— Three full and one half baths

- Double gable with palladian, clerestory window and wrap-around Porch provide country appeal

- First floor enjoys nine foot ceilings throughout

- Palladian windows flood two-story Foyer and Great Room with natural light

- Both Master Bedroom and Great Room access covered, rear Porch

- One upstairs Bedroom offers private Bath and walk-in closet

FIRST FLOOR — 1,346 SQ. FT.
SECOND FLOOR — 836 SQ. FT.

TOTAL LIVING AREA:
2,182 SQ. FT.

Two-Story Foyer Adds to Elegance

Price Code: D

■ This plan features:

— Three bedrooms

— Two full baths

■ Two-story foyer with curved staircase

■ Formal Dining and Living Rooms to either side of the Foyer

■ Family Room enhanced by fireplace and access to Sundeck

■ Country-sized Kitchen with bright Breakfast Area, adjoins Dining Room and Utility/Garage entry

■ French doors lead into plush Master Bedroom with decorative ceiling and large Master Bath

■ Three additional bedrooms share a full Bath and Bonus Room

■ An optional basement, slab or crawl-space foundation — please specify when ordering

An
EXCLUSIVE DESIGN
By Jannis Vann & Associates, Inc.

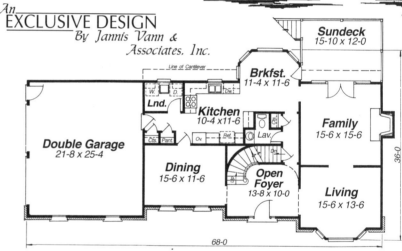

SECOND FLOOR

FIRST FLOOR — 1,277 SQ. FT.
SECOND FLOOR — 1,177 SQ. FT.
BONUS ROOM — 392 SQ. FT.
GARAGE — 572 SQ. FT

TOTAL LIVING AREA:
2,454 SQ. FT.

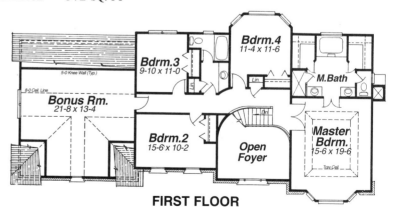

FIRST FLOOR

To order your Blueprints, call 1-800-235-5700

Build With Budget

PRICE CODE: A

- This plan features:
  - Three bedrooms
  - One full and one three-quarter baths
- Easy-care tiled Entry into spacious Living Room with raised hearth fireplace and access to Terrace
- Formal Dining Room overlooking rear yard adjoins Living Room and Kitchen
- Eat-in, country Kitchen with built-in Pantry
- Master Bedroom offers double closet, private Bath and access to Terrace
- Two additional Bedrooms share a full Bath

MAIN FLOOR — 1,267 SQ. FT.
BASEMENT — 1,267 SQ. FT.
GARAGE — 467 SQ. FT.

TOTAL LIVING AREA:
1,267 SQ. FT.

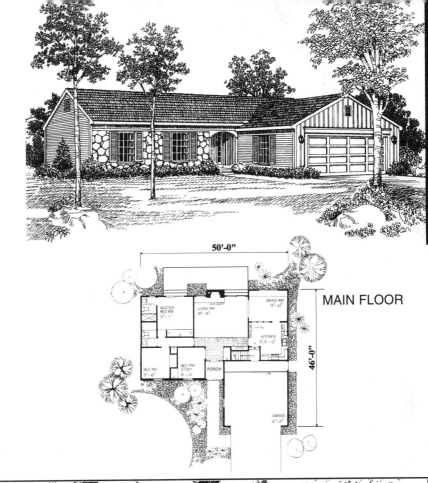

MAIN FLOOR

Central Courtyard Features Pool

PRICE CODE: C

- This plan features:
  - Three bedrooms
  - One full and one three-quarter baths
- A central Courtyard complete with a pool
- A secluded Master Bedroom accented by a skylight, a spacious walk-in closet, and a private Bath
- A convenient Kitchen easily serving the Patio for comfortable outdoor entertaining
- A detached two-car Garage

MAIN FLOOR — 2,194 SQ. FT.
GARAGE — 576 SQ. FT.

TOTAL LIVING AREA:
2,194 SQ. FT.

ZIP QUOTE
HOME COST CALCULATOR
see order pages for details

MAIN FLOOR

To order your Blueprints, call 1-800-235-5700

PLAN NO. 98208

Impressive Staircase
PRICE CODE: E

■ This plan features:
— Four bedrooms
— Three full and one half baths
■ The Foyer is surrounded by columns and is highlighted by an impressive staircase
■ Both the Family Room and the Keeping Room feature fireplaces
■ A Solarium is connected to the well-appointed Kitchen
■ The second floor Master Suite has a sunny Sitting Area
■ A hall with a barrel vaulted ceiling connects the Master Suite to its Bath
■ The Laundry Room is located near the Bedrooms for maximum convenience
■ An optional basement and a crawl space foundation — please specify when ordering
■ No materials list is available for this plan

FIRST FLOOR — 1,431 SQ. FT.
SECOND FLOOR — 1,519 SQ. FT.
BONUS — 153 SQ. FT.
BASEMENT — 1,431 SQ. FT.
GARAGE — 458 SQ. FT.

TOTAL LIVING AREA:
2,950 SQ. FT.

SECOND FLOOR

FIRST FLOOR

PLAN NO. 94640

Family Room at the Heart of the Home
PRICE CODE: D

■ This plan features:
— Three bedrooms
— Three full baths
■ The Living Room and Dining Room are to the right and left of the Foyer
■ The Dining Room with French doors opens to the Kitchen
■ An extended counter maximizes the work space in the Kitchen
■ The Breakfast Room includes access to the Utility Room and to the secondary Bedroom wing
■ The Master Bedroom is equipped with a double vanity bath, two walk-in closets and a linear closet
■ A cozy fireplace and a decorative ceiling highlight the Family Room
■ Secondary Bedrooms have easy access to two full Baths
■ No materials list is available for this plan

MAIN FLOOR — 2,558 SQ. FT.
GARAGE — 549 SQ. FT.

TOTAL LIVING AREA:
2,558 SQ. FT.

MAIN FLOOR

264

To order your Blueprints, call 1-800-235-5700

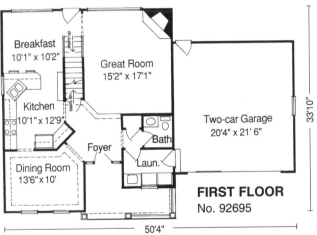

Breakfast
10'1" x 10'2"

Great Room
15'2" x 17'1"

Kitchen
10'1" x 12'9"

Two-car Garage
20'4" x 21' 6"

Foyer

Bath

Laun.

Dining Room
13'6" x 10'

33'10"

FIRST FLOOR
No. 92695

50'4"

SECOND FLOOR

Bath

Master Bedroom
15'2" x 14'6"

Bedroom
10'1" x 11'6"

walk-in closet

Bath

Bedroom
13'6" x 10'0"

TOTAL LIVING AREA:
1,704 SQ. FT.

Enchanting Elevation
Price Code: B

■ This plan features:

— Three bedrooms

— One full, one three quarter , and one half baths

■ The covered front Porch provides a warm welcome

■ The large Foyer showcases interesting angled entries to the rooms beyond

■ The Dining Room has a tray ceiling and is directly connected to the Kitchen

■ The Great Room has a corner fireplace

■ The Kitchen features a serving bar

■ The Breakfast Nook has to the rear yard and stairs to the second floor

■ Upstairs, find three Bedrooms, all with ample closet space and two Baths

■ No materials list is available for this plan

FIRST FLOOR — 906 SQ. FT.
SECOND FLOOR — 798 SQ. FT.
BASEMENT — 906 SQ. FT.
GARAGE — 437 SQ. FT.

Country Farmhouse with Modern Touches

Price Code: C

- This plan features:
- — Three bedrooms
- — Three full baths
- An old-fashioned Porch surrounding this Saltbox design with two convenient entrances
- A central Foyer with a curved staircase opening to a Sunken Living Room with a heat-circulating fireplace
- A formal Dining Room with a sliding glass door to the Terrace and separated from Living Room by a railing
- Family Room with a built-in entertainment center is conveniently located near the Mudroom and Foyer
- U-shaped Kitchen serving both the Dining Room and Dinette with ease
- An expansive Master Suite with two closets, a dressing area, and a private Bath highlighted by skylights
- Two additional, roomy bedrooms sharing a full hall bath

FIRST FLOOR — 1,238 SQ. FT.
SECOND FLOOR — 797 SQ. FT.
BASEMENT — 1,159 SQ. FT.
GARAGE — 439 SQ. FT.

TOTAL LIVING AREA:
2,035 SQ. FT.

SECOND FLOOR

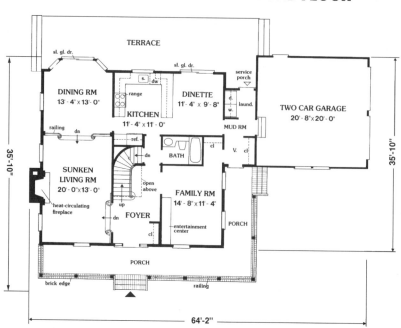

FIRST FLOOR

To order your Blueprints, call 1-800-235-5700

Open Floor Plan

Price Code: C

FIRST FLOOR
No. 96528

SECOND FLOOR

■ This plan features:

— Three bedrooms

— Two full baths

■ Great Room open to the Dining Room separated from the Kitchen by only an extended counter

■ A corner fireplace accenting the Great Room

■ U-shaped Kitchen maximizing counter area for an abundance of work space

■ Master Suite with lavish Bath and a walk-in closet

■ Second floor terrace accessed from the Master Suite

FIRST FLOOR — 1,455 SQ. FT.
SECOND FLOOR — 561 SQ. FT.
GARAGE — 584 SQ. FT.

TOTAL LIVING AREA:
2,016 SQ. FT.

Four Bedroom Brick

Price Code: E

- This plan features:
  - Four bedrooms
  - Two full and one half baths
- Arched entry into pillared Foyer with angled staircase
- Formal Living and Dining rooms enhanced by pillars and expansive views of rear grounds
- Country-size Kitchen offers work island, large walk-in Pantry, bright Breakfast Area, serving counter to Family Room, and adjoining Utility/Garage entry
- Private first floor Master Bedroom boasts a fireplace and lavish Bath with a corner whirlpool tub
- Three additional Bedrooms on second floor share a double vanity Bath
- No materials list is available for this plan

FIRST FLOOR — 1,910 SQ. FT.
SECOND FLOOR — 834 SQ. FT.
GARAGE — 489 SQ. FT.

TOTAL LIVING AREA:
2,744 SQ. FT.

© Larry E. Belk

FIRST FLOOR
WIDTH 64-8
DEPTH 54-2

SECOND FLOOR

To order your Blueprints, call 1-800-235-5700

High Impact Angles
PRICE CODE: A

This plan features:
- Two or Three bedrooms
- Two full baths
- Soaring ceilings to give the house a spacious, contemporary feeling
- A fireplaced Great Room adjoining a convenient Kitchen, with a sunny Breakfast Nook
- Sliding glass doors opening onto an angular Deck
- A Master Suite with vaulted ceilings and a private Bath

MAIN FLOOR — 1,368 SQ. FT.

TOTAL LIVING AREA:
1,368 SQ. FT.

Main Floor Plan

Superb Southern Styling
PRICE CODE: E

- This plan features:
- Four bedrooms
- Three full baths
- Terrific front Porch and dormers create a homey Southern style
- A corner fireplace enhancing the Family Room
- A cooktop island and a peninsula counter adding to the efficiency of the Kitchen
- Convenient peninsula counter separates the Kitchen from the Breakfast Room
- Lavish Master Suite includes a whirlpool tub and a walk-in closet
- Secondary Bedrooms located in close proximity to a full Bath
- An optional crawl space or slab foundation — please specify when ordering
- No materials list is available for this plan

FIRST FLOOR — 2,135 SQ. FT.
SECOND FLOOR — 538 SQ. FT.
BONUS — 225 SQ. FT.
GARAGE — 436 SQ. FT.

TOTAL LIVING AREA:
2,673 SQ. FT.

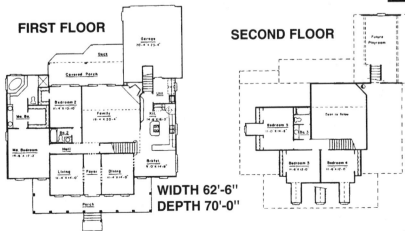

FIRST FLOOR

SECOND FLOOR

WIDTH 62'-6"
DEPTH 70'-0"

To order your Blueprints, call 1-800-235-5700

Quoin Accents
Distinguish this Plan
PRICE CODE: A

■ This plan features:
— Three bedrooms
— Two full baths
■ A traditional brick elevation with quoin accents
■ A large Family Room with a corner fireplace and direct access to the outside
■ An arched opening leading to the Breakfast Area
■ A bay window illuminating the Breakfast Area with natural light
■ An efficiently designed, U-shaped Kitchen with ample cabinet and counter space
■ A Master Suite with a private master Bath
■ Two additional Bedrooms that share a full hall Bath
■ No material list is available for this plan

MAIN FLOOR — 1,142 SQ. FT.
GARAGE — 428 SQ. FT.

TOTAL LIVING AREA:
1,142 SQ. FT.

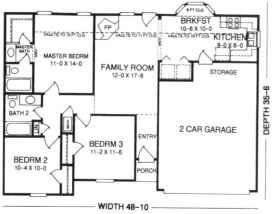

MAIN FLOOR

European Flair
PRICE CODE: B

■ This plan features:
— Three bedrooms
— Two full baths
■ Large fireplace serving as an attractive focal point for the vaulted Family Room
■ Decorative column defining the elegant Dining Room
■ Kitchen including a serving bar for the Family Room and a Breakfast Area
■ Master Suite topped by a tray ceiling over the Bedroom and a vaulted ceiling over the five-piece Master Bath
■ Optional bonus room for future expansion
■ An optional basement or crawl space foundation — please specify when ordering
■ No material list is available for this plan

MAIN FLOOR — 1,544 SQ. FT.
BONUS ROOM — 284 SQ. FT.
GARAGE — 440 SQ. FT.

TOTAL LIVING AREA:
1,544 SQ. FT.

© Frank Betz Associates

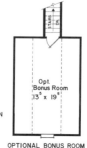

To order your Blueprints, call 1-800-235-5700

This plan cannot be built within a 25 mile radius of Cedar Rapids, IA.

SECOND FLOOR

TOTAL LIVING AREA:
3,397 SQ. FT.

ZIP QUOTE
HOME COST CALCULATOR
see order pages for details

Contemporary Plan With An Old-Fashioned Look

Price Code: F

■ This plan features:

— Four bedrooms

— Three full and one half baths

■ Gracious entry with arched window, sidelights and two-story Foyer

■ Formal Dining Room and quiet Study have decorative windows

■ Convenient Kitchen with cooktop island, opens to Eating Area

■ Expansive Family Room accented by cozy fireplace

■ Secluded Master Bedroom offers a bright Sitting Area

■ No materials list is available for this plan

MAIN FLOOR — 2,385 SQ. FT.
SECOND FLOOR — 1,012 SQ. FT.
GARAGE — 846 SQ. FT.
BASEMENT — 2,385 SQ. FT.

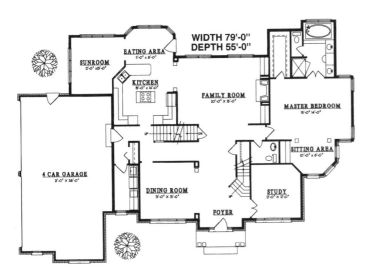

WIDTH 79'-0"
DEPTH 55'-0"

MAIN FLOOR

Stately Columns and Keystones

Price Code: E

- This plan features:
  - Four bedrooms
  - Three full and one half baths
- Gracious two-story Foyer opens to vaulted Living Room and arched Dining Room
- Expansive, two-story Grand Room with impressive fireplace between outdoor views
- Spacious Kitchen with a work island and Breakfast Area
- Private Master Bedroom offers a decorative ceiling, two walk-in closets and vanities, and a garden window tub
- Three second floor Bedrooms with great closets, share two full Baths
- No materials list is available for this plan

FIRST FLOOR — 2,115 SQ. FT.
SECOND FLOOR — 914 SQ. FT.
BASEMENT — 2,115 SQ. FT.
GARAGE — 448 SQ. FT.

TOTAL LIVING AREA:
3,029 SQ. FT.

FIRST FLOOR

SECOND FLOOR

An
EXCLUSIVE DESIGN
By Garrell Associates Inc

To order your Blueprints, call 1-800-235-5700

© 1991 Donald A. Gardner Architects, Inc.

Deck Includes Spa

Price Code: D

■ This plan features:
— Three bedrooms
— Two full and one half baths

■ An exterior Porch giving the home a traditional flavor

■ Great Room highlighted by a fireplace and a balcony above as well as a pass-through into the Kitchen

■ Kitchen Eating Area with sky lights and bow windows overlooking the Deck with a Spa

■ Two additional Bedrooms with a full Bath on the second floor

■ Master Suite on the first floor and naturally illuminated by two skylights

■ An optional basement or a crawl space foundation — please specify when ordering

FIRST FLOOR — 1,325 SQ. FT.
SECOND FLOOR — 453 SQ. FT.

TOTAL LIVING AREA:
1,778 SQ. FT.

FIRST FLOOR

48-4

© 1991 Donald A Gardner Architects, Inc.

ZIP QUOTE
HOME COST CALCULATOR
see order pages for details

SECOND FLOOR

To order your Blueprints, call 1-800-235-5700

Elegant Elevation

Price Code: D

- This plan features:
- — Four bedrooms
- — Two full and one half baths
- A wide-apron staircase and plant shelf highlight open Foyer
- Bay window in formal Dining Room
- Expansive Family Room with focal point fireplace and view of rear yard
- Hub Kitchen with Breakfast Area, Garage entry, Laundry, and peninsula counter/snackbar
- Master Bedroom with sloped ceiling, large walk-in closet and plush Bath
- Three additional Bedrooms share a double vanity Bath with skylight
- No materials list is available for this plan

FIRST FLOOR — 1,309 SQ. FT.
SECOND FLOOR — 1,119 SQ. FT.
BASEMENT — 1,277 SQ. FT.
GARAGE — 452 SQ. FT.

Bedroom
11'6" x 12'0"

Master Bedroom
15'0" x 14'5"

walk-in closet

slope ceiling

slope ceiling

Bath

Bedroom
11'8" x 11'0"

Balcony

Bath

stairs dn

Bedroom
11'4" x 13'6"

Foyer Below

plant shelf

slope ceiling

slope ceiling

SECOND FLOOR

TOTAL LIVING AREA:
2,428 SQ. FT.

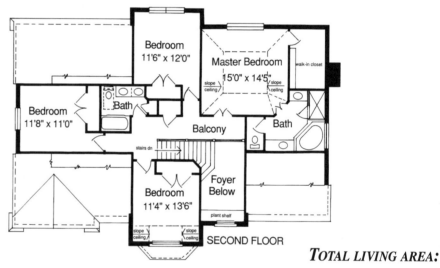

Laun.

Bath

Breakfast
11'4" x 10'4"

Family Room
17'5" x 15'4"

Kitchen
15'6" x 10'6"

Two-car Garage
19'8" x 23'0"

stairs dn

stairs up

Living Room
11'6" x 15'6"

arched ceiling

high ceiling

Dining Room
13'6" x 14'2"

Foyer

Porch

FIRST FLOOR

WIDTH 54' - 6"
DEPTH 41' - 10"

To order your Blueprints, call 1-800-235-5700

A Private Guest Suite

PRICE CODE: E

This plan features:
- Four bedrooms
- Three full and one half baths
- Columns accent the entrance to this grand home
- The Living Room and the Dining Room both provide an open space for entertaining
- A warm fireplace accents the Living Room
- The Kitchen with its center island flows into the Breakfast Area
- The Master Suite has decorative ceilings above it
- A private Guest Suite is perfect for visiting relatives
- An optional basement or crawl space foundation — please specify when ordering
- No materials list is available for this plan

FIRST FLOOR — 1,920 SQ. FT.
SECOND FLOOR — 912 SQ. FT.
BASEMENT — 1,920 SQ. FT.
GARAGE — 538 SQ. FT.

TOTAL LIVING AREA:
2,832 SQ. FT.

SECOND FLOOR

FIRST FLOOR

Porches Expands Living Space

PRICE CODE: C

This plan features:
- Three bedrooms
- Two full and one half baths
- Porches on the front and the rear of this home expand the living space to the outdoors
- The rear Porch is accessed directly from the Great Room
- The spacious Great Room is enhanced by a twelve foot ceiling and a fireplace
- The well-appointed Kitchen has an extended counter/eating bar and easy access to the Dining Room
- Secondary Bedrooms have a full Bath located between the rooms
- The Master Suite is enhanced by his-n-her walk-in closets, a whirlpool tub, and a separate shower
- There is a bonus room for the future expansion

MAIN FLOOR — 2,089 SQ. FT.
BONUS ROOM — 497 SQ. FT.

TOTAL LIVING AREA:
2,089 SQ. FT.

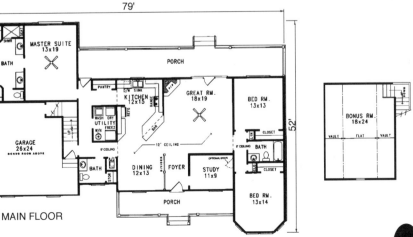

MAIN FLOOR

To order your Blueprints, call 1-800-235-5700

Stone and Siding
PRICE CODE: E

- This plan features:
  — Four bedrooms
  — Three full and one half baths
- Attractive styling using a combination of stone and siding and a covered Porch add to the curb appeal
- Former Foyer giving access to the bedroom wing, Library or Activity Room
- Activity Room showcasing a focal point fireplace and including direct access to the rear Deck and the Breakfast Room
- Breakfast Room is topped by a vaulted ceiling and flows into the Kitchen
- A snack bar/peninsula counter highlights the Kitchen which also includes a built-in Pantry.
- A secluded guest Bedroom suite is located off the Kitchen Area
- Master Suite topped by a tray ceiling and pampered by five-piece Bath

MAIN FLOOR — 2,690 SQ. FT.
BASEMENT — 2,690 SQ. FT.
GARAGE — 660 SQ. FT.

TOTAL LIVING AREA:
2,690 SQ. FT.

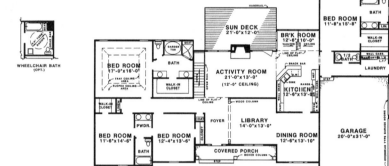

MAIN AREA

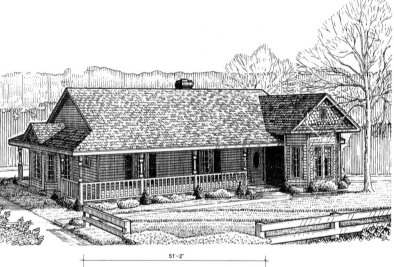

Casual Living
Inside and Out
PRICE CODE: B

- This plan features:
  — Three bedrooms
  — Two full baths
- A Living Room with a ten foot ceiling and a cozy corner fireplace
- An enormous Dining Area that is able to handle even the largest family dinners
- A large rear Porch that is perfect for outdoor dining
- A conveniently placed Laundry Room
- His-n-her walk-in closets and a double vanity in the Master Bath
- Secondary Bedrooms that share a full hall Bath with a double vanity
- No materials list is available for this plan

MAIN AREA — 1,772 SQ. FT.

TOTAL LIVING AREA:
1,772 SQ. FT.

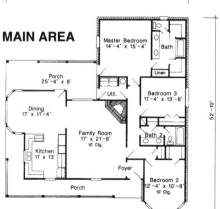

MAIN AREA

To order your Blueprints, call 1-800-235-5700

An
EXCLUSIVE DESIGN
By Patrick Morabito,
A.I.A. Architect

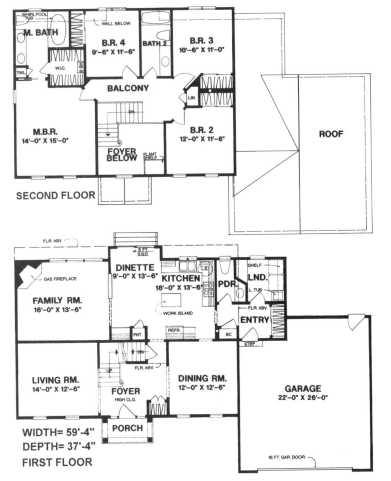

SECOND FLOOR

WIDTH= 59'-4"
DEPTH= 37'-4"
FIRST FLOOR

Speaking of Colonials

Price Code: C

- This plan features:
- — Four bedrooms
- — Two full and one half baths
- Entry Porch leads into central Foyer between formal Living and Dining Rooms
- Comfortable Family Room with a corner fireplace and back yard view
- Hub Kitchen with a work island, Pantry, Dinette Area with outdoor access, and nearby Laundry and Garage entry
- Corner Master Bedroom offers a walk-in closet and a double vanity Bath with a whirlpool tub
- No materials list is available for this plan

FIRST FLOOR — 1,110 SQ. FT.
SECOND FLOOR — 992 SQ. FT.
BASEMENT — 1,110 SQ. FT.
GARAGE — 530 SQ. FT.

TOTAL LIVING AREA:
2,102 SQ. FT.

To order your Blueprints, call 1-800-235-5700

Angles and Windows
Add Eye Appeal

Price Code: C

■ This plan features:

— Four or five bedrooms

— Two full baths

■ A unique, eye catching design with decorative windows wrapping around a natural stone chimney

■ A dramatic Living Room and Dining Room "L" with a 16 foot ceiling

■ A well-equipped Kitchen with a unusual curved glass Dinette

■ A Master Bedroom and second Bedroom on the first floor sharing a luxurious Bath

■ Three additional Bedrooms, on the second floor, sharing a full hall Bath

FIRST FLOOR — 1,345 SQ. FT.
SECOND FLOOR — 656 SQ. FT.
BASEMENT — 1,359 SQ. FT.
GARAGE — 467 SQ. FT.

TOTAL LIVING AREA:
2,001 SQ. FT.

SECOND FLOOR

dinette roof
BED RM #4
12'-4" x 10'-5"
whirlpool tub
BATH
roof
STORAGE
roof
slope ceiling
cl. cl.
open
low wall
H.
down
lin.
BED RM #3
14'-4" x 14'
upper part of living room
cl.
STUDY OR BED RM 5
16'-8" x 9'-2"
cl.
slope ceiling
STORAGE
roof

flat roof
garage roof
trellis beams

FIRST FLOOR

58'-0"

steps
TERRACE
DINETTE
9' x 8'-6"
2x6 studs for added insulation
sl. gl. dr.
MUD RM laundry
w. d.
service entry
DINING RM
13' x 11'
KITCHEN
10'-10" x 9'
range
ck.
BATH
whirlpool tub
BED RM #2
12' x 11'
dw
ref.
lin.
cl.
heat-circulating fireplace
LIVING RM
22'-6" x 15'
down
H.
cl. cl. cl.
MASTER BED RM
16'-4" x 11'-6"
up
cl. VEST.
TWO CAR GARAGE
20' x 19'-4"
trellis above
posts
storage, bicycles etc.

49'-0"

To order your Blueprints, call 1-800-235-5700

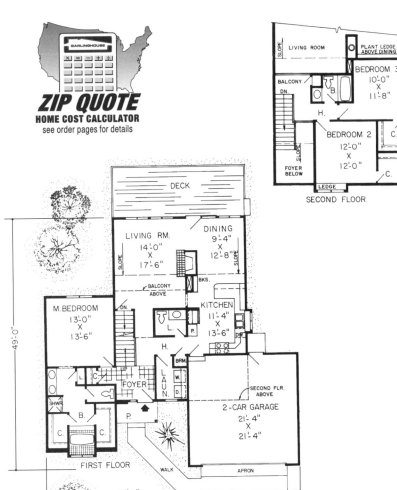

Wonderful Views Everywhere

Price Code: C

■ This plan features:

— Three bedrooms

— Two full and one half baths

■ A fireplaced Living Room with a sloped ceiling

■ A second floor balcony

■ A huge Master Bedroom featuring a lavish Bath

■ Walk-in closets for all Bedrooms

FIRST FLOOR — 1,277 SQ. FT.
SECOND FLOOR — 616 SQ. FT.
BASEMENT — 1,265 SQ. FT.
GARAGE — 477 SQ. FT.
PORCH — 32 SQ. FT.

TOTAL LIVING AREA:
1,893 SQ. FT.

An
EXCLUSIVE DESIGN
By Karl Kreeger

Quality Inside and Out

Price Code: E

- This plan features:
- — Three bedrooms
- — Two full and one half baths
- A spacious Entry/Gallery opens to Living Room with focal point fireplace
- Country Kitchen with work island opens to Breakfast bay, Family Room, Dining Room, Utility and Garage entry
- Expansive Family Room offers a vaulted ceiling, third fireplace and access to Patio
- Private Master Bedroom suite with a vaulted ceiling, lavish bath and walk-in closet
- Two second floor bedrooms share a double vanity bath
- No materials list available for this plan

MAIN FLOOR — 2,273 SQ. FT.
UPPER FLOOR — 562 SQ. FT.
GARAGE — 460 SQ. FT.
FOUNDATION —BASEMENT, SLAB OR
CRAWL SPACE

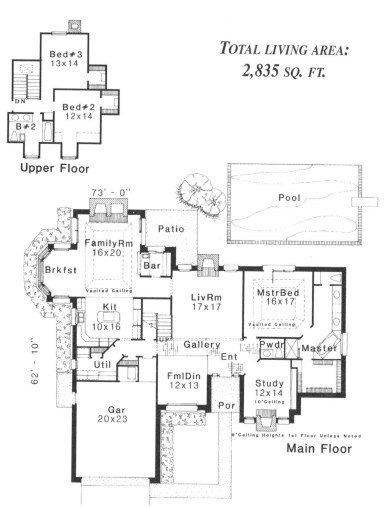

TOTAL LIVING AREA:
2,835 SQ. FT.

To order your Blueprints, call 1-800-235-5700

Compact Plan

PRICE CODE: C

PLAN NO. 93085

■ This plan features:
— Three bedrooms
— Two full baths
■ Roomy front Porch adding outdoor living area
■ Dining Room and Great Room visible from the Foyer through a series of elegant archways
■ Angled Counter opening to the Great Room from the Kitchen
■ Master Suite with a luxurious, private Bath including a whirlpool tub, a separate shower and an enormous walk-in closet
■ Two additional Bedrooms sharing a full Bath
■ No materials list is available for this plan

MAIN FLOOR — 1,955 SQ. FT.
GARAGE — 517 SQ. FT.

TOTAL LIVING AREA:
1,955 SQ. FT.

MAIN FLOOR

Exterior Shows
Attention to Detail

PRICE CODE: D

PLAN NO. 94811

■ This plan features:
— Three bedrooms
— Two full baths
■ Privately located Master Suite is complimented by a luxurious Bath with two walk-in closets
■ Two additional Bedrooms have ample closet space and share a full Bath
■ The Activity Room has a sloped ceiling, large fireplace and is accented with columns
■ Access to Sun Deck from the Dining Room
■ The island Kitchen and Breakfast Area have access to Garage for ease when bringing in groceries

MAIN FLOOR — 2,165 SQ. FT.
GARAGE — 484 SQ. FT.

TOTAL LIVING AREA:
2,165 SQ. FT.

MAIN FLOOR

To order your Blueprints, call 1-800-235-5700

Wood Siding and Stone Accents

PRICE CODE: B

- This plan features:
  - Three bedrooms
  - Two full and one half baths
- Columns with stone pedestals support the covered front Porch
- The Living Room overlooks the front Porch and has a stone fireplace
- The Dining Room has sliders to the rear yard
- The Kitchen has a convenient arrangement, plus a door to the Garage
- The Master Bedroom is located on the First Floor and has it's own Bath
- Upstairs find two more Bedrooms that share a full Bath
- No materials list is available for this plan

FIRST FLOOR — 934 SQ. FT.
SECOND FLOOR — 581 SQ. FT.
BASEMENT — 928 SQ. FT.
GARAGE — 509 SQ. FT.

TOTAL LIVING AREA:
1,515 SQ. FT.

60'6"

WHIRLPOOL

MASTER BATH

P.R.

DINING ROOM 9'0" x 11'8"

SLIDERS

KITCHEN 9'0" x 11'8"

DW

DN

2 CAR GARAGE 23'2" x 22'2"

33'6"

MASTER BEDROOM 12'0" x 15'6"

CL

DN

UP

CL

LIVING ROOM 18'0" x 12'0"

FIREPLACE

PORTICO

FIRST FLOOR

BATH

HALL

DN

BEDROOM 12'0" x 11'0"

CL

CL

BEDROOM 15'8" x 11'0"

SECOND FLOOR

Open Plan is Full of Air & Light

PRICE CODE: B

- This plan features:
  - Three bedrooms
  - Two full and one half baths
- Foyer open to the Family Room and highlighted by a fireplace
- Dining Room with a sliding glass door to rear yard adjoins Family Room
- Kitchen and Nook in an efficient open layout
- Second Floor Master Suite topped by tray ceiling over the Bedroom and a vaulted ceiling over the lavish Bath
- Two additional Bedrooms sharing a full Bath in the hall
- An optional basement or crawl space foundation — please specify when ordering
- No materials list is available for this plan

FIRST FLOOR — 767 SQ. FT.
SECOND FLOOR — 738 SQ. FT.
BONUS ROOM — 240 SQ. FT.
BASEMENT — 767 SQ. FT.

TOTAL LIVING AREA:
1,505 SQ. FT.

© Frank Betz Associates

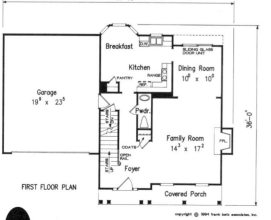

47'-10"

Breakfast

D.W.

Kitchen

RANGE

SLIDING GLASS DOOR UNIT

Dining Room 10⁰ x 10⁰

PANTRY

REF.

Garage 19⁹ x 23⁵

STAIRS DN

Pwdr.

36'-0"

COATS

OPEN RAIL

STAIRS

Family Room 14³ x 17²

FPL

Foyer

FIRST FLOOR PLAN

Covered Porch

copyright © 1994 frank betz associates, inc.

PLANT SHELF ABOVE

SHWR.

W.i.c.

Vaulted M.Bath

TRAY CLG.

LINEN

Opt. Bonus Room 19⁹ x 11⁵

LIN.

W. D.

Master Suite 12⁰ x 16⁰

Bath

SECOND FLOOR PLAN

Bedroom 2 12⁰ x 10⁰

Bedroom 3 10⁵ x 10⁰

To order your Blueprints, call 1-800-235-5700

© 1994 Donald A. Gardner Architects, Inc.

P. NATHAN

PLAN NO. 96408

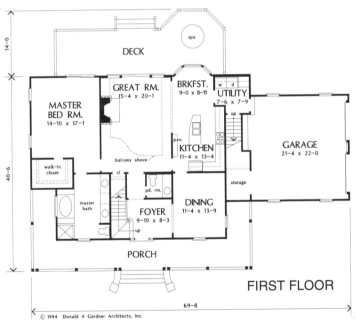

FIRST FLOOR

© 1994 Donald A Gardner Architects, Inc.

- DECK
- spa
- GREAT RM. 15-4 x 20-1
- BRKFST. 9-0 x 8-11
- UTILITY 7-6 x 7-9
- w d
- MASTER BED RM. 14-10 x 17-1
- balcony above
- KITCHEN 11-4 x 13-4
- pan.
- GARAGE 21-4 x 22-0
- walk-in closet
- cl
- storage
- master bath
- pd. rm.
- DINING 11-4 x 13-9
- FOYER 9-10 x 8-3
- up
- PORCH
- 14-0
- 40-6
- 69-8

SECOND FLOOR

- great room below
- attic storage
- cl
- BED RM. 11-4 x 10-0
- attic storage
- skylights
- BONUS RM. 22-10 x 13-4
- down
- lin.
- railing
- BED RM. 11-4 x 10-0
- down
- BED RM. 11-4 x 13-8
- cl
- foyer below
- cl
- attic storage

Four Bedroom Country Classic

Price Code: E

- ■ This plan features:
  - — Four bedrooms
  - — Two full and one half baths
- ■ Foyer open to the Dining Room creating a hall with a balcony over the vaulted Great Room
- ■ Great Room opens to the Deck and to the island Kitchen with convenient Pantry
- ■ Nine foot ceilings on the first floor expand volume
- ■ Master Suite pampered by a whirlpool tub, double vanity, separate shower, and access to the Deck
- ■ Bonus room to be finished now or later

FIRST FLOOR — 1,499 SQ. FT.
SECOND FLOOR — 665 SQ. FT.
GARAGE & STORAGE — 567 SQ. FT.
BONUS ROOM — 380 SQ. FT.

TOTAL LIVING AREA:
2,164 SQ. FT.

To order your Blueprints, call 1-800-235-5700

283

Spectacular Stucco and Stone

Price Code: E

- ■ This plan features:
- — Three bedrooms
- — Two full and one half baths
- ■ Two-story glass entry opens to Great Room with an inviting fireplace
- ■ Open Kitchen and Morning Room with pantry, cooktop island, fireplace and skylights
- ■ Master Bedroom has a bay window, two walk-in closets and a private bath
- ■ Two second floor bedrooms with walk-in closets and vanities, have private access to a full bath
- ■ Optional second floor plan adds another bedroom, bath and Bonus Room
- ■ An optional basement or crawl space foundation — please specify when ordering
- ■ No materials list is available for this plan

FIRST FLOOR — 1,719 SQ. FT.
SECOND FLOOR — 608 SQ. FT.
BONUS — 630 SQ. FT.

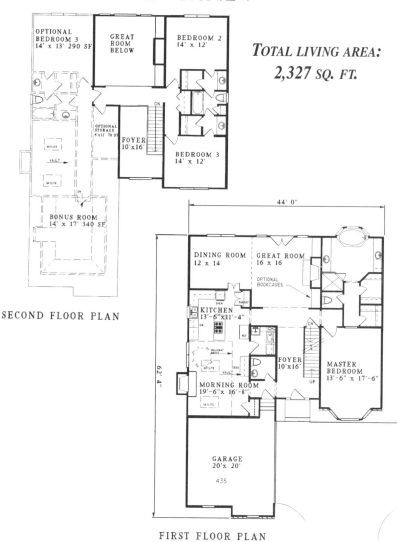

TOTAL LIVING AREA:
2,327 SQ. FT.

SECOND FLOOR PLAN

FIRST FLOOR PLAN

To order your Blueprints, call 1-800-235-5700

© 1992 Donald A. Gardner Architects, Inc.

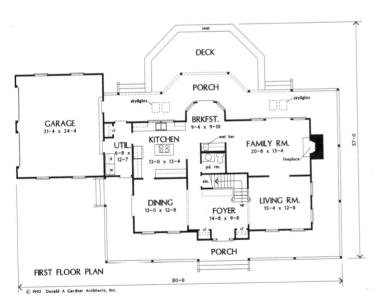

FIRST FLOOR PLAN

© 1992 Donald A Gardner Architects, Inc.

DECK

seat

PORCH

skylights

skylights

BRKFST.
9-4 x 9-10

FAMILY RM.
20-8 x 13-4

KITCHEN
13-0 x 13-4

wet bar

fireplace

UTIL.
6-8 x
12-7

pd. rm.

sto.

GARAGE
21-4 x 24-4

DINING
13-0 x 12-8

FOYER
14-8 x 9-8

up

LIVING RM.
15-4 x 12-8

cl

cl

PORCH

80-0

57-0

SECOND FLOOR PLAN

walk-in
closet

lin.

master bath

bath

skylight

BED RM.
11-8 x 11-8

cl

cl

MASTER
BED RM.
13-0 x 19-0

down

BED RM.
12-4 x 10-0

BED RM.
15-4 x 12-0

cl

Grand Four Bedroom Farmhouse

Price Code: F

■ This plan features:

— Four bedrooms

— Two full and one half baths

■ Double gables, wrap-around Porch and custom window details add appeal to farmhouse

■ Formal Living and Dining rooms connected by Foyer in front, while casual living areas expand rear

■ Efficient Kitchen with island cooktop and easy access to all eating areas

■ Fireplace, wetbar and rear Porch and Deck provide great entertainment space

■ Spacious Master Bedroom features walk-in closet and pampering Bath

FIRST FLOOR — 1,357 SQ. FT.
SECOND FLOOR — 1,204 SQ. FT.
GARAGE & STORAGE — 546 SQ. FT.

TOTAL LIVING AREA:
2,561 SQ. FT.

285

To order your Blueprints, call 1-800-235-5700

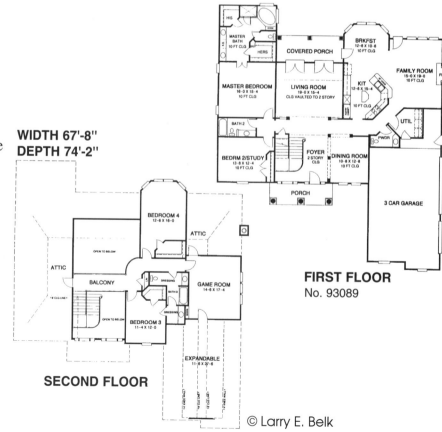

A Commanding Presence

Price Code: F

■ This plan features:

— Four bedrooms

— Three full baths and one half bath

■ An arresting double arch gives this home a commanding presence

■ Two-story Foyer opens the view directly through the Living Room

■ The use of square columns to define the Dining Room add an air of elegance

■ Kitchen/Breakfast area and Family Room are conveniently grouped

■ The Master Bedroom has an elegantly appointed Master Bath

MAIN FLOOR — 2,469 SQ. FT.
SECOND FLOOR — 1,025 SQ. FT.
BONUS ROOM — 320 SQ. FT.
GARAGE — 795 SQ. FT.

TOTAL LIVING AREA:
3,494 SQ. FT.

WIDTH 67'-8"
DEPTH 74'-2"

FIRST FLOOR
No. 93089

HIS

MASTER BATH
10 FT CLG

HERS

COVERED PORCH

BRKFST
12-6 X 10-6
10 FT CLG

FAMILY ROOM
15-0 X 19-0
10 FT CLG

FP

MASTER BEDROOM
16-0 X 15-4
10 FT CLG

LIVING ROOM
19-0 X 15-4
CLG VAULTED TO 2 STORY

KIT
12-6 X 15-4
10 FT CLG

BATH 2

UTIL

PWDR

BEDRM 2/STUDY
13-8 X 12-4
10 FT CLG

FOYER
2 STORY
CLG

DINING ROOM
10-8 X 12-8
10 FT CLG

PORCH

3 CAR GARAGE

SECOND FLOOR

BEDROOM 4
12-6 X 16-0

ATTIC

OPEN TO BELOW

ATTIC

BALCONY

GAME ROOM
14-6 X 17-4

DRESSING

BATH 3

DRESSING

OPEN TO BELOW

BEDROOM 3
11-4 X 12-0

DRESSING

EXPANDABLE
11-6 X 27-6

© Larry E. Belk

To order your Blueprints, call 1-800-235-5700

Quaint Front Porch and Lovely Details
PRICE CODE: C

This plan features:
- Four bedrooms
- Two full and one half baths
- A Covered Porch and Victorian touches create unique elevation
- A one and a half story entry hall leads into formal Dining Room
- A volume ceiling above abundant windows and a see-through fireplace highlight the Great Room
- Kitchen/Breakfast Area shares the fireplace and has a snack bar, desk, walk-in Pantry and abundant counter space
- Laundry Area provides access to Garage and side yard also
- Secluded Master Suite crowned by a vaulted ceiling and a luxurious Bath
- Three additional Bedrooms on the second floor share a full Bath

FIRST FLOOR — 1,421 SQ. FT.
SECOND FLOOR — 578 SQ. FT.
BASEMENT — 1,421 SQ. FT.
GARAGE — 480 SQ. FT.

TOTAL LIVING AREA: 1,999 SQ. FT.

FIRST FLOOR

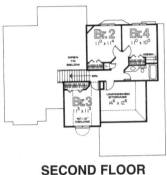

SECOND FLOOR

© design basics, inc.

Elegant Exterior Attracts Attention
PRICE CODE: D

This plan features:
- Three bedrooms
- Three full baths
- The exterior is highlighted by a high columned Porch and many windows
- The Receiving Room is graced by a see-through fireplace that is shared with the Great Room
- The Great Room is spacious and opens onto the Verandah
- The Kitchen/Dining Area adjoins the Great Room adding a spacious feeling to the home
- A vaulted ceiling, a private whirlpool Bath and a Lounging Room are in the Master Suite
- Two additional Bedrooms have access to a full Bath

MAIN FLOOR — 2,289 SQ. FT.
GARAGE — 758 SQ. FT.

TOTAL LIVING AREA: 2,289 SQ. FT.

MAIN FLOOR

To order your Blueprints, call 1-800-235-5700

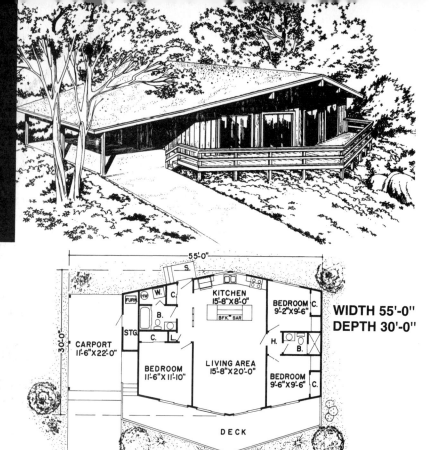

Design Features Six Sides

PRICE CODE: A

- This plan features:
  — Three bedrooms
  — One full and one three-quarter baths
- Active living areas centrally located between two quiet Bedroom and Bath areas
- A Living Room that can be closed off from the Bedroom wings giving privacy to both areas
- A bath located behind a third Bedroom
- A bedroom complete with washer/dryer facilities

MAIN FLOOR — 1,040 SQ. FT.
DECK — 258 SQ. FT.
CARPORT — 230 SQ. FT.

TOTAL LIVING AREA:
1,040 SQ. FT.

WIDTH 55'-0"
DEPTH 30'-0"

MAIN FLOOR

Executive Features

PRICE CODE: E

- This plan features:
  — Four bedrooms
  — Three full and one half baths
- High volume ceilings
- An extended staircase highlights the Foyer as columns define the Dining Room and the Grand Room
- A massive glass exterior rear wall and high ceiling in the Master Bedroom
- His-n-her walk-in closets and a lavish five-piece bath highlight the Master Bedroom
- The island Kitchen, Keeping Room and Breakfast Room create an open living space
- A fireplace accents both the Keeping Room and the two-story Grand Room
- Three additional Bedrooms with private Bathroom access and ample closet space
- An optional basement or crawl space foundation — please specify when ordering
- No materials list is available for this plan

FIRST FLOOR — 2,035 SQ. FT.
SECOND FLOOR — 1,028 SQ. FT.
BASEMENT — 2,035 SQ. FT.
GARAGE — 530 SQ. FT.

TOTAL LIVING AREA:
3,063 SQ. FT.

WIDTH 56'-0"
DEPTH 62'-6"

FIRST FLOOR PLAN

SECOND FLOOR PLAN

To order your Blueprints, call 1-800-235-5700

Farmhouse Flavor

Price Code: D

- This plan features:
  - Three or four bedrooms
  - Two full and one half baths

- A country-styled, three-sided porch, providing a warm welcome

- A central staircase dominating the central Foyer, surrounded by the formal Living and Dining Rooms

- A decorative ceiling treatment adding elegance to the formal Dining Room

- A quiet Den with built-in bookcases and a walk-in closet may also be used as a fourth bedroom

- A spacious island Kitchen with a pantry, and a cheerful Breakfast area with a decorative ceiling

- A Sun Room highlighted by skylights and a plant shelf

- A convenient first floor Master Suite with a skylight in the private bath

- Two additional bedrooms, sharing a full bath loaded with intriguing angles

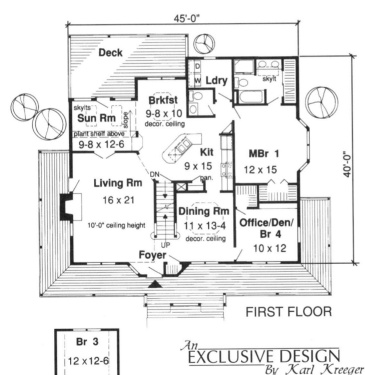

45'-0"

Deck

Ldry
skylt

Brkfst
9-8 x 10
decor. ceiling

Sun Rm
skylts
slope
plant shelf above
9-8 x 12-6

Kit
9 x 15
pan.

MBr 1
12 x 15

Living Rm
16 x 21
DN
10'-0" ceiling height

Dining Rm
11 x 13-4
decor. ceiling

Office/Den/
Br 4
10 x 12

UP

Foyer

40'-0"

FIRST FLOOR

Br 3
12 x 12-6

lin.

DN

Br 2
11 x 12-8

lin.

slope

SECOND FLOOR

An
EXCLUSIVE DESIGN
By Karl Kreeger

FIRST FLOOR — 1,698 SQ. FT.
SECOND FLOOR — 601 SQ. FT.
BASEMENT — 1,681 SQ. FT.
GARAGE — 616 SQ. FT.

TOTAL LIVING AREA:
2,299 SQ. FT.

Rustic Styling

Price Code: B

■ This plan features:

— Two bedrooms

— Two full baths

■ A large Sun Deck wraps around this rustic home

■ The Living Room and Dining Room are combined

■ The Living Room has a gas fireplace and sliders to the Deck

■ The large Kitchen features an angled counter

■ There is a Bedroom, Bath and a Utility Room on the first floor

■ Upstairs the Master Bedroom has two closets and a private Deck

■ Relax in the whirlpool tub in the Master Bath

■ An optional basement or crawl space foundation — please specify when ordering

FIRST FLOOR — 1,064 SQ. FT.
SECOND FLOOR — 613 SQ. FT.

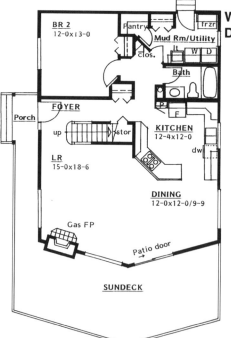

WIDTH 28'-0"
DEPTH 40'-0"

FIRST FLOOR
No. 99914

TOTAL LIVING AREA:
1,677 SQ. FT.

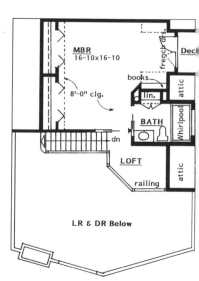

SECOND FLOOR

To order your Blueprints, call 1-800-235-5700

UPPER FLOOR PLAN

MAIN FLOOR PLAN

Dramatic Two-Story Arched Window

Price Code: D

■ This plan features:

— Three bedrooms

— Two full and one half baths

■ A spacious Family Room/Kitchen combination

■ A sunken Living Room with a warm and cozy fireplace

■ An impressive Dining Room with a vaulted ceiling in close proximity to the Kitchen

■ A Master Suite with a walk-in closet, a double-vanity bath, and a private deck

■ Please specify a basement, slab, or crawl space foundation when ordering

MAIN FLOOR — 1,416 SQ. FT.
UPPER FLOOR — 1,056 SQ. FT.
GARAGE — 504 SQ. FT. OR
729 SQ. FT. WITH OPTION

TOTAL LIVING AREA:
2,472 SQ. FT.

© 1995 Donald A. Gardner Architects, Inc.

Designed for Today's Family

Price Code: E

■ This plan features:

— Three bedrooms

— Two full and one half baths

■ Volume and nine foot ceilings add elegance to a comfortable, open floor plan

■ Secluded Bedrooms designed for pleasant retreats at the end of the day

■ Airy Foyer topped by a vaulted dormer sends natural light streaming in

■ Formal Dining Room delineated from the Foyer by columns topped with a tray ceiling

■ Extra flexibility in the front Bedroom as it could double as a Study

■ Tray ceiling, skylights and a garden tub, in the Bath highlight the Master Suite

MAIN FLOOR — 2,192 SQ. FT.
GARAGE & STORAGE — 582 SQ. FT.
BONUS — 390 SQ. FT.

TOTAL LIVING AREA:
2,192 SQ. FT.

ZIP QUOTE
HOME COST CALCULATOR
see order pages for details

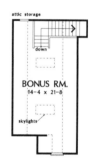

attic storage

down

BONUS RM.
14-4 x 21-8

skylights

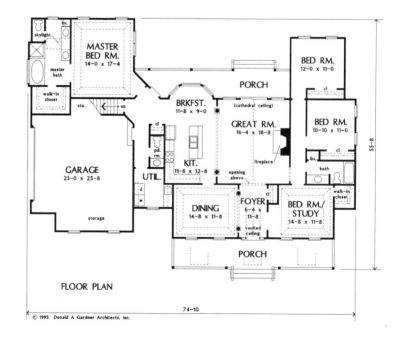

FLOOR PLAN

© 1995 Donald A Gardner Architects, Inc.

Spacious Living Room
PRICE CODE: D

■ This plan features:
— Four bedrooms
— Three full and one half baths
■ The spacious Living Room is topped by a decorative ceiling treatment and is enhanced by a corner fireplace
■ The Kitchen boasts a built-in desk and an angled counter/snack bar
■ There is direct access to the formal Dining Room and the Breakfast Nook from the Kitchen
■ The secluded Master Suite has two walk-in closets and a five-piece Bath
■ Three additional Bedrooms, located at the opposite side of the home, each have private access to the full Bath
■ An optional basement or a crawl space foundation — please specify when ordering

MAIN FLOOR — 2,483 SQ. FT.
GARAGE — 504 SQ. FT.

TOTAL LIVING AREA:
2,483 SQ. FT.

MAIN FLOOR

Country Influence
PRICE CODE: D

■ This plan features:
— Four bedrooms
— Two full and one half baths
■ An optional walk-out basement that can be included if built on a sloping lot
■ Master Bedroom located on the first floor and includes his-n-her walk-in closets and a roomy Bath
■ Optional basement space can be used as a Game Room/Media Room or a Home Office
■ No material list is available for this plan

FIRST FLOOR — 1,732 SQ. FT.
SECOND FLOOR — 818 SQ. FT.
BASEMENT — 592 SQ. FT.

TOTAL LIVING AREA:
2,550 SQ. FT.

SECOND FLOOR

GROUND FLOOR

WALK OUT BASEMENT PLAN

To order your Blueprints, call 1-800-235-5700

European Flavor
PRICE CODE: B

■ This plan features:
— Three bedrooms
— Two full baths
■ A covered entry reveals a foyer inside with a 14-foot ceiling
■ The Family Room has a vaulted ceiling, a fireplace, and a French door to the rear yard
■ The Breakfast Area has a tray ceiling and a bay of windows that overlooks the backyard
■ The Kitchen has every imaginable convenience including a walk-in Pantry
■ The Dining Room is delineated by columns and has a plant shelf above it
■ The privately located Master Suite has a tray ceiling, a walk in closet and a private Bath
■ Two other Bedrooms share a full Bath on the opposite side of the home
■ No materials list is available for this plan
■ An optional basement or crawl space foundation — please specify when ordering

MAIN FLOOR — 1,779 SQ. FT.
BASEMENT — 1,818 SQ. FT.
GARAGE — 499 SQ. FT.

TOTAL LIVING AREA:
1,779 SQ. FT.

© Frank Betz Associates

Brick Accents
and Dormer Windows
PRICE CODE: C

■ This plan features:
— Four bedrooms
— Two full and one half baths
■ A detailed Covered Porch leads into easy-care Entry
■ Formal Dining Room welcomes guests with decorative windows
■ A well integrated Family Room, Kitchen and Breakfast Area accommodate many family activities
■ A private Master Bedroom suite accented by a transom window and plush Bath with a whirlpool tub
■ Three secondary Bedrooms share a full Bath and an unfinished Storage Room

FIRST FLOOR — 1,348 SQ. FT.
SECOND FLOOR — 609 SQ. FT.
STORAGE ROOM — 341 SQ. FT.
BASEMENT — 1,348 SQ. FT.
GARAGE — 566 SQ. FT.

TOTAL LIVING AREA:
1,957 SQ. FT.

© design basics, inc.

SECOND FLOOR

FIRST FLOOR

To order your Blueprints, call 1-800-235-5700

© 1995 Donald A Gardner Architects, Inc.

ZIP QUOTE
HOME COST CALCULATOR
see order pages for details

Cathedral Ceiling

Price Code: C

■ This plan features:

— Four bedrooms

— Two full baths

■ Cathedral ceiling expanding the Great room, Dining Room and Kitchen

■ A versatile Bedroom or Study topped by a cathedral ceiling accented by double circle-top windows

■ Master Suite complete with a cathedral ceiling, including a Bath with a garden tub, linen closet and a walk-in closet

MAIN FLOOR — 1,417 SQ. FT.
GARAGE — 441 SQ. FT.

TOTAL LIVING AREA:
1,417 SQ. FT.

DECK

storage

DINING
11-0 x 11-2
(cathedral ceiling)

fireplace

GREAT RM.
16-4 x 15-0
(cathedral ceiling)

walk-in closet

MASTER BED RM.
12-4 x 15-0
(cathedral ceiling)

master bath

GARAGE
20-8 x 20-4

KIT.
10-8 x 11-6

FOYER
7-8 x 7-8

UTIL.

w d

cl

bath

lin.

cl

PORCH

cl

BED RM./STUDY
11-0 x 11-0
(cathedral ceiling)

BED RM.
12-4 x 11-0

FLOOR PLAN

8-0

39-0

69-0

© 1995 Donald A Gardner Architects, Inc.

To order your Blueprints, call 1-800-235-5700

295

© 1997 Donald A Gardner Architects, Inc.

Columns Punctuate the Interior Space

Price Code: E

■ This plan features:

— Three bedrooms

— Two full and one half baths

■ A two-story Great Room and two-story Foyer, both with dormer windows, welcome natural light into this graceful country classic with a wrap-around Porch

■ Large Kitchen, featuring a center cooking island with counter and large Breakfast Area, opens to the Great Room for easy entertaining

■ Columns punctuate the interior spaces and a separate Dining Room provides a formal touch to the plan

■ Master Bedroom suite, privately situated on the first floor, has a double vanity, garden tub, and separate shower

FIRST FLOOR — 1,618 SQ. FT.
SECOND FLOOR — 570 SQ. FT.
BONUS ROOM — 495 SQ. FT.
GARAGE & STORAGE — 649 SQ. FT.

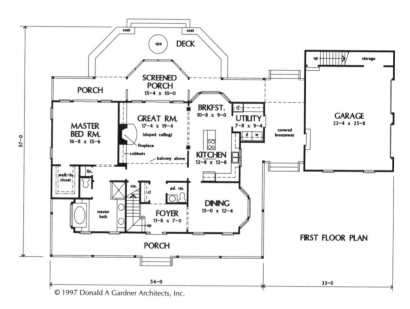

FIRST FLOOR PLAN

© 1997 Donald A Gardner Architects, Inc.

ZIP QUOTE
HOME COST CALCULATOR
see order pages for details

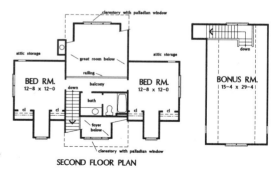

SECOND FLOOR PLAN

TOTAL LIVING AREA:
2,188 SQ. FT.

Above Expectations

Price Code: E

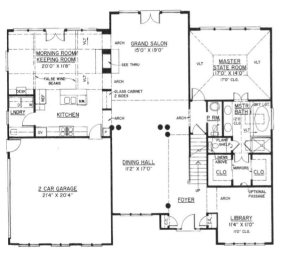

FIRST FLOOR
No. 98212

TOTAL LIVING AREA:
2,707 SQ. FT.

WIDTH 54'-4"
DEPTH 46'-4"

SECOND FLOOR

■ This plan features:

— Four bedrooms

— Three full and one half baths

■ The two-story Foyer leads through an arched opening to the Library on the right

■ The Dining Hall has a front and side wall the rest of the space is delineated by columns

■ The Grand Salon shares a fireplace with the Keeping Room that is entered through arched openings

■ From the Kitchen you may see into the Keeping Room with its beamed ceiling

■ The Master State Room has a vaulted ceiling, a walk-in closet and a luxurious bath

■ An optional basement or slab foundation — please specify when ordering

■ No materials list is available for this plan

FIRST FLOOR — 1,809 SQ. FT.
SECOND FLOOR — 898 SQ. FT.
BASEMENT — 1,809 SQ. FT.
GARAGE — 425 SQ. FT.

© 1995 Donald A. Gardner Architects, Inc.

Casually Elegant

Price Code: D

- This plan features:
- — Three bedrooms
- — Two full baths
- Arched windows, dormers and charming front and back Porches with columns creating Country flavoring
- Central Great Room topped by a cathedral ceiling, a fireplace and a clerestory window
- Breakfast Bay for casual dining is open to the Kitchen
- Columns accenting the entryway into the formal Dining Room
- Cathedral ceiling crowning the Master Bedroom
- Master Bath with skylights, whirlpool tub, shower, and a double vanity
- Two additional Bedrooms sharing a Bath located between the rooms

MAIN FLOOR — 1,561 SQ. FT.
GARAGE & STORAGE — 346 SQ. FT.

ZIP QUOTE
HOME COST CALCULATOR
see order pages for details

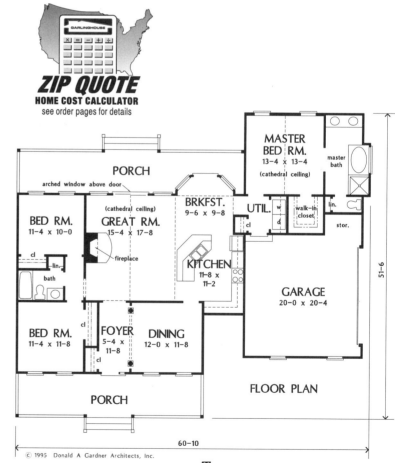

© 1995 Donald A Gardner Architects, Inc.

TOTAL LIVING AREA:
1,561 SQ. FT.

To order your Blueprints, call 1-800-235-5700

Fieldstone Facade and Arched Windows

PRICE CODE: C

This plan features:
- Three bedrooms
- Two full baths
- Inviting covered Porch shelters entrance
- Expansive Great Room enhanced by warm fireplace and three transom windows
- Breakfast Area adjoins Great Room giving a feeling of more space
- An efficient Kitchen with counter snack bar and nearby Laundry and Garage entry
- A first floor Master Bedroom suite with an arched window below a sloped ceiling and a double vanity Bath
- Two additional Bedrooms share a bonus area and a full Bath on the second floor

FIRST FLOOR — 1,405 SQ. FT.
SECOND FLOOR — 453 SQ. FT.
BONUS ROOM — 300 SQ. FT.
BASEMENT — 1,405 SQ. FT.
GARAGE — 490 SQ. FT.

TOTAL LIVING AREA:
1,858 SQ. FT.

ZIP QUOTE
HOME COST CALCULATOR
see order pages for details

FIRST FLOOR

SECOND FLOOR

© design basics, inc.

Traditional Look

PRICE CODE: C

This plan features:
- Three bedrooms
- Two full baths
- Foyer opens into formal Dining Room and dramatic Great Room with a fireplace framed by windows
- Country-size Kitchen with an island/snackbar, bright Breakfast Area, and nearby screen Porch and Laundry/Garage entry
- Comfortable Master Bedroom with a large walk-in closet and double vanity Bath with whirlpool tub
- Two additional Bedrooms with large closets, share full Bath
- No materials list is available for this plan

MAIN FLOOR — 2,176 SQ. FT.
GARAGE — 961 SQ. FT.
BASEMENT — 2,176 SQ. FT.

TOTAL LIVING AREA:
2,176 SQ. FT.

WIDTH 73'-0"
DEPTH 58'-8"

MAIN FLOOR

To order your Blueprints, call 1-800-235-5700

PLAN NO. 24911

Vintage America
PRICE CODE: E

- This plan features:
— Four bedrooms
— Two full and one half baths
- Wide front Porch framing the front of the home
- Huge Great Room opening through classic arches to the Kitchen and Breakfast Room
- Kitchen with all the amenities, a large work island complete with cooktop and raised eating bar
- Luxurious Master Suite with his-n-her vanities and closets
- A second large covered Porch at the rear of the home
- All Bedrooms feature picturesque dormer windows, perfect for a built-in window seat or toy box
- No materials list is available for this plan

FIRST FLOOR — 1,785 SQ. FT.
SECOND FLOOR — 830 SQ. FT.
BONUS ROOM — 280 SQ. FT.
GARAGE — 583 SQ. FT.

TOTAL LIVING AREA:
2,615 SQ. FT.

© Larry E. Belk

PLAN NO. 24311

Room for More
PRICE CODE: A

- This plan features:
— Two bedrooms
— Two full baths
- A Living Room with a fireplace and access to two Decks, expanding the outdoor living space
- An efficient Kitchen opening to the Dining Area
- A Master Bedroom, including a private Bath with a corner spa/ tub

MAIN AREA — 1,127 SQ. FT.

TOTAL LIVING AREA:
1,127 SQ. FT.

ZIP QUOTE
HOME COST CALCULATOR
see order pages for details

An
EXCLUSIVE DESIGN
By Marshall Associates

300

To order your Blueprints, call 1-800-235-5700

An Elegant and Stylish Manner

Price Code: C

■ This plan features:

— Three bedrooms

— Two full and one half baths

■ Brick trim, sidelights and a transom window at the front door

■ A high ceiling through the Foyer and Great Room

■ A cozy fireplace and a built-in entertainment center in the Great Room

■ Kitchen serving the formal Dining Room and the Breakfast Area

■ A whirlpool tub, shower stall, his-n-her vanities and a spacious walk-in closet in the Master Suite

■ Study Loft overlooking the Great Room

■ No materials list is available for this plan

FIRST FLOOR — 1,524 SQ. FT.
SECOND FLOOR — 558 SQ. FT.
BONUS — 267 SQ. FT.
BASEMENT — 1,460 SQ. FT.

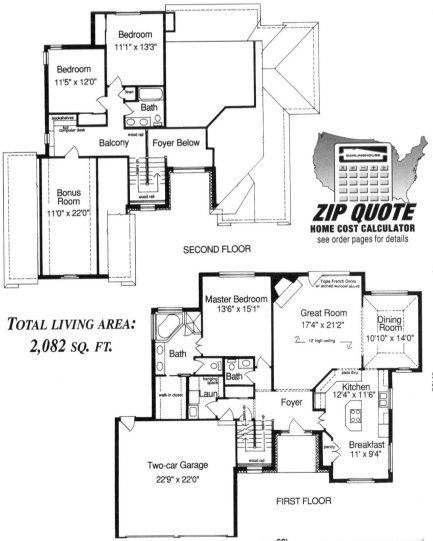

TOTAL LIVING AREA: 2,082 SQ. FT.

ZIP QUOTE
HOME COST CALCULATOR
see order pages for details

SECOND FLOOR

FIRST FLOOR

To order your Blueprints, call 1-800-235-5700

301

A Warm Welcome

Price Code: D

- ■ This plan features:
- — Three bedrooms
- — Two full and one half baths
- ■ An open Kitchen with a pantry, work island and bright Breakfast area
- ■ A vaulted ceiling in the Sun Room
- ■ A tray ceiling in the formal Dining Room with easy access to the Kitchen
- ■ A fireplace and a built-in wetbar in the informal Family Room
- ■ A vaulted ceiling in the Master Suite with his-n-her walk-in closets and double vanity Bath
- ■ A barrel vaulted ceiling in the front bedroom
- ■ A second floor Laundry Room

MAIN FLOOR — 1,336 SQ. FT.
UPPER FLOOR — 1,015 SQ. FT.
BASEMENT — 1,336 SQ. FT.
GARAGE — 496 SQ. FT.

TOTAL LIVING AREA:
2,351 SQ. FT.

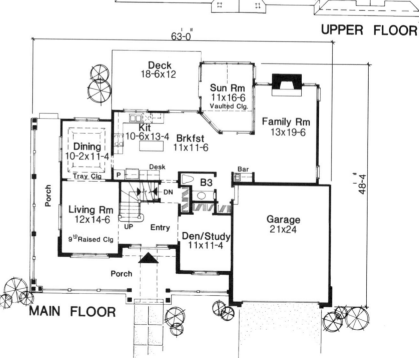

UPPER FLOOR

MAIN FLOOR

To order your Blueprints, call 1-800-235-5700

© 1995 Donald A Gardner Architects, Inc.

PLAN NO. 99858

ZIP QUOTE
HOME COST CALCULATOR
see order pages for details

TOTAL LIVING AREA:
1,253 SQ. FT.

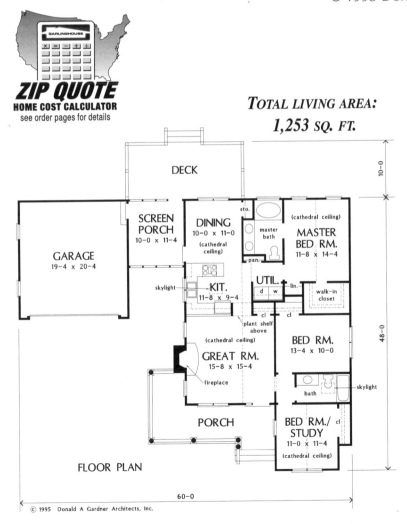

FLOOR PLAN

© 1995 Donald A Gardner Architects, Inc.

Amenities Normally Found In Larger Homes

Price Code: C

■ This plan features:

— Three bedrooms

— Two full baths

■ A continuous cathedral ceiling in the Great Room, Kitchen, and Dining Room giving a spacious feel to this efficient plan

■ Skylighted Kitchen with a seven foot high wall by the Great Room and a popular plant shelf

■ Master Suite opens up with a cathedral ceiling and contains walk-in and linen closets and a private Bath with garden tub and dual vanity

■ Cathedral ceiling as the crowning touch to the front Bedrooms/Study

MAIN FLOOR — 1,253 SQ. FT.
GARAGE & STORAGE — 420 SQ. FT.

To order your Blueprints, call 1-800-235-5700

303

Built-In Entertainment Center for Family Fun

Price Code: C

■ This plan features:

— Four bedrooms

— Two full and one half baths

■ A heat-circulating fireplace in the Living Room framed by decorative pilasters that support dropped beams

■ A convenient Mudroom providing access to the two-car Garage

■ A spacious Master Suite with a separate Dressing Area

FIRST FLOOR — 1,094 SQ. FT.
SECOND FLOOR — 936 SQ. FT.
BASEMENT — 1,022 SQ. FT.
GARAGE — 441 SQ. FT.

TOTAL LIVING AREA:
2,030 SQ. FT.

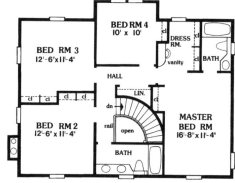

SECOND FLOOR PLAN

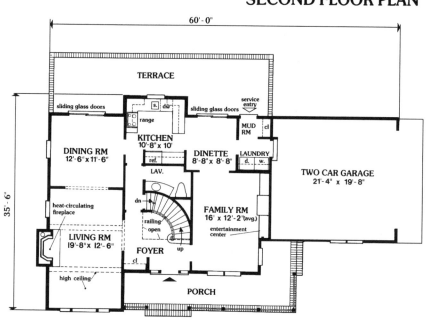

FIRST FLOOR PLAN

To order your Blueprints, call 1-800-235-5700

Keystone Accents

PRICE CODE: E

This plan features:
- Four bedrooms
- Two full and one three-quarter baths
- Welcoming entrance with sidelights and two-story Foyer with a lovely, landing staircase
- Open Living Room flows into Dining Room framed by columns and a step ceiling
- Convenient Kitchen with built-in Pantry, work island, Dining Area and access to back yard
- Expansive Family Room accented by columns and an inviting fireplace topped by a cathedral ceiling
- Private Study with closet offers multiple uses
- Spacious Master Bedroom with two closets and a pampering Bath
- Three additional Bedrooms share a full Bath and a Bonus Room
- No materials list is available for this plan

FIRST FLOOR — 1,431 SQ. FT.
SECOND FLOOR — 1,189 SQ. FT.
BONUS — 333 SQ. FT.
BASEMENT — 1,431 SQ. FT.
GARAGE — 476 SQ. FT.

TOTAL LIVING AREA: 2,620 SQ. FT.

Second floor

WIDTH 66'-0"
DEPTH 41'-0"

First floor

Friendly Front Porch

PRICE CODE: C

This plan features:
- Three bedrooms
- One full and one half baths
- Country, homey feeling with wrap-around Porch
- Adjoining Living Room and Dining Room creates spacious feeling
- Efficient Kitchen easily serves Dining Area with extended counter and a built-in Pantry
- Spacious Family Room with optional fireplace and access to Laundry/Garage entry
- Large Master Bedroom with a walk-in closet and access to a full Bath, offers a private Bath option
- Two additional bedrooms with ample closets and full Bath access
- No materials list is available for this plan

FIRST FLOOR — 900 SQ. FT.
SECOND FLOOR — 676 SQ. FT.
BASEMENT — 900 SQ. FT.
GARAGE — 448 SQ. FT.

TOTAL LIVING AREA: 1,576 SQ. FT.

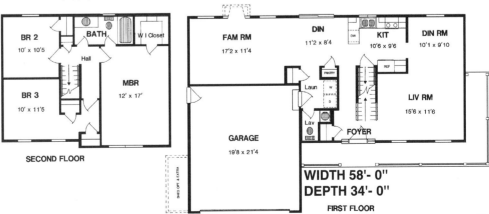

SECOND FLOOR

WIDTH 58'- 0"
DEPTH 34'- 0"

FIRST FLOOR

PLAN NO. 97108

Classic Ranch
PRICE CODE: B

- This plan features:
  - Three bedrooms
  - Two full baths
- A fabulous Great Room with a step ceiling and a cozy fireplace
- An elegant arched soffit connects the Great Room to the Dining Room
- The Kitchen has wrap-around counters, a center island and a Nook
- The Master Bedroom is completed with a walk-in closet and a private Bath
- Two additional Bedrooms with ample closet space share a full Bath
- No materials list is available for this plan

MAIN FLOOR — 1,794 SQ. FT.
BASEMENT — 1,794 SQ. FT.

TOTAL LIVING AREA:
1,794 SQ. FT.

MAIN FLOOR PLAN

PLAN NO. 93265

An EXCLUSIVE DESIGN
By Jannis Vann & Associates, Inc.

Plan for the Future
PRICE CODE: A

- This plan features:
  - Three bedrooms
  - Two full baths
- Entry leads up to Living Area accented by a vaulted ceiling and arched window
- Compact, efficient Kitchen with serving counter/snack-bar, serves Dining Area and Deck beyond
- Comfortable Master Bedroom with a walk-in closet and double vanity Bath with a window tub
- Two additional Bedrooms with large closets, share a full Bath
- Entry leads down to Laundry, Garage and future Playroom
- No materials list is available for this plan

MAIN FLOOR — 1,269 SQ. FT.
FINISHED STAIRCASE — 56 SQ. FT.
BASEMENT — 382 SQ. FT.
GARAGE — 598 SQ. FT.

TOTAL LIVING AREA:
1,325 SQ. FT.

FIRST FLOOR

SECOND FLOOR

ZIP QUOTE
HOME COST CALCULATOR
see order pages for details

306

To order your Blueprints, call 1-800-235-5700

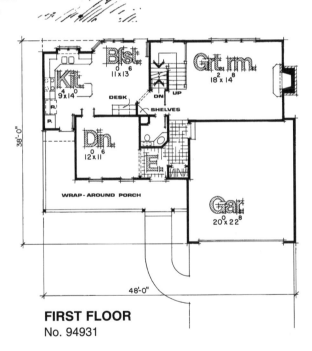

FIRST FLOOR
No. 94931

SECOND FLOOR

© design basics, inc.

Traditional Country Home

Price Code: C

■ This plan features:

— Four bedrooms

— Two full and one half baths

■ Wraparound Porch accesses tiled Entry and Kitchen

■ Expansive Great Room with triple window, inviting fireplace and landing staircase

■ Large Kitchen with built-in Pantry and desk, work island and bright Breakfast Area

■ Private Master Bedroom with decorative ceiling and deluxe Bath

■ Three secondary Bedrooms share a double vanity Bath

FIRST FLOOR — 927 SQ. FT.
SECOND FLOOR — 1,163 SQ. FT.
GARAGE — 463 SQ. FT.
BASEMENT — 927 SQ. FT.

TOTAL LIVING AREA:
2,090 SQ. FT.

To order your Blueprints, call 1-800-235-5700

© 1996 Donald A Gardner Architects, Inc.

Great As A Mountain Retreat

Price Code: D

ZIP QUOTE
HOME COST CALCULATOR
see order pages for details

■ This plan features:

— Three bedrooms

— Two full baths

■ Board and batten siding, stone, and stucco combine to give this popular plan a casual feel

■ User friendly Kitchen with huge pantry for ample storage and island counter

■ Casual family meals in sunny Breakfast bay; formal gatherings in the columned Dining area

■ Master Suite is topped by a deep tray ceiling, has a large walk-in closet, an extravagant private bath and direct access to back porch

MAIN FLOOR — 1,912 SQ. FT.
GARAGE — 580 SQ. FT.
BONUS — 398 SQ. FT.

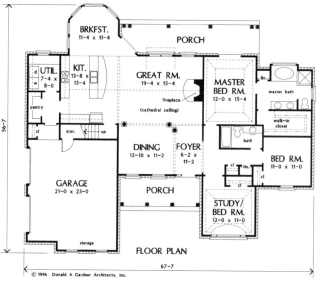

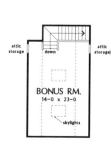

© 1996 Donald A Gardner Architects, Inc.

TOTAL LIVING AREA:
1,912 SQ. FT.

To order your Blueprints, call 1-800-235-5700

© 1992 Donald A Gardner Architects, Inc.

Classic Farmhouse

Price Code: C

- **This plan features:**
  - — Three bedrooms
  - — Two full and one half baths
- Covered Porch gives a classic country farmhouse look, and includes multiple dormers, a great layout for entertaining, and a bonus room
- Clerestory dormer window bathes the two-story Foyer in natural light
- Large Great Room with fireplace opens to the Dining/Breakfast /Kitchen space, which leads to a spacious Deck with optional Spa and seating for easy indoor/outdoor entertaining
- First floor Master Suite offers privacy and luxury with a separate shower, whirlpool tub, and a double vanity

FIRST FLOOR — 1,145 SQ. FT.
SECOND FLOOR — 518 SQ. FT.
BONUS ROOM — 380 SQ. FT.
GARAGE & STORAGE — 509 SQ. FT.

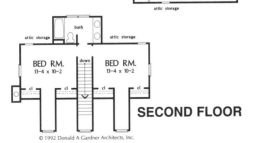

ZIP QUOTE
HOME COST CALCULATOR
see order pages for details

FIRST FLOOR

seat
spa
DECK
storage
GARAGE
21-0 x 21-8
BRKFST.
10-10 7-6
DINING
12-4 x 11-6
KITCHEN
13-2 x 8-2
pd. rm.
UTIL
walk-in closet
master bath
GREAT RM.
13-4 x 19-4
fireplace
MASTER BED RM.
13-4 X 13-0
up
PORCH
56-6
59-4
up

© 1992 Donald A Gardner Architects, Inc.

attic storage
skylights
down BONUS RM.
24-8 x 14-4
attic storage

attic storage
bath
attic storage
BED RM.
13-4 x 10-2
down
BED RM.
13-4 x 10-2
cl   cl   cl   cl

SECOND FLOOR

© 1992 Donald A Gardner Architects, Inc.

TOTAL LIVING AREA:
1,663 SQ. FT.

© Larry E. Belk

Inviting Elevation

Price Code: E

- ■ This plan features:
- — Four bedrooms
- — Three full baths
- ■ An angled see-through fireplace serves the Great Room, Breakfast Room and Kitchen
- ■ Kitchen has an abundance of cabinet and counter space, a walk-in Pantry and a built-in desk
- ■ The Master Suite is highlighted by a Sitting Area
- ■ The second Bedroom conveniently located on the first floor can used as a Guest Room, Nursery or Study
- ■ A large expandable area is available for future use
- ■ No material list is available for this plan

FIRST FLOOR — 2,028 sq. ft.
SECOND FLOOR — 558 sq. ft.
BONUS — 272 sq. ft.
GARAGE — 551 sq. ft.

TOTAL LIVING AREA:
2,586 SQ. FT.

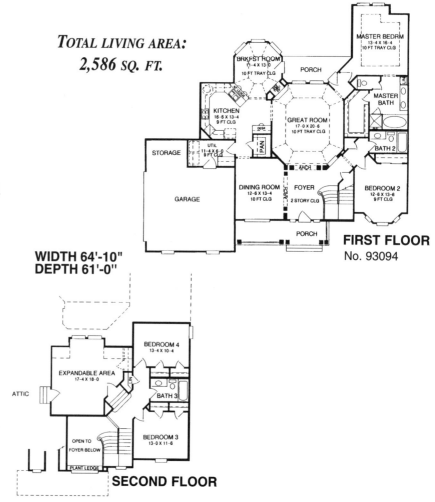

WIDTH 64'-10"
DEPTH 61'-0"

FIRST FLOOR
No. 93094

SECOND FLOOR

To order your Blueprints, call 1-800-235-5700

Many Amenities
PRICE CODE: A

■ This plan features:
– Three bedrooms
– Two full baths

■ A column supported covered entry greets you

■ Inside a tiled foyer with a vaulted ceiling leads to the Great Room

■ A corner fireplace and a wall of windows distinguished the Great Room

■ The Dining Room has a cathedral ceiling and an access door to the rear yard

■ Wrap-around counters provide working convenience in the Kitchen

■ The Master Bedroom is secluded and has an enormous walk-in closet

■ The secondary Bedrooms are located on the opposite side of the home

■ A two-car Garage completes this home

■ No material list is available for this plan

MAIN FLOOR — 1,416 SQ. FT.
BASEMENT — 1,416 SQ. FT.

TOTAL LIVING AREA:
1,416 SQ. FT.

MAIN FLOOR

For the Growing Family
PRICE CODE: C

■ This plan features:
– Three bedrooms
– Three full baths

■ Formal areas are located to either side of the impressive two-story Foyer

■ An open rail staircase adorning the Living Room while the Dining Room features easy access to the Kitchen

■ Kitchen equipped with a corner double sink and a wrap-around snack bar is open to the Family Room and Breakfast Area

■ Fireplace in the Family Room giving warmth and atmosphere to living space

■ Secondary Bedroom or Study privately located in the left rear corner of the home with direct access to a full Bath

■ Master Suite decorated by a tray ceiling in the Bedroom and a vaulted ceiling in the master Bath

FIRST FLOOR — 1,103 SQ. FT.
SECOND FLOOR — 759 SQ. FT.
BASEMENT — 1,103 SQ. FT.
GARAGE — 420 SQ. FT.

TOTAL LIVING AREA:
1,862 SQ. FT.

© Frank Betz Associates

FIRST FLOOR

SECOND FLOOR

Easy Living Ranch
PRICE CODE: B

■ This plan features:
— Three bedrooms
— Two full baths
■ Distinct exterior features, including vinyl siding, a series of gables, an arched window in the Dining Room and a protected front door with sidelights
■ Dining Room with a 14-foot ceiling
■ Directly behind the Dining Room is the Kitchen with a serving bar
■ Breakfast Area with easy access to the Great Room
■ Master Bedroom crowned in a tray ceiling
■ Master Bath including a large walk-in closet and separate shower and garden tub
■ No material list is available for this plan
MAIN FLOOR — 1,590 SQ. FT.

TOTAL LIVING AREA:
1,590 SQ. FT.

MAIN FLOOR

Pleasing to the Eye
PRICE CODE: E

■ This plan features:
— Four bedrooms
— Two full and one three-quarter baths
■ The attractive elevation of this home hides a luxurious interior
■ The Living Room has a fireplace, a vaulted ceiling, and is punctuated by columns
■ The Dining room has a wall of windows and is located convenient to the Kitchen
■ The Family Room also has a fireplace, but with book shelves set between it
■ The Breakfast Area is designed in a pretty bay shape
■ The Kitchen has plenty of space for multiple chefs
■ Three Bedrooms on the Second Floor share a Bath
■ The Master Suite has a vaulted ceiling and a Sitting Area
■ The Master Bath includes dual walk in closets and a whirlpool tub
■ There is no materials list available for this plan
FIRST FLOOR — 1,431 SQ. FT.
SECOND FLOOR — 1,335 SQ. FT.
BASEMENT — 1,431 SQ. FT.
GARAGE — 463 SQ. FT.

TOTAL LIVING AREA:
2,766 SQ. FT.

SECOND FLOOR

FIRST FLOOR

To order your Blueprints, call 1-800-235-5700

© design basics, inc.

Gar.
19⁸ x 23⁴

30'-0"

Kit.
9⁰ x 13⁶

Bfst.
10⁰ x 13⁰

COVERED PORCH

W. D.

SERVERY

R. P.

DN

Grt. rm.
14⁰ x 19⁴

Din.
14⁰ x 10⁰

UP

TRANSOM

STOOP

56'-0"

FIRST FLOOR
No. 94944

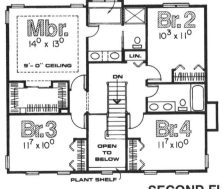

WHIRLPOOL

Mbr.
14⁰ x 13⁰

9'-0" CEILING

Br. 2
10³ x 11⁰

LIN.

DN

Br. 3
11⁷ x 10⁰

OPEN TO BELOW

Br. 4
11⁷ x 10⁰

PLANT SHELF

SECOND FLOOR

Spectacular Sophistication

Price Code: C

■ This plan features:

— Four bedrooms

— Two full and one half baths

■ Open Foyer with circular window and a plant shelf leads into the Dining Room

■ Great Room with an inviting fireplace and windows front and back

■ Open Kitchen has a work island and accesses the Breakfast Area

■ Master Bedroom features a nine-foot boxed ceiling, a walk-in closet and whirlpool Bath

■ Three additional Bedrooms share a full Bath with a double vanity

FIRST FLOOR — 941 SQ. FT.
SECOND FLOOR — 992 SQ. FT.
BASEMENT — 941 SQ. FT.
GARAGE — 480 SQ. FT.

TOTAL LIVING AREA:
1,933 SQ. FT.

Infinite Possibilities

Price Code: D

- This plan features:
  - — Three bedrooms
  - — Two full and one half baths
- A dramatic vaulted entry
- An arched floor-to-ceiling window, a vaulted ceiling, and a fireplace in the Living Room
- A formal Dining Room adjoining the Living Room
- An open layout between the Kitchen, eating Nook and the Family Room making for a spacious atmosphere
- A peninsula counter in the efficient Kitchen
- Direct access to the patio from the Family Room which also has a fireplace
- A Master Suite with a vaulted ceiling, walk-in closet and private Master Bath
- An optional basement, slab or crawl space foundation - please specify when ordering

FIRST FLOOR — 1,290 SQ. FT.
UPPER FLOOR — 932 SQ. FT.
BONUS ROOM — 228 SQ. FT.

TOTAL LIVING AREA:
2,222 SQ. FT.

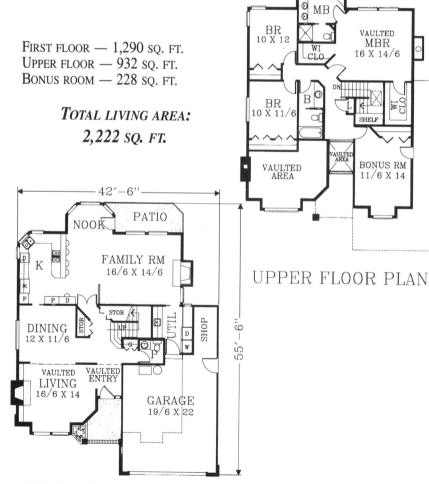

UPPER FLOOR PLAN

FIRST FLOOR PLAN

French Flavor

Price Code: E

- ■ This plan features:
- — Four bedrooms
- — Three full baths
- ■ Porch entry into open Foyer with a lovely, landing staircase
- ■ Elegant columns define Dining and Den area for gracious entertaining
- ■ Efficient, U-shaped Kitchen with a serving counter, Eating Bay, and nearby Utility Area and Garage
- ■ Decorative ceiling tops Master Bedroom offering a huge walk-in closet and plush Bath
- ■ Three additional Bedrooms with walk-in closets, access full Baths
- ■ An optional crawl space or slab foundation — please specify when ordering

FIRST FLOOR — 1,911 SQ. FT.
SECOND FLOOR — 579 SQ. FT.
GARAGE — 560 SQ. FT.

TOTAL LIVING AREA:
2,490 SQ. FT.

second floor

br 3
13⁶ x 12

WIDTH 57'-10"
DEPTH 56'-10"

br 4
12 x 12

open to foyer

first floor

porch
33 x 10

eating
14 x 10

util
8 x 10

kit
14 x 12

sto
6 x 8

den
19 x 20

mbr
14 x 16

garage
22 x 22

dining
12 x 14

foy

br 2
12 x 14

porch   4 x 21

Classic Exterior with Modern Interior

Price Code: C

- This plan features:
- — Three or four bedrooms
- — Two full and one half baths

- Front Porch leads into an open Foyer and Great Room

- An efficient Kitchen with a cooktop island, walk-in Pantry, a bright Dining Area and nearby Screened Porch, Laundry and Garage entry

- Deluxe Master Bedroom wing with a decorative ceiling, large walk-in closet and plush Bath

- Two or three Bedrooms on the second floor share a double vanity Bath

- No materials list is available for this plan

FIRST FLOOR — 1,348 SQ. FT.
SECOND FLOOR — 528 SQ. FT.
BASEMENT — 1,300 SQ. FT.
BONUS — 195 SQ. FT.

TOTAL LIVING AREA:
1,876 SQ. FT.

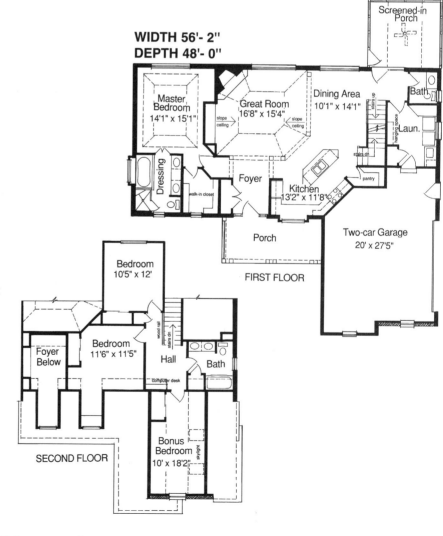

WIDTH 56'- 2"
DEPTH 48'- 0"

Screened-in Porch

Master Bedroom 14'1" x 15'1"

Great Room 16'8" x 15'4"

Dining Area 10'1" x 14'1"

Bath

slope ceiling

slope ceiling

Laun.

Dressing

Foyer

Kitchen 13'2" x 11'8"

pantry

walk-in closet

stairs dn

Porch

Two-car Garage 20' x 27'5"

FIRST FLOOR

Bedroom 10'5" x 12'

Foyer Below

Bedroom 11'6" x 11'5"

Hall

Bath

computer desk

wood rail

stairs dn

SECOND FLOOR

Bonus Bedroom 10' x 18'2"

skylight

To order your Blueprints, call 1-800-235-5700

Triple Arched Porch

PRICE CODE: B

PLAN NO. 98474

This plan features:
- Four bedrooms
- Three full baths
- A triple arched front porch, segmented arched window keystones and shutters accent the exterior
- An impressive two-story Foyer adjoins the elegant Dining Room
- The Family Room, Breakfast Room and Kitchen have an open layout
- The Study/Bedroom Floor is topped by a vaulted ceiling and is located close to a full Bath
- The Master Suite is topped by a tray ceiling while there is a vaulted ceiling over the Bath
- An optional Bonus Room offers expansion for future needs
- An optional basement or crawl space foundation — please specify when ordering
- No materials list is available for this plan

FIRST FLOOR — 972 SQ. FT.
SECOND FLOOR — 772 SQ. FT.
BONUS ROOM — 358 SQ. FT.
BASEMENT — 972 SQ. FT.
GARAGE — 520 SQ. FT.

TOTAL LIVING AREA:
1,744 SQ. FT.

© Frank Betz Associates

Rewards of Success

PRICE CODE: D

PLAN NO. 93254

This plan features:
- Three bedrooms
- Three full baths
- Formal areas, the Living Room and Dining Room, located in the front of the house, each enhanced by a bay window
- An expansive Family Room, including a fireplace flanked by windows, at the rear of the house
- An open layout between the Family Room, Breakfast Bay and the Kitchen
- A lavish Master Suite crowned by a decorative ceiling and pampered by a private Master Bath
- Two additional Bedrooms, one has use of a full hall Bath the other has a private Bath

FIRST FLOOR — 1,282 SQ. FT.
SECOND FLOOR — 1,227 SQ. FT.
BONUS ROOM — 314 SQ. FT.
GARAGE — 528 SQ. FT.
BASEMENT — 1,154 SQ. FT.

TOTAL LIVING AREA:
2,509 SQ. FT.

An
EXCLUSIVE DESIGN
By Jannis Vann & Associates, Inc.

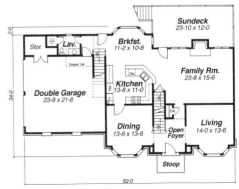

To order your Blueprints, call 1-800-235-5700

PLAN NO. 9403

Fabulous Family Room
PRICE CODE: B

■ This plan features:
— Three bedrooms
— Two full and one half baths
■ Attractive bay, transom and dormer windows add to appeal of this home
■ Split Entry leads up to an open, formal Living Room highlighted by a lovely, bay window and cozy fireplace
■ Convenient Dining Room opens to Living Room, Deck and Kitchen
■ Corner Master Bedroom features a walk-in closet and private bath
■ Two additional bedrooms with dormer windows and ample closets, share a full bath
■ Spacious Family Room with another bay window, fireplace and outdoor access, shares Lower level with Laundry and Garage
■ No materials list is available for this plan

MAIN FLOOR — 1,196 SQ. FT.
LOWER LEVEL — 486 SQ. FT.
DECK — 162 SQ. FT.
GARAGE — 715 SQ. FT.

TOTAL LIVING AREA:
1,682 SQ. FT.

WIDTH 44'- 0"
DEPTH 32'- 0"

MAIN FLOOR

LOWER LEVEL

PLAN NO. 94949

Quaint, Cozy Exterior
PRICE CODE: B

■ This plan features:
— Four bedrooms
— Two full and one half baths
■ Covered Porch leads into tiled Entry with banister staircase
■ Formal Dining Room doubles as a Parlor
■ Compact Kitchen serving counter/snackbar, Pantry and Breakfast Area with back yard access
■ Spacious Family Room with an inviting fireplace and triple window
■ Corner Master Bedroom offers a roomy walk-in closet and a pampering Path
■ Three additional Bedrooms with ample closets, share a full Bath

FIRST FLOOR — 866 SQ. FT.
SECOND FLOOR — 905 SQ. FT.
BASEMENT — 866 SQ. FT.
GARAGE — 541 SQ. FT.

TOTAL LIVING AREA:
1,771 SQ. FT.

© design basics, inc.

SECOND FLOOR

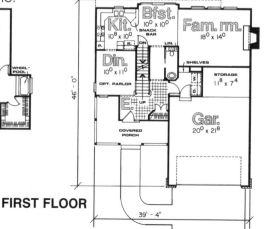

FIRST FLOOR

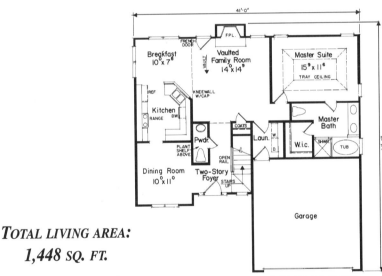

FIRST FLOOR
No. 96528

TOTAL LIVING AREA:
1,448 SQ. FT.

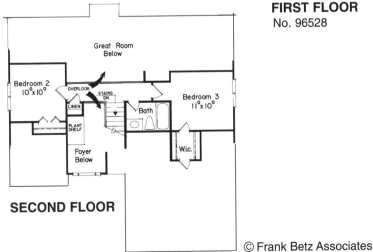

SECOND FLOOR

© Frank Betz Associates

Stylish Smaller Home
Price Code: A

■ This plan features:

— Three bedrooms

— Two full and one half baths

■ Two-story Foyer leads into the Family Room with a vaulted ceiling

■ A cozy atmosphere created by a fireplace in the Family Room

■ Breakfast Room adjoins the Family Room and the Kitchen

■ An extended counter adds to the work area of the Kitchen

■ A tray ceiling and a private master Bath in the Master Suite

■ Two additional Bedroom with ample closet space sharing the full Bath in the hall

■ An optional basement, crawl space or slab foundation — please specify when ordering

■ No materials list is available for this plan

FIRST FLOOR — 1,049 SQ. FT.
SECOND FLOOR — 399 SQ. FT.
BASEMENT — 1,051 SQ. FT.
GARAGE — 400 SQ. FT.

© 1996 Donald A. Gardner Architects, Inc.

Home Builders on a Budget

Price Code: C

ZIP QUOTE
HOME COST CALCULATOR
see order pages for details

- ■ This plan features:
- — Three bedrooms
- — Two full baths
- ■ Down-sized country plan for home builder on a budget
- ■ Columns punctuate open, one-level floor plan and connect Foyer with clerestory window dormers
- ■ Front Porch and large, rear Deck extend living space outdoors
- ■ Tray ceilings decorate Master Bedroom, Dining Room and Bedroom/Study
- ■ Private Master Bath features garden tub, double vanity, separate shower and skylights

MAIN FLOOR — 1,498 SQ. FT.
GARAGE & STORAGE — 427 SQ. FT.

TOTAL LIVING AREA:
1,498 SQ. FT.

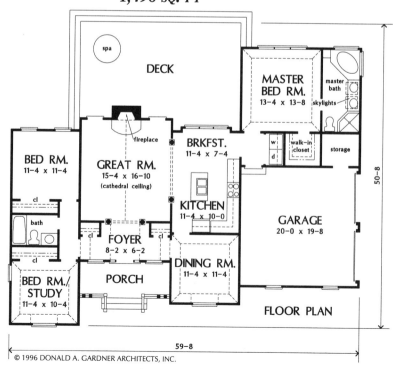

© 1996 DONALD A. GARDNER ARCHITECTS, INC.

To order your Blueprints, call 1-800-235-5700

©1994 Donald A. Gardner Architects, Inc.

Exciting Ceilings Add Appeal

Price Code: C

- This plan features:
  — Three bedrooms
  — Two full baths
- Open design enhanced by cathedral and tray ceilings above arched windows
- Foyer with columns defining Great Room with central fireplace and Deck access
- Cooktop island in Kitchen provides cooks with convenience and company
- Ultimate Master Bedroom suite offers walk-in closet, tray ceiling, and whirlpool bath
- Front Bedroom/Study offers multiple uses with tray ceiling and arched window

MAIN FLOOR — 1,475 SQ. FT.
GARAGE & STORAGE — 478 SQ. FT.

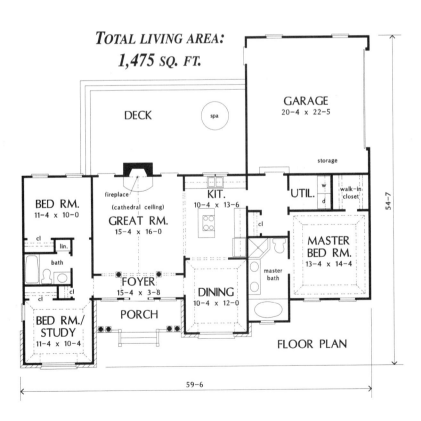

TOTAL LIVING AREA:
1,475 SQ. FT.

DECK

spa

GARAGE
20-4 x 22-5

storage

fireplace
(cathedral ceiling)

KIT.
10-4 x 13-6

UTIL.

w
d

walk-in
closet

BED RM.
11-4 x 10-0

cl   lin.

bath

GREAT RM.
15-4 x 16-0

cl

MASTER
BED RM.
13-4 x 14-4

master
bath

cl

FOYER
15-4 x 3-8

DINING
10-4 x 12-0

BED RM./
STUDY
11-4 x 10-4

PORCH

FLOOR PLAN

54-7

59-6

Spacious Family Living

Price Code: D

■ This plan features:

— Four bedrooms

— Two full and one half baths

■ Front Porch welcomes friends and family home

■ Entry opens to spacious Living Room with a tiered ceiling and Dining Room beyond

■ Hub Kitchen easily serves the Dining Room, the Breakfast bay and the Family Room

■ Corner Master Bedroom has access to a private Bath

■ Three additional Bedrooms share a double vanity Bath

FIRST FLOOR — 1,269 SQ. FT.
SECOND FLOOR — 1,034 SQ. FT.
BASEMENT — 1,269 SQ. FT.
GARAGE — 485 SQ. FT.

TOTAL LIVING AREA :
2,303 SQ. FT.

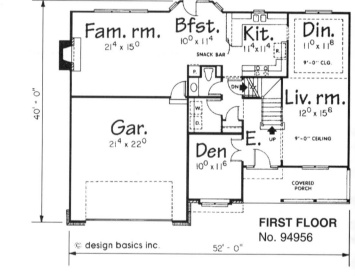

FIRST FLOOR
No. 94956

© design basics inc.

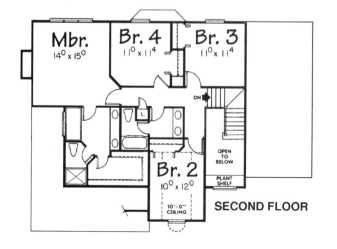

SECOND FLOOR

ZIP QUOTE
HOME COST CALCULATOR
see order pages for details

To order your Blueprints, call 1-800-235-5700

Family Get-Away

PRICE CODE: B

This plan features:

Three bedrooms

Two full and one half baths

A wrap-around Porch for views and visiting provides access into the Great Room and Dining Area

A spacious Great Room with a two-story ceiling and dormer window above a massive fireplace

A combination Dining/Kitchen with an island work area and breakfast bar opening to a Great Room and adjacent to the Laundry/Storage and half Bath area

A private two-story Master Bedroom with a dormer window, walk-in closet, double vanity Bath and optional Deck with hot tub

Two additional Bedrooms on the second floor sharing a full Bath

FIRST FLOOR — 1,061 SQ. FT.

SECOND FLOOR — 499 SQ. FT.

BASEMENT — 1,061 SQ. FT.

TOTAL LIVING AREA:
1,560 SQ. FT.

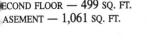

ZIP QUOTE
HOME COST CALCULATOR
see order pages for details

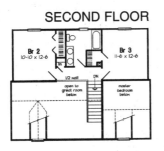
SECOND FLOOR

Alternate Foundation Plan

FIRST FLOOR

Balcony Overlooks
Living Room Below

PRICE CODE: A

This plan features:

- Three bedrooms
- Two full and one half baths
- A vaulted ceiling Living Room with a balcony above and a fireplace
- An efficient, well-equipped Kitchen with stovetop island and easy flow of traffic into the Dining Room
- A deck accessible from the Living Room
- A luxurious Master Suite with a bay window seat, walk-in closet, Dressing Area, and a private shower
- Two additional Bedrooms that share a full hall Bath

MAIN FLOOR — 674 SQ. FT.

UPPER FLOOR — 677 SQ. FT.

BASEMENT — 674 SQ. FT.

TOTAL LIVING AREA:
1,351 SQ. FT.

PLAN NO.90356

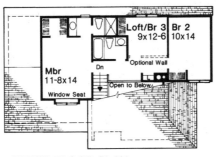
UPPER FLOOR PLAN

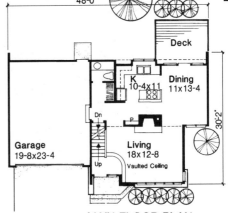
MAIN FLOOR PLAN

Refinement with Brilliancy
PRICE CODE: E

■ This plan features:
— Four bedrooms
— Three full baths
■ Two-story foyer dominated by an open rail staircase
■ Two story Family Room enhanced by a fireplace
■ Walk-in pantry and ample counter space highlighting the Breakfast room
■ Secluded Study easily becoming an additional bedroom with a private bath
■ Second floor Master Suite with tray ceiling, bayed sitting area and a vaulted ceiling over the private bath
■ An optional basement, slab or crawl space foundation – please specify when ordering
■ No material list is available for this plan

FIRST FLOOR — 1,548 SQ. FT.
SECOND FLOOR — 1,164 SQ. FT.
BONUS — 198 SQ. FT.
BASEMENT — 1,548 SQ. FT.
GARAGE — 542 SQ. FT.

TOTAL LIVING AREA:
2,712 SQ. FT.

PLAN NO. 24706

© Frank Betz Associates

FIRST FLOOR PLAN

SECOND FLOOR PLAN

Country Porch
Topped by Dormer
PRICE CODE: A

■ This plan features:
— Three bedrooms
— Two full baths
■ Front Porch offers outdoor living and leads into tiled entry and spacious Living Room with focal point fireplace
■ Side entrance leads into Utility Room and central Foyer with a landing staircase
■ Country-size Kitchen with cooktop island, bright Breakfast Area and access to Deck
■ Second floor Master Bedroom offers lovely dormer window, vaulted ceiling, walk-in closet and double vanity Bath
■ Two additional Bedrooms with ample closets, share a full Bath

FIRST FLOOR — 1,035 SQ. FT.
SECOND FLOOR — 435 SQ. FT.
BASEMENT — 1,018 SQ. FT.

TOTAL LIVING AREA:
1,470 SQ. FT.

FIRST FLOOR

Alternate Foundation Plan

SECOND FLOOR

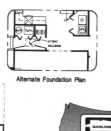

To order your Blueprints, call 1-800-235-5700

SECOND FLOOR

TOTAL LIVING AREA:
2,594 SQ. FT.

© design basics, inc.

FIRST FLOOR

WRAP-AROUND COVERED PORCH

56'-0"

Welcoming Wrap-Around Porch

Price Code: D

■ This plan features:

— Four bedrooms

— Two full and one half baths

■ Front Porch accesses tiled entry

■ Formal Living and Dining Rooms connected by French doors

■ Kitchen with serving counter/snackbar, pantry, Breakfast Area and Sun Room

■ Sunken Family Room with beamed ceiling and inviting fireplace

■ Master Bedroom with decorative ceiling and French doors into spacious Dressing Area with a whirlpool window tub and large walk-in closet

■ Three additional Bedrooms, one with an optional Play Area, share a double vanity Bath

FIRST FLOOR — 1,322 SQ. FT.
SECOND FLOOR — 1,272 SQ. FT.
BASEMENT — 1,322 SQ. FT.
GARAGE — 468 SQ. FT.

To order your Blueprints, call 1-800-235-5700

© 1993 Donald A. Gardner Architects, Inc.

B. NATHAN

Quaint and Cozy

Price Code: D

- ■ This plan features:
- — Three bedrooms
- — Two full and one half baths
- ■ Spacious floor plan with large Great Room crowned by cathedral ceiling
- ■ Central Kitchen with angled counter opens to the Breakfast Area and Great Room for easy entertaining
- ■ Privately located Master Bedroom has a cathedral ceiling and nearby access to the Deck with an optional Spa
- ■ Operable skylights over the tub accent the luxurious Master Bath
- ■ Bonus room over the Garage makes expanding easy
- ■ An optional crawl space or basement foundation—please specify when ordering

MAIN FLOOR — 1,864 SQ. FT.
GARAGE — 614 SQ. FT.
BONUS — 420 SQ. FT.

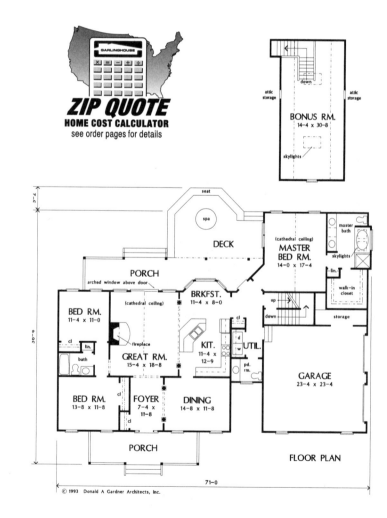

TOTAL LIVING AREA:

1,864 SQ. FT.

To order your Blueprints, call 1-800-235-5700

© 1997 Donald A Gardner Architects, Inc.

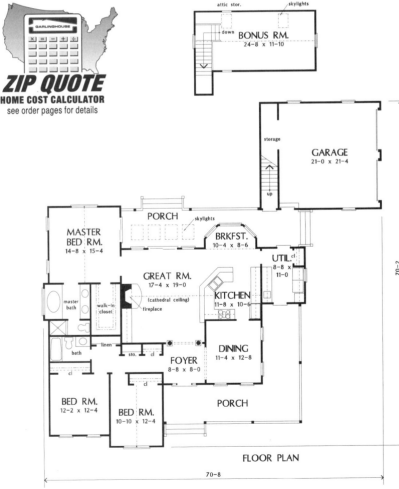

ZIP QUOTE
HOME COST CALCULATOR
see order pages for details

Country Style Home With Corner Porch

Price Code: D

■ This plan features:

— Three bedrooms

— Two full baths

■ Dining Room has four floor to ceiling windows that overlook front Porch

■ Great Room topped by a cathedral ceiling, enhanced by a fireplace, and sliding doors to the back Porch

■ Utility Room located near Kitchen and Breakfast Nook

■ Master Bedroom has a walk in closet and private Bath

■ Two additional Bedrooms with ample closet space share a full Bath

■ A skylight bonus room over the two-car Garage

MAIN FLOOR — 1,815 SQ. FT.
GARAGE — 522 SQ. FT.
BONUS — 336 SQ. FT.

TOTAL LIVING AREA:
1,815 SQ. FT.

© 1996 Donald A. Gardner Architects, Inc.

Compact Plan

Price Code: C

- This plan features:
- — Three bedrooms
- — Two full baths
- A Great Room topped by a cathedral ceiling, combining with the openness of the adjoining Dining Room and Kitchen, to create a spacious living area
- A bay window enlarging the Dining Room and a palladian window allowing ample light into the Great Room
- An efficient U-shaped Kitchen leading directly to the garage, convenient for unloading groceries
- A Master Suite highlighted by ample closet space and a private a skylit Bath enhanced by a dual vanity and a separate tub and shower

MAIN FLOOR — 1,372 SQ. FT.
GARAGE & STORAGE — 537 SQ. FT.

TOTAL LIVING AREA:
1,372 SQ. FT.

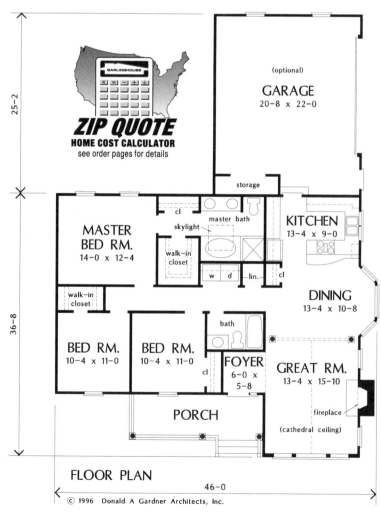

ZIP QUOTE
HOME COST CALCULATOR
see order pages for details

25–2

36–8

(optional)
GARAGE
20–8 x 22–0

storage

MASTER BED RM.
14–0 x 12–4

cl
skylight
master bath
walk-in closet
w d lin. cl

KITCHEN
13–4 x 9–0

walk-in closet

BED RM.
10–4 x 11–0

BED RM.
10–4 x 11–0

bath

FOYER
6–0 x 5–8

cl

DINING
13–4 x 10–8

GREAT RM.
13–4 x 15–10

fireplace

(cathedral ceiling)

PORCH

FLOOR PLAN

46–0

© 1996 Donald A Gardner Architects, Inc.

To order your Blueprints, call 1-800-235-5700

Inviting Front Porch

PRICE CODE: B

This plan features:

- Three bedrooms
- Two full and one half baths
- Detailed gables and inviting front Porch create a warm welcoming facade
- Open foyer features an angled staircase, a half Bath and a coat closet
- The expansive, informal living area at the rear of the home features a fireplace and opens onto the Sun Deck
- The efficient Kitchen has easy access to both the formal and informal Dining Areas
- Master Bedroom includes a walk-in closet and compartmented private Bath
- Two secondary Bedrooms share a Bath with a double vanity
- No materials list is available for this plan

FIRST FLOOR — 797 SQ. FT.

SECOND FLOOR — 886 SQ. FT.

BASEMENT — 797 SQ. FT.

GARAGE — 414 SQ. FT.

TOTAL LIVING AREA: 1,683 SQ. FT.

An EXCLUSIVE DESIGN
By Jannis Vann & Associates, Inc.

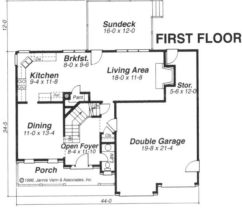

FIRST FLOOR

SECOND FLOOR

A-Frame for Year-Round Living

PRICE CODE: B

- This plan features:
- Three bedrooms
- One full and one three-quarter baths
- A vaulted ceiling in the Living Room with a massive fireplace
- A wrap-around Sun Deck that gives you a lot of outdoor living space
- A luxurious Master Suite complete with a walk-in closet, full Bath and private Deck
- Two additional Bedrooms that share a full hall Bath

MAIN FLOOR — 1,238 SQ. FT.

LOFT — 464 SQ. FT.

BASEMENT — 1,175 SQ. FT.

TOTAL LIVING AREA: 1,702 SQ. FT.

An EXCLUSIVE DESIGN
By Westhome Planners, Ltd.

WIDTH 34'-0"
DEPTH 56'-0"

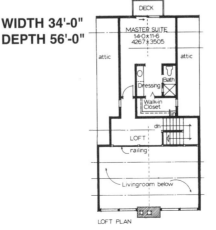

LOFT PLAN

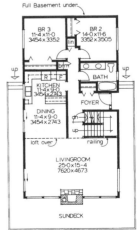

MAIN FLOOR

Open Space Living
PRICE CODE: B

- This plan features:
  — Three bedrooms
  — Two full and one half baths
- A wrap-around Deck providing outdoor living space, ideal for a sloping lot
- Two and a half-story glass wall and two separate atrium doors providing natural light for the Living/Dining Room area
- An efficient galley Kitchen with easy access to the Dining Area
- A Master Bedroom with a half Bath and ample closet space
- Another Bedroom on the first floor adjoins a full hall Bath
- A second floor Bedroom/Studio, with a private Deck, adjacent to a full hall bath and a Loft area

FIRST FLOOR — 1,086 SQ. FT.
SECOND FLOOR — 466 SQ. FT.
BASEMENT — 1,080 SQ. FT.

TOTAL LIVING AREA:
1,552 SQ. FT.

FIRST FLOOR

SECOND FLOOR

An
EXCLUSIVE DESIGN
By Westhome Planners, Ltd.

A Livable Home
PRICE CODE: E

- This plan features:
  — Four bedrooms
  — Two full, one three-quarter and one half baths
- The Master Bedroom is complete with a tray ceiling, two walk-in closets, and a large Bath
- Three additional Bedrooms upstairs, all have ample closet space and share two full Baths
- The Dining and Living rooms both have decorative windows that let in plenty of light
- The Family Room has a beamed ceiling and a fireplace
- This home has a three-car Garage with plenty of storage space
- No materials list is available for this plan

FIRST FLOOR — 1,400 SQ. FT.
SECOND FLOOR — 1,315 SQ. FT.
BASEMENT — 1,400 SQ. FT.
GARAGE — 631 SQ. FT.

TOTAL LIVING AREA:
2,715 SQ. FT.

© Carmichael & Dame

SECOND FLOOR

FIRST FLOOR

ZIP QUOTE
HOME COST CALCULATOR
see order pages for details

© 1990 Donald A. Gardner Architects, Inc.

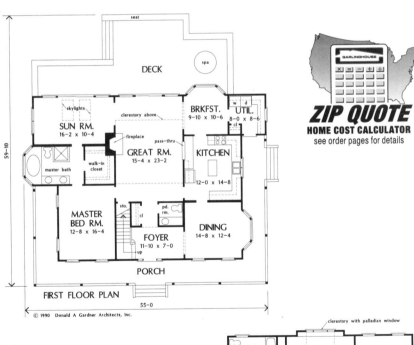

FIRST FLOOR PLAN

© 1990 Donald A Gardner Architects, Inc.

SECOND FLOOR PLAN

ZIP QUOTE
HOME COST CALCULATOR
see order pages for details

Stately Elegance

Price Code: F

■ This plan features:
— Four bedrooms

— Three full and one half baths

■ Impressive double gable roof with front and rear palladian windows and wrap-around Porch

■ Vaulted ceilings in two-story Foyer and Great Room accommodates Loft/Study Area

■ Spacious, first floor Master Bedroom suite offers walk-in closet and luxurious Bath

■ Living space expanded outdoors by wrap-around Porch and large Deck

■ Upstairs, one of three Bedrooms could be a second master suite

FIRST FLOOR — 1,734 SQ. FT.
SECOND FLOOR — 958 SQ. FT.

TOTAL LIVING AREA:
2,692 SQ. FT.

PLAN NO. 99424

Stately Exterior with an Open Interior

Price Code: E

■ This plan features:

— Four bedrooms

— Two full and one half baths

■ Open entry accented by a lovely landing staircase and access to quiet Study and formal Dining Room

■ Central Family Room with an inviting fireplace and a cathedral ceiling extending into Kitchen

■ Spacious Kitchen offers a work island/snackbar, built-in Pantry, glass Breakfast Area and nearby Porch, Utilities and Garage entry

■ Secluded Master Bedroom enhanced by a large walk-in closet and lavish Bath

■ No materials list is available for this plan

FIRST FLOOR — 1,906 SQ. FT.
SECOND FLOOR — 749 SQ. FT.
BASEMENT — 1,906 SQ. FT.
GARAGE — 682 SQ. FT.

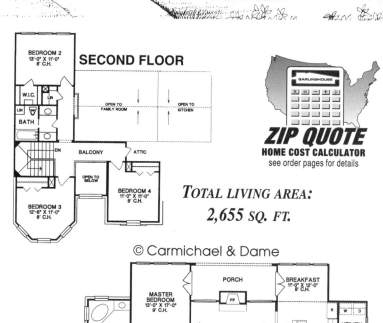

SECOND FLOOR

BEDROOM 2
13'-0" X 11'-0"
8' C.H.

W.I.C. LN

LN

BATH

DN   BALCONY   ATTIC

OPEN TO
BELOW

BEDROOM 3
12'-6" X 11'-0"
8' C.H.

OPEN TO
FAMILY ROOM

OPEN TO
KITCHEN

BEDROOM 4
11'-0" X 11'-0"
8' C.H.

ZIP QUOTE
HOME COST CALCULATOR
see order pages for details

TOTAL LIVING AREA:
2,655 SQ. FT.

© Carmichael & Dame

MASTER
BEDROOM
13'-0" X 17'-0"
9' C.H.

PORCH

FP

BREAKFAST
11'-0" X 12'-0"
9' C.H.

MASTER
BATH

FAMILY ROOM
19'-0" X 15'-0"
11'-19' C.H.

R W D

UTILITY

PWDR

KITCHEN
13'-4" X 15'-0"
11'-19' C.H.

SERV.
ENTRY PANT

MASTER
CLOSET

UP DN

GALLERY
9' C.H.

BUTLER'S

ENTRY
18' C.H.

DINING ROOM
11'-0" X 13'-0"
9' C.H.

57'-1 1/2"

STUDY
12'-6" X 13'-0"
9' C.H.

PORCH

3-CAR GARAGE
9' C.H.

FIRST FLOOR

65'-3"

332

To order your Blueprints, call 1-800-235-5700

© Frank Betz Associates

FIRST FLOOR
No. 97210

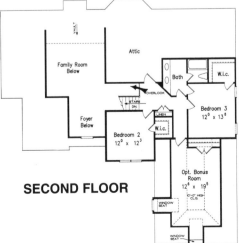

SECOND FLOOR

TOTAL LIVING AREA:
2,601 SQ. FT.

Notable Exterior

Price Code: E

■ This plan features:

— Four bedrooms

— Three full baths

■ Two story foyer adds a feeling of volume

■ Family Room topped by vaulted ceiling and accented by a fireplace

■ Formal Living Room with an eleven-foot ceiling

■ Private Master Suite with a five-piece Bath and a large walk-in closet

■ Rear Bedroom/Study located close a full bath

■ Two more Bedrooms on the second floor are close to a full Bath

■ No materials list is available for this plan

■ An optional basement or crawl space foundation — please specify when ordering

FIRST FLOOR — 2,003 SQ. FT.
SECOND FLOOR — 598 SQ. FT.
BONUS — 321 SQ. FT.
BASEMENT — 2,003 SQ. FT.
GARAGE — 546 SQ. FT.

To order your Blueprints, call 1-800-235-5700

Discriminating Taste

Price Code: C

- ■ This plan features:
- — Three bedrooms
- — Two full and one half baths
- ■ Inside, high ceilings and open spaces are featured
- ■ A fireplace warms the Kitchen, Breakfast Nook and Keeping Room
- ■ The Dining Room has sliding doors to the rear Patio
- ■ The Master Bedroom has been placed in a secluded location and has a private Bath
- ■ Two additional Bedrooms have walk in closets and share a full Bath
- ■ There is a two-car Garage with storage space
- ■ An optional basement or slab foundation — please specify when ordering
- ■ No materials list is available for this plan

MAIN FLOOR — 2,006 SQ. FT.
GARAGE — 376 SQ. FT.

WIDTH 46'-6"
DEPTH 65'-6"

MAIN FLOOR
No. 98222

TOTAL LIVING AREA:
2,006 SQ. FT.

To order your Blueprints, call 1-800-235-5700

Attention to Details
PRICE CODE: B

This plan features:
- Three bedrooms
- Two full and one half baths
- Foyer, Family Room, and Dining Room have 15'8" ceilings
- Breakfast Room and the Master Bath have vaulted ceilings
- Master Suite topped by a tray ceiling
- Arched openings to the Dining Room from the Family Room and Foyer
- Split Bedroom floor plan, affording additional privacy to the Master Suite
- Master Suite enhanced by a five-piece master Bath and a walk-in closet
- An optional basement or crawl space foundation — please specify when ordering
- No materials list is available for this plan

MAIN FLOOR — 1,575 SQ. FT.
BASEMENT — 1,612 SQ. FT.
GARAGE — 456 SQ. FT.

TOTAL LIVING AREA:
1,575 SQ. FT.

© Frank Betz Associates

Beautiful Arched Window
PRICE CODE: C

This plan features:
- Three bedrooms
- Two full baths
- Ten-foot ceilings topping the Entry and the Great Room
- A see-through fireplace is shared between the Great Room and the Hearth Room
- Built-in entertainment center and a bayed window highlighting the Hearth Room
- Breakfast Room and Hearth Room in an open layout separated by only a snack bar in the Kitchen
- Built-in Pantry and corner sinks enhancing efficiency in the Kitchen
- Split Bedroom plan assuring homeowner's privacy in the Master Suite which includes a decorative ceiling, private Bath and a large walk-in closet
- Two additional Bedrooms at the opposite side of the home share a full, skylit Bath in the hall

MAIN FLOOR — 1,911 SQ. FT.
GARAGE — 481 SQ. FT.

TOTAL LIVING AREA:
1,911 SQ. FT.

© design basics, inc.

MAIN FLOOR

To order your Blueprints, call 1-800-235-5700

A Very Distinctive Ranch
PRICE CODE: C

■ This plan features:
— Three bedrooms
— Two full and one half baths
■ This hip roofed ranch has an exterior mixing brick and siding
■ The recessed entrance has sidelights which work to create a formal Entry
■ The formal Dining Room has a butler's Pantry for added convenience
■ The Great Room features a vaulted ceiling and a fireplace for added atmosphere
■ The large open Kitchen has ample cupboard space and a spacious Breakfast Area
■ The Master Suite includes a walk-in closet, private Bath and an elegant bay window
■ A Laundry Room is on the Main Floor between the three-car Garage and the Kitchen

MAIN FLOOR — 1,947 SQ. FT.
BASEMENT — 1,947 SQ. FT.

TOTAL LIVING AREA:
1,947 SQ. FT.

MAIN FLOOR PLAN

Living Large
PRICE CODE: F

■ This plan features:
— Four bedrooms
— Three full and one half baths
■ A Box bay windows in the Dining room and the Parlor add character to this home
■ Inside the two-story Foyer find a grand staircase and columns to separate the space
■ The Family Room shares a see-through fireplace with the Parlor
■ The Kitchen is open to the interesting Breakfast Nook
■ The Master Bedroom has a sitting area with a fireplace as well as a sumptuous bath
■ Three large additional Bedrooms all have walk in closets
■ A three-car Garage completes this home plan
■ An optional basement or slab foundation available — please specify when ordering
■ No materials list is available for this plan

FIRST FLOOR — 1,597 SQ. FT.
SECOND FLOOR — 1,859 SQ. FT.
BONUS — 200 SQ. FT.
GARAGE — 694 SQ. FT.
BASEMENT — 1,597 SQ. FT.

TOTAL LIVING AREA:
3,456 SQ. FT.

FIRST FLOOR　　　**SECOND FLOOR**

To order your Blueprints, call 1-800-235-5700

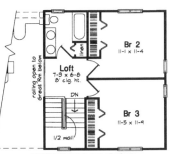

SECOND FLOOR

Br 2
11-1 x 11-4

Loft
7-3 x 6-8
8' clg. ht.

linen

railing open to
Great Rm below

DN

Br 3
11-5 x 11-9

1/2 wall

TOTAL LIVING AREA:
1,855 SQ. FT.

LOWER FLOOR

Railing

COV'RD
DECK
7-10 x 6-10

STORAGE

M.P. Tub

Glass Block

linen

MASTER
BR
11-10 x 15-0
Flat Clg. @ 8'

Dining Room Below

LOFT
7-10 x 11-4

Railing

Great Room Below

DN

STORAGE

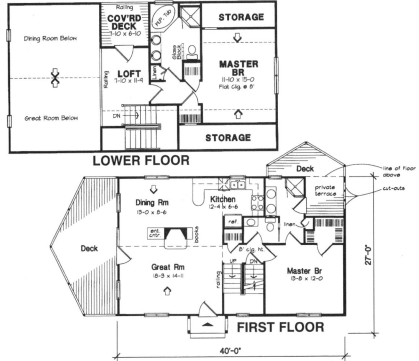

FIRST FLOOR

Deck

line of floor above

cut-outs

private terrace

Dining Rm
13-0 x 8-6

Kitchen
12-4 x 6-6

ref.

linen

ent. cntr.

books

8' clg. ht.

Deck

Great Rm
18-3 x 14-11

UP

DN

railing

Master Br
13-8 x 12-0

27'-0"

40'-0"

Spectacular Scenes

Price Code: C

- ■ This plan features:
- — Three bedrooms
- — Two full and one half baths

- ■ Covered Entry into exceptional Great Room and Dining Room with central fireplace, glass floor to vaulted ceiling and Deck access Room/Dining Room

- ■ Efficient Kitchen with a peninsula counter serving Dining Room

- ■ First floor Master Bedroom a private Deck, walk-in closet and double vanity Bath

- ■ Two second floor Bedrooms with large closets, share a double vanity Bath

- ■ Lower level Recreation Room with utilities, Unfinished Basement and Patio access

- ■ No materials list is available for this plan

FIRST FLOOR — 913 SQ. FT.
SECOND FLOOR — 516 SQ. FT.
LOWER FLOOR — 426 SQ. FT.
BASEMENT — 487 SQ. FT.

Ideal for a Sloping Lot

Price Code: B

- This plan features:
- — Three bedrooms
- — Two full baths
- Double French doors with arched transom windows access an elevated Deck
- Spacious feeling created by open Great Room, Dining area and Kitchen
- Two first floor bedrooms with ample closets, share a full bath
- Secluded Master Bedroom with Covered Deck, bath, storage and a Loft
- Lower level offers an optional Recreation Room with Patio, fireplace and wet bar
- No materials list available with this plan

FIRST FLOOR — 1,062 SQ. FT.
SECOND FLOOR — 500 SQ. FT.
OPTIONAL REC ROOM — 678 SQ. FT.
BASEMENT — 384 SQ. FT.

TOTAL LIVING AREA:
1,562 SQ. FT.

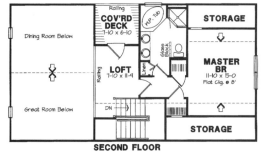

SECOND FLOOR

WIDTH 45'-5"
DEPTH 27'-0"

FIRST FLOOR

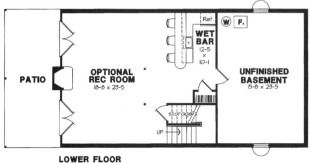

LOWER FLOOR

To order your Blueprints, call 1-800-235-5700

Country Home with Victorian Accents

Price Code: C

■ This plan features:

— Three bedrooms

— Two full and one half baths

■ Friendly front porch shelters entrance into Living and Dining rooms defined by columns and a cozy fireplace

■ L-shaped Kitchen with built-in planning desk and easy access to Dining Room, Family Room and Utility and Garage entry

■ Expansive Family Room with glass access to rear Deck

■ Master Bedroom highlighted by a lovely oval window above a window seat and book shelves, a double vanity bath and a large walk-in closet

■ Two additional bedrooms share full bath

■ No materials list is available for this plan

First Floor

FIRST FLOOR — 909 SQ. FT.
SECOND FLOOR — 913 SQ. FT.
GARAGE — 600 SQ. FT.
FOUNDATION — BASEMENT, SLAB OR CRAWL SPACE

TOTAL LIVING AREA:
1,822 SQ. FT.

Alternate Foundation Plan

Second Floor

Bricks and Arches
Detail this Ranch

Price Code: D

■ This plan features:

— Two bedrooms

— Two full and one half baths

■ A Master Bedroom with a vaulted ceiling, luxurious bath, complimented by a skylit walk-in closet

■ A second Bedroom shares a full Bath with the Den/optional Bedroom, which has built-in curio cabinets

■ Columns and arched windows define the elegant Dining Room

■ A Great Room shares a see-through fireplace with the Hearth Room, which also has a built-in entertainment center

■ A gazebo-shaped Nook opening into the Kitchen with a center island, snack bar and desk

MAIN FLOOR — 2,512 SQ. FT.
GARAGE — 783 SQ. FT.

TOTAL LIVING AREA:
2,512 SQ. FT.

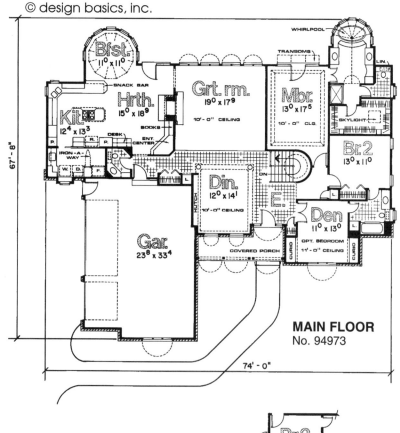

© design basics, inc.

MAIN FLOOR
No. 94973

OPTION

To order your Blueprints, call 1-800-235-5700

Luxurious Appointments

PRICE CODE: F

This plan features:

- Five bedrooms
- Four full and one half baths
- Formal areas located conveniently to promote elegant entertaining and family interaction
- Arched openings from the Foyer into the formal Dining Room and the Living Room
- Decorative columns highlighting the entrance to the Breakfast Room
- Two-Story ceiling topping the Family Room, highlighted by a fireplace
- Efficiency emphasized in the island Kitchen with a walk-in Pantry and abundant counter space
- Master Suite with lavish Bath topped by a vaulted ceiling
- An optional basement or crawl space foundation — please specify when ordering
- No material list is available for this plan

FIRST FLOOR — 1,527 SQ. FT.
SECOND FLOOR — 1,495 SQ. FT.
BASEMENT — 1,527 SQ. FT.
GARAGE — 440 SQ. FT.

TOTAL LIVING AREA:
3,022 SQ. FT.

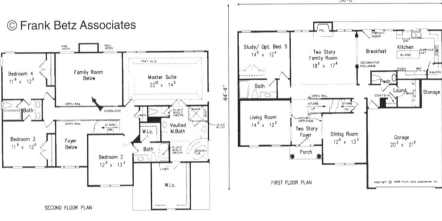

© Frank Betz Associates

Compact and Convenient Colonial

PRICE CODE: A

This plan features:

- Three bedrooms
- Two full and one half baths
- Traditional Entry with landing staircase, closet and powder room
- Living Room with focal point fireplace opens to formal Dining Room for ease in entertaining
- Efficient, L-shaped Kitchen with built-in Pantry, eating Nook and Garage entry
- Corner Master Bedroom with private Bath and attic access
- Two additional Bedrooms with ample closets share a double vanity Bath

FIRST FLOOR — 624 SQ. FT.
SECOND FLOOR — 624 SQ. FT.
GARAGE — 510 SQ. FT.

TOTAL LIVING AREA:
1,248 SQ. FT.

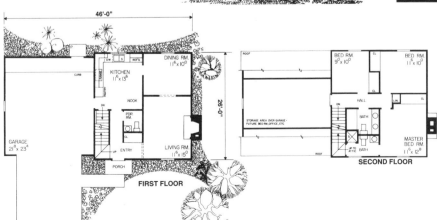

To order your Blueprints, call 1-800-235-5700

PLAN NO. 97213

Towering Windows
PRICE CODE: B

- This plan features:
  — Three bedrooms
  — Two full baths
- A wrap-around Deck above a three car garage with plenty of work/storage space
- Both the Dining and Living areas claim vaulted ceiling above French doors to the Deck
- A octagon-shaped Kitchen with a view, a cooktop peninsula and an open counter to the Dining area
- A Master Bedroom on the upper floor, with an over-sized closet, a private bath and an optional Loft
- Two additional bedrooms sharing a full hall bath
- An optional slab or crawlspace foundation — please specify when ordering
- No materials list is available for this plan

MAIN FLOOR — 1,329 SQ. FT.
UPPER FLOOR — 342 SQ. FT.
GARAGE — 885 SQ. FT.
DECK — 461 SQ. FT.

TOTAL LIVING AREA:
1,671 SQ. FT.

LOWER FLOOR

MAIN FLOOR PLAN

UPPER FLOOR

PLAN NO. 99238

Economical Vacation Home Provides Viewing Deck
PRICE CODE: A

- This plan features:
  — Three bedrooms
  — Two full baths
- A large rectangular Living Room with a fireplace at one end and plenty of room for separate activities at the other end
- A galley-style Kitchen with adjoining Dining area
- A second-floor Master Bedroom with a children's dormitory across the hall
- A second-floor deck outside the Master Bedroom

FIRST FLOOR — 784 SQ. FT.
SECOND FLOOR — 504 SQ. FT.

TOTAL LIVING AREA:
1,288 SQ. FT.

FIRST FLOOR

SECOND FLOOR

To order your Blueprints, call 1-800-235-5700

© Frank Betz Associates

43'-0"

RADIUS WDW.

Vaulted M. Bath

TRAY CLG.

Master Suite 11⁶ x 15⁰

FPL.

FRENCH DOOR

PLANT SHELF ABOVE

Vaulted Breakfast

VAULT

Vaulted Family Room 13⁷ x 18⁶

PLANT SHELF ABOVE

W.i.c.

PASS THRU

Kitchen

REF.

D.W. RANGE

33'-6"

Bath

LINEN

COATS

PAN.

Bedroom 3 11' x 10⁰

Bedroom 2 11' x 10⁰

STAIRS UP

STAIRS DN.

Foyer

Vaulted Dining Room 11⁵ x 11⁸

RADIUS WDW

UPPER FLOOR PLAN
No. 98487

TOTAL LIVING AREA:
1,401 SQ. FT.

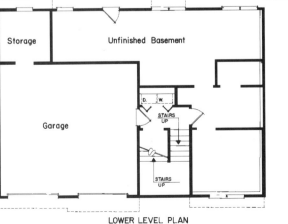

Storage

Unfinished Basement

Garage

D. W.

STAIRS UP

STAIRS UP

LOWER LEVEL PLAN

Voluminous Vaulted Ceilings

Price Code: A

■ This plan features:

— Three bedrooms

— Two full baths

■ The Dining Room, Family Room and Breakfast Nook have vaulted ceilings

■ The Family Room has a rear wall fireplace with a French door to one side

■ There is a plant shelf above the entrance to the Nook

■ With an angle at one end a new twist is placed on this galley style Kitchen

■ The Master Suite has a tray ceiling as well as a private Bath

■ Two identical Bedrooms are located next to each other and share a Bath in the hall

■ On the lower level find the garage and plenty of unfinished space

■ No materials list is available for this plan

UPPER FLOOR — 1,349 SQ. FT.
FINISHED STAIRCASE — 52 SQ. FT.
BASEMENT — 871 SQ. FT.
GARAGE — 478 SQ. FT.

To order your Blueprints, call 1-800-235-5700

First Floor Master Suite

Price Code: C

- This plan features:
- — Three bedrooms
- — Two full and one half baths
- The front Porch and dormer add to the country appeal of this home
- An elegant Dining Room is topped by a decorative ceiling and has direct Kitchen access
- The Kitchen/Breakfast Room includes a cooktop island and a vaulted ceiling
- The Great Room is accented by a vaulted ceiling and a fireplace
- A double door entrance, a box bay window and a vaulted ceiling are featured in the Master Suite
- Two additional Bedrooms share use of the full Bath in the hall

FIRST FLOOR — 1,490 SQ. FT.
SECOND FLOOR — 436 SQ. FT.
BASEMENT — 1,490 SQ. FT.
GARAGE — 400 SQ. FT.

TOTAL LIVING AREA:
1,926 SQ. FT.

FIRST FLOOR
No. 98357

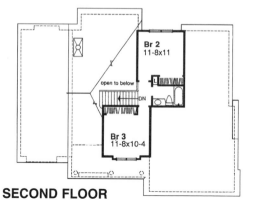

SECOND FLOOR

To order your Blueprints, call 1-800-235-5700

An
EXCLUSIVE DESIGN
By Patrick Morabito.
A.I.A. Architect

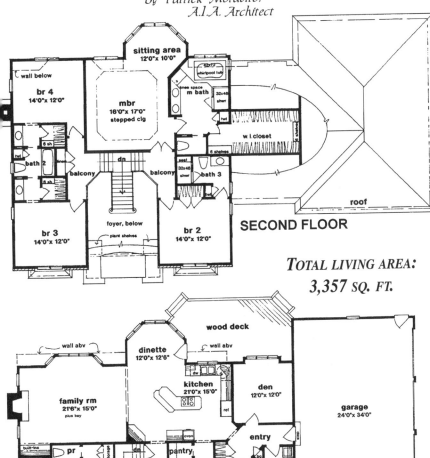

sitting area
12'0"x 10'0"

32x12
whirlpool tub

br 4
14'0"x 12'0"

knee space
m bath 32x48
shwr

mbr
16'0"x 17'0"
stepped clg

w.l.closet

6 shelves

bath 2
6 sh

balcony

balcony

seat
32x48
shwr
bath 3

roof

br 3
14'0"x 12'0"

foyer, below
plant shelves

br 2
14'0"x 12'0"

SECOND FLOOR

TOTAL LIVING AREA:
3,357 SQ. FT.

wood deck

dinette
12'0"x 12'6"

wall abv
wall abv

family rm
21'6"x 15'0"
plus bay

kitchen
21'0"x 15'0"

den
12'0"x 12'0"

garage
24'0"x 34'0"

built-ins
pr
built-ins
gas fireplace

pantry

entry

oven
ref

living rm
14'0"x 17'6"

foyer
high clg

dining rm
14'0"x 15'6"
stepped clg

laund
w
d

porch

(3) 9 ft garage door

porch

FIRST FLOOR
WIDTH= 77'-8"
DEPTH= 46'-0"

Exceptional Entrance

Price Code: F

■ This plan features:

— Four bedrooms

— Three full and one half baths

■ Grand Foyer with a transom window and banister staircase with balcony

■ Formal Living Room with a decorative window, fireplace and built-ins

■ Formal Dining Room accented by decorative ceiling and box window

■ Family Room with an inviting fireplace and beautiful bay window

■ Hub Kitchen with angled, cooktop island/snackbar, bright Dinette with Deck access and nearby Den, Laundry and Garage entry

■ Master Bedroom offers a stepped ceiling, glass Sitting Area, a whirlpool bath, and a large walk-in closet

■ No materials list is available for this plan

FIRST FLOOR — 1,880 SQ. FT.
SECOND FLOOR — 1,477 SQ. FT.
GARAGE — 816 SQ. FT.
BASEMENT — 1,880 SQ. FT.

345

Family Room with a Fireplace

Price Code: D

- This plan features:
  — Four bedrooms
  — Two full and one half baths
- An island Kitchen with a built-in Pantry, double sink and a convenient Dinette Area
- A cozy fireplace enhances the Family Room
- A formal Living Room and Dining Room
- A luxurious Master Suite with an ultra Bath and walk-in closet
- Three additional Bedrooms share a full hall Bath
- No materials list is available for this plan

FIRST FLOOR — 1,228 SQ. FT.
SECOND FLOOR — 1,191 SQ. FT.
BASEMENT — 1,228 SQ. FT.
GARAGE — 528 SQ. FT.

An EXCLUSIVE DESIGN
By Patrick Morabito,
A.I.A. Architect

FIRST FLOOR
No. 93319

TOTAL LIVING AREA:
2,419 SQ. FT.

SECOND FLOOR

To order your Blueprints, call 1-800-235-5700

Ten Foot Entry
PRICE CODE: B

This plan features:
- Three bedrooms
- Two full baths
- Large volume Great Room highlighted by a fireplace flanked by windows
- See-through wetbar enhancing the Breakfast Area and the Dining Room
- Decorative ceiling treatment giving elegance to the Dining Room
- Fully equipped Kitchen with a planning desk and a Pantry
- Roomy Master Bedroom has a volume ceiling and special amenities; a skylighted dressing Bath area, plant shelf, a large walk-in closet, a double vanity and a whirlpool tub
- Secondary Bedrooms with ample closets sharing a convenient hall Bath

MAIN FLOOR — 1,604 SQ. FT.
GARAGE — 466 SQ. FT.
FOUNDATION — BASEMENT ONLY

TOTAL LIVING AREA
1,604 SQ. FT.

© design basics, inc.

MAIN FLOOR

Welcoming Front Porch
PRICE CODE: D

This plan features:
- Three bedrooms
- Two full and one half baths
- The covered front Porch provides a warm welcome
- The Great Room has a fireplace with built in cabinets to one side
- Enter the nook through and arched soffit, the Kitchen is just beyond
- Access the screen Porch from the nook
- The Master Bedroom has a tray ceiling, a walk in closet, and a private Bath
- Located upstairs for privacy are the secondary Bedrooms
- This home has a three car Garage
- There is no materials list available for this plan

FIRST FLOOR — 1,835 SQ. FT.
SECOND FLOOR — 573 SQ. FT.
BASEMENT — 1,835 SQ. FT.

TOTAL LIVING AREA:
2,408 SQ. FT.

FIRST FLOOR

SECOND FLOOR

To order your Blueprints, call 1-800-235-5700

Country Charm
PRICE CODE: A

■ This plan features:
— Three bedrooms
— Two full baths

■ Ten-foot high ceilings in the Living Room, Family Room, and Dinette Area

■ A heat-circulating fireplace

■ A Master Bath with separate stall shower and whirlpool tub

■ A two-car Garage with access through a Mudroom

MAIN FLOOR — 1,203 SQ. FT.
BONUS AREA — 676 SQ. FT.
GARAGE — 509 SQ. FT.

TOTAL LIVING AREA:
1,203 SQ. FT.

MAIN FLOOR

45'-0"
Deck
Br 2 11x10
Br 3 10x10
Dining 10x10
Kit 10-6 x11
M. Suite 11x14-6 vaulted
Entry DN UP
Living 12x14-6 vaulted
26'-8"

LOWER FLOOR

Garage 23-6x21-8
Mechanical
Optional
UP
Bonus Space

Stunning Family Plan
PRICE CODE: C

■ This plan features:
— Four bedrooms
— Two full and one half baths

■ Windows, brick, and columns combine to create an eye-catching elevation

■ A pair of columns greets you as you enter the Living Room

■ The formal Dining Room is located just steps away from the Kitchen

■ Set on a unique angle the Family Room has a rear wall fireplace

■ The open Kitchen has a center island, which makes for easy meal prep

■ Set away from the active areas the Master Bedroom is a quiet retreat

■ Three additional Bedrooms are located in their own wing of the home

■ A Patio in the rear and a two-car Garage complete this home plan

■ No materials list is available for this plan

MAIN FLOOR — 2,194 SQ. FT.
GARAGE — 462 SQ. FT.

TOTAL LIVING AREA :
2,194 SQ. FT.

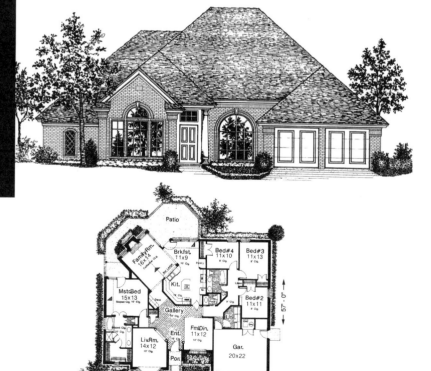

Floor Plan

Patio
FamilyRm. 16x14
Brkfst 11x9
Bed#4 11x10
Bed#3 11x13
MstrBed 15x13
Kit.
Bed#2 11x11
Gallery
Ent.
FmlDin. 11x12
Util.
LivRm. 14x12
Por.
Gar. 20x22
57'-0"
60'-0"

To order your Blueprints, call 1-800-235-5700

SECOND FLOOR

© design basics, inc.

FIRST FLOOR

ZIP QUOTE
HOME COST CALCULATOR
see order pages for details

Glorious Gables

Price Code: F

■ This plan features:

— Four bedrooms

— Two full, one three-quarter and one half baths

■ Arched ceiling topping decorative windows

■ Hub Kitchen with angled, work island/snackbar

■ Comfortable Family Room with hearth fireplace framed by decorative windows

■ Private Master Bedroom Suite offers a Sitting Area, two walk-in closets, and luxurious Bath

■ Three additional Bedrooms with ample closets and private access to a full Bath

FIRST FLOOR — 1,709 SQ. FT.
SECOND FLOOR — 1,597 SQ. FT.
GARAGE — 721 SQ. FT.
BASEMENT — 1,709 SQ. FT.

TOTAL LIVING AREA:
3,306 SQ. FT.

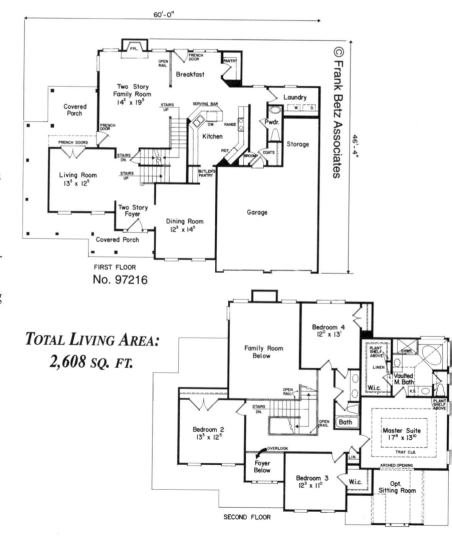

Two-Story Family Room

Price Code: E

■ This plan features:

— Four bedrooms

— Two full and one half baths

■ The Family Room has a fireplace and a French door to the Porch

■ The Breakfast Nook is separated from the Family Room by an open rail

■ The Kitchen features a convenient serving bar for quick meals and snacks

■ The hall from the Kitchen to the Dining Room has a butler's Pantry

■ The second floor Master Suite has a tray ceiling and an optional plan for a Sitting Area

■ No materials list is available for this plan

FIRST FLOOR — 1,351 SQ. FT.
SECOND FLOOR — 1,257 SQ. FT.
BONUS — 115 SQ. FT.
GARAGE — 511 SQ. FT.
BASEMENT — 1,351 SQ. FT.

60'-0"

© Frank Betz Associates

46'-4"

FPL
FRENCH DOOR
OPEN RAIL
PANTRY
Breakfast
Two Story Family Room 14² x 19³
Covered Porch
STAIRS UP
SERVING BAR
Laundry W. D.
FRENCH DOOR
D.W. RANGE
Pwdr.
Kitchen
Storage
FRENCH DOORS
STAIRS DN.
REF.
BROOM
COATS
Living Room 13³ x 12⁵
STAIRS UP
BUTLER'S PANTRY
Garage
Two Story Foyer
Dining Room 12³ x 14⁵
Covered Porch

FIRST FLOOR
No. 97216

TOTAL LIVING AREA: 2,608 SQ. FT.

Bedroom 4 12⁰ x 13¹
Family Room Below
PLANT SHELF ABOVE
LINEN
Vaulted M. Bath
W.i.c.
OPEN RAIL
STAIRS DN.
OPEN RAIL
Bath
PLANT SHELF ABOVE
Bedroom 2 13³ x 12⁵
Master Suite 17³ x 13¹⁰
OVERLOOK
TRAY CLG.
Foyer Below
LIN
ARCHED OPENING
Bedroom 3 12³ x 11¹⁰
W.i.c.
Opt. Sitting Room

SECOND FLOOR

To order your Blueprints, call 1-800-235-5700

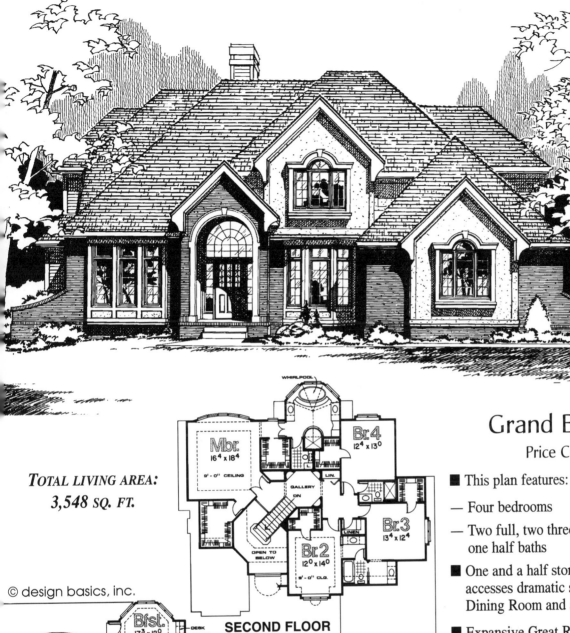

TOTAL LIVING AREA:
3,548 SQ. FT.

© design basics, inc.

SECOND FLOOR

FIRST FLOOR

Grand Entrance

Price Code: F

■ This plan features:

— Four bedrooms

— Two full, two three-quarter and one half baths

■ One and a half story, glass Entry accesses dramatic staircase, formal Dining Room and a Den

■ Expansive Great Room features a lovely bow window, raised hearth fireplace and wetbar

■ Convenient Kitchen with a bright Breakfast Bay, work island/snack bar,

■ Sumptuous Master Bedroom offers a bow window, two spacious walk-in closets and vanities

■ Three comfortable secondary Bedrooms with walk-in closets and private Bath access

MAIN FLOOR — 1,871 SQ. FT.
SECOND FLOOR — 1,677 SQ. FT.
BASEMENT — 1,871 SQ. FT.
GARAGE — 779 SQ. FT.

To order your Blueprints, call 1-800-235-5700

Timeless Beauty

Price Code: E

- ■ This plan features:
- — Four bedrooms
- — Two full, two three-quarter and one half bath
- ■ Two-story entry hall accesses formal Dining and Living room
- ■ Spacious Great Room with cathedral ceiling, fireplace between floor to ceiling windows
- ■ Ideal Kitchen with built-in desk and Pantry
- ■ Master Bedroom wing offers a decorative ceiling, and luxurious Dressing/Bath Area
- ■ Three second floor Bedrooms with roomy closets and private Baths

FIRST FLOOR — 2,063 SQ. FT.
SECOND FLOOR — 894 SQ. FT.
GARAGE — 666 SQ. FT.
BASEMENT — 2,063 SQ. FT.

TOTAL LIVING AREA:
2,957 SQ. FT.

© design basics, inc.

To order your Blueprints, call 1-800-235-5700

Expansive Windows Compliment Leisure Living

PRICE CODE: C

This plan features:
 Three bedrooms
 Three full baths
Wrap-around Deck expands Living outdoors and provides multiple access to Living Room
Impressive fieldstone fireplace with log holder warms Living/Dining Room below cathedral ceiling
Efficient L-shaped Kitchen with built-in counter table and Laundry with built-in Pantry
Master Bedroom suite with double windows and plush, double vanity Bath
Second Bedroom on first floor and another Bedroom on second floor each have access to full Baths
Side entrance into Vestibule with Gear Equipment Area and Foyer with two closetssw

FIRST FLOOR — 1,361 SQ. FT.
LOFT FLOOR — 453 SQ. FT.
BASEMENT — 694 SQ. FT.

TOTAL LIVING AREA:
1,814 SQ. FT.

Dramatic Windows and Gables

PRICE CODE: D

© 1991 Donald A. Gardner Architects, Inc.

This plan features:
– Three bedrooms
– Two full and one half baths
■ The barrel vaulted entrance is flanked by columns
■ Interior columns add elegance while visually dividing the Foyer from the Dining Room and the Great Room from the Kitchen
■ The Great Room is enlarged by its cathedral ceiling and a bank of windows
■ An angled center island and breakfast counter in the Kitchen
■ The first floor Master Suite has his-n-her closets plus a garden tub with skylight above
■ An optional basement or crawl space foundation — please specify when ordering

FIRST FLOOR — 1,416 SQ. FT.
SECOND FLOOR — 445 SQ. FT.
BONUS — 284 SQ. FT.
GARAGE — 485 SQ. FT.

TOTAL LIVING AREA:
1,861 SQ. FT.

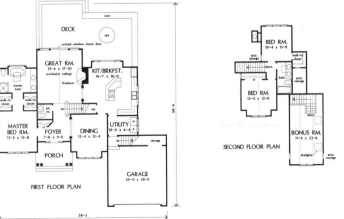

To order your Blueprints, call 1-800-235-5700

Small With Room To Grow

PRICE CODE: B

■ This plan features:
— Three bedrooms
— Two full baths
■ A Master Suite with a vaulted ceiling and its own skyli
  Bath
■ A fireplaced Living Room with a sloped ceiling
■ Efficient Kitchen with a Breakfast Nook
■ Options for growth on the lower level

MAIN FLOOR — 1,321 SQ. FT.
LOWER FLOOR — 286 SQ. FT.
GARAGE — 655 SQ. FT.

TOTAL LIVING AREA:
1,607 SQ. FT.

MAIN FLOOR

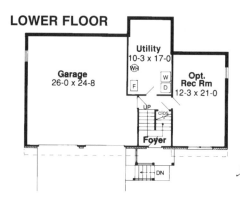

LOWER FLOOR

ZIP QUOTE
HOME COST CALCULATOR
see order pages for details

An
EXCLUSIVE DESIGN
By Karl Kreeger

© design basics, inc.

Grandeur Personified

PRICE CODE: F

■ This plan features:
— Four bedrooms
— Two full, one three- quarter and two half baths
■ A Master Bedroom topped by a decorative ceiling and a
  luxurious Bath
■ Upstairs, three additional Bedrooms with ample closet
  space and two full Baths
■ French doors and an arched window accenting the Den
■ A Dining Room with a built in hutch and an adjacent
  butler's Pantry
■ A Great Room with an 11-foot ceiling has bowed tran-
  som windows and a fireplace

FIRST FLOOR — 2,375 SQ. FT.
SECOND FLOOR — 1,073 SQ. FT.
BASEMENT — 2,375 SQ. FT.
GARAGE — 672 SQ. FT.

TOTAL LIVING AREA:
3,448 SQ. FT.

SECOND FLOOR

FIRST FLOOR

© Frank Betz Associates

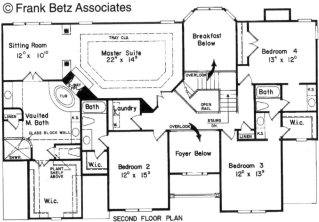

Sitting Room
12⁰ x 10¹⁰

TRAY CLG.

Master Suite
22⁴ x 14⁸

Breakfast
Below

Bedroom 4
13⁴ x 12⁰

3-WAY FPL.

OVERLOOK

Bath

Bath

LINEN

Vaulted
M. Bath

TUB

K.S.

Laundry

OPEN
RAIL

K.S.

GLASS BLOCK WALL

W.

STAIRS
DN.

W.i.c.

SHWR.

OVERLOOK

LINEN

K.S.

PLANT
SHELF
ABOVE

W.i.c.

Bedroom 2
12⁰ x 15³

Foyer Below

Bedroom 3
12⁰ x 13⁹

W.i.c.

SECOND FLOOR PLAN

Exquisite Detail

Price Code: F

■ This plan features:

— Four bedrooms

— Three full and one half baths

■ Two-story Foyer

■ Formal Living Room with access to Covered Porch

■ Radius windows and arches enhance Family Room

■ Kitchen with Pantry and cooktop/serving bar

■ Master Bedroom offers a tray ceiling and a cozy Sitting Room

■ An optional basement or crawl space foundation — please specify when ordering

FIRST FLOOR — 1,418 SQ. FT.
SECOND FLOOR — 1,844 SQ. FT.
BASEMENT — 1,418 SQ. FT.
GARAGE — 840 SQ. FT.

TOTAL LIVING AREA:
3,262 SQ. FT.

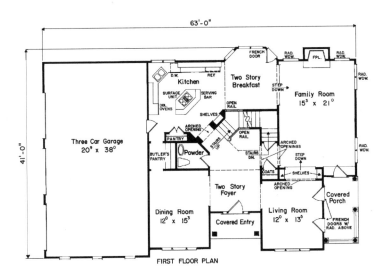

63'-0"

41'-0"

FRENCH
DOOR

RAD.
WDW.

FPL.

RAD.
WDW.

Kitchen

D.W.

REF.

Two Story
Breakfast

STEP
DOWN

RAD.
WDW.

Family Room
15³ x 21⁰

SURFACE
UNIT

SERVING
BAR

OPEN
RAIL

DBL.
OVENS

SHELVES

Three Car Garage
20⁹ x 38⁰

ARCHED
OPENING

PANTRY

OPEN
RAIL

STAIRS
UP

STAIRS
DN.

ARCHED
OPENINGS

RAD.
WDW.

BUTLER'S
PANTRY

Powder

STEP
DOWN

COATS

SHELVES

Two Story
Foyer

ARCHED
OPENING

Dining Room
12⁰ x 15³

Covered Entry

Living Room
12⁰ x 13⁶

Covered
Porch

FRENCH
DOORS W/
RAD. ABOVE

FIRST FLOOR PLAN

To order your Blueprints, call 1-800-235-5700

PLAN NO. 98401

Stately Structure

Price Code: F

■ This plan features:

— Five bedrooms

— Four full baths

■ Two-story Foyer with a banister staircase and decorative window

■ Two-story Family Room with a focal point fireplace framed by windows

■ Kitchen with a cooktop island/serving bar and nearby Dining Room

■ Elegant Master Bedroom offers a see-thru fireplace shared with Bath

■ Three additional Bedrooms with walk-in closets and private access to a full Bath

■ An optional basement or crawl space foundation — please specify when ordering

FIRST FLOOR — 1,665 SQ. FT.
SECOND FLOOR — 1,554 SQ. FT.
BASEMENT — 1,665 SQ. FT.
GARAGE — 462 SQ. FT.

TOTAL LIVING AREA:
3,219 SQ. FT.

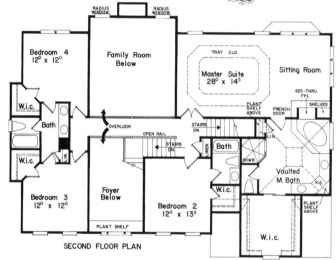

SECOND FLOOR PLAN

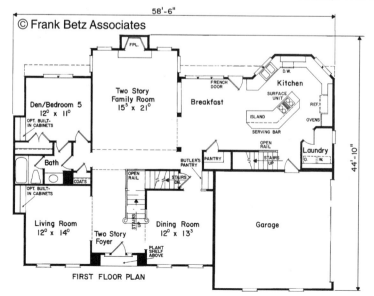

© Frank Betz Associates

FIRST FLOOR PLAN

356

To order your Blueprints, call 1-800-235-5700

A Grand Presence

PRICE CODE: F

This plan features:

Four bedrooms

Two full and one half baths

A gourmet Kitchen with a cooktop island and built-in
Pantry and planning desk

A formal Living Room with a fireplace that can be seen
from the Foyer

Pocket doors that separate the formal Dining Room from
the informal Dinette Area

A balcony overlooking the Family Room

An expansive Family Room with a fireplace and a
built-in entertainment center

A luxuriant Master Bath that highlights the Master Suite

Three additional Bedrooms that share use of a
compartmented full hall Bath

No materials list is available for this plan

FIRST FLOOR — 2,093 SQ. FT.

SECOND FLOOR — 1,527 SQ. FT.

BASEMENT — 2,093 SQ. FT.

GARAGE — 816 SQ. FT.

TOTAL LIVING AREA:
3,620 SQ. FT.

An
EXCLUSIVE DESIGN
By Patrick Morabito,
A.I.A. Architect

Home on a Hill

PRICE CODE: A

This plan features:

– Two bedrooms

– Two full baths

Sweeping panels of glass and a wood stove, creating
atmosphere for the Great Room

An open plan that draws the Kitchen into the warmth of
the Great Room's wood stove

A sleeping Loft that has a full Bath all to itself

MAIN FLOOR — 988 SQ. FT.

UPPER FLOOR — 366 SQ. FT.

BASEMENT — 742 SQ. FT.

GARAGE — 283 SQ. FT.

TOTAL LIVING AREA:
1,354 SQ. FT.

UPPER FLOOR PLAN

MAIN FLOOR PLAN

PLAN NO.98406

PLAN NO.91026

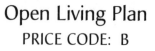

Open Living Plan
PRICE CODE: B

- This plan features:
  - Three bedrooms
  - Two full and one half baths
- Kitchen, Breakfast Bay, and Family Room blend into a spacious open living area
- Convenient Laundry Center is tucked into the rear of the Kitchen
- Luxurious Master Suite is topped by a tray ceiling while a vaulted ceiling is in the Bath
- Two roomy secondary Bedrooms share the full Bath in the hall
- An optional basement, crawl space or slab foundation - please specify when ordering

FIRST FLOOR — 828 SQ. FT.
SECOND FLOOR — 772 SQ. FT.
BASEMENT — 828 SQ. FT.
GARAGE — 473 SQ. FT.

TOTAL LIVING AREA:
1,600 SQ. FT

© Frank Betz Associates

52'-4"

Garage

Breakfast
W. D.
FRENCH DOOR

Family Room
17⁰ x 12⁸
FPL

Kitchen
RANGE
D.W.
PANTRY
REF.

Pwdr.

STAIRS UP
OPEN RAIL
STAIRS DN

COATS
NICHE

Dining Room
11' x 10⁰

Two Story Foyer

Living Room
11' x 10⁰

Covered Porch

34'-0"

FIRST FLOOR

SHWR
TUB
VAULT VAULT
Vaulted Master Bath
LINEN

TRAY CEILING
Master Suite
16⁹ x 12⁸

PLANT SHELF ABOVE
W.i.c.

Bath

STAIRS DN
OPEN RAIL

Bedroom 2
11⁸ x 10⁰

OVERLOOK
Foyer Below
PLANT SHELF

Bedroom 3
11' x 10⁰

PLANT SHELF

SECOND FLOOR

One Floor Comfort
PRICE CODE: B

- This plan features:
  - Three bedrooms
  - Two full baths
- Arched windows, keystones, and shutters highlight the exterior
- The Great Room and the Breakfast Nook feature vaulted ceilings
- There is direct access from the Dining Room to the Kitchen
- The Kitchen has a space saving Pantry and plenty of counter space
- Both secondary Bedrooms have spectacular front wall windows
- The Master Suite is enormous and features a glass walled Sitting Area
- A walk-in closet, a dual vanity and a whirlpool tub highlights the Master Bath
- This home has a convenient drive under Garage
- No materials list is available for this plan

MAIN FLOOR — 1,743 SQ. FT.
BASEMENT — 998 SQ. FT.
GARAGE — 763 SQ. FT.

TOTAL LIVING AREA:
1,743 SQ. FT.

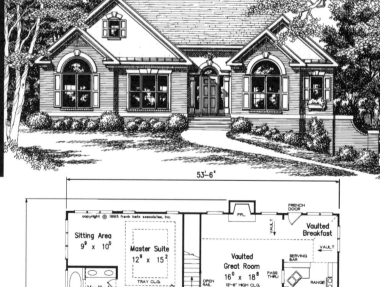

53'-6"

copyright © 1995 frank betz associates, inc.

Sitting Area
9⁹ x 10⁰

Master Suite
12⁹ x 15²
TRAY CLG.

Vaulted M.Bath
PLANT SHELF ABOVE
SHWR

W.i.c.

COATS
LINEN
LINEN

OPEN RAIL
STAIRS DN

Bath

FPL
FRENCH DOOR
VAULT
Vaulted Breakfast
VAULT

Vaulted Great Room
16⁰ x 18⁸
13'-6" HIGH CLG.

SERVING BAR
PASS THRU

Kitchen
RANGE
DW.
REF.

Foyer
13'-6" HIGH CLG.

PANTRY

Dining Room
11⁵ x 12⁰
11'-0" HIGH CLG.

Laun.
VLT
VLT

39'-4"

Vaulted Bedroom 2
12⁴ x 11²
11'-0" HIGH CLG.
VLT.

Bedroom 3
11⁰ x 11²
VLT.

MAIN FLOOR

© Frank Betz Associates

To order your Blueprints, call 1-800-235-5700

© Frank Betz Associates

Stately Stone and Stucco

Price Code: F

- ■ This plan features:
- — Four bedrooms
- — Three full and one half baths
- ■ Two story Foyer with angled staircase
- ■ Expansive two story Great Room enhanced by a fireplace
- ■ Convenient Kitchen with a cooktop island
- ■ Open Keeping Room accented by a wall of windows and backyard access
- ■ Master Suite wing offers a tray ceiling, a plush Bath and roomy walk-in closet
- ■ An optional basement, slab or crawl space foundation — please specify when ordering

FIRST FLOOR — 2,130 SQ. FT.
SECOND FLOOR — 897 SQ. FT.
BASEMENT — 2,130 SQ. FT.
GARAGE — 494 SQ. FT.

TOTAL LIVING AREA:
3,027 SQ. FT.

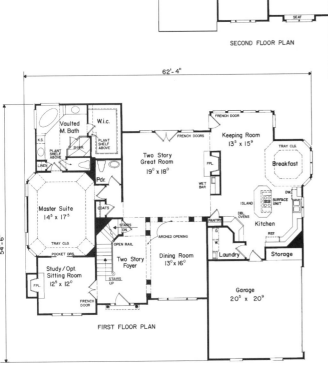

© Frank Betz Associates

Luxurious Yet Cozy

Price Code: F

■ This plan features:

— Four bedrooms

— Three full and one half baths

■ Covered Porch leads into two-story Foyer and Living Room

■ Decorative columns define Dining Room and Great Room

■ Open and convenient Kitchen with a work island

■ Corner Master Suite includes a cozy fireplace

■ Three second floor Bedrooms with walk-in closets

■ An optional basement, slab or crawl space foundation — please specify when ordering

FIRST FLOOR — 2,467 SQ. FT.
SECOND FLOOR — 928 SQ. FT.
BONUS — 296 SQ. FT.
BASEMENT — 2,467 SQ. FT.
GARAGE — 566 SQ. FT.

TOTAL LIVING AREA:
3,395 SQ. FT.

SECOND FLOOR

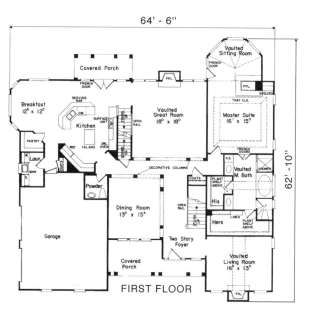

FIRST FLOOR

To order your Blueprints, call 1-800-235-5700

Amenities Galore
and Room to Grow
PRICE CODE: A

This plan features:
- Three bedrooms (future five)
- Two full baths (future three)
- A front door Porch that shelters your arrival and adds a traditional flavor
- A Foyer stairway that ascends to a unique and spacious Living/Dining Room
- An L-shaped Kitchen complete with built-in Pantry, double sink, and a convenient snack bar for informal meals
- A Covered Sun Deck accessed by both Kitchen and Dining Room extending entertainment possibilities
- A large Master Suite with a walk-in closet and private full Bath
- A basement ready to finish into a spacious Family Room, two additional bedrooms, and a Bath/Utility Room

Main Area — 1,269 SQ. FT.
Basement — 1,034 SQ. FT.
Garage — 462 SQ. FT.

TOTAL LIVING AREA:
1,269 SQ. FT.

An
EXCLUSIVE DESIGN
By Westhome Planners, Ltd.

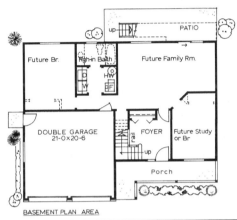

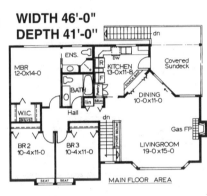

WIDTH 46'-0"
DEPTH 41'-0"

Spectacular Curving
Stairway
PRICE CODE: E

This plan features:
- Four bedrooms
- Two full, one three-quarter and one half baths
- Spacious formal entry with arched transom, is enhanced by curved staircase
- Great Room is inviting with a cozy fireplace, a wetbar and triple arched windows
- Open Kitchen, Breakfast and Hearth area combine efficiency and comfort for all
- Master Bedroom retreat offers a private back door, a double walk-in closet and a whirlpool Bath
- Generous closets and Baths enhance the three second floor Bedrooms

First Floor — 2,252 SQ. FT.
Second Floor — 920 SQ. FT.
Basement — 2,252 SQ. FT.
Garage — 646 SQ. FT.

TOTAL LIVING AREA:
3,172 SQ. FT.

© design basics, inc.

ZIP QUOTE
HOME COST CALCULATOR
see order pages for details

SECOND FLOOR

FIRST FLOOR

Living Room Features
Exposed Beams
PRICE CODE: C

- This plan features:
  - Three bedrooms
  - Two full baths
- A covered Porch shelters the entry to this home
- The large Living room with exposed beams includes a fireplace and built-ins
- The bright Dining Room is located next to the Kitchen which features a center island
- The Bedroom wing features three spacious Bedrooms and two full Baths
- The two-car Garage has a handy Workshop Area
- An optional crawl space or slab foundation available — please specify when ordering
- No materials list is available for this plan

MAIN FLOOR — 1,876 SQ. FT.
GARAGE — 619 SQ. FT.

TOTAL LIVING AREA:
1,876 SQ. FT.

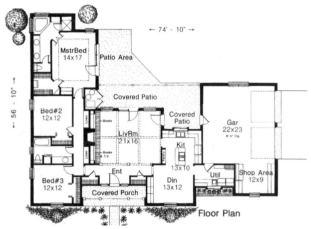

Floor Plan

Country Elegance
PRICE CODE: B

- This plan features:
  - Three bedrooms
  - Two full and one half baths
- Welcoming front Porch leads into open entry with landing staircase and convenient closet
- Expansive Living Room/Dining Area highlighted by multiple windows front and back
- Comfortable Family Room with gas fireplace, sliding glass door to Patio and adjoining Kitchen, Laundry and Garage
- Efficient U-shaped Kitchen with built-in desk and eating bar
- Private Master Bedroom with an arched window and plush Bath and walk-in closet
- Two additional Bedrooms with large closets share a full Bath
- Bonus room with another arched window and storage space offers many options
- No materials list is available for this plan

FIRST FLOOR — 913 SQ. FT.
SECOND FLOOR — 771 SQ. FT.
GARAGE — 483 SQ. FT.

TOTAL LIVING AREA:
1,684 SQ. FT.

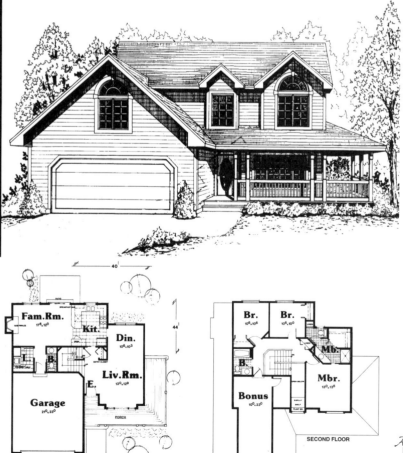

MAIN AREA

SECOND FLOOR

An
EXCLUSIVE DESIGN
By Independent Designs

To order your Blueprints, call 1-800-235-5700

An
EXCLUSIVE DESIGN
By Patrick Morabito,
A.I.A. Architect

FIRST FLOOR
WIDTH= 63'-0"
DEPTH= 47'-0"

TOTAL LIVING AREA:
1,961 SQ. FT.

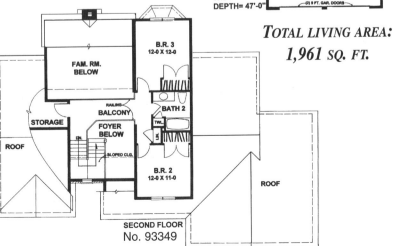

SECOND FLOOR
No. 93349

Conventional and Classic Comfort

Price Code: C

■ This plan features:

— Three bedrooms

— Two full and one half baths

■ Cozy Porch accesses two-story Foyer with decorative window

■ Formal Dining Room accented by a recessed window adjoins Kitchen

■ Spacious Family Room crowned by a vaulted ceiling over a hearth fireplace

■ Efficient Kitchen with an extended counter/eating bar and bright Dinette Area with bay window and access to Deck

■ Convenient Laundry, Powder Room and Garage entry near Kitchen

■ First floor Master Bedroom with walk-in closet and Master Bath with double vanity

■ Two additional Bedrooms and a full bath complete second floor

FIRST FLOOR — 1,454 SQ. FT.
SECOND FLOOR — 507 SQ. FT.
BASEMENT — 1,454 SQ. FT.
GARAGE — 624 SQ. FT.

© Frank Betz Associates

Regal Residence

Price Code: F

■ This plan features:

— Five bedrooms

— Four full baths

■ Keystone, arched windows accent entrance into two-story Foyer

■ Spacious Family Room is enhanced by a fireplace

■ Kitchen with a cooktop island/serving bar and a walk-in Pantry

■ First floor Guest Room/Study adjoins a full Bath

■ Master Suite offers a tray ceiling and a vaulted Bath with a radius window

■ Three additional Bedrooms have walk-in closets

■ An optional basement or crawl space foundation — please specify when ordering

FIRST FLOOR — 1,488 SQ. FT.
SECOND FLOOR — 1,551 SQ. FT.
BASEMENT — 1,488 SQ. FT.
GARAGE — 667 SQ. FT.

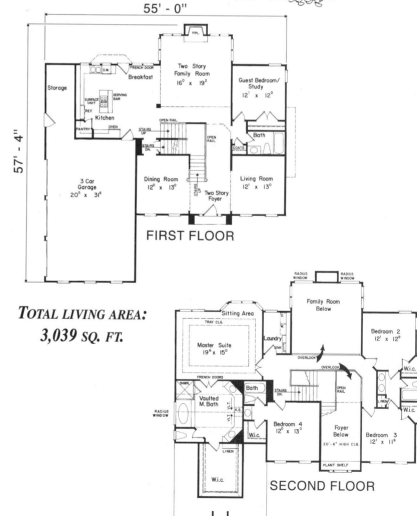

TOTAL LIVING AREA: 3,039 SQ. FT.

To order your Blueprints, call 1-800-235-5700

Rustic Retreat

PRICE CODE: A

◀ This plan features:
- Two bedrooms
- One full bath

A wrap-around deck equipped with a built-in bar-b-que for easy outdoor living

An entry, in a wall of glass, opens the living area to the outdoors

A large fireplace in the living area opens into an efficient Kitchen, with a built-in Pantry, that serves the Nook area

■ Two Bedrooms share a centrally located full Bath with a window tub

A Loft area ready for multiple uses

MAIN FLOOR — 789 SQ. FT.

LOFT — 108 SQ. FT.

TOTAL LIVING AREA:
897 SQ. FT.

An
EXCLUSIVE DESIGN
By Marshall Associates

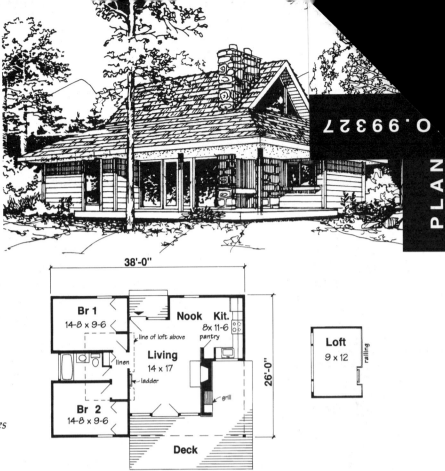

PLAN NO. 99327

Main Floor

Elegant Stone Two–Story

PRICE CODE: E

■ This plan features:
— Four bedrooms
— Two full and one half baths

■ The two-story entry leads directly into the Great Room

■ The Kitchen has a center island and is open to the large Nook

■ The Master Bedrooms has an access door to the rear Deck

■ Upstairs are two Bedrooms that are serviced by a full Bath

■ Also upstairs is a large Game Room for all the kid's toys

■ A Three-Season Porch with a cathedral ceiling rounds out this plan

■ No materials list is available for this plan

MAIN FLOOR — 2,039 SQ. FT.

SECOND FLOOR — 613 SQ. FT.

TOTAL LIVING AREA:
2,652 SQ. FT.

PLAN NO. 99149

WIDTH 69'-8"
DEPTH 72'-0"

FIRST FLOOR

SECOND FLOOR

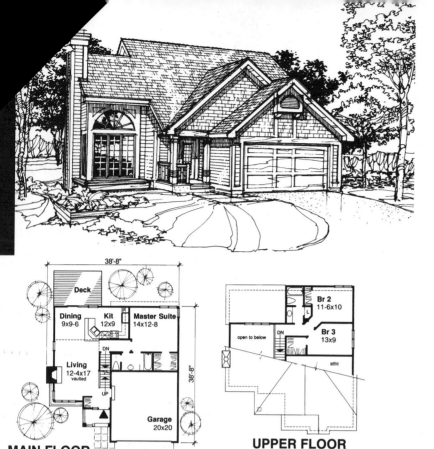

PLAN N

Tradition Combined with Contemporary
PRICE CODE: A

- This plan features:
  — Three bedrooms
  — Two full baths
- A vaulted ceiling in the Entry
- A formal Living Room with a fireplace and a half-round transom
- A Dining Room with sliders to the Deck and easy access to the Kitchen
- A main floor Master Suite with corner windows, a closet and private Bath access
- Two additional Bedrooms that share a full hall Bath

MAIN FLOOR — 858 SQ. FT.
UPPER FLOOR — 431 SQ. FT.
BASEMENT — 858 SQ. FT.
GARAGE — 400 SQ. FT.

TOTAL LIVING AREA:
1,289 SQ. FT.

MAIN FLOOR

UPPER FLOOR

PLAN NO. 90378

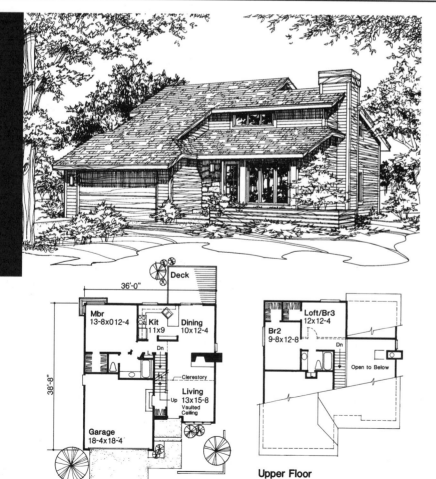

Lots of Space in this Small Package
PRICE CODE: A

- This plan features:
  — Two or three bedrooms
  — Two full baths
- A Living Room with dynamic, soaring angles and a fireplace
- A first floor Master Suite with full Bath and walk in closet
- Walk-in closets in all Bedrooms

MAIN FLOOR — 878 SQ. FT.
UPPER FLOOR — 405 SQ. FT.

TOTAL LIVING AREA:
1,283 SQ. FT.

Main Floor

Upper Floor

HOME COST CALCULATOR
see order pages for details

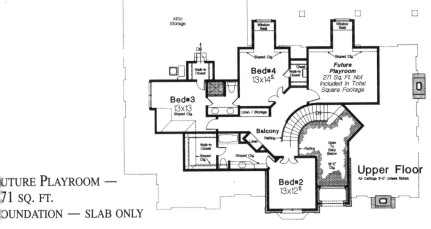

FUTURE PLAYROOM —
71 SQ. FT.
FOUNDATION — SLAB ONLY

TOTAL LIVING AREA:
3,480 SQ. FT.

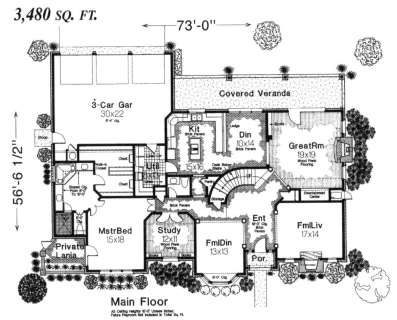

Country Estate Home
Price Code: F

■ This plan features:
— Four bedrooms
— Three full and one half baths

■ Impressive two-story Entry with a lovely curved staircase

■ Formal Living and Dining rooms have columns and decorative windows

■ Wood plank flooring, a large fireplace and Veranda access accent Great Room

■ Hub Kitchen with brick pavers, extended serving counter, bright Breakfast area, and nearby Utility/Garage entry

■ Private Master Bedroom suite offers a Private Lanai and plush dressing area with an enormous walk-in closet

■ Three second floor bedrooms with walk-in closets and private access to a full bath

■ Future Playroom offers many options

■ No materials list is available for this plan

MAIN FLOOR — 2,441 SQ. FT.
SECOND FLOOR — 1,039 SQ. FT.
GARAGE — 660 SQ. FT.

To order your Blueprints, call 1-800-235-5700

Drive Under Garage

Price Code: A

■ This plan features:

— Three bedrooms

— Two full baths

■ Porch shelters Entry into Living Area with an inviting fireplace topped by a vaulted ceiling

■ Convenient Dining Area opens to Living Room, Kitchen and Sundeck

■ Efficient, U-shaped Kitchen serves Dining Area and Sun Deck beyond

■ Pampering Master Bedroom with a vaulted ceiling, two closets and a double vanity Bath

■ Two additional Bedrooms share a full Bath and convenient Laundry Center

MAIN FLOOR — 1,208 SQ. FT.
BASEMENT — 728 SQ. FT.
GARAGE — 480 SQ. FT.

TOTAL LIVING AREA:
1,208 SQ. FT.

An
EXCLUSIVE DESIGN
By Jannis Vann &
Associates, Inc.

Sundeck
10-0 x 10-0

10-0

M.Bath

Bedroom 2

Opt. Plant Shelf
Open To Bdrm.

Vaulted Ceil.

Bath 2

W. D.

Kitchen
8-0 x 10-0

Dw.

Dining
10-4 x 10-0

Ref.

Master Bedroom
11-6 x 14-6

Cls.

Down

Family Room
18-4 x 13-0

Vaulted Ceil.

29-0

Bedroom 3
11-0 x 10-0

Entry

© 1989, Jannis vann & Associates, Inc.

48-0

2-4

MAIN AREA

Brick and Stucco
PRICE CODE: F

This plan features:
- Four bedrooms
- Two full, two three-quarter and one half baths
- The brick, stucco wing walls, and dual chimneys add elegant eye appeal to this home
- A large front Courtyard adds intrigue to front of the home
- The spider beamed Den with French doors includes arched transom windows
- The formal Dining Room opens to a dramatic high ceiling in the entry
- The Great Room features a fireplace wall with entertainment center, bookcases and wetbar
- Informal areas include the gazebo shaped Dinette, Kitchen with wrapping counters, large island/snack bar, walk-in Pantry, and private stairs accessing the second floor
- Each secondary Bedroom includes a walk-in closet, a built-in desk and a private Bath
- The exquisite first floor Master Suite includes a Sitting Room with a built-in bookcase and a fireplace

FIRST FLOOR — 2,603 SQ. FT.
SECOND FLOOR — 1,020 SQ. FT.
BASEMENT — 2,603 SQ. FT.
GARAGE — 801 SQ. FT.

TOTAL LIVING AREA: 3,623 SQ. FT.

© design basics, inc.

SECOND FLOOR

FIRST FLOOR

PLAN NO. 91002

Three Porches Offer Outdoor Charm
PRICE CODE: A

This plan features:
- Three bedrooms
- Two full baths
- An oversized log burning fireplace in the spacious Living/Dining Area which is two stories high with sliding glass doors
- Three Porches offering the maximum in outdoor living space
- A private Bedroom located on the second floor
- An efficient Kitchen including an eating bar and access to the covered Dining Porch

FIRST FLOOR — 974 SQ. FT.
SECOND FLOOR — 300 SQ. FT.

TOTAL LIVING AREA: 1,274 SQ. FT.

PLAN NO. 90048

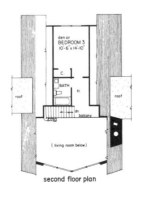

second floor plan

first floor plan

Lovely Second Home
PRICE CODE: A

- This plan features:
— Three bedrooms
— One full and one three-quarter baths
- Firedrum fireplace warming both entryway and Living Room
- Dining and Living rooms opening onto the Deck, which surrounds the house on three sides

MAIN FLOOR — 808 SQ. FT.
UPPER FLOOR — 288 SQ. FT.

TOTAL LIVING AREA:
1,096 SQ. FT.

MAIN FLOOR PLAN

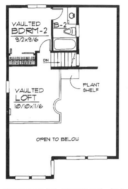

UPPER FLOOR PLAN

Old Fashioned With Contemporary Interior
PRICE CODE: C

- This plan features:
— Four bedrooms
— Three full baths
- A two-story Foyer is flanked by the Living Room and the Dining Room
- The Family Room features a fireplace and a French doo
- The bayed Breakfast Nook and Pantry are adjacent to th Kitchen
- The Master Suite with a trayed ceiling has an attached Bath with a vaulted ceiling and radius window
- Upstairs are two additional Bedrooms, a full Bath, a Laundry closet and a Bonus Room
- An optional basement, crawl space or slab foundation available — please specify when ordering this plan

FIRST FLOOR — 1,135 SQ. FT.
SECOND FLOOR — 917 SQ. FT.
BONUS — 216 SQ. FT.
BASEMENT — 1,135 SQ. FT.
GARAGE — 452 SQ. FT.

TOTAL LIVING AREA:
2,052 SQ. FT.

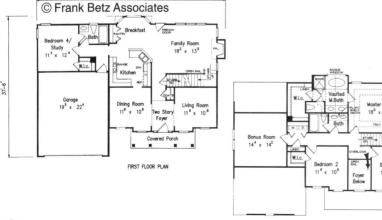

© Frank Betz Associates

FIRST FLOOR PLAN

SECOND FLOOR PLAN

To order your Blueprints, call 1-800-235-5700

ZIP QUOTE
HOME COST CALCULATOR
see order pages for details

SECOND FLOOR

FIRST FLOOR

Stucco, Brick and Elegant Details

Price Code: E

■ This plan features:

— Four bedrooms

— Three full and one half baths

■ Majestic Entry opens to Den and Dining Room

■ Expansive Great Room shares a see-thru fireplace with the Hearth Room

■ Lovely Hearth Room enhanced by three skylights above triple arched windows

■ Hub Kitchen has a work island/snack bar

■ Sumptuous Master Bedroom Suite with corner windows and two closets

FIRST FLOOR — 2,084 SQ. FT.
SECOND FLOOR — 848 SQ. FT.
BASEMENT — 2,084 SQ. FT.
GARAGE — 682 SQ. FT.

TOTAL LIVING AREA:
2,932 SQ. FT.

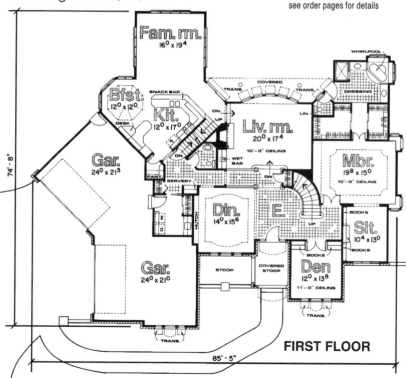

"English Manor" House

Price Code: F

- ■ This plan features:
- — Four bedrooms
- — Two full, one three quarter and one half baths
- ■ Covered stoop and impressive entry with columns and a curved staircase
- ■ Double doors open to Den with built-in shelves and triple, transom window
- ■ Formal Dining Room accented by a decorative ceiling
- ■ Spectacular bow window and a raised, hearth fireplace highlight Living Room
- ■ Ideal Kitchen with walk-in Pantry
- ■ Master Suite with a charming Sitting Area

FIRST FLOOR — 2,813 SQ. FT.
SECOND FLOOR — 1,091 SQ. FT.
BASEMENT — 2,813 SQ. FT.
GARAGE — 1,028 SQ. FT.

TOTAL LIVING AREA:
3,904 SQ. FT.

© design basics, inc.

SECOND FLOOR

ZIP QUOTE
HOME COST CALCULATOR
see order pages for details

FIRST FLOOR

To order your Blueprints, call 1-800-235-5700

Four Bedroom
1-1/2 Story Design
PRICE CODE: B

This plan features:
 Three bedrooms
 Two full baths
A vaulted ceiling in the Great Room and a fireplace
An efficient Kitchen with a peninsula counter and double sink
A Family Room with easy access to the wood Deck
A Master Bedroom with private Bath entrance
Convenient Laundry facilities outside the Master Bedroom
Two additional Bedrooms upstairs with walk-in closets and the use of the full hall Bath

AIN FLOOR — 1,062 SQ. FT.
PPER FLOOR — 469 SQ. FT.

TOTAL LIVING AREA:
1,531 SQ. FT.

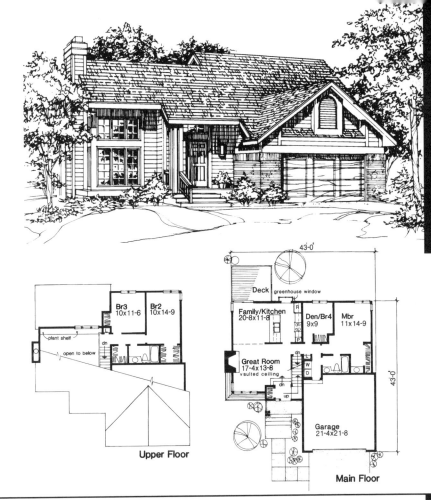
Upper Floor

Main Floor

Lap of Luxury
PRICE CODE: D

This plan features:
- Four bedrooms
- Three full baths
Entertaining in grand style in the formal Living Room, the Dining Room, or under the covered Patio in the backyard
A Family Room crowned in a cathedral ceiling, enhanced by a center fireplace, and built-in book shelves
An efficient Kitchen highlighted by a wall oven, plentiful counter space and a Pantry
A Master Bedroom with a Sitting Area, huge walk in closet, private Bath, and access to a covered lanai
A secondary Bedroom wing containing three additional Bedrooms with ample closet space, and two full Baths
No materials list is available for this plan

MAIN FLOOR — 2,445 SQ. FT.
GARAGE — 630 SQ. FT.

TOTAL LIVING AREA:
2,445 SQ. FT.

ZIP QUOTE
HOME COST CALCULATOR
see order pages for details

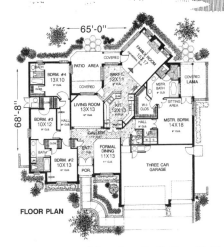

FLOOR PLAN

To order your Blueprints, call 1-800-235-5700

PLAN NO. 97254

© Frank Betz Associates

Elegant Ceiling Treatments

PRICE CODE: B

■ This plan features:
— Three bedrooms
— Two full baths
■ A cozy wrapping front Porch sheltering entrance
■ Dining Room defined by columns at the entrances
■ Kitchen highlighted by a peninsula counter/serving ba
■ Breakfast Room flowing from the Kitchen
■ Vaulted ceiling highlighting the Great Room which als
includes a fireplace
■ Master Suite crowned in a tray ceiling over the
Bedroom, a Sitting Room and plush Master Bath
■ Two additional Bedrooms are located at the other side
the house
■ An optional basement or crawl space foundation —
please specify when ordering
■ No materials list is available for this plan

MAIN FLOOR — 1,692 SQ. FT.
BONUS ROOM — 358 SQ. FT.
BASEMENT — 1,705 SQ. FT.
GARAGE — 472 SQ. FT.

TOTAL LIVING AREA:
1,692 SQ. FT.

PLAN NO. 20148

Hillside Haven

PRICE CODE: B

■ This plan features:
— Three bedrooms
— Two full baths
■ A well-appointed Kitchen that adjoins a cheerful, six-sided Breakfast Room with access to the wrap-around Deck
■ A decorative ceiling in the formal Dining Room which flows into the Living Room
■ A sky-lit Living Room with a built-in wetbar and a fire-place
■ A Master Suite with a decorative ceiling, a window sea a walk-in closet, and a private Master Bath
■ Two additional Bedrooms with ample closet space that share a full hall Bath

MAIN FLOOR — 1,774 SQ. FT.
GARAGE — 551 SQ. FT.
BASEMENT — 1,399 SQ. FT.

TOTAL LIVING AREA:
1,774 SQ. FT.

Slab/Crawl Space Option

ZIP QUOTE
HOME COST CALCULATOR
see order pages for details

An
EXCLUSIVE DESIGN
By Karl Kreeger

MAIN FLOOR

374

To order your Blueprints, call 1-800-235-5700

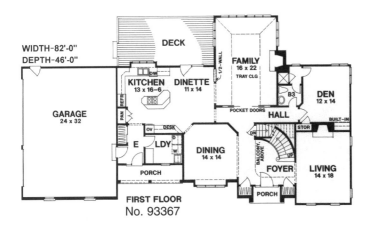

WIDTH-82'-0"
DEPTH-46'-0"

DECK

FAMILY
16 x 22
TRAY CLG

KITCHEN
13 x 16-6

DINETTE
11 x 14

DEN
12 x 14

GARAGE
24 x 32

POCKET DOORS

HALL

BUILT-IN

STOR

OV

DESK

E

LDY

DINING
14 x 14

BALCONY
ABOVE

FOYER

LIVING
14 x 18

PORCH

PORCH

FIRST FLOOR
No. 93367

An
EXCLUSIVE DESIGN
By Patrick Morabito,
A.I.A. Architect

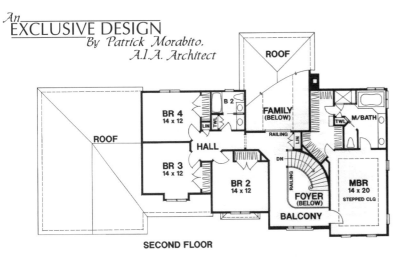

ROOF

BR 4
14 x 12

B 2

FAMILY
(BELOW)

M/BATH

ROOF

RAILING

HALL

BR 3
14 x 12

DN

BR 2
14 x 12

RAILING

FOYER
(BELOW)

MBR
14 x 20
STEPPED CLG

BALCONY

SECOND FLOOR

Outstanding Family Home

Price Code: F

■ This plan features:

— Four bedrooms

— Three full baths

■ Sheltered entrance into an open Foyer

■ Formal Living and Dining rooms off Foyer

■ Pocket doors open to expansive Family Room with a hearth fireplace

■ Spacious Kitchen/Dinette with cooktop/ snackbar

■ Quiet, corner Den with built-ins

■ Private Master Bedroom offers a stepped ceiling, a huge walk-in closet and a plush Bath

■ Three additional Bedrooms share a double vanity Bath

FIRST FLOOR — 1,895 SQ. FT.
SECOND FLOOR — 1,463 SQ. FT.
BASEMENT — 1,895 SQ. FT.
GARAGE — 768 SQ. FT.

TOTAL LIVING AREA:
3,358 SQ. FT.

Open Plan Accented By Loft, Windows and Decks

Price Code: C

- This plan features:
- — Three bedrooms
- — Two full and one half baths

- A fireplaced Family Room and Dining Room

- A large Kitchen sharing a preparation/eating bar with Dining Room

- A first floor Master Bedroom featuring two closets and a five-piece bath

- An ample Utility Room designed with a pantry and room for a freezer, a washer and dryer, plus a furnace and a hot water heater

MAIN FLOOR — 1,280 SQ. FT.
UPPER LOFT — 735 SQ. FT.
GREENHOUSE — 80 SQ. FT.

TOTAL LIVING AREA:
2,015 SQ. FT.

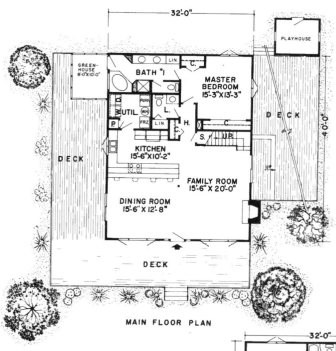

MAIN FLOOR PLAN

ZIP QUOTE
HOME COST CALCULATOR
see order pages for details

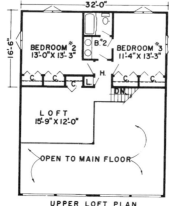

UPPER LOFT PLAN

To order your Blueprints, call 1-800-235-5700

Appealing Master Suite

PRICE CODE: A

This plan features:

- Three bedrooms
- Two full baths
- Sheltered Entry into spacious Living Room with a corner fireplace and Patio access
- Efficient Kitchen with a serving counter for Dining Area and nearby Utility/Garage entry
- Private Master Bedroom offers a vaulted ceiling and pampering Bath with dual vanity and walk-in closets and a garden window tub
- Two additional Bedrooms with ample closets, share a full Bath
- No materials list is available for this plan

MAIN FLOOR — 1,198 SQ. FT.

TOTAL LIVING AREA:
1,198 SQ. FT.

PLAN NO. 92239

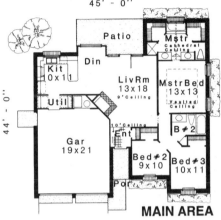

Welcoming Exterior

PRICE CODE: F

- This plan features:
  - Four bedrooms
  - Two full and one half baths
- Columns between the Foyer and Living Room/Study hint at all the extras in this four Bedroom country estate with a warm, welcoming exterior
  - Transom windows over French doors open up the Living Room/Study to the front Porch, while a generous Family Room accesses the covered back Porch
- Deluxe Master Suite is topped by a tray ceiling and includes a Bath with a sunny garden tub bay and ample closet space
- Bonus room is accessed from the second floor and ready to expand family living space for future needs

FIRST FLOOR — 1,483 SQ. FT.
SECOND FLOOR — 1,349 SQ. FT.
BONUS — 486 SQ. FT.
GARAGE — 738 SQ. FT.

TOTAL LIVING AREA:
2,832 SQ. FT.

PLAN NO. 96403

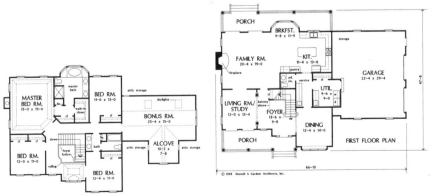

Traditional Ranch
PRICE CODE: B

- This plan features:
  - Three bedrooms
  - Two full baths
- A large front palladium window that gives this home great curb appeal, and allows a view of the front yard from the Living Room
- A vaulted ceiling in the Living Room, adding to the architectural interest and the spacious feel of the room
- Sliding glass doors in the Dining Room that lead to a wood Deck
- A built-in Pantry, double sink and breakfast bar in the efficient Kitchen
- A Master Suite that includes a walk-in closet and a private Bath with a double vanity
- Two additional Bedrooms that share a full hall Bath

MAIN AREA — 1,568 SQ. FT.
GARAGE — 509 SQ. FT.
BASEMENT — 1,568 SQ. FT.

TOTAL LIVING AREA:
1,568 SQ. FT.

MAIN AREA

Main Floor

ZIP QUOTE
HOME COST CALCULATOR
see order pages for details

An
EXCLUSIVE DESIGN
By Karl Kreeger

Tailored for a View to the Side
PRICE CODE: D

- This plan features:
  - Three or four bedrooms
  - Three full and one half baths
- A designed for a homesite with a view to the side, perfect for entertaining and everyday living
- A sheltered entrance with windows over the door and a side light
- A large entry Foyer highlighted by a ceiling dome and French doors leading to the private Study or Guest Bedroom with a vaulted ceiling
- An elegant formal Dining Room with a high ceiling and a columned and arched entrance
- A sunken Great Room with a tray ceiling, arched and columned openings and a cozy fireplace
- A Breakfast Room, with an optional planning desk, opens to the Kitchen via the eating bar
- An island and walk-in Pantry adding to the Kitchen's efficiency
- A tray ceiling and lavish bath pamper the owner in the Master Suite
- Two additional Bedrooms that share a split vanity Bath
- No materials list is available for this plan

MAIN FLOOR — 2,579 SQ. FT.
GARAGE — 536 SQ. FT.

TOTAL LIVING AREA:
2,579 SQ. FT.

Main Level Floor Plan

An
EXCLUSIVE DESIGN
By Building Science Associates

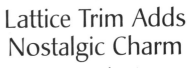

Garage
19-8x23-4

Deck

Brkfst
10-6x14-6

Dining
11x13-4

Kitchen

Living Rm
18x12-8
vaulted

48'-0"

29'-10"

FIRST FLOOR

MBr
11-8x13

Loft/
Br 3
9x11

Br 2
10x9-8

skylight

open to below

SECOND FLOOR

Lattice Trim Adds Nostalgic Charm

Price Code: A

■ This plan features:

— Three bedrooms

— Two full and one half baths

■ Wood and fieldstone exterior

■ A vaulted Living Room with balcony view and floor to ceiling corner window treatment

■ A Master Suite with private Bath and Dressing Area

■ A two-car Garage with access to Kitchen

FIRST FLOOR — 668 SQ. FT.
SECOND FLOOR — 691 SQ. FT.
GARAGE — 459 SQ. FT.

TOTAL LIVING AREA:
1,359 SQ. FT.

Interesting Detailing

Price Code: C

■ This plan features:

— Three bedrooms

— Two full and one half baths

■ Double door entry into Foyer and Living Room beyond

■ Formal Living Room with patio access, shares see-through fireplace with Family Room

■ Open and efficient Kitchen with pantry, peninsula snackbar, Dining Room and patio beyond, and nearby laundry and service entry

■ Private Master Bedroom pampered with two walk-in closets and a dressing area with a double vanity and whirlpool tub

■ Two additional bedrooms with arched windows, share a full bath

FIRST FLOOR — 1,182 SQ. FT.
SECOND FLOOR — 927 SQ. FT.
FOUNDATION — BASEMENT ONLY

TOTAL LIVING AREA:
2,109 SQ. FT.

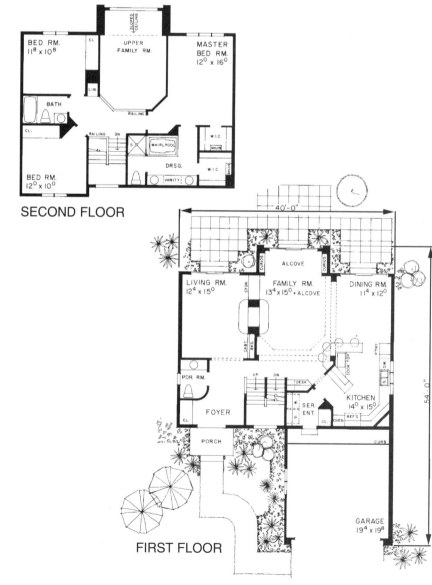

SECOND FLOOR

FIRST FLOOR

To order your Blueprints, call 1-800-235-5700

Country Style Charm
PRICE CODE: C

This plan features:
 Three bedrooms
 Two full baths
 Brick accents, front facing gable, and railed wrap-around covered Porch
 A built-in range and oven in a L-shaped Kitchen
 A Nook with garage access for convenient unloading of groceries and other supplies
 A bay window wrapping around the front of the formal Living Room
 A Master Suite with French doors opening to the Deck

MAIN AREA — 1,857 SQ. FT.
GARAGE — 681 SQ. FT.

TOTAL LIVING AREA:
1,857 SQ. FT.

WIDTH 51'-6"
DEPTH 65'-0"

Symmetrical and Stately
PRICE CODE: E

This plan features:
- Four bedrooms
- Two full and one half baths
- Double column Porch leads into the open Foyer, the Dining Room accented by an arched window and pillars, and a spacious Den
- Decorative ceiling crowns the Den with a hearth fireplace, built-in shelves and window access to the rear Porch
- Large, efficient Kitchen with a peninsula serving counter, a Breakfast Area, adjoining the Utility and the Garage
- Master Bedroom suite with a decorative ceiling, two vanities and a large walk-in closet
- Three additional Bedrooms with double closets share a full Bath
- An optional slab or crawl space foundation — please specify when ordering

MAIN AREA — 2,387 SQ. FT.
GARAGE — 505 SQ. FT.

TOTAL LIVING AREA:
2,387 SQ. FT.

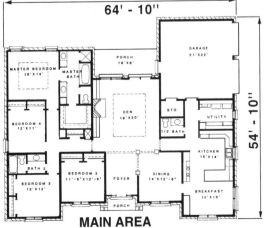

MAIN AREA

PLAN NO. 93048

WIDTH 49–10

© Larry E. Belk

MAIN AREA

BRKFST. RM 9–4 X 11–0 10 FT CLG · SLOPE

KITCHEN 9–6 X 11–0 · 10 FT CLG

STORAGE

GARAGE

LIVING RM 14–6 X 17–8 10 FT CLG

FP

MASTER BEDRM 14–8 X 12–6 10 FT CLG

MASTER BATH

SHLV

DEPTH 40–6

FOYER

BATH 2

PORCH

BEDRM 2 10–0 X 11–0

LIN

BEDRM 3 11–0 X 10–0

OPTIONAL BAY WINDOW

For First Time Buyers
PRICE CODE: A

■ This plan features:
— Three bedrooms
— Two full baths
■ An efficiently designed Kitchen with a corner sink, ample counter space and a peninsula counter
■ A sunny Breakfast Room with a convenient hide-away Laundry Center
■ An expansive Family Room that includes a corner fireplace and direct access to the Patio
■ A private Master Suite with a walk-in closet and a double vanity Bath
■ Two additional Bedrooms, both with walk-in closets, that share a full hall Bath
■ No materials list is available for this plan

MAIN AREA — 1,310 SQ. FT.
GARAGE — 449 SQ. FT.

TOTAL LIVING AREA:
1,310 SQ. FT.

PLAN NO. 91418

FLOOR PLAN

COVERED PATIO

PATIO

READING NOOK

VAULTED MBR 16/6 X 14 AVG

W1 CLO

VAULTED GREAT ROOM 22 X 24 AVG

DINE 10 X 12 AVG

MB

BR 11 X 9/6

VAULTED FOYER

KIT

R

BATH

BR 11 X 9/6

UTIL

NOOK 10/8 X 9/6

PLANTER

UTIL D W

ALTERNATE BASEMENT PLAN

GARAGE 20 X 20

65'-0"

44'-0"

Carefree Comfort
PRICE CODE: B

■ This plan features:
— Three bedrooms
— Two full baths
■ A dramatic vaulted Foyer
■ A range top island Kitchen with a sunny eating Nook surrounded by a built-in planter
■ A vaulted ceiling in the Great Room with a built-in bar and corner fireplace
■ A bayed Dining Room that combines with the Great Room for a spacious feeling
■ A Master Bedroom with a private reading Nook, vaulted ceiling, walk-in closet, and a well-appointed private Bath
■ Two additional Bedrooms sharing a full hall Bath
■ An optional basement, slab or crawl space foundation — please specify when ordering

MAIN FLOOR — 1,665 SQ. FT.

TOTAL LIVING AREA:
1,665 SQ. FT.

An
EXCLUSIVE DESIGN
By Westhome Planners, Ltd.

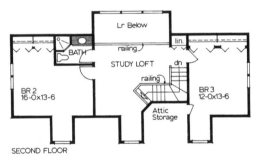

STUDY LOFT

Lr Below
railing
lin.

BATH

BR 2
16-0x13-6

dn
railing

BR 3
12-0x13-6

Attic
Storage

SECOND FLOOR

Room to Grow

Price Code: E

■ This plan features:

— Three bedrooms

— Three full baths

■ A corner gas fireplace in the spacious Living Room

■ A Master Suite including a private Bath with a whirlpool tub, separate shower and a double vanity

■ An island Kitchen that is well-equipped to efficiently serve both formal Dining Room and informal Nook

■ Two additional bedrooms sharing a full bath on the second floor

FIRST FLOOR — 1,837 SQ. FT.
SECOND FLOOR — 848 SQ. FT.
BASEMENT — 1,803 SQ. FT.
BONUS ROOM — 288 SQ. FT.

TOTAL LIVING AREA:
2,685 SQ. FT.

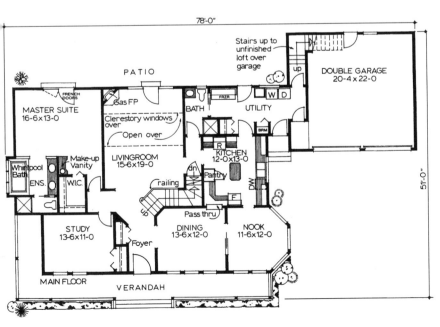

78'-0"

Stairs up to unfinished loft over garage

PATIO

DOUBLE GARAGE
20-4 x 22-0

up

FRENCH DOORS

Gas FP

BATH

UTILITY

W D

FRZR

MASTER SUITE
16-6 x 13-0

Clerestory windows over

Open over

LIVINGROOM
15-6 x 19-0

KITCHEN
12-0x13-0

BRM

R

51'-0"

Whirlpool Bath

Make-up Vanity

railing

dn

Pantry

DW

ENS.

W.I.C.

Pass thru

F

up

STUDY
13-6 x 11-0

DINING
13-6 x 12-0

NOOK
11-6 x 12-0

Foyer

MAIN FLOOR

VERANDAH

©1997 Donald A. Gardner Architects, Inc.

Wrapping Front Porch and Gabled Dormers

Price Code: F

■ This plan features:

— Four bedrooms

— Three full baths

■ Generous Great Room with a fireplace, cathedral ceiling, and a balcony above

■ Flexible Bedroom/Study having a walk-in closet and an adjacent full Bath

■ Master Suite with a sunny bay window and a private Bath topped by a cathedral ceiling and highlighted by his-n-her vanities, and a separate tub and shower

■ Two additional Bedrooms, each with dormer windows, share a full bath with a cathedral ceiling, palladian window and a double vanity

■ Bonus room over the Garage for future expansion

FIRST FLOOR — 1,939 SQ. FT.
SECOND FLOOR — 657 SQ. FT.
GARAGE & STORAGE — 526 SQ. FT.
BONUS ROOM — 386 SQ. FT.

TOTAL LIVING AREA:
2,596 SQ. FT.

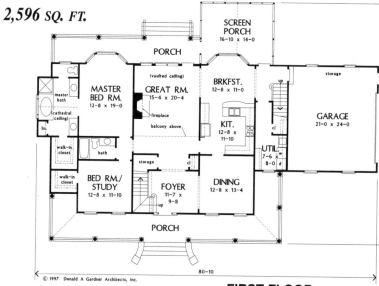

FIRST FLOOR
No. 96411

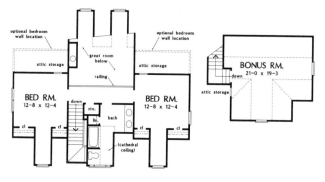

SECOND FLOOR

384

To order your Blueprints, call 1-800-235-5700

Attractive Exterior

PRICE CODE: C

This plan features:
Three bedrooms
Two full baths
In the gallery columns separate space into the Great
Room and the Dining Room
Access to backyard covered patio from bayed Breakfast
Nook
The large Kitchen is a chef's dream with lots of counter
space and a Pantry
The Master Bedroom is removed from traffic areas and
contains a luxurious Master Bath
A hall connects the two secondary Bedrooms which
share a full skylit Bath

MAIN FLOOR — 2,167 SQ. FT.
GARAGE — 690 SQ. FT.

TOTAL LIVING AREA:
2,167 SQ. FT.

MAIN FLOOR

Demonstrative Detail

PRICE CODE: C

This plan features:
Three bedrooms
Two full and one half baths
Keystone arched windows, stone and stucco combine
with shutters and a flower box to create an eye-catching
elevation
The Foyer accesses the Dining Room, Family Room or
the Master Suite
The Family Room has a sloped ceiling and is accented
by a fireplace with windows to either side
The Kitchen/Breakfast Area has easy access to the rear
Porch
Two roomy Bedrooms on the second floor share the full
hall Bath
An optional Bonus Area over the Garage offers
possibilities for future expansion

FIRST FLOOR — 1,317 SQ. FT.
SECOND FLOOR — 537 SQ. FT.
BONUS — 312 SQ. FT.
BASEMENT — 1,317 SQ. FT.

TOTAL LIVING AREA:
1,854 SQ. FT.

An
EXCLUSIVE DESIGN
By Greg Marquis

Southern Hospitality
PRICE CODE: B

■ This plan features:
— Three bedrooms
— Two full and one half baths

■ Inviting atmosphere enhanced by Porch surrounding shading home

■ Two-story entry hall graced by a landing staircase and arched window

■ Double doors access to Porch from Family Great Room Dining Room and Master Suite

■ Country Kitchen with cooktop island/snackbar, eating alcove and archway to Family Room with cozy fireplace

■ First floor Master Suite with bay window, walk-in closet and pampering Bath

■ Two double dormer Bedrooms on second floor catch breezes and share a full Bath

FIRST FLOOR — 1171 SQ. FT.
SECOND FLOOR — 600 SQ. FT.

TOTAL LIVING AREA:
1,771 SQ. FT.

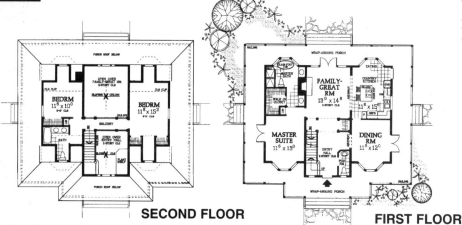

SECOND FLOOR

FIRST FLOOR

Covered Porch with Columns
PRICE CODE: C

■ This plan features:
— Three bedrooms
— Two full baths

■ The foyer with 12′ ceiling leads past decorative columns into the Family Room with a center fireplace

■ The Living Room and Dining Room are linked by the Foyer and have windows overlooking the front Porch

■ The Kitchen has a serving bar and is adjacent to the Breakfast Nook which has a French door that opens to the backyard

■ The private Master Suite has a tray ceiling, a vaulted bath with a double vanity, and a walk in closet

■ The two other Bedrooms share a full Bath

■ An optional basement, slab, or crawl space foundation — please specify when ordering

MAIN FLOOR — 1,856 SQ. FT.
GARAGE — 429 SQ. FT.
BASEMENT — 1,856 SQ. FT.

TOTAL LIVING AREA:
1,856 SQ. FT.

FLOOR PLAN

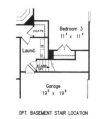

OPT. BASEMENT STAIR LOCATION

© Frank Betz Associates

To order your Blueprints, call 1-800-235-5700

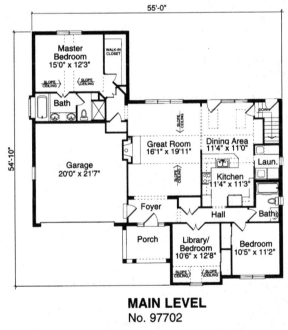

55'-0"

Master Bedroom
15'0" x 12'3"

WALK-IN CLOSET

SLOPE CEILING   SLOPE CEILING

Bath

SLOPE CEILING

54'-10"

Garage
20'0" x 21'7"

Great Room
16'1" x 19'11"

Dining Area
11'4" x 11'0"

DOWN

Laun.

Kitchen
11'4" x 11'3"

Foyer

Hall

Bath

Porch

Library/
Bedroom
10'6" x 12'8"

Bedroom
10'5" x 11'2"

SLOPE CEILING   SLOPE CEILING

MAIN LEVEL
No. 97702

Basement Storage

Media Area

Rec. Room
32'6" x 36'6"

Bar

up

LOWER LEVEL

Billiard Area

TOTAL LIVING AREA:
1,601 SQ. FT.

Exciting Facade
Price Code: B

■ This plan features:

— Three bedrooms

— Two full baths

■ Brick, stone and siding combine to create an exciting facade

■ A covered Porch shelters the entry through the front door with sidelights

■ The sloping ceiling and a fireplace make the Great Room impressive

■ Skylights brighten the Dining Area

■ The large Kitchen is well planned for meal preparation

■ The Master Bedroom is located for privacy and has a large Bath and closet

■ Both secondary Bedrooms have front wall windows to maximize illumination

■ A plan for the lower level is included that calls for a future recreation space

■ No materials list is available for this plan

MAIN LEVEL — 1,601 SQ. FT.
BASEMENT — 1,601 SQ. FT.
GARAGE — 426 SQ. FT.

Opulence and Grandeur

Price Code: F

■ This plan features:

— Four bedrooms

— Three full and one half baths

■ Dramatic two-story glass Entry with a curved staircase

■ Both Living and Family rooms offer high ceilings, decorative windows and large fireplaces

■ Large, but efficient Kitchen with a cook-top serving island, walk-in pantry, bright Breakfast area and Patio access

■ Lavish Master Bedroom with a cathedral ceiling, two walk-in closets, and large bath

■ Two additional bedrooms with ample closets, share a double vanity bath

■ A materials list is not available for this plan

FIRST FLOOR — 2,506 SQ. FT.
SECOND FLOOR — 1,415 SQ. FT.
GARAGE — 660 SQ. FT.
FOUNDATION — BASEMENT OR SLAB

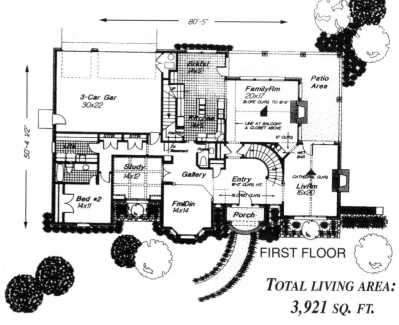

FIRST FLOOR

TOTAL LIVING AREA:
3,921 SQ. FT.

ZIP QUOTE
HOME COST CALCULATOR
see order pages for details

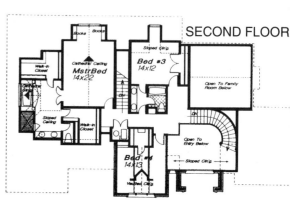

SECOND FLOOR

To order your Blueprints, call 1-800-235-5700

Spectacular Traditional
PRICE CODE: B

This plan features:
- Three bedrooms
- Two full baths
- The use of gable roofs and the blend of stucco and brick to form a spectacular exterior
- A high vaulted ceiling and a cozy fireplace, with built-in cabinets in the Den
- An efficient, U-shaped Kitchen with an adjacent Dining Area
- A Master Bedroom, with a raised ceiling, that includes a private Bath and a walk-in closet
- Two family Bedrooms that share a full hall Bath
- An optional slab or crawl space foundation — please specify when ordering

MAIN AREA — 1,237 SQ. FT.
GARAGE — 436 SQ. FT.

TOTAL LIVING AREA:
1,237 SQ. FT.

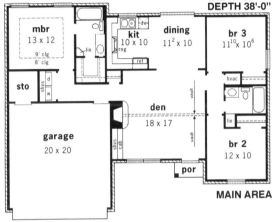

WIDTH 50'-0"
DEPTH 38'-0"

MAIN AREA

Enhanced by a Columned Porch
PRICE CODE: C

This plan features:
- Three bedrooms
- Two full baths
- A Great Room with a fireplace and decorative ceiling
- A large efficient Kitchen with Breakfast Area
- A Master Bedroom with a private Master Bath and walk-in closet
- A formal Dining Room conveniently located near the Kitchen
- Two additional Bedrooms with walk-in closets and use of full hall Bath
- An optional slab or crawl space foundation — please specify when ordering

MAIN FLOOR — 1,754 SQ. FT.
GARAGE — 552 SQ. FT.

TOTAL LIVING AREA:
1,754 SQ. FT.

MAIN FLOOR

Easy Living Design
PRICE CODE: A

■ This plan features:
— Three bedrooms
— Two full baths
■ A handicaped Master Bath plan is available
■ Vaulted Great Room, Dining Room and Kitchen Areas
■ A Kitchen accented with angles and an abundance of cabinets for storage
■ A Master Bedroom with an ample sized wardrobe, large covered private Deck, and private Bath

MAIN FLOOR — 1,345 SQ. FT.

TOTAL LIVING AREA:
1,345 SQ. FT.

WIDTH 47'-8"
DEPTH 56'-0"

ALTERNATE BATH

MAIN FLOOR

Attractive Roof Lines
PRICE CODE: A

■ This plan features:
— Three bedrooms
— One full and one three-quarter baths baths
■ An open floor plan shared by the sunken Living Room, Dining and Kitchen areas
■ An unfinished daylight Basement which will provide future bedrooms, a bathroom and laundry facilities
■ A Master Suite with a big walk- in closet and a private bath featuring a double shower

MAIN AREA — 1,396 SQ. FT.
GARAGE — 389 SQ. FT.
BASEMENT — 1,396 SQ. FT.

TOTAL LIVING AREA:
1,396 SQ. FT.

WIDTH 48'-0"
DEPTH 54'-0"

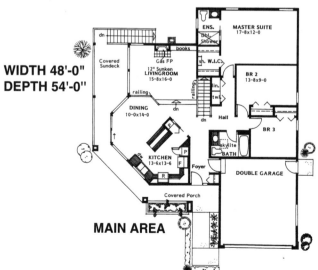

MAIN AREA

An
EXCLUSIVE DESIGN
By Westhome Planners, Ltd.

To order your Blueprints, call 1-800-235-5700

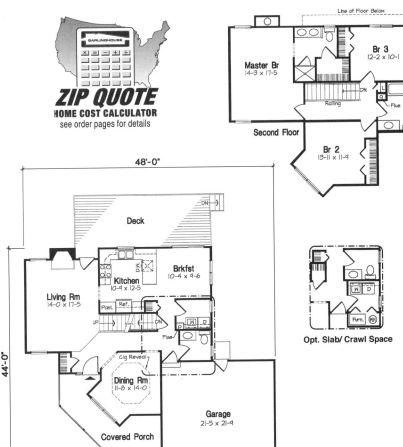

Line of Floor Below

Master Br
14-3 x 17-5

Br 3
12-2 x 10-1

DN

Railing

Flue

Second Floor

Br 2
13-11 x 11-9

Opt. Slab/ Crawl Space

48'-0"

44'-0"

Deck

DN

Brkfst
10-4 x 9-6

Kitchen
10-9 x 12-5

Living Rm
14-0 x 17-5

Pant. | Ref.

UP

DN

Flue

Clg Reveal

Dining Rm
11-8 x 14-0

Garage
21-5 x 21-9

Covered Porch

First Floor

Covered Porch on Farm Style Traditional

Price Code: B

■ This plan features:
— Three bedrooms
— Two full and one half baths

■ A Dining Room with bay window and elevated ceiling

■ A Living Room complete with gas light fireplace

■ A two-car Garage

■ Ample storage space throughout the home

FIRST FLOOR — 909 SQ. FT
SECOND FLOOR — 854 SQ. FT.
BASEMENT — 899 SQ. FT.
GARAGE — 491 SQ. FT.

TOTAL LIVING AREA:
1,763 SQ. FT.

An
EXCLUSIVE DESIGN
By Karl Kreeger

© 1994 Donald A. Gardner Architects, Inc.

The Great Outdoors

Price Code: F

- This plan features:

— Four bedrooms

— Two full and one half baths

- Bay windows and a long, skylit, screened Porch make this four Bedroom country home a haven for outdoor enthusiasts

- Foyer is open to take advantage of the light from the central dormer with palladian window

- Vaulted ceiling in the Great Room adds vertical drama to the room

- Contemporary Kitchen is open to the Great Room creating a feeling of additional space

- Master Suite is privately tucked away with a large luxurious Bath complete with a bay window, corner shower, and a garden tub

FIRST FLOOR — 1,907 SQ. FT.
SECOND FLOOR — 656 SQ. FT.
BONUS ROOM — 467 SQ. FT.
GARAGE & STORAGE — 580 SQ. FT.

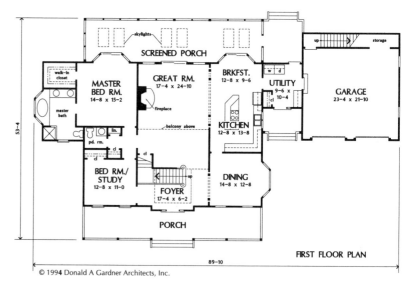

© 1994 Donald A Gardner Architects, Inc.

FIRST FLOOR PLAN

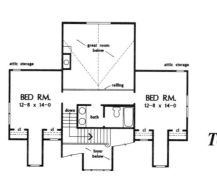

SECOND FLOOR PLAN

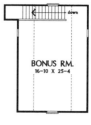

TOTAL LIVING AREA:
2,563 SQ. FT.

To order your Blueprints, call 1-800-235-5700

An Open Concept Home
PRICE CODE: A

This plan features:

Three bedrooms

Two full baths

An angled Entry creating the illusion of space

Two square columns that flank the bar and separate the Kitchen from the Living Room

A Dining Room that may service both formal and informal occasions

A Master Bedroom with a large walk-in closet

A large Master Bath with double vanity, linen closet and whirlpool tub/shower combination

Two additional Bedrooms that share a full Bath

No materials list is available for this plan

Ａin Floor — 1,282 sq. ft.

ＡRAGE — 501 sq. ft.

TOTAL LIVING AREA:
1,282 SQ. FT.

© Larry E. Belk

WIDTH 48–10

MAIN FLOOR

Perfect Plan for Busy Family
PRICE CODE: B

This plan features:

- Three bedrooms

- Two full baths

Covered Entry opens to vaulted Foyer and Family Room

Spacious Family Room with a vaulted ceiling, central fireplace and expansive back yard views

Angular and efficient Kitchen with an eating bar, built-in desk, Dining area with outdoor access, and nearby Laundry and Garage entry

Secluded Master Bedroom with a large walk-in closet and double vanity Bath

Two additional Bedrooms with ample closets and easy access to a full Bath

Plenty of room for growing family to expand on lower level

No materials list is available for this plan

ＭAIN FLOOR — 1,756 sq. ft.

ＢASEMENT — 1,756 sq. ft.

TOTAL LIVING AREA:
1,756 SQ. FT.

MAIN FLOOR PLAN

PLAN NO.93021

Cabin in the Country
PRICE CODE: A

- This plan features:
  — Two bedrooms
  — One full and one half baths
- A screened Porch for enjoyment of your outdoor surroundings
- A combination Living and Dining Area with cozy fireplace for added warmth
- An efficiently laid out Kitchen with a built-in Pantry
- Two large Bedrooms located at the rear of the home
- An optional slab or crawl space foundation — please specify when ordering

MAIN FLOOR — 928 SQ. FT.
SCREENED PORCH — 230 SQ. FT.

TOTAL LIVING AREA:
928 SQ. FT.

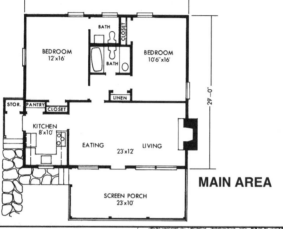

MAIN AREA

PLAN NO.93411

First Floor Master Suite
PRICE CODE: B

- This plan features:
  — Three bedrooms
  — Two full and one half baths
- Children have their own floor, while adults receive the privacy they deserve in the first floor Master Suite
- An open layout between the Kitchen and Dining Room adds a spacious feeling to the home
- The cooktop island/snack bar expands work space in the Kitchen
- A pass-through into the Family Room offers convenience
- The Family Room includes a fireplace and views to the front yard
- Two secondary Bedrooms share the full Bath in the hall
- No materials list is available for this plan

FIRST FLOOR — 1,229 SQ. FT.
SECOND FLOOR — 551 SQ. FT.
BASEMENT — 1229 SQ. FT.
GARAGE — 569 SQ. FT.

An
EXCLUSIVE DESIGN
By Greg Marquis

TOTAL LIVING AREA:
1,780 SQ. FT.

To order your Blueprints, call 1-800-235-5700

SECOND FLOOR

ZIP QUOTE
HOME COST CALCULATOR
see order pages for details

Alternate Crawl/Slab Plan

Gingerbread Charm

Price Code: D

■ This plan features:

— Three bedrooms

— Two full and one half baths

■ A wrap-around Porch and rear Deck adding lots of outdoor living space

■ A formal Parlor and Dining Room just off the central entry

■ A Family Room with a fireplace

■ A Master Suite complete with a five-sided Sitting Nook, walk-in closets and a sunken tub

FIRST FLOOR — 1,260 SQ. FT.
SECOND FLOOR — 1,021 SQ. FT.
BASEMENT — 1,186 SQ. FT.
GARAGE — 851 SQ. FT.

TOTAL LIVING AREA:
2,281 SQ. FT.

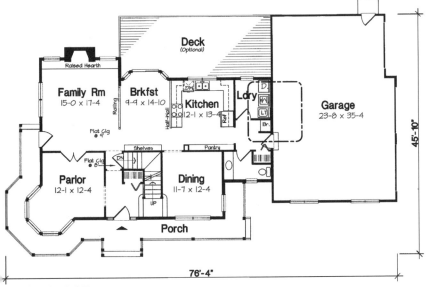

FIRST FLOOR

Inviting Covered Porch

Price Code: C

- ■ This plan features:
- — Four bedrooms
- — Two full and one half baths
- ■ Interesting staircase with landing in volume Entry
- ■ Ten foot ceiling above transom windows and hearth fireplace accent the Great Room
- ■ Island counter/snack bar, Pantry and desk featured in Kitchen/Breakfast Area
- ■ Kitchen conveniently accesses Laundry Area and Garage
- ■ Master Bedroom suite features decorative ceiling to walk-in closets and double vanity Bath with a whirlpool tub
- ■ Three additional Bedrooms with ample closets share a full Bath

FIRST FLOOR — 944 SQ. FT.
SECOND FLOOR — 987 SQ. FT.
BASEMENT — 944 SQ. FT.
GARAGE — 557 SQ. FT.

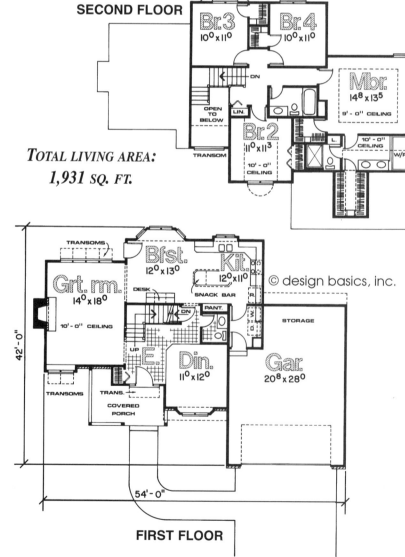

SECOND FLOOR

TOTAL LIVING AREA:
1,931 SQ. FT.

© design basics, inc.

FIRST FLOOR

To order your Blueprints, call 1-800-235-5700

Comfortable Design Encourages Relaxation

PRICE CODE: E

This plan features:

Four bedrooms

Three full bathrooms

A wide front Porch providing a warm welcome

Center dormer lighting Foyer, as columns punctuate the entry to the Dining Room and Great Room

Spacious Kitchen with angled countertop and open to the Breakfast Bay

Tray ceilings adding elegance to the Dining Room and the Master Bedroom

Master Suite, privately located, features an arrangement for physically challenged

Two Bedrooms share a third full Bath with a linen closet

Skylit bonus room is located over the Garage

MAIN FLOOR — 2,349 SQ. FT.

BONUS — 435 SQ. FT.

GARAGE — 615 SQ. FT.

TOTAL LIVING AREA:
2,349 SQ. FT.

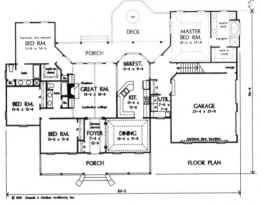

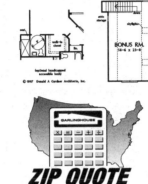

Your Classic Hideaway

PRICE CODE: B

This plan features:

- Three bedrooms

- Two full baths

A lovely fireplace in the Living Room which is both cozy and a source of heat for the core area

An efficient country Kitchen, connecting the large Dining and Living Rooms

A lavish Master Suite enhanced by a step-up sunken tub, more than ample closet space, and separate shower

A screened Porch and Patio Area for outdoor living

An optional basement, slab or crawl space foundation — please specify when ordering

MAIN AREA — 1,773 SQ. FT.

SCREENED PORCH — 240 SQ. FT.

TOTAL LIVING AREA:
1,773 SQ. FT.

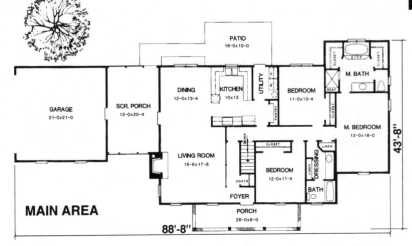

PLAN NO. 98409

Classically Detailed
PRICE CODE: D

- This plan features:
  - Four bedrooms
  - Two full and one half baths
- Keystones and columns accent the front triple arched Porch
- On either side of the two-story Foyer are arched openings to the formal areas
- The Family room has a rear wall fireplace set between bank of windows
- The Kitchen has a convenient center island and is open to the Nook
- The Master Suite has a tray ceiling and an optional Sitting Room
- Bedroom number two has a window seat in the front of the room
- An optional basement, slab or crawl space foundation please specify when ordering

FIRST FLOOR — 1,200 SQ. FT.
SECOND FLOOR — 1,168 SQ. FT.
BASEMENT — 1,200 SQ. FT.
GARAGE — 527 SQ. FT.

TOTAL LIVING AREA:
2,368 SQ. FT.

SECOND FLOOR PLAN

© Frank Betz Associates

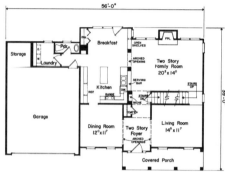

FIRST FLOOR PLAN

PLAN NO. 90682

Inviting Porch Adorns Affordable Home
PRICE CODE: A

- This plan features:
  - Three bedrooms
  - Two full baths
- A large and spacious Living Room that adjoins the Dining Room for ease in entertaining
- A private Bedroom wing offering a quiet atmosphere
- A Master Bedroom with his-n-her closets and a private Bath
- An efficient Kitchen with a walk-in Pantry

MAIN AREA — 1,243 SQ. FT.
BASEMENT — 1,103 SQ. FT.
GARAGE — 490 SQ. FT.

TOTAL LIVING AREA:
1,243 SQ. FT.

MAIN AREA

To order your Blueprints, call 1-800-235-5700

Easy Traffic Flow
Price Code: C

- This plan features:
- — Four bedrooms
- — Two full and one half baths
- Covered Porch welcomes all and shelters entry
- Formal Dining Room highlighted by a boxed window
- Fireplace and a wall of windows accent the Family Room
- Bayed Breakfast Area with access to back yard part of the efficient Kitchen
- Kitchen adjoins Dining Room, half-Bath, Laundry and Garage entry
- Master Bedroom Suite offers two walk-in closets and a double vanity Bath
- Three additional Bedrooms share a full hall Bath

FIRST FLOOR — 925 SQ. FT.
SECOND FLOOR — 960 SQ. FT.
BONUS — 258 SQ. FT.
BASEMENT — 925 SQ. FT.
GARAGE — 455 SQ. FT.

SECOND FLOOR

Br. 3
$10^0 \times 11^6$

Br. 4
$10^0 \times 11^6$

Mbr.
$12^0 \times 16^0$

Br. 2
$10^0 \times 11^8$
$10'-0''$ CLG.

DN

PLANT SHELF

TOTAL LIVING AREA:
1,885 SQ. FT.

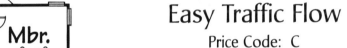

Fam. rm.
$18^0 \times 14^0$

Bfst.
$10^6 \times 15^0$

Kit.
$9^0 \times 11^6$

R.
W.
D.

© design basics, inc.

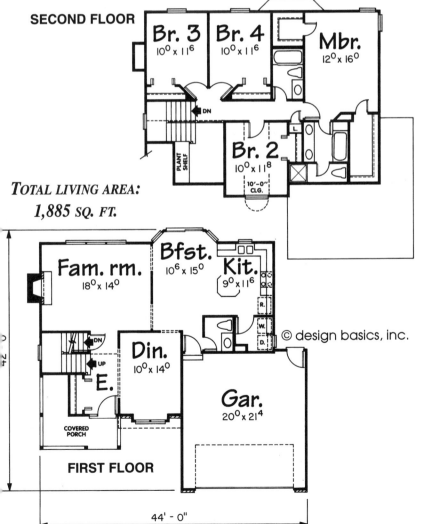

Din.
$10^0 \times 14^0$

E.

DN
UP

Gar.
$20^0 \times 21^4$

COVERED PORCH

FIRST FLOOR

44' - 0"

Distinctive Brick with Room to Expand

Price Code: E

An **EXCLUSIVE DESIGN**
By Jannis Vann & Associates, Inc

■ This plan features:

— Four bedrooms

— Two full and one half baths

■ Arched entrance with decorative glass leads into two-story Foyer

■ Formal Dining Room with tray ceiling above decorative window

■ Kitchen with island cooktop and built-in desk and Pantry

■ Master Bedroom wing topped by tray ceiling with French door to Patio, and a lavish Bath

■ Second Floor optional space for Storage and future Bedroom with full Bath

■ An optional basement, slab or crawl-space foundation — please specify when ordering

FIRST FLOOR — 2,577 SQ. FT.
SECOND FLOOR — 68 SQ. FT.
BONUS — 619 SQ. FT.
BASEMENT — 2,561 SQ. FT.
GARAGE — 560 SQ. FT.

FIRST FLOOR

SECOND FLOOR

TOTAL LIVING AREA:
2,645 SQ. FT.

To order your Blueprints, call 1-800-235-5700

Tandem Garage
PRICE CODE: B

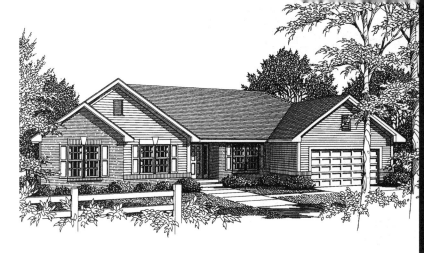

This plan features:
- Three bedrooms
- Two full baths
- Open Foyer leads into spacious Living highlighted by a wall of windows
- Country-size Kitchen with efficient, U-shaped counter, work island, eating Nook with back yard access, and nearby Laundry/Garage entry
- French doors open to pampering Master Bedroom with window alcove, walk-in closet and double vanity Bath
- Two additional Bedrooms with large closets, share a full Bath
- No materials list is available for this plan

MAIN FLOOR — 1,761 SQ. FT.
GARAGE — 658 SQ. FT.
BASEMENT — 1,761 SQ. FT.

TOTAL LIVING AREA:
1,761 SQ. FT.

ZIP QUOTE
HOME COST CALCULATOR
see order pages for details

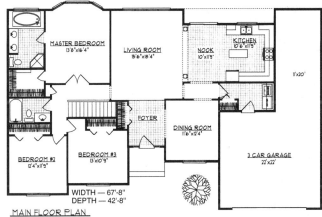

MAIN FLOOR PLAN

WIDTH — 67'-8"
DEPTH — 42'-8"

Wide Open and Convenient
PRICE CODE: B

This plan features:
- Three bedrooms
- Two full baths
- Vaulted ceilings in the Dining Room and Master Bedroom
- A sloped ceiling in the fireplaced Living Room
- A skylight illuminating the Master Bath
- A large Master Bedroom with a walk-in closet

MAIN FLOOR — 1,737 SQ. FT.
BASEMENT — 1,727 SQ. FT.
GARAGE — 484 SQ. FT.

TOTAL LIVING AREA:
1,737 SQ. FT.

ZIP QUOTE
HOME COST CALCULATOR
see order pages for details

An EXCLUSIVE DESIGN
By Karl Kreeger

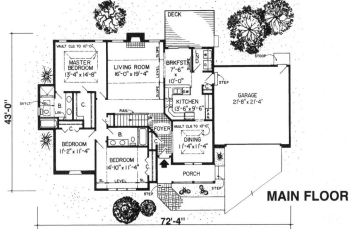

MAIN FLOOR

Open & Airy
PRICE CODE: C

- This plan features:
  — Three bedrooms
  — Two full and one half baths
- The Foyer is naturally lit by a dormer window above
- Family Room is highlighted by two front windows and fireplace
- Kitchen includes an angled extended counter/snack bar and an abundance of counter/cabinet space
- Dining Area opens to the Kitchen, for a more spacious feeling
- The roomy Master Suite is located on the first floor and has a private five-piece Bath plus a walk-in closet
- Laundry Room doubles as a Mudroom from the side entrance
- No materials list is available for this plan

FIRST FLOOR — 1,271 SQ. FT.
SECOND FLOOR — 537 SQ. FT.
BASEMENT — 1,271 SQ. FT.
GARAGE — 555 SQ. FT.

TOTAL LIVING AREA:
1,808 SQ. FT.

An
EXCLUSIVE DESIGN
By Greg Marquis

Quaint Starter Home
PRICE CODE: A

- This plan features:
  — Three bedrooms
  — Two full baths
- A vaulted ceiling giving an airy feeling to the Dining and Living Rooms
- A streamlined Kitchen with a comfortable work area, a double sink and ample cabinet space
- A cozy fireplace in the Living Room
- A Master Suite with a large closet, French doors leading to the Batio and a private Bath
- Two additional Bedrooms sharing a full bath
- No materials list is available for this plan

MAIN AREA — 1,050 SQ. FT.
GARAGE — 261 SQ. FT.

TOTAL LIVING AREA:
1,050 SQ. FT.

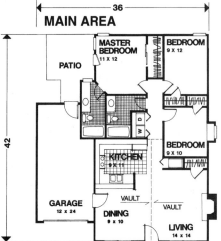

To order your Blueprints, call 1-800-235-5700

© 1994 Donald A. Gardner Architects, Inc.

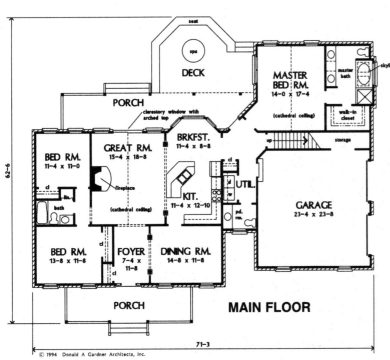

MAIN FLOOR

© 1994 Donald A Gardner Architects, Inc.

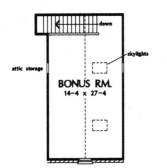

Mixture of Traditional and Country Charm

Price Code: D

- ■ This plan features:
- — Three bedrooms
- — Two full and one half baths
- ■ Stairs to the skylit bonus room located near the Kitchen and Master Suite
- ■ Master Suite crowned in cathedral ceilings has a skylit Bath that contains a whirlpool tub and dual vanity
- ■ Great Room, topped by a cathedral ceiling and highlighted by a fireplace, is adjacent to the country Kitchen
- ■ Two additional Bedrooms share a hall Bath

MAIN FLOOR — 1,954 SQ. FT.
GARAGE — 649 SQ. FT.
BONUS ROOM — 436 SQ. FT.

TOTAL LIVING AREA:
1,954 SQ. FT.

Country Style For Today

Price Code: D

■ This plan features:

— Three bedrooms

— Two full and one half baths

■ A wide wrap-around porch for a farmhouse style

■ A spacious Living Room with double doors and a large front window

■ A garden window over the double sink in the huge, country Kitchen with two islands, one a butcher block, and the other an eating bar

■ A corner fireplace in the Family Room enjoyed throughout the Nook and Kitchen, thanks to an open layout

■ A Master Suite with a spa tub, and a huge walk-in closet as well as a shower and double vanities

FIRST FLOOR — 1,785 SQ. FT.
SECOND FLOOR — 621 SQ. FT.

TOTAL LIVING AREA:
2,406 SQ. FT.

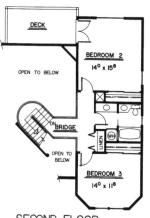

SECOND FLOOR

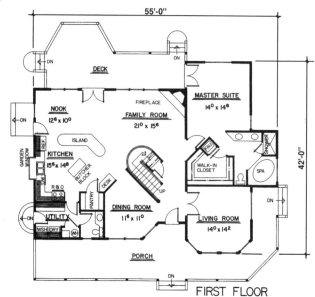

FIRST FLOOR

Skylight Brightens Master Bedroom

PRICE CODE: B

This plan features:

Three bedrooms

One full and one three-quarter baths

A covered Porch entry

A foyer separating the Dining Room from the Breakfast Area and Kitchen

A Living Room enhanced by a vaulted beam ceiling and a fireplace

A Master Bedroom with a decorative ceiling and a skylight in the private Bath

An optional Deck accessible through sliding doors off the Master Bedroom

MAIN AREA — 1,686 SQ. FT.

GARAGE — 484 SQ. FT.

BASEMENT — 1,676 SQ. FT.

TOTAL LIVING AREA:
1,686 SQ. FT.

ZIP QUOTE
HOME COST CALCULATOR
see order pages for details

An EXCLUSIVE DESIGN
By Karl Kreeger

MAIN AREA

Rocking Chair Living

PRICE CODE: B

This plan features:

- Three bedrooms
- Two full baths
- A massive fireplace separating Living and Dining Rooms
- An isolated Master Suite with a walk-in closet and compartmentalized Bath
- A galley-type Kitchen between the Breakfast Room and Dining Room
- An optional basement, slab or crawl space foundation — please specify when ordering

MAIN AREA — 1,670 SQ. FT.

BASEMENT — 1,670 SQ. FT.

GARAGE — 427 SQ. FT.

TOTAL LIVING AREA:
1,670 SQ. FT.

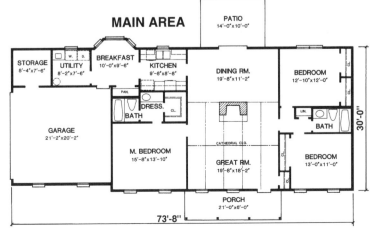

MAIN AREA

© 1992 Donald A. Gardner Architects, Inc.

Stately Home
PRICE CODE: F

- This plan features:
  - Four bedrooms
  - Two full and one half baths
- An elegant brick exterior and careful detailing
- Light floods through the arched window in the clerestory dormer above the Foyer
- Great Room topped by a cathedral ceiling boasting built-in cabinets and bookshelves
- Through glass doors capped by an arched window the Sun Room is access from the Great Room
- Both the Dining Room and the Bedroom/Study have tray ceilings
- Master Suite includes a fireplace, access to the Deck, his-n-her vanities, a shower and a whirlpool tub
- An optional basement or crawl space foundation — please specify when ordering

MAIN FLOOR — 2,526 SQ. FT.
GARAGE — 611 SQ. FT.

TOTAL LIVING AREA:
2,526 SQ. FT.

ALTERNATE PLAN FOR BASEMENT

FLOOR PLAN

French Country Styling
PRICE CODE: F

- This plan features:
  - Four bedrooms
  - Three full and one half baths
- Brick and stone blend masterfully for an impressive French Country exterior
- Separate Master Suite with expansive Bath and closet
- Study containing a built-in desk and bookcase
- Angled island Kitchen highlighted by walk-in Pantry and open to the Breakfast Bay
- Fantastic Family Room including a brick fireplace and built-in entertainment center
- Three additional Bedrooms with private access to a full Bath
- No material list is available for this plan

MAIN FLOOR — 3,352 SQ. FT.
GARAGE — 672 SQ. FT.

TOTAL LIVING AREA:
3,352 SQ. FT.

MAIN FLOOR

ZIP QUOTE
HOME COST CALCULATOR
see order pages for details

To order your Blueprints, call 1-800-235-5700

FIRST FLOOR — 2,553 SQ. FT.
SECOND FLOOR — 1,260 SQ. FT.
GARAGE — 714 SQ. FT.

TOTAL LIVING AREA:
3,813 SQ. FT.

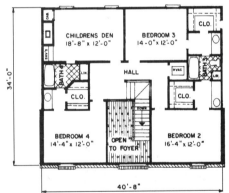

CHILDRENS DEN
18'-8" x 12'-0"

BEDROOM 3
14'-0" x 12'-0"

HALL

BEDROOM 4
14'-4" x 12'-0"

OPEN TO FOYER

BEDROOM 2
16'-4" x 12'-0"

34'-0"

40'-8"

SECOND FLOOR PLAN

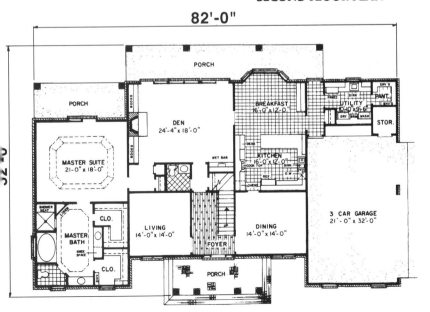

82'-0"

PORCH

PORCH

DEN
24'-4" x 18'-0"

BREAKFAST
16'-0" x 12'-0"

UTILITY
10'-0" x 9'-0"

PANT.

STOR.

MASTER SUITE
21'-0" x 18'-0"

WET BAR

KITCHEN
16'-0" x 12'-0"

SHOWER SEAT

MASTER BATH

CLO.

LIVING
14'-0" x 14'-0"

FOYER

DINING
14'-0" x 14'-0"

3 CAR GARAGE
21'-0" x 32'-0"

CLO.

PORCH

FIRST FLOOR PLAN

Traditional Elegance

Price Code: F

■ This plan features:

— Four bedrooms

— Three full and one half baths

■ A elegant entrance leading into a two story Foyer with an impressive staircase highlighted by a curved window

■ Floor to ceiling windows in both the formal Living and Dining Rooms

■ A spacious Den with a hearth fireplace, built-in book shelves, and a wetbar

■ A large, efficient Kitchen, a bright Breakfast area, and access to the Dining Room, Utility Room, walk-in Pantry and Garage

■ A grand Master Suite with decorative ceilings, a private Porch, an elaborate Bath and two walk-in closets

■ Three additional Bedrooms on the second floor with walk-in closets, sharing adjoining, full Baths and a ideal Children's Den

■ An optional crawl space or slab foundation — please specify when ordering

Letting the Light In

Price Code: B

- **This plan features:**
- — Four bedrooms
- — Two full baths

- **Covered Porch** leads into easy-care tile Entry with angled staircase

- **Vaulted Ceiling** tops decorative corner windows and cozy wood stove in Living Room

- **Sliding glass door** to rear yard brightens Dining Room and adjoining Living Room and Kitchen

- **Efficient Kitchen** with built-in Pantry, pass-through counter and plant shelf window

- **Two first floor Bedrooms** with ample closets, share a full Bath and Utility Area

- **French doors** lead into private Master Bedroom with skylight Bath

- **Loft/Bedroom** overlooking Living Room offers many options

- **No materials list** is available for this plan

FIRST FLOOR — 1076 SQ. FT.
SECOND FLOOR — 449 SQ. FT.
GARAGE — 495 SQ. FT.

TOTAL LIVING AREA:
1,525 SQ. FT.

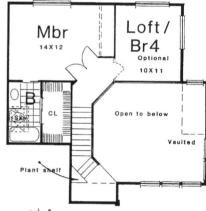

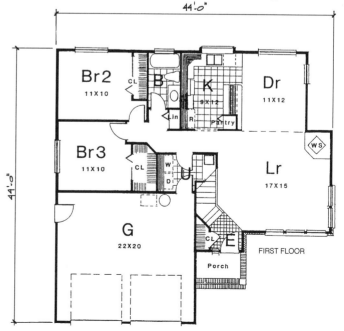

Definitely Detailed
PRICE CODE: C

This plan features:
- Three bedrooms
- Two full baths
- An artistically detailed brick exterior adds to the appeal of this home
- The Foyer is separated from the Great room by columns
- The Great Room has a wall of windows and a warming fireplace
- The Dining Room has a sloped ceiling and is adjacent to the Kitchen
- The Kitchen is arranged in a U-shape and features a center island plus a walk-in Pantry
- The Bedrooms are all on one side of the home for privacy
- An optional plan for the basement includes a Recreation Room, an Exercise Room, and a Bath
- No materials list is available for this plan

FIRST FLOOR — 1,963 SQ. FT.
LOWER LEVEL — 1,963 SQ. FT.

TOTAL LIVING AREA:
1,963 SQ. FT.

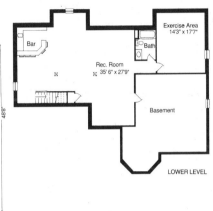

For an Established Neighborhood
PRICE CODE: A

This plan features:
- Three bedrooms
- Two full baths
- A covered entrance sheltering and welcoming visitors
- An expansive Living Room enhanced by natural light streaming in from the large front window
- A bayed formal Dining Room with direct access to the Sun Deck and the Living Room for entertainment ease
- An efficient, galley Kitchen, convenient to both formal and informal eating areas, and equipped with a double sink and adequate counter and storage space
- An informal Breakfast Room with direct access to the Sun Deck
- A large Master Suite equipped with a walk-in closet and a full private Bath
- Two additional Bedrooms that share a full hall Bath

MAIN FLOOR — 1,276 SQ. FT.
FINISHED STAIRS — 16 SQ. FT.
BASEMENT — 392 SQ. FT.
GARAGE — 728 SQ. FT.

TOTAL LIVING AREA:
1,292 SQ. FT.

An
EXCLUSIVE DESIGN
By Jannis Vann & Associates, Inc.

ZIP QUOTE
HOME COST CALCULATOR
see order pages for details

Cute Cottage
PRICE CODE: A

- This plan features:
  - Three bedrooms
  - Two full baths
- A cute covered front Porch adds character to this cottage plan
- The large Living Room has a 10-foot ceiling and a side wall fireplace
- The Kitchen is open to the Dining Room
- The Kitchen is equipped with a center island, a planning desk, and a cooktop
- A convenient Laundry Room is located off of the Kitchen
- The Master Bedroom has a walk in closet and a full Bath
- Two secondary Bedrooms are identical in size and share a Bath in the hall
- There is a detached two-car Barage with this plan
- No materials list is available for this plan

MAIN FLOOR — 1,393 SQ. FT.
GARAGE — 528 SQ. FT.

TOTAL LIVING AREA:
1,393 SQ. FT.

MAIN AREA

An
EXCLUSIVE DESIGN
By Greg Marquis

Traditional Brick with Detailing
PRICE CODE: D

- This plan features:
  - Three bedrooms
  - Two full baths
- Covered entry leads into the Foyer, the formal Dining Room and the Den
- Expansive Den with a decorative ceiling over a hearth fireplace and sliding glass doors to the rear yard
- Country Kitchen with a built-in Pantry, double ovens and a cooktop island easily serves the Breakfast Area and Dining Room
- Private Master Bedroom suite with a decorative ceiling, a walk-in closet, a double vanity and a whirlpool tub
- Two additional Bedrooms share a full Bath
- An optional slab or crawl space foundation — please specify when ordering

MAIN FLOOR — 1,869 SQ. FT.
GARAGE — 561 SQ. FT.

TOTAL LIVING AREA:
1,869 SQ. FT.

WIDTH 74'-10"
DEPTH 40'-4"

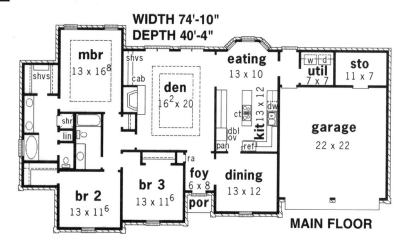

MAIN FLOOR

To order your Blueprints, call 1-800-235-5700

© 1996 Donald A Gardner Architects, Inc.

Easy, Economical Building

Price Code: D

■ This plan features:
— Three bedrooms
— Two full baths

■ Many architectural elements offer efficient and economical design

■ Great Room vaulted ceiling gracefully arches to include arched window dormer

■ Open Kitchen with angled counter easily serves Breakfast Area

■ Tray ceilings enhance Dining Room, front Bedroom and Master Bedroom

■ Private Master Bath includes garden tub, double vanity and skylight

■ An optional basement or crawl space foundation—please specify when ordering

MAIN FLOOR — 1,959 SQ. FT.
BONUS ROOM — 385 SQ. FT.
GARAGE & STORAGE — 484 SQ. FT.

TOTAL LIVING AREA:
1,959 SQ. FT.

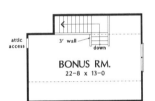

BONUS RM.
22-8 x 13-0
attic access
3' wall
down

FLOOR PLAN

© 1996 Donald A Gardner Architects, Inc.

Elegant Brick
Two-Story

Price Code: D

■ This plan features:

— Four bedrooms

— Two full and one half baths

■ A large two-story Great Room with a fireplace and access to a wood Deck

■ A secluded Master Suite with two walk-in closets and a private, lavish, Master Bath

■ A large island Kitchen serving the formal Dining Room and the sunny Breakfast Nook with ease

■ Three additional Bedrooms, two with walk-in closets, sharing a full hall Bath

■ An optional bonus room with a private entrance from below

■ An optional basement or crawl space foundation — please specify when ordering

FIRST FLOOR — 1,637 SQ. FT.
SECOND FLOOR — 761 SQ. FT.
BONUS — 453 SQ. FT.

TOTAL LIVING AREA:
2,398 SQ. FT.

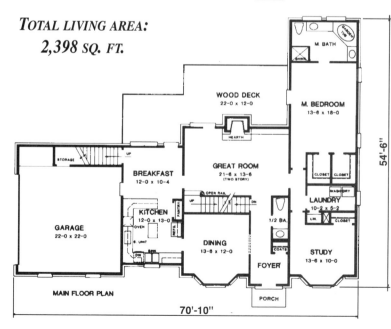

To order your Blueprints, call 1-800-235-5700

Traditional Ranch
PRICE CODE: D

This plan features:

Three bedrooms

Two full baths

A tray ceiling in the Master Suite that is equipped with his-n-her walk-in closets and a private Master Bath with a cathedral ceiling

A formal Living Room with a cathedral ceiling

A decorative tray ceiling in the elegant formal Dining Room

A spacious Family Room with a vaulted ceiling and a fireplace

A modern, well-appointed Kitchen with snack bar and bayed Breakfast Area

Two additional Bedrooms that share a full hall Bath each having a walk-in closet

MAIN FLOOR — 2,275 SQ. FT.

GARAGE — 512 SQ. FT.

BASEMENT — 2,207 SQ. FT.

TOTAL LIVING AREA:
2,275 SQ. FT.

PLAN NO. 92404

Comfortable, Easy Living
PRICE CODE: G

This plan features:

- Five bedrooms

- Three full and one half baths

Great Room is overlooked by a curved balcony and features a fireplace with built-ins on either side

Spacious and efficient Kitchen equipped with a cooktop island has direct access to Breakfast Room and Dining Room

Swing Room, Bedroom/Study, with private full Bath and closet

Master Suite pampered by lavish Bath and large walk-in closet

Three additional second floor Bedrooms, each with ample storage, share a full Bath in the hall

FIRST FLOOR — 2,176 SQ. FT.

SECOND FLOOR — 861 SQ. FT.

BONUS ROOM — 483 SQ. FT.

GARAGE — 710 SQ. FT.

TOTAL LIVING AREA:
3,037 SQ. FT.

©1993 Donald A. Gardner Architects, Inc.

PLAN NO. 96444

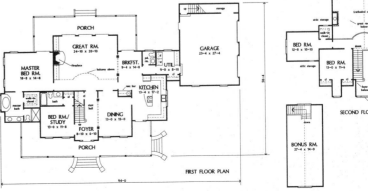

To order your Blueprints, call 1-800-235-5700

For the Young at Heart
PRICE CODE: A

- This plan features:
  - Three bedrooms
  - Two full baths
- Arched transom windows, divided-light windows, bay windows and a covered Porch entry
- A Great Room with a vaulted ceiling, a fireplace and a transom window
- A Kitchen with a vaulted ceiling and a Breakfast Area with sliding doors to the Deck
- A Master Suite with ample closet space and a private Master Bath

MAIN FLOOR — 1,307 SQ. FT.
BASEMENT — 1,307 SQ. FT.
GARAGE — 374 SQ. FT.

TOTAL LIVING AREA:
1,307 SQ. FT.

Floor Plan

Inexpensive Ranch Design
PRICE CODE: A

- This plan features:
  - Three bedrooms
  - Two full baths
- A large picture window brightening the Breakfast Area
- A well planned Kitchen
- A Living Room which is accented by an open beam across the sloping ceiling and wood burning fireplace
- A Master Bedroom with an extremely large Bath Area

MAIN AREA — 1,500 SQ. FT.
BASEMENT — 1,500 SQ. FT.
GARAGE — 482 SQ. FT.

TOTAL LIVING AREA:
1,500 SQ. FT.

MAIN AREA

ZIP QUOTE
HOME COST CALCULATOR
see order pages for details

An
EXCLUSIVE DESIGN
By Karl Kreeger

To order your Blueprints, call 1-800-235-5700

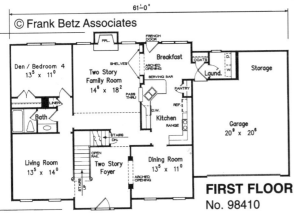

© Frank Betz Associates

61'-0"

FIRST FLOOR
No. 98410

Den / Bedroom 4
13⁵ x 11⁰

Two Story
Family Room
14⁶ x 18²

Breakfast

Storage

Laund.

Garage
20⁸ x 20⁶

Bath

Living Room
13⁵ x 14⁰

Two Story
Foyer

Kitchen

Dining Room
13⁵ x 11⁰

TOTAL LIVING AREA:
2,389 SQ. FT.

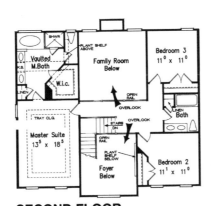

SECOND FLOOR

Vaulted
M.Bath

Family Room
Below

Bedroom 3
11⁰ x 11⁰

Master Suite
13⁵ x 18⁵

Foyer
Below

Bath

Bedroom 2
11¹ x 11⁰

SECOND FLOOR WITH BONUS ROOM

Bedroom 3
11⁰ x 12⁴

Bath

Bonus Room
12¹⁰ x 20⁵

Bedroom 2
13⁵ x 12³

A Magnificent Manor
Price Code: D

■ This plan features:
— Three bedrooms
— Three full baths

■ The two-story Foyer is dominated by a lovely staircase

■ The formal Living Room is located directly off the Foyer

■ An efficient Kitchen accesses the Dining Room for ease in serving

■ The Breakfast Area is separated from the Kitchen by an extended counter/serving bar

■ The two-story Family Room is highlighted by a fireplace that is framed by windows

■ A tray ceiling crowns the Master Bedroom while a vaulted ceiling tops the Master Bath

■ An optional basement or crawl space foundation — please specify when ordering

FIRST FLOOR — 1,428 SQ. FT.
SECOND FLOOR — 961 SQ. FT.
BONUS — 472 SQ. FT.
BASEMENT — 1,428 SQ. FT.
GARAGE — 507 SQ. FT.

Double Decks Adorn Luxurious Master Suite

Price Code: E

- This plan features:
- — Three bedrooms
- — Two full and one half baths
- Abundant windows, indoor planters and three decks uniting every room with the outdoors
- An efficient Kitchen with direct access to the Nook and the formal Dining Room
- A wood stove warming the spacious Family Room
- A secluded Master Suite with private deck, Den and master bath
- An optional basement, slab or crawl space foundation — please specify when ordering

MAIN FLOOR — 1,985 SQ. FT.
UPPER FLOOR — 715 SQ. FT.

TOTAL LIVING AREA:
2,700 SQ. FT.

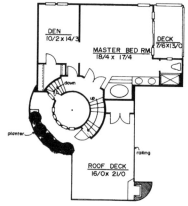

UPPER FLOOR

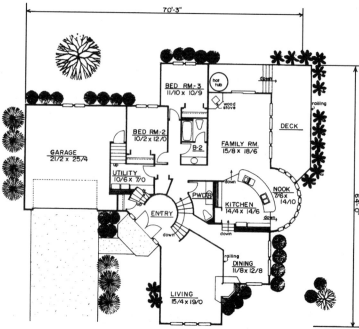

MAIN FLOOR

To order your Blueprints, call 1-800-235-5700

Backyard Views
PRICE CODE: B

PLAN NO.9

is plan features:

ree bedrooms

o full baths

nt Porch accesses open Foyer, and spacious Dining
om and Great Room with sloped ceilings

rner fireplace, windows and atrium door to Patio
hance Great Room

nvenient Kitchen with a Pantry, peninsula serving
nter for bright Breakfast Area and nearby
undry/Garage entry

xurious Bath, walk-in closet and backyard view
ered in Master Bedroom

o additional Bedrooms, one with an arched window,
are a full Bath

materials list is available for this plan

N AREA — 1,746 SQ. FT.

EMENT — 1,697 SQ. FT.

AGE — 480 SQ. FT.

TOTAL LIVING AREA:
1,746 SQ. FT.

ZIP QUOTE
HOME COST CALCULATOR
see order pages for details

WIDTH: 65' - 10"
DEPTH: 56' - 0"

MAIN AREA

Compact Country Cottage
PRICE CODE: C

PLAN NO.99856

his plan features:

hree bedrooms

wo full baths

oyer opening to a large Great Room with a fireplace
nd a cathedral ceiling

fficient U-shaped Kitchen with peninsula counter
xtending work space and separating it from the Dining
Room

wo front Bedrooms, one with a bay window, the other
with a walk-in closet, sharing a full Bath in the hall

Master Suite located to the rear with a walk-in closet and
private Bath with a double vanity

Partially covered Deck with skylights accessible from
he Dining Room, Great Room and the Master Bedroom

AIN FLOOR — 1,310 SQ. FT.

RAGE & STORAGE — 455 SQ. FT.

TOTAL LIVING AREA:
1,310 SQ. FT.

91 Donald A. Gardner Architects, Inc.

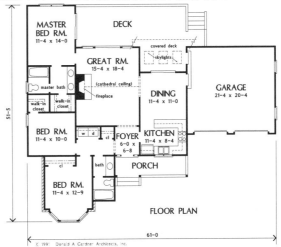

FLOOR PLAN

A Nest for Empty-Nesters

PRICE CODE: A

■ This plan features:
— Two bedrooms
— One full bath
■ An economical design
■ A covered Sun Deck adding outdoor living space
■ A Mudroom/Laundry area inside the side door, trapping dirt before it can enter the house
■ An open layout between the Living Room with fireplace Dining Room and Kitchen

MAIN FLOOR — 884 SQ. FT.

TOTAL LIVING AREA:
884 SQ. FT.

MAIN FLOOR

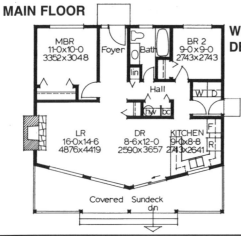

WIDTH 34'- 0"
DEPTH 28'- 0"

MBR 11-0x10-0 3352x3048
Foyer
Bath
BR 2 9-0x9-0 2743x2743
lin
Hall
W D
hw bc
LR 16-0x14-6 4876x4419
DR 8-6x12-0 2590x3657
KITCHEN 9-0x8-8 2743x2641
F R

Covered Sundeck
dn

An
EXCLUSIVE DESIGN
By Westhome Planners, Ltd.

Style and Convenience

PRICE CODE: A

■ This plan features:
—Three bedrooms
—Two full baths
■ Large front windows, dormers and an old-fashioned Porch giving a pleasing style to the home
■ A vaulted ceiling topping the Foyer flowing into the Family Room which is highlighted by a fireplace
■ A Formal Dining Room flowing from the Family Room crowned in an elegant vaulted ceiling
■ An efficient Kitchen enhanced by a Pantry, a pass through to the Family Room and direct access to the Dining Room and Breakfast Room
■ A decorative tray ceiling, a five-piece private Bath and walk-in closet in the Master Suite
■ Two additional Bedrooms, roomy in size, share the full Bath in the hall
■ An optional basement or crawl space foundation — please specify when ordering

MAIN FLOOR — 1,373 SQ. FT.
BASEMENT — 1,386 SQ. FT.

TOTAL LIVING AREA:
1,373 SQ. FT.

WIDTH 50'-4"
DEPTH 45'-0"

Porch
Breakfast
Bedroom 3 11⁶ x 11⁰
W.i.c.
PLANT SHELF ABOVE
Vaulted M. Bath
SHWR
Vaulted Dining Room 10' x 12⁶
Kitchen
PANTRY
PLANT SHELF ABOVE
LINEN
Bath
Master Suite 14⁶ x 14⁰
TRAY CLG.
PASS THRU
REF
DW
RANGE
FPL
Vaulted Family Room 16⁶ x 12⁶
COATS
Bedroom 2 11⁰ x 10⁰
Garage 19⁵ x 21⁶
OPT. STAIRS TO BSMT.
Vaulted Foyer
Porch

FLOOR PLAN

GARAGE LOCATION WITH BASEMENT

© Frank Betz Associates

To order your Blueprints, call 1-800-235-5700

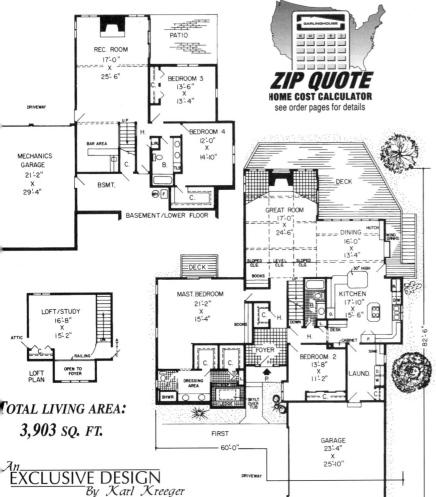

ZIP QUOTE
HOME COST CALCULATOR
see order pages for details

REC. ROOM 17'-0" X 25'-6"

PATIO

BEDROOM 3 13'-6" X 13'-4"

BEDROOM 4 12'-0" X 14'-10"

DRIVEWAY

MECHANICS GARAGE 21'-2" X 29'-4"

BAR AREA

BSMT.

BASEMENT/LOWER FLOOR

LOFT/STUDY 16'-8" X 15'-2"

ATTIC

LOFT PLAN

OPEN TO FOYER

RAILING

DECK

GREAT ROOM 17'-0" X 24'-6"

DINING 16'-0" X 13'-4"

KITCHEN 17'-10" X 15'-6"

MAST. BEDROOM 21'-2" X 15'-4"

DECK

FOYER

DRESSING AREA

SHWR

LEDGE

SKYLT OVER TUB

BEDROOM 2 13'-8" X 11'-2"

LAUND.

FIRST

GARAGE 23'-4" X 25'-10"

DRIVEWAY

60'-0"

82'-6"

TOTAL LIVING AREA: 3,903 SQ. FT.

An EXCLUSIVE DESIGN *By Karl Kreeger*

Loft Overlooks Foyer
Price Code: F

■ This plan features:
— Four bedrooms
— Three full baths

■ Enormous rooms and two Garages

■ An island Kitchen with an eating peninsula for informal dining

■ Great Room with a massive fireplace and open-beamed ceiling

■ A large wrap-around Deck to expand the outdoor living area

■ A Master Bedroom suite with a private Deck, two large walk-in closets, and a lavish sky-lit tub

■ A large Recreation Room on the lower floor with access to the rear Patio

FIRST FLOOR — 2,367 SQ. FT.
LOWER FLOOR — 1,241 SQ. FT.
BASEMENT (UNFINISHED) — 372 SQ. FT.
LOFT — 295 SQ. FT.
GARAGE (UPPER) — 660 SQ. FT.
GARAGE (LOWER) — 636 SQ. FT.

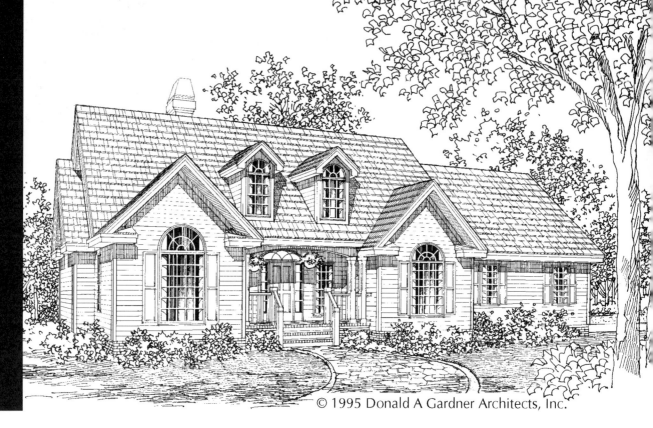

© 1995 Donald A Gardner Architects, Inc.

Great Room With Columns

Price Code: D

TOTAL LIVING AREA:
1,879 SQ. FT.

■ This plan features:

— Three bedrooms

— Two full baths

■ Great Room crowned with a cathedral ceiling and accented by columns and a fireplace

■ Tray ceilings and arched picture windows accent front Bedroom and the Dining Room

■ Secluded Master Suite highlighted by a tray ceiling and contains a Bath with skylight, a garden tub and spacious walk-in closet

■ Two additional Bedrooms share a full Bath

■ An optional crawl space or basement foundation — please specify when ordering this plan

MAIN FLOOR — 1,879 SQ. FT.
GARAGE — 485 SQ. FT.
BONUS — 360 SQ. FT.

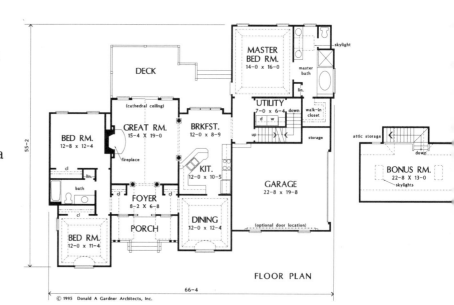

FLOOR PLAN

© 1995 Donald A Gardner Architects, Inc.

To order your Blueprints, call 1-800-235-5700

Charming Southern Traditional

PRICE CODE: B

This plan features:

Three bedrooms

Two full baths

A covered front Porch with striking columns, brick quoins, and dentil molding

A spacious Great Room with vaulted ceilings, a fireplace, and built-in cabinets

A Utility Room adjacent to the Kitchen which leads to the two-car Garage and Storage Rooms

A Master Bedroom including a large walk-in closet and a compartmentalized Bath

An optional slab or crawl space foundation — please specify when ordering

MAIN FLOOR — 1,271 SQ. FT.

GARAGE — 506 SQ. FT.

TOTAL LIVING AREA:
1,271 SQ. FT.

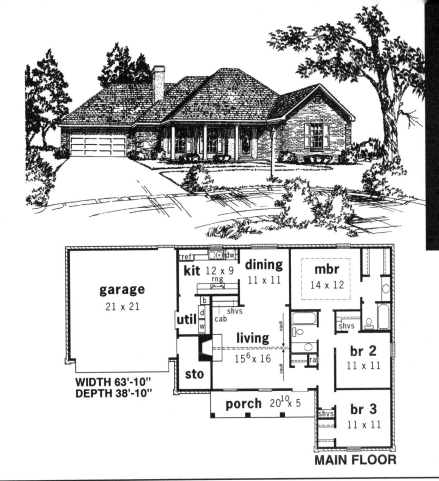

MAIN FLOOR

- garage 21 x 21
- kit 12 x 9
- dining 11 x 11
- mbr 14 x 12
- util
- living 15⁶ x 16
- sto
- br 2 11 x 11
- br 3 11 x 11
- porch 20¹⁰ x 5

WIDTH 63'-10"
DEPTH 38'-10"

Plush Master Bedroom Wing

PRICE CODE: C

This plan features:

- Three bedrooms

- Two full baths

A raised, tile Foyer with a decorative window leading into an expansive Living Room, accented by a tiled fireplace and framed by French doors

An efficient Kitchen with a walk-in Pantry and serving bar adjoining the Breakfast and Utility Areas

A private Master Bedroom, crowned by a stepped ceiling, offering an atrium door to outside, a huge, walk-in closet and a luxurious Bath

Two additional Bedrooms with walk-in closets, share a full hall Bath

No materials list is available for this plan

MAIN FLOOR — 1,849 SQ. FT.

GARAGE — 437 SQ. FT.

TOTAL LIVING AREA:
1,849 SQ. FT.

MAIN FLOOR

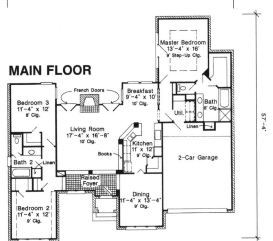

- Master Bedroom 13'-4" x 16' 9' Step-Up Clg.
- Breakfast 9'-4" x 10' 10' Clg.
- Bath 8' Clg.
- Util.
- Linen
- Bedroom 3 11'-4" x 12' 8' Clg.
- French Doors
- Living Room 17'-4" x 16'-8" 10' Clg.
- Kitchen 11' x 12' 9' Clg.
- Books
- Bath 2
- Linen
- 2-Car Garage
- Raised Foyer
- Dining 11'-4" x 13'-4" 9' Clg.
- Bedroom 2 11'-4" x 12' 9' Clg.

60'

57'-4"

Old World Flavor
PRICE CODE: A

- This plan features:
  - Three bedrooms
  - Two full baths
- Timely floor plan easily supports a busy family's contemporary lifestyle
- Generous center island Kitchen facilitates quick meal preparation
- Vaulted ceiling in the flexible Living Room/Study
- One walk-in closet and a private Bath compliment the Master Suite
- No material list is available for this plan

MAIN FLOOR — 1,475 SQ. FT.
GARAGE & STORAGE — 455 SQ. FT.

TOTAL LIVING AREA: 1,475 SQ. FT.

MAIN FLOOR

An EXCLUSIVE DESIGN
By Greg Marquis

Charm and Efficiency
PRICE CODE: C

- This plan features:
  - Three bedrooms
  - Two full and one half baths
- This attractive home will fit the lifestyle of a growing family of an empty nester
- The open floor plan maximizes interaction when entertaining
- The Master Bedroom is located in the rear of the home for privacy
- Upstairs are the secondary Bedrooms, a Bath, and a Lo
- A convenient half Bath is located on the first floor near the living space
- A two-car Garage accesses the Laundry Room
- No materials list is available for this plan

FIRST FLOOR — 1,283 SQ. FT.
SECOND FLOOR — 615 SQ. FT.
BASEMENT — 1,283 SQ. FT.
GARAGE — 420 SQ. FT.

TOTAL LIVING AREA: 1,898 SQ. FT.

FIRST FLOOR

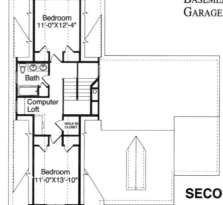

SECOND FLOOR

To order your Blueprints, call 1-800-235-5700

©1993 Donald A. Gardner Architects, Inc.

B. NATHAN

FIRST FLOOR
No. 96446

DECK
spa
covered porch
covered porch
DINING 12-0 x 12-8
KIT. 10-6 x 16-4
BRKFST. 10-7 x 9-8
pd. rm.
up
storage
d w
cl
GARAGE 23-4 x 22-0
54-4
GREAT RM. 15-4 x 19-8
walk-in closet
master bath
fireplace
MASTER BED RM. 15-4 x 14-4
FOYER 7-0 x 6-0
up
cl
PORCH
72-8

SECOND FLOOR

bath
attic storage
attic storage
BED RM. 15-4 x 11-0
BED RM. 15-4 x 11-0
down
lin.
cl   cl
cl   cl
foyer below

down
BONUS RM. 13-4 x 25-8

Perfect for the Growing Family
Price Code: E

■ This plan features:
— Three bedrooms
— Two full and one half baths

■ Natural light fills the two-story foyer through a palladian window in dormer above

■ Dining Room and Great Room adjoin for entertaining possibilities

■ U-shaped Kitchen with a curved counter opens to a large Breakfast Area

■ Master Suite, situated downstairs for privacy with generous walk-in closet, double vanity, separate shower and a whirlpool tub

■ An optional basement or crawl space foundation — please specify when ordering

FIRST FLOOR — 1,484 SQ. FT.
SECOND FLOOR — 660 SQ. FT.
BONUS ROOM — 389 SQ. FT.
GARAGE — 600 SQ. FT.

TOTAL LIVING AREA:
2,144 SQ. FT.

423

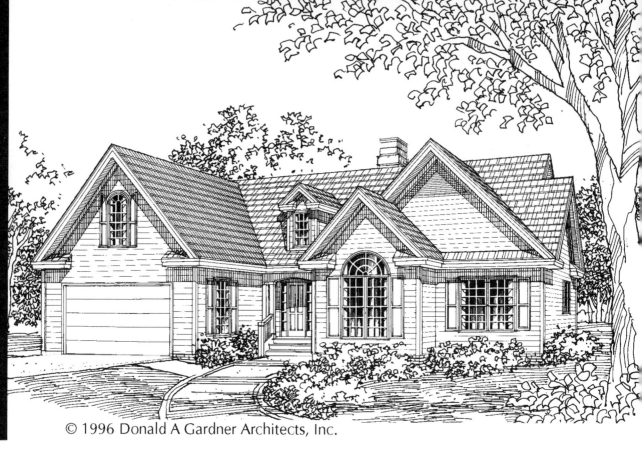

© 1996 Donald A Gardner Architects, Inc.

Sunny Dormer
Brightens Foyer

Price Code: C

■ This plan features:

— Three bedrooms

— Two full baths

■ Today's comforts with cost effective construction

■ Open Great room, Dining Room, and Kitchen topped by a cathedral ceiling emphasizing spaciousness

■ Adjoining Deck providing extra living or entertaining room

■ Front Bedroom crowned in cathedral ceiling and pampered by a private Bath with garden tub, dual vanity and a walk-in closet

■ Skylit bonus room above the garage offering flexibility and opportunity for growth

MAIN FLOOR — 1,386 SQ. FT.
GARAGE — 517 SQ. FT.
BONUS ROOM — 314 SQ. FT.

ZIP QUOTE
HOME COST CALCULATOR
see order pages for details

TOTAL LIVING AREA:
1,386 SQ. FT.

BONUS RM.
12-0 x 20-8
(cathedral ceiling)
down
attic storage
skylights

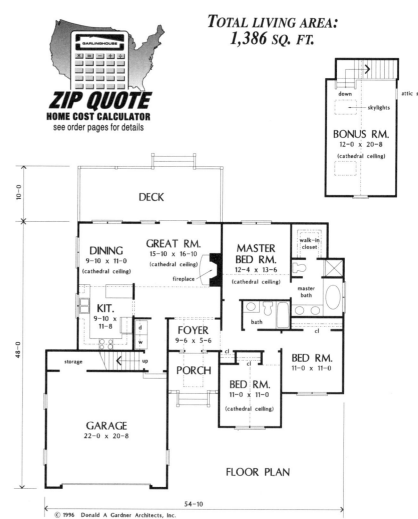

FLOOR PLAN

DECK

DINING
9-10 x 11-0
(cathedral ceiling)

GREAT RM.
15-10 x 16-10
(cathedral ceiling)
fireplace

MASTER
BED RM.
12-4 x 13-6
(cathedral ceiling)

walk-in closet

master bath

KIT.
9-10 x 11-8

d
w

FOYER
9-6 x 5-6

bath

cl

BED RM.
11-0 x 11-0

storage
up

PORCH

cl

cl

BED RM.
11-0 x 11-0
(cathedral ceiling)

GARAGE
22-0 x 20-8

10-0

48-0

54-10

© 1996 Donald A Gardner Architects, Inc.

To order your Blueprints, call 1-800-235-5700

Ranch Provides Great Kitchen Area

PRICE CODE: A

This plan features:
 Three bedrooms
 Two full baths
 A Dining Room with sliding glass doors to the backyard
 Access to the Garage through the Laundry Room
 A Master Bedroom with a private full Bath
 A two-car Garage

MAIN FLOOR — 1,400 SQ. FT.
BASEMENT — 1,400 SQ. FT.
GARAGE — 528 SQ. FT.

TOTAL LIVING AREA:
1,400 SQ. FT.

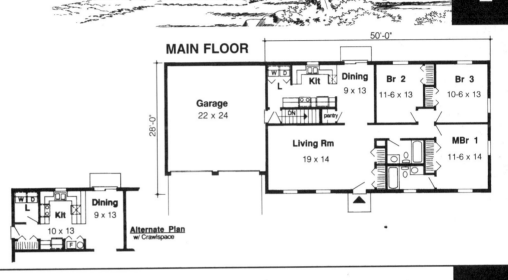

MAIN FLOOR

50'-0"

28'-0"

Garage
22 x 24

W D
L
Kit
Dining
9 x 13

Br 2
11-6 x 13

Br 3
10-6 x 13

DN
pantry

Living Rm
19 x 14

MBr 1
11-6 x 14

W D
L
Kit
10 x 13
Dining
9 x 13
F

Alternate Plan
w/ Crawlspace

Mind Your Manor

PRICE CODE: F

This plan features:
- Five bedrooms
- Two full, one three-quarter and one half baths
 From the front covered Porch enter into the Entry/Gallery which features a grand spiral staircase
 In the front of the house find the formal Living Room and Dining Room, each with two palladian windows
 The Study has built in book cases centered between a window
 The large Family Room has a fireplace and a built in stereo cabinet
 The bayed Breakfast Nook has a door that leads into the backyard covered Patio
 The first floor Master Bedroom has two walk in closets with a built-in chest of drawers and a Bath with a cathedral ceiling
 An optional slab or a crawl space foundation — please specify when ordering
 No materials list is available for this plan

FIRST FLOOR — 2,208 SQ. FT.
SECOND FLOOR — 1,173 SQ. FT.
BONUS — 224 SQ. FT.
GARAGE — 520 SQ. FT.

TOTAL LIVING AREA:
3,381 SQ. FT.

72'-0"

63'-10"

Covered Patio

MstrBed
14 x 18

Brkfst
12 x 10

FamilyRm
16 x 17

Kit
14 x 12

Study
14 x 11

Gallery

Gar
20 x 26

Util

LivRm
15 x 12

Ent

FrmlDin
15 x 12

Covered Porch

Main Floor

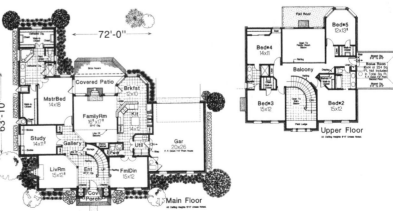

Bed#5
12 x 13

Bed#4
14 x 11

Bonus Room

Balcony

Bed#3
15 x 12

Bed#2
15 x 12

Upper Floor

To order your Blueprints, call 1-800-235-5700

Family Favorite
PRICE CODE: A

- This plan features:
- — Three bedrooms
- — Two full baths
- An open arrangement with the Dining Room that combines with ten foot ceilings to make the Living Room seem more spacious
- Glass on three sides of the Dining Room which overlooks the deck
- An efficient, compact Kitchen with a built-in pantry a peninsula counter
- A Master Suite with a romantic window seat, a compartmentalized private bath and a walk-in closet
- Two additional bedrooms that share a full hall closet

MAIN FLOOR — 1,359 SQ. FT.
GARAGE — 501 SQ. FT.
FOUNDATION — BASEMENT, SLAB OR CRAWL SPACE

An
EXCLUSIVE DESIGN
By Karl Kreeger

MAIN FLOOR

Crawl Space/Slab Option

Br #2
10-10 x 11-10

Den/Br #3
10-0 x 11-10

Optional Door Location

Deck

Dining
11-0 x 11-2

Kit
10-0 x 11-2

Ldry

Living Rm
14-10 x 17-0
10' clg

MBr #1
11-7 x 13-0

Garage
20-4 x 21-8

58'-0"

34'-4"

Seat

TOTAL LIVING AREA:
1,359 SQ. FT.

GARLINGHOUSE
ZIP QUOTE
HOME COST CALCULATOR
see order pages for details

No Wasted Space
PRICE CODE: A

- This plan features:
- — Three bedrooms
- — Two full baths
- A centrally located Great Room with a cathedral ceiling exposed wood beams, and large areas of fixed glass
- The Living and Dining areas separated by a massive stone fireplace
- A secluded Master Suite with a walk-in closet and private Master Bath
- An efficient Kitchen with a convenient laundry area
- An optional basement, slab or crawl space foundation - please specify when ordering

MAIN AREA — 1,454 SQ. FT.

TOTAL LIVING AREA:
1,454 SQ. FT.

MAIN AREA

67'-0"

CARPORT
20'-0" x 20'-0"

KITCHEN
15'-2" x 8'-8"

DINING
15'-0" x 12'-0"

BEDROOM
15'-2" x 11'-0"

STORAGE   STORAGE

M. BEDROOM
15'-2" x 13'-6"

CATHEDRAL CEILING
LIVING
15'-0" x 21'-10"

BEDROOM
12'-8" x 11'-0"

BATH

34'-10"

DECK

To order your Blueprints, call 1-800-235-5700

ZIP QUOTE
HOME COST CALCULATOR
see order pages for details

An
EXCLUSIVE DESIGN
By Jannis Vann & Associates, Inc.

SECOND FLOOR

Bth.2
Lin.
Linen
Bdrm. 3
11-6 x 10-0
M.Bath
Coffered Ceil.
Bonus
15-10 x 17-4
8' Ceil.
W. D. Cab.
Low Wall
Bdrm. 2
11-6 x 11-0
Master Bdrm.
11-6 x 17-2
Tray Ceil.
Low Storage
Open Foyer

FIRST FLOOR

10-0
32-0
©1996, Jannis Vann & Associates, Inc.
Double Garage
21-8 x 21-4
Sundeck
16-0 x 12-0
Brkfst.
8-8 x 9-6
Kit.
10-9 x 9-6
Ref.
Family Rm.
18-0 x 13-6
Pant.
Cts.
Lav.
W/H
Dining
11-4 x 11-6
Living
13-6 x 13-6
Open Foyer
9-8 x 12-0
Stoop
58-4

A Modern Look At Colonial Styling
Price Code: C

■ This plan features:
— Three bedrooms
— Two full and one half baths

■ Brick detailing and keystones

■ Two-story Foyer opens to formal Living and Dining rooms

■ Expansive Family Room with a hearth fireplace between built-in shelves

■ U-shaped Kitchen with Breakfast Alcove, and nearby Garage entry

■ Elegant Master Bedroom with a large walk-in closet and a double vanity Bath

■ Two additional Bedrooms share a full Bath, Laundry and bonus area

FIRST FLOOR — 987 SQ. FT.
SECOND FLOOR — 965 SQ. FT.
FINISHED STAIRCASE — 72 SQ. FT.
BONUS — 272 SQ. FT.
BASEMENT — 899 SQ. FT.

TOTAL LIVING AREA:
2,024 SQ. FT.

Ceiling Treatments
Add Interest

Price Code: B

- ■ This plan features:
- — Three bedrooms
- — Two full baths
- ■ A vaulted ceiling over the Family Room and a tray ceiling over the Master Suite
- ■ Decorative columns accenting the entrance into the Dining Room
- ■ Great Room with a pass through from the Kitchen and a fireplace framed by a window to one side and a French door
- ■ A built-in Pantry and desk adding convenience to the Kitchen
- ■ An optional basement, crawl space or slab foundation — please specify when ordering

MAIN FLOOR — 1,553 SQ. FT.
BASEMENT — 1,605 SQ. FT.
GARAGE — 434 SQ. FT.

TOTAL LIVING AREA :
1,553 SQ. FT.

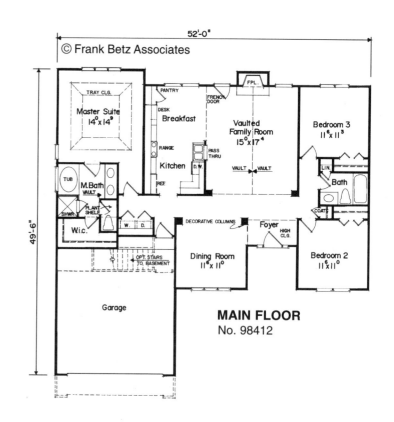

© Frank Betz Associates

52'-0"

49'-6"

TRAY CLG.

Master Suite
14⁰x14⁹

M.Bath
VAULT

TUB

SHWR

PLANT SHELF

W.i.c.

PANTRY

DESK

Breakfast

RANGE

Kitchen

REF.

D.W.

PASS THRU

FPL

FRENCH DOOR

Vaulted Family Room
15⁰x17⁴

VAULT   VAULT

Bedroom 3
11⁶x11³

LIN.

Bath

COATS

W.   D.

OPT. STAIRS TO BASEMENT

DECORATIVE COLUMNS

Dining Room
11⁶x11⁰

Foyer
HIGH CLG.

Bedroom 2
11⁶x11⁰

Garage

MAIN FLOOR
No. 98412

To order your Blueprints, call 1-800-235-5700

Impeccable Style
PRICE CODE: C

This plan features:
- Three bedrooms
- Two full and one half baths

Brick, stone, and interesting rooflines showcase the impeccable style of this home

Inside a deluxe staircase highlights the Foyer

The Dining room has a bay window at one end and columns at the other

The U-shaped Kitchen has an island in its center

The two-story Great Room has a warm fireplace

The shape of the Master Bedroom adds to its character

Upstairs find two Bedrooms and a full Bath

No materials list is available for this plan

FIRST FLOOR — 1,706 SQ. FT.
SECOND FLOOR — 492 SQ. FT.
BASEMENT — 1,706 SQ. FT.

TOTAL LIVING AREA:
2,198 SQ. FT.

Cozy Cottage
PRICE CODE: A

This plan features:
- Three bedrooms
- One full baths

Quaint front Porch giving this home a cottage styled exterior

Family Room highlighted by a cozy fireplace flanked by windows

Efficient L-shaped, eat-in Kitchen with window above the double sink

First floor Bedroom in close proximity to the Bathroom

Two additional Bedrooms on the second floor

No materials list is available for this plan

FIRST FLOOR — 728 SQ. FT.
SECOND FLOOR — 300 SQ. FT.

TOTAL LIVING AREA:
1,028 SQ. FT.

An
EXCLUSIVE DESIGN
By Greg Marquis

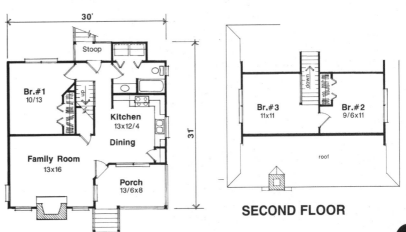

FIRST FLOOR

SECOND FLOOR

Delightful, Compact Home

PRICE CODE: A

■ This plan features:
— Three bedrooms
— Two full baths
■ A fireplaced Living Room brightened by a wonderful picture window
■ A counter island featuring double sinks separating the Kitchen and Dining areas
■ A Master Bedroom that includes a private Master Bath and double closets
■ Two additional Bedrooms with ample closet space that share a full Bath

MAIN FLOOR — 1,146 SQ. FT.

TOTAL LIVING AREA:
1,146 SQ. FT.

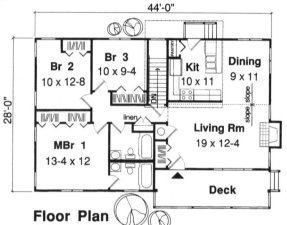

44'-0"

28'-0"

Br 2
10 x 12-8

Br 3
10 x 9-4

Kit
10 x 11

Dining
9 x 11

linen

MBr 1
13-4 x 12

Living Rm
19 x 12-4

Deck

Floor Plan

slab/crawlspace option

ZIP QUOTE
HOME COST CALCULATOR
see order pages for details

Compact Ranch

PRICE CODE: A

■ This plan features:
— Three bedrooms
— Two full baths
■ A Great Room and Dining area with vaulted ceilings, and a fireplace in the Great Room
■ A Kitchen and sunny Breakfast area with access to a rear Deck
■ A Master Suite with a private full Bath and one wall of closet space

MAIN AREA — 1,325 SQ. FT.
GARAGE — 390 SQ. FT.

TOTAL LIVING AREA:
1,325 SQ. FT.

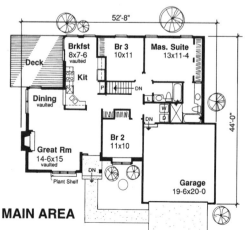

52'-8"

44'-0"

Deck

Brkfst
8x7-6
vaulted

Br 3
10x11

Mas. Suite
13x11-4

Kit

Dining
vaulted

Br 2
11x10

Great Rm
14-6x15
vaulted

Plant Shelf

Garage
19-6x20-0

MAIN AREA

To order your Blueprints, call 1-800-235-5700

PLAN NO. 91517

MAIN FLOOR — 1,022 SQ. FT.
UPPER FLOOR — 813 SQ. FT.
BASEMENT — 1,077 SQ. FT.

TOTAL LIVING AREA:
1,835 SQ. FT.

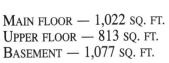

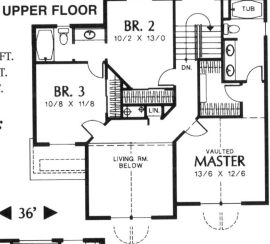

UPPER FLOOR

BR. 2
10/2 X 13/0

TUB

BR. 3
10/8 X 11/8

LIN.

DN.

LIVING RM.
BELOW

VAULTED
MASTER
13/6 X 12/6

◀ 36' ▶

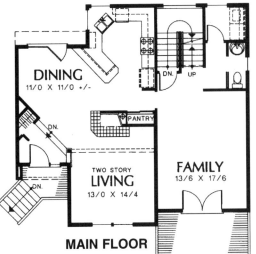

MAIN FLOOR

DINING
11/0 X 11/0 +/-

PANTRY

DN.

UP

DN.

TWO STORY
LIVING
13/0 X 14/4

FAMILY
13/6 X 17/6

DN.

3'

TWO CAR GARAGE BELOW

Designed for Sloping Lot

Price Code: C

- ■ This plan features:
  - — Three bedrooms
  - — Two full and one half baths
- ■ An impressive elevation accented by palladium windows and a raised entrance
- ■ Two-story Living Room with corner fireplace opens to Dining Area and Kitchen for ease in entertaining
- ■ Expansive Dining Area with atrium door to rear yard
- ■ Efficient Kitchen with built-in Pantry and angled serving counter
- ■ Comfortable Family Room with French doors to raised Deck and easy access to Laundry and half Bath
- ■ Secluded Master suite with arched window below vaulted ceiling, walk-in closet and double vanity Bath
- ■ Two additional Bedrooms with ample closets share a full Bath

© 1996 Donald A. Gardner Architects, Inc.

B. NATHAN

Dramatic Dormers

Price Code: D

■ This plan features:

— Three bedrooms

— Two full baths

■ A Foyer open to the dramatic dormer, defined by columns

■ A Dining Room augmented by a tray ceiling

■ A Great Room expanded into the open Kitchen and the Breakfast Room

■ A privately located Master Suite, topped by a tray ceiling in the Bedroom and pampered by a garden tub with a picture window as the focal point of the Master Bath

■ Two additional Bedrooms, located at the opposite side of the home from the Master Suite, sharing a full Bath and linen closet

MAIN FLOOR — 1,685 SQ. FT.
GARAGE & STORAGE — 536 SQ. FT.
BONUS — 331 SQ. FT.

ZIP QUOTE
HOME COST CALCULATOR
see order pages for details

TOTAL LIVING AREA:
1,685 SQ. FT.

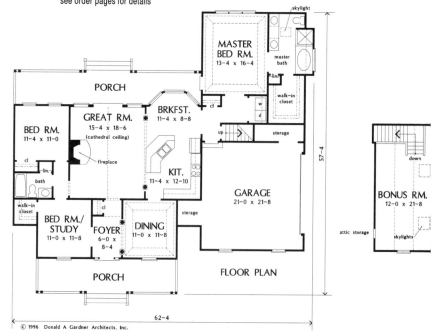

© 1996 Donald A Gardner Architects, Inc.

Great Room Heart of Home

PRICE CODE: A

This plan features:

- Three bedrooms
- Two full baths
- Sheltered Porch leads into the Entry with arches and a Great Room
- Spacious Great Room with a ten foot ceiling above a wall of windows and rear yard access
- Efficient Kitchen with a built-in Pantry, a laundry closet and a Breakfast Area accented by a decorative window
- Bay of windows enhances the Master Bedroom suite with a double vanity Bath and a walk-in closet
- Two additional Bedrooms with ample closets, share a full Bath
- No materials list is available for this plan

MAIN AREA — 1,087 SQ. FT.

TOTAL LIVING AREA:
1,087 SQ. FT.

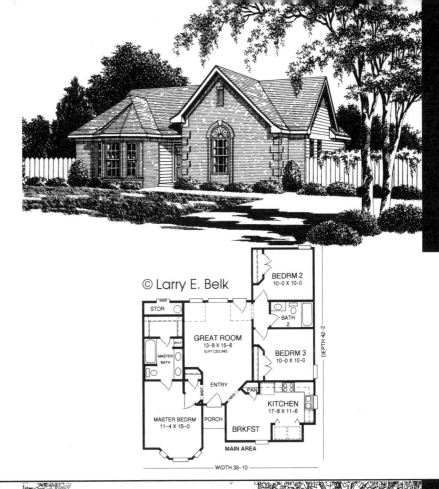

© Larry E. Belk

Rustic Simplicity

PRICE CODE: C

This plan features:

- Three bedrooms
- Two full and one half baths
- The central living area is large and boasts a cathedral ceiling, exposed wood beams and a clerestory
- A long screened Porch has a bank of skylights
- The open Kitchen contains a convenient serving and eating counter
- The generous Master Suite opens to the screened Porch, and is enhanced by a walk-in closet and a whirlpool tub
- Two more Bedrooms share a second full Bath

MAIN FLOOR — 1,426 SQ. FT.

TOTAL LIVING AREA:
1,426 SQ. FT.

© 1987 Donald A. Gardner Architects, Inc.

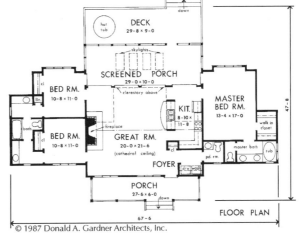

© 1987 Donald A. Gardner Architects, Inc.

To order your Blueprints, call 1-800-235-5700

Sense of Spaciousness
PRICE CODE: D

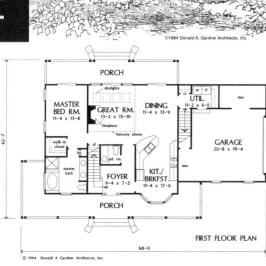

©1994 Donald A. Gardner Architects, Inc.

- This plan features:
— Three bedrooms
— Two full and one half baths
- Creative use of natural lighting gives a feeling of spaciousness to this Country home
- Traffic flows easily from the bright Foyer into the Great Room which has a vaulted ceiling and skylights
- The open floor plan is efficient for Kitchen/Breakfast Area and the Dining Room
- Master Bedroom Suite features a walk-in closet and a private Bath with whirlpool tub
- Two second floor Bedrooms with storage access share full Bath

FIRST FLOOR — 1,180 SQ. FT.
SECOND FLOOR — 459 SQ. FT.
BONUS ROOM — 385 SQ. FT.
GARAGE & STORAGE — 533 SQ. FT.

TOTAL LIVING AREA:
1,639 SQ. FT.

FIRST FLOOR PLAN

© 1994 Donald A Gardner Architects, Inc.

SECOND FLOOR PLAN

Elegant Victorian
PRICE CODE: D

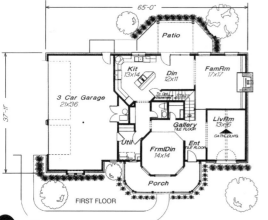

- This plan features:
— Three bedrooms
— Two full and one half baths
- Sit and relax on the front Porch at the end of the day with family and friends
- Serve guests dinner in the bayed Dining Room and the gather in the Living Room which features a cathedral ceiling
- There is plenty of space for activities in the Family Room which is accented by a fireplace
- The Master Bedroom has a Sitting Area, walk-in closet and a private Bath
- Two additional Bedrooms share a full Bath, and there a bonus room upstairs for future expansion
- This plan features a three car Garage with space for storage
- A basement or a slab foundation — please specify when ordering
- No material list is available for this plan

FIRST FLOOR — 1,447 SQ. FT.
SECOND FLOOR — 1,008 SQ. FT.
GARAGE — 756 SQ. FT.

FIRST FLOOR

ZIP QUOTE
HOME COST CALCULATOR
see order pages for details

SECOND FLOOR

TOTAL LIVING AREA:
2,455 SQ. FT.

An EXCLUSIVE DESIGN
By Greg Marquis

Cozy See-Through Fireplace

Price Code: B

■ This plan features:

— Three bedrooms

— Two full baths

■ Spacious Family Room enhanced by a see-through fireplace and a pass-through from the Kitchen

■ Dining Area has access to the outside

■ Kitchen including a work island, a double sink and direct access to the laundry room

■ Master Suite is located to the rear of the home and can be accessed from the Dining Area

■ Compartmental Bath and a walk-in closet highlight the Master Suite

■ Two additional Bedrooms have walk-in closets and easy access to the full Bath in the hall

■ No materials list is available for this plan

MAIN FLOOR — 1,655 SQ. FT.
GARAGE — 484 SQ. FT.

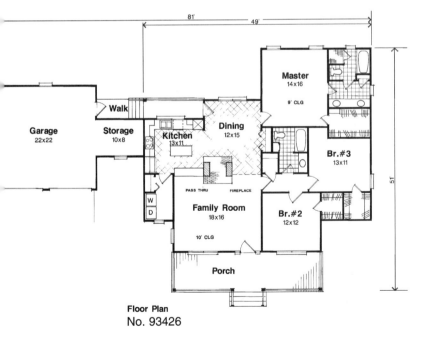

Floor Plan
No. 93426

TOTAL LIVING AREA:
1,655 SQ. FT.

Designed for a Narrow Lot

Price Code: B

■ This plan features:

— Three bedrooms

— Two full and one half baths

■ Enter the home through the front door with transom and sidelights

■ The Great Room with its corner fireplace is just steps beyond the Foyer

■ The Dining Room accesses the rear Patio

■ The Kitchen is spacious enough for multiple chefs to stir the soup

■ The Bedrooms are all on the second floor and have ample closets

■ A Bonus Room is accessed from the second floor

■ No materials list is available for this plan

FIRST FLOOR — 798 SQ. FT.
SECOND FLOOR — 777 SQ. FT.
BONUS — 242 SQ. FT.
BASEMENT — 798 SQ. FT.

FIRST FLOOR
No. 97712

TOTAL LIVING AREA:
1,575 SQ. FT.

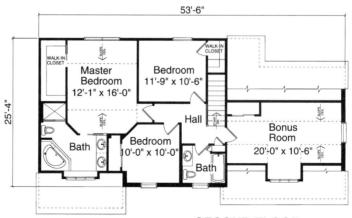

SECOND FLOOR

Charming Country Style
PRICE CODE: B

This plan features:
- Three bedrooms
- Two full baths

Spacious Great Room enhanced by a fireplace and transom windows

Breakfast Room with a bay window and direct access to the Kitchen

Snack bar extending work space in the Kitchen

Master Suite enhanced by a crowning in a boxed nine foot ceiling, a compartmental whirlpool Bath and a large walk-in closet

Second floor balcony overlooking the U-shaped stairs and Entry

Two second floor Bedrooms share a full hall Bath

FIRST FLOOR — 1,191 SQ. FT.
SECOND FLOOR — 405 SQ. FT.
BASEMENT — 1,191 SQ. FT.
GARAGE — 454 SQ. FT.

TOTAL LIVING AREA:
1,596 SQ. FT.

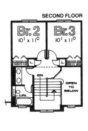

ZIP QUOTE
HOME COST CALCULATOR
see order pages for details

© design basics, inc.

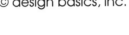

Split Bedroom Plan
PRICE CODE: A

This plan features:
- Three bedrooms
- Two full baths

A tray ceiling giving a decorative touch the Master Bedroom and a vaulted ceiling topping the five-piece Master Bath

A full Bath located between the secondary Bedrooms

A corner fireplace and a vaulted ceiling highlighting the heart of the home, the Family Room

A wetbar, serving bar to the Family Room and a built-in Pantry adding to the convenience of the Kitchen

A formal Dining Room crowned in an elegant high ceiling

An optional basement, slab, or crawl space foundation — please specify when ordering

MAIN FLOOR — 1,429 SQ. FT.
BASEMENT — 1,429 SQ. FT.
GARAGE — 438 SQ. FT.

TOTAL LIVING AREA:
1,429 SQ. FT.

© Frank Betz Associates

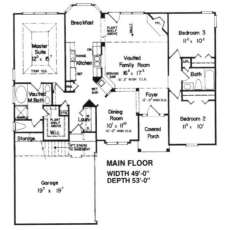

To order your Blueprints, call 1-800-235-5700

"How to obtain a construction cost calculation based on labor rates and building material costs in your Zip Code area!"

ZIP-QUOTE!
HOME COST CALCULATOR

ZIP QUOTE
HOME COST CALCULATOR

WHY?

Do you wish you could quickly find out the building cost for your new home without waiting for a contractor to compile hundreds of bids? Would you like to have a benchmark to compare your contractor(s) bids against? *Well, Now You Can!!,* with **Zip-Quote** Home Cost Calculator. Zip-Quote is only available for zip code areas within the United States.

HOW?

Our new **Zip-Quote** Home Cost Calculator will enable you to obtain the calculated building cost to construct your new home, based on labor rates and building material costs within your zip code area, without the normal delays or hassles usually associated with the bidding process. Zip-Quote can be purchased in two separate formats, an itemized or a bottom line format.

"How does **Zip-Quote** actually work?" When you call to order, you must choose from the options available, for your specific home, in order for us to process your order. Once we receive your **Zip-Quote** order, we process your specific home plan building materials list through our Home Cost Calculator which contains up-to-date rates for all residential labor trades and building material costs in your zip code area. "The result?" A calculated cost to build your dream home in your zip code area. This calculation will help you (as a consumer or a builder) evaluate your building budget. This is a valuable tool for anyone considering building a new home.

All database information for our calculations is furnished by Marshall & Swift, L.P. For over 60 years, Marshall & Swift L.P. has been a leading provider of cost data to professionals in all aspects of the construction and remodeling industries.

OPTION 1

The **Itemized Zip-Quote** is a detailed building material list. Each building material list line item will separately state the labor cost, material cost and equipment cost (if applicable) for the use of that building material in the construction process. Each category within the building material list will be subtotaled and the entire Itemized cost calculation totaled at the end. This building materials list will be summarized by the individual building categories and will have additional columns where you can enter data from your contractor's estimates for a cost comparison between the different suppliers and contractors who will actually quote you their products and services.

OPTION 2

The **Bottom Line Zip-Quote** is a one line summarized total cost for the home plan of your choice. This cost calculation is also based on the labor cost, material cost and equipment cost (if applicable) within your local zip code area.

COST

The price of your **Itemized Zip-Quote** is based upon the pricing schedule of the plan you have selected, in addition to the price of the materials list. Please refer to the pricing schedule on our order form. The price of your initial **Bottom Line Zip-Quote** is $29.95. Each additional **Bottom Line Zip-Quote** ordered in conjunction with the initial order is only $14.95. **Bottom Line Zip-Quote** may be purchased separately and does NOT have to be purchased in conjunction with a home plan order.

FYI

An **Itemized Zip-Quote** Home Cost Calculation can ONLY be purchased in conjunction with a Home Plan order. The **Itemized Zip-Quote** can not be purchased separately. The **Bottom Line Zip-Quote** can be purchased separately and doesn't have to be purchased in conjunction with a home plan order. Please consult with a sales representative for current availability. If you find within 60 days of your order date that you will be unable to build this home, then you may exchange the plans and the materials list towards the price of a new set of plans (see order info pages for plan exchange policy). The **Itemized Zip-Quote** and the **Bottom Line Zip-Quote** are NOT returnable. The price of the initial **Bottom Line Zip-Quote** order can be credited towards the purchase of an **Itemized Zip-Quote** order only. Additional **Bottom Line Zip-Quote** orders, within the same order can not be credited. Please call our Customer Service Department for more information.

Zip-Quote is available for plans where you see this symbol. Please call for current availability.

ZIP QUOTE
HOME COST CALCULATOR

SOME MORE INFORMATION

The Itemized and Bottom Line Zip-Quotes give you approximate costs for constructing the particular house in your area. These costs are not exact and are only intended to be used as a preliminary estimate to help determine the affordability of a new home and/or a guide to evaluate the general competitiveness of actual price quotes obtained through local suppliers and contractors. However, Zip-Quote cost figures should never be relied upon as the only source of information in either case. Land, sewer systems, site work, landscaping and other expenses are not included in our building cost figures. The Garlinghouse Company and Marshall & Swift L.P. can not guarantee any level of data accuracy or correctness in a Zip-Quote and disclaim all liability for loss with respect to the same, in excess of the original purchase price of the Zip-Quote product. All Zip-Quote calculations are based upon the actual blueprint materials list with options as selected by customer and do not reflect any differences that may be shown on the published house renderings, floor plans, or photographs.

438

Seismic Engineer...

...for

The Garlinghouse Company has teamed with Parker [...] premiere Engineering firm in Southern California, to [...] vices to the Southwestern Sunbelt market. We are now able to [...] seismic engineering for any plan that appears in this publication. Seismic engin... can be provided with, or without, specific soils information, depending on your local building needs.

Our extensive engineering packages will come to you complete with 3 sets of stamped and signed blueprints, 1 set of reproducible vellums, and 3 sets of stamped and signed structural calculations!

Parker Resnick Structural Engineering, located in Los Angeles California will help make building your dream home a reality. Through this exclusive offer, we are able to provide these services at very reasonable prices.

Price Code	*Without Specific Soils Information*	*With Specific Soils Information*
A	$1020	$1500
B	$1080	$1590
C	$1160	$1720
D	$1250	$1840
E	$1360	$2000
F	$1490	$2200
G	$1620	$2400
H	$1760	$2600

NOTE: Seismic engineering pricing is in addition to the cost of a reproducible vellum.

You will be required to provide all applicable soils reports (if they are required in your area) before any specific foundation engineering can begin. Once we have received your order or approved soils reports, please allow 10-14 additional business days for delivery. Check with your local building department to find out your exact requirements before placing your order.

The above pricing includes shipping from Parker Resnick Structural Engineering to you. All plan check revisions, site visits or field questions will be billable at $100.00 per hour. Site visit billing will include travel time. Seismic engineering is a custom professional service and is locally specific. Please note that all fees for this service are non-refundable upon commencement of any engineering.

We are proud to offer these engineering services to you at these very competitive rates.

ML Materials List Available   **ZIP** Zip Quote Available   **RRR** Right Reading Reverse   **DUP** Duplex Plan

Everything You Need...
...to Make Your Dream Come True

You pay only a fraction of the original cost for home designs by respected professionals.

You've Picked Your Dream Home!

You can already see it standing on your lot... you can see yourselves in your new home... enjoying family, entertaining guests, celebrating holidays. All that remains ahead are the details. That's where we can help. Whether you plan to build-it-yourself, be your own contractor, or hand your plans over to an outside contractor, your Garlinghouse blueprints provide the perfect beginning for putting yourself in your dream home right away.

We even make it simple for you to make professional design modifications. We can also provide a materials list for greater economy.

My grandfather, L.F. Garlinghouse, started a tradition of quality when he founded this company in 1907. For over 90 years, homeowners and builders have relied on us for accurate, complete, professional blueprints. Our plans help you get results fast... and save money, too! These pages will give you all the information you need to order. So get started now... I know you'll love your new Garlinghouse home!

Sincerely,

Whtn Garling

EXTERIOR ELEVATIONS

Elevations are scaled drawings of the front, rear, left and right sides of a home. All of the necessary information pertaining to the exterior finish materials, roof pitches and exterior height dimensions of your home are defined.

CABINET PLANS

These plans, or in some cases elevations, will detail the layout of the kitchen and bathroom cabinets at a larger scale. This gives you an accurate layout for your cabinets or an ideal starting point for a modified custom cabinet design. Available for most plans in our collection. You may also show the floor plan without a cabinet layout. This will allow you to start from scratch and design your own dream kitchen.

TYPICAL WALL SECTION

This section is provided to help your builder understand the structural components and materials used to construct the exterior walls of your home. This section will address insulation, roof components, and interior and exterior wall finishes. Your plans will be designed with either 2x4 2x6 exterior walls, but most professional contractors can easily adapt the plans to the wall thickness you require. Available for most plans in our collection.

FIREPLACE DETAILS

If the home you have chosen includes a fireplace, the fireplace detail will show typical methods to construct the firebox, hearth and flue chase for masonry units, or a wood frame chase for a zero-clearance unit. Available for most plans in our collection.

FOUNDATION PLAN

These plans will accurately dimension the footprint of your home including load bearing points and beam placement if applicable. The foundation style will vary from plan to plan. Your local climatic conditions will dictate whether a basement, slab or crawlspace is best suited for your area. In most cases, if your plan comes with one foundation style, a professional contractor can easily adapt the foundation plan to an alternate style.

ROOF PLAN

The information necessary to construct the roof will be included with your home plans. Some plans will reference roof trusses, while many others contain schematic framing plans. These framing plans will indicate the lumber sizes necessary for the rafters and ridgeboards based on the designated roof loads.

TYPICAL CROSS SECTION

A cut-away cross-section through the entire home shows your building contractor the exact correlation of construction components at all levels of the house. It will help to clarify the load bearing points from the roof all the way down to the basement.

DETAILED FLOOR PLANS

The floor plans of your home accurately dimension the positioning of all walls, doors, windows, stairs and permanent fixtures. They will show you the relationship and dimensions of rooms, closets and traffic patterns. The schematic of the electrical layout may be included in the plan. This layout is clearly represented and does not hinder the clarity of other pertinent information shown. All these details will help your builder properly construct your new home.

STAIR DETAILS

If stairs are an element of the design you have chosen, the plans will show the necessary information to build these, either through a stair cross section, or on the floor plans. Either way, the information provides your builders the essential reference points that they need to build the stairs.

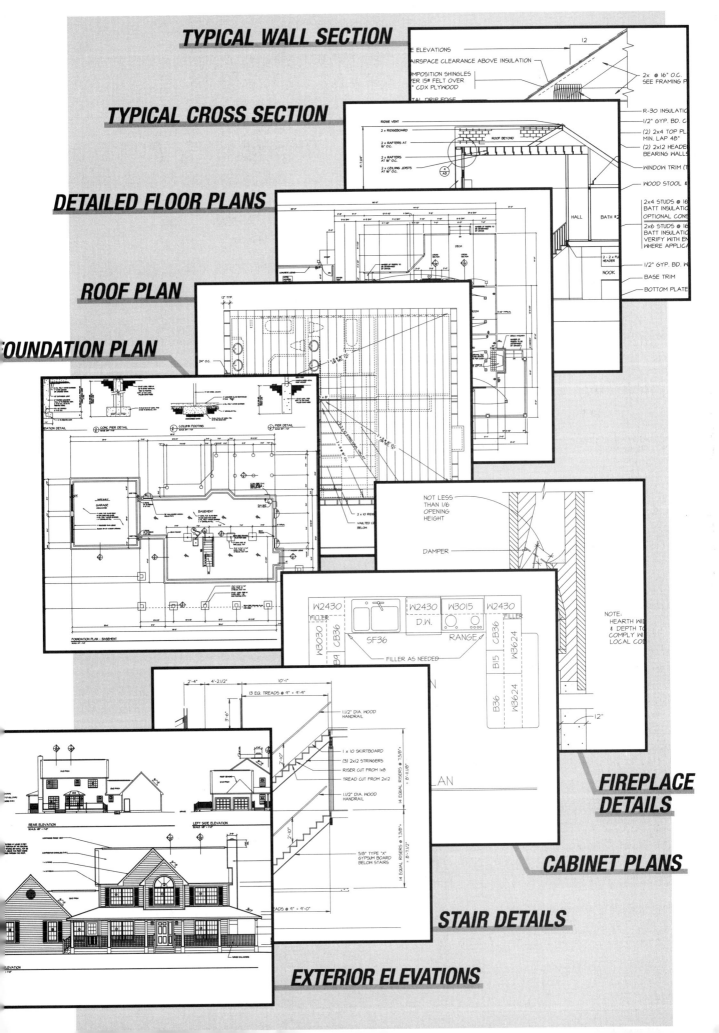

TYPICAL WALL SECTION

TYPICAL CROSS SECTION

DETAILED FLOOR PLANS

ROOF PLAN

FOUNDATION PLAN

FIREPLACE DETAILS

CABINET PLANS

STAIR DETAILS

EXTERIOR ELEVATIONS

Garlinghouse Options & Extras
...Make Your Dream A Home

Reversed Plans Can Make Your Dream Home Just Right!

"That's our dream home...if only the garage were on the other side!"

You could have exactly the home you want by flipping it end-for-end. Check it out by holding your dream home page of this book up to a mirror. Then simply order your plans "reversed." We'll send you one full set of mirror-image plans (with the writing backwards) as a master guide for you and your builder.

The remaining sets of your order will come as shown in this book so the dimensions and specifications are easily read on the job site...but most plans in our collection come stamped "REVERSED" so there is no construction confusion.

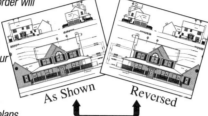

As Shown   Reversed

We can only send reversed plans with multiple-set orders. There is a $50 charge for this service.

Some plans in our collection are available in Right Reading Reverse. Right Reading Reverse plans will show your home in reverse, with the writing on the plan being readable. This easy-to-read format will save you valuable time and money. Please contact our Customer Service Department at (860) 343-5977 to check for Right Reading Reverse availability. (There is a $125 charge for this service.)

Specifications & Contract Form

We send this form to you free of charge with your home plan order. The form is designed to be filled in by you or your contractor with the exact materials to use in the construction of your new home. Once signed by you and your contractor it will provide you with peace of mind throughout the construction process.

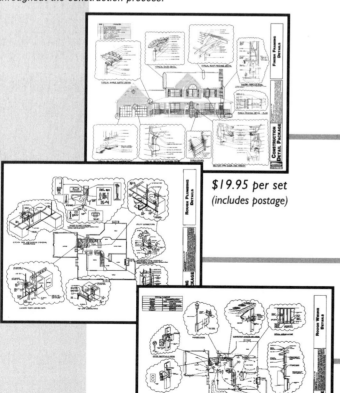

$19.95 per set
(includes postage)

Remember To Order Your Materials List

It'll help you save money. Available at a modest additional charge, the Materials List gives the quantity, dimensions, and specifications for the major materials needed to build your home. You will get faster, more accurate bids from your contractors and building suppliers — and avoid paying for unused materials and waste. Materials Lists are available for all home plans except as otherwise indicated, but can only be ordered with a set of home plans. Due to differences in regional requirements and homeowner or builder preferences... electrical, plumbing and heating/air conditioning equipment specifications are not designed specifically for each plan. However, non-plan specific detailed typical prints of residential electrical, plumbing and construction guidelines can be provided. Please see below for additional information. If you need a detailed materials cost you might need to purchase a Zip Quote. (Details follow)

Detail Plans Provide Valuable Information About Construction Techniques

Because local codes and requirements vary greatly, we recommend that you obtain drawings and bids from licensed contractors to do your mechanical plans. However, if you want to know more about techniques — and deal more confidently with subcontractors — we offer these remarkably useful detail sheets. These detail sheets will aid in your understanding of these technical subjects. **The detail sheets are not specific to any one home plan and should be used only as a general reference guide.**

RESIDENTIAL CONSTRUCTION DETAILS

Ten sheets that cover the essentials of stick-built residential home construction. Details foundation options — poured concrete basement, concrete block, or monolithic concrete slab. Shows all aspects of floor, wall and roof framing. Provides details for roof dormers, overhangs, chimneys and skylights. Conforms to requirements of Uniform Building code or BOCA code. Includes a quick index and a glossary of terms.

RESIDENTIAL PLUMBING DETAILS

Eight sheets packed with information detailing pipe installation methods, fittings, and sized. Details plumbing hook-ups for toilets, sinks, washers, sump pumps, and septic system construction. Conforms to requirements of National Plumbing code. Color coded with a glossary of terms and quick index.

RESIDENTIAL ELECTRICAL DETAILS

Eight sheets that cover all aspects of residential wiring, from simple switch wiring to service entrance connections. Details distribution panel layout with outlet and switch schematics, circuit breaker and wiring installation methods, and ground fault interrupter specifications. Conforms to requirements of National Electrical Code. Color coded with a glossary of terms.

Modifying Your Favorite Design, Made *EASY!*

OPTION #1

Modifying Your Garlinghouse Home Plan

Simple modifications to your dream home, including minor non-structural changes and material substitutions, can be made between you and your builder by marking the changes directly on your blueprints. However, if you are considering making significant changes to your chosen design, we recommend that you use the services of The Garlinghouse Co. Design Staff. We will help take your ideas and turn them into a reality, just the way you want. Here's our procedure!

When you place your Vellum order, you may also request a free Garlinghouse Modification Kit. In this kit, you will receive a red marking pencil, furniture cut-out sheet, ruler, a self addressed mailing label and a form for specifying any additional notes or drawings that will help us understand your design ideas. Mark your desired changes directly on the Vellum drawings. NOTE: Please use only a **red pencil** to mark your desired changes on the Vellum. Then, return the redlined Vellum set in the original box to The Garlinghouse Company, 282 Main Street Extension, Middletown, CT 06457. **IMPORTANT:** Please **roll** the Vellums for shipping, **do not fold** the Vellums for shipping.

We also offer modification estimates. We will provide you with an estimate to draft your changes based on your specific modifications before you purchase the vellums, for a $50 fee. After you receive your estimate, if you decide to have The Garlinghouse Company Design Staff do the changes, the $50 estimate fee will be deducted from the cost of your modifications. If, however, you choose to use a different service, the $50 estimate fee is non-refundable. (Note: Personal checks cannot be accepted for the estimate.)

Within 5 days of receipt of your plans, you will be contacted by a member of The Garlinghouse Co. Design Staff with an estimate for the design services to draw those changes. A 50% deposit is required before we begin making the actual modifications to your plans.

Once the design changes have been completed to your vellum plan, a representative from The Garlinghouse Co. Design Staff will call to inform you that your modified Vellum plan is complete and will be shipped as soon as the final payment has been made. For additional information call us at 1-860-343-5977. Please refer to the Modification Pricing Guide for estimated modification costs. Please call for Vellum modification availability for plan numbers 85,000 and above.

OPTION #2

Reproducible Vellums for Local Modification Ease

If you decide not to use the Garlinghouse Co. Design Staff for your modifications, we recommend that you follow our same procedure of purchasing our Vellums. You then have the option of using the services of the original designer of the plan, a local professional designer, or architect to make the modifications to your plan.

With a Vellum copy of our plans, a design professional can alter the drawings just the way you want, then you can print as many copies of the modified plans as you need to build your house. And, since you have already started with our complete detailed plans, the cost of those expensive professional services will be significantly less than starting from scratch. Refer to the price schedule for Vellum costs. Again, please call for Vellum availability for plan numbers 85,000 and above.

IMPORTANT RETURN POLICY: Upon receipt of your Vellums, if for some reason you decide you do not want the modified plan, then simply return the Kit and the unopened Vellums. Reproducible Vellum copies of our home plans are copyright protected and only sold under the terms of a license agreement that you will receive with your order. Should you not agree to the terms, then the Vellums may be returned, **unopened,** for a full refund less the shipping and handling charges, plus a 15% restocking fee. For any additional information, please call us at 1-860-343-5977.

MODIFICATION PRICING GUIDE

CATEGORIES	ESTIMATED COST
KITCHEN LAYOUT — PLAN AND ELEVATION	$175.00
BATHROOM LAYOUT — PLAN AND ELEVATION	$175.00
FIREPLACE PLAN AND DETAILS	$200.00
INTERIOR ELEVATION	$125.00
EXTERIOR ELEVATION — MATERIAL CHANGE	$140.00
EXTERIOR ELEVATION — ADD BRICK OR STONE	$400.00
EXTERIOR ELEVATION — STYLE CHANGE	$450.00
NON BEARING WALLS (INTERIOR)	$200.00
BEARING AND/OR EXTERIOR WALLS	$325.00
WALL FRAMING CHANGE — 2X4 TO 2X6 OR 2X6 TO 2X4	$240.00
ADD/REDUCE LIVING SPACE — SQUARE FOOTAGE	QUOTE REQUIRED
NEW MATERIALS LIST	QUOTE REQUIRED
CHANGE TRUSSES TO RAFTERS OR CHANGE ROOF PITCH	$300.00
FRAMING PLAN CHANGES	$325.00
GARAGE CHANGES	$325.00
ADD A FOUNDATION OPTION	$300.00
FOUNDATION CHANGES	$250.00
RIGHT READING PLAN REVERSE	$575.00
ARCHITECTS SEAL (Available for most states)	$300.00
ENERGY CERTIFICATE	$150.00
LIGHT AND VENTILATION SCHEDULE	$150.00

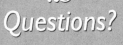

Questions?

Call our customer service department at *1-860-343-5977*

IMPORTANT INFORMATION TO READ BEFORE YOU PLACE YOUR ORDER

How Many Sets Of Plans Will You Need?

The Standard 8-Set Construction Package

Our experience shows that you'll speed every step of construction and avoid costly building errors by ordering enough sets to go around. Each tradesperson wants a set — the general contractor and all subcontractors; foundation, electrical, plumbing, heating/air conditioning and framers. Don't forget your lending institution, building department and, of course, a set for yourself.
* Recommended for Construction *

The Minimum 4-Set Construction Package

If you're comfortable with arduous follow-up, this package can save you a few dollars by giving you the option of passing down plan sets as work progresses. You might have enough copies to go around if work goes exactly as scheduled and no plans are lost or damaged by subcontractors. But for only $50 more, the 8-set package eliminates these worries. * Recommended for Bidding *

The Single Study Set

We offer this set so you can study the blueprints to plan your dream home in detail. They are stamped "study set-not for construction", and you cannot build a home from a them. In pursuant to copyright laws, it is illegal to reproduce any blueprint.

An Important Note About Building Code Requirements:

All plans are drawn to conform to one or more of the industry's major national building standards. However, due to the variety of local building regulations, your plan may need to be modified to comply with local requirements — snow loads, energy loads, seismic zones, etc. Do check them full and consult your local building officials.

A few states require that all building plans used be drawn by an architect registered in that state. While having your plans reviewed and stamped by such an architect may be prudent, laws requiring non-conforming plans like ours to be completely redrawn forces you to unnecessarily pay very large fees. If your state has such a law, we strongly recommend you contact your state representative to protest.

The rendering, floor plans, and technical information contained within t publication are not guaranteed to be totally accurate. Consequently, no info mation from this publication should be used either as a guide to constructi a home or for estimating the cost of building a home. Complete blueprints must be purchased for such purposes.

Order Form

Plan prices guaranteed until 3/26/00 —After this date call for updated pricing

Order Code No. **H9BS2**

____ set(s) of blueprints for plan #_____ $_____

____ Vellum & Modification kit for plan #_____ $_____

____ Additional set(s) @ $35 each for plan #_____ $_____

____ Mirror Image Reverse @ $50 each $_____

____ Right Reading Reverse @ $125 each $_____

____ Materials list for plan #_____ $_____

____ Detail Plans @ $19.95 each
     ❏ Construction   ❏ Plumbing   ❏ Electrical $_____

____ Bottom line ZIP Quote @ $29.95 for plan #_____ $_____

____ Additional Bottom Line Zip Quote
     @ $14.95 for plan(s) #_____

_____ $_____

____ Itemized ZIP Quote for plan(s) #_____ $_____

Shipping (see charts on opposite page) $_____

Subtotal $_____

Sales Tax   (CT residents add 6% sales tax, KS residents add 6.15% sales tax) (Not required for other states) $_____

TOTAL AMOUNT ENCLOSED $_____

Send your check, money order or credit card information to:
(No C.O.D.'s Please)

Please submit all United States & Other Nations orders to:

Garlinghouse Company
P.O. Box 1717
Middletown, CT. 06457

Please Submit all Canadian plan orders to:

Garlinghouse Company
60 Baffin Place, Unit #5
Waterloo, Ontario N2V 1Z7

ADDRESS INFORMATION:

NAME: _____

STREET: _____

CITY: _____ STATE: _____ ZIP: _____

DAYTIME PHONE: _____

Credit Card Information

Charge To: ❏ Visa   ❏ Mastercard

Card # | | | | | | | | | | | | | | | | |

Signature _____ Exp. ____/____

Please submit all Canadian plan orders to:
Garlinghouse Company
60 Baffin Place, Unit #5, Waterloo, Ontario N2V 1Z7
Canadian Customers Only: 1-800-561-4169/Fax #: 1-800-719-3291
Customer Service #: 1-519-746-4169

ORDER TOLL FREE — 1-800-235-5700
Monday-Friday 8:00 a.m. to 8:00 p.m. Eastern Time
or FAX your Credit Card order to 1-860-343-5984
All foreign residents call 1-800-343-5977

Please have ready: 1. Your credit card number   2. The plan number   3. The order code number ⇨ H9BS2

Garlinghouse 1999 Blueprint Price Code Schedule

Additional sets with original order $35

PRICE CODE	A	B	C	D	E	F	G	H
8 SETS OF SAME PLAN	$405	$445	$490	$530	$570	$615	$655	$695
4 SETS OF SAME PLAN	$355	$395	$440	$480	$520	$565	$605	$645
1 SINGLE SET OF PLANS	$305	$345	$390	$430	$470	$515	$555	$595
VELLUMS	$515	$560	$610	$655	$700	$750	$795	$840
MATERIALS LIST	$60	$60	$65	$65	$70	$70	$75	$75
ITEMIZED ZIP QUOTE	$75	$80	$85	$85	$90	$90	$95	$95

Shipping — (Plans 1-84999)

	1-3 Sets	4-6 Sets	7+ & Vellums
Standard Delivery (UPS 2-Day)	$25.00	$30.00	$35.00
Overnight Delivery	$35.00	$40.00	$45.00

International Shipping & Handling

	1-3 Sets	4-6 Sets	7+ & Vellums
Regular Delivery Canada (7-10 Days)	$25.00	$30.00	$35.00
Express Delivery Canada (5-6 Days)	$40.00	$45.00	$50.00
Overseas Delivery Airmail (2-3 Weeks)	$50.00	$60.00	$65.00

Shipping — (Plans 85000-99999)

	1-3 Sets	4-6 Sets	7+ & Vellums
Ground Delivery (7-10 Days)	$15.00	$20.00	$25.00
Express Delivery (3-5 Days)	$20.00	$25.00	$30.00

Our Reorder and Exchange Policies:

If you find after your initial purchase that you require additional sets of plans you may purchase them from us at special reorder prices (please call for pricing details) provided that you reorder within 6 months of your original order date. There is a $28 reorder processing fee that is charged on all reorders. For more information on reordering plans please contact our Customer Service Department (860) 343-5977.

We want you to find your dream home from our wide selection of home plans. However, if for some reason you find that the plan you have purchased from us does not meet your needs, then you may exchange that plan for any other plan in our collection. We allow you sixty days from your original invoice date to make an exchange. At the time of the exchange you will be charged a processing fee of 15% of the total amount of your original order plus the difference in price between the plans (if applicable) plus the cost to ship the new plans to you. Call our Customer Service Department at (860) 343-5977 for more information. Please Note: Reproducible vellums can only be exchanged if they are unopened.

Important Shipping Information

Please refer to the shipping charts on the order form for service availability for your specific plan number. Our delivery service must have a street address or Rural Route Box number — never a post office box. (PLEASE NOTE: Supplying a P.O. Box number only will delay the shipping of your order.) Use a work address if no one is home during the day.

Orders being shipped to APO or FPO must go via First Class Mail. Please include the proper postage.

For our International Customers, only Certified bank checks and money orders are accepted and must be payable in U.S. currency. For speed, we ship international orders Air Parcel Post. Please refer to the chart for the correct shipping cost.

Important Canadian Shipping Information

To our friends in Canada, we have a plan design affiliate in Kitchener, Ontario. This relationship will help you avoid the delays and charges associated with shipments from the United States. Moreover, our affiliate is familiar with the building requirements in your community and country. We prefer payments in U.S. Currency. If you, however, are sending Canadian funds please add 40% to the prices of the plans and shipping fees.

Ignoring Copyright Laws Can Be
A $1,000,000 Mistake

Recent changes in the US copyright laws allow for statutory penalties of up to **$100,000** per incident for copyright infringement involving any of the copyrighted plans found in this publication. The law can be confusing. So, for your own protection, take the time to understand what you can and cannot do when it comes to home plans.

···WHAT YOU CANNOT DO···

You Cannot Duplicate Home Plans

Purchasing a set of blueprints and making additional sets by reproducing the original is **illegal**. If you need multiple sets of a particular home plan, then you must purchase them.

You Cannot Copy Any Part of a Home Plan to Create Another

Creating your own plan by copying even part of a home design found in this publication is called "creating a derivative work" and is **illegal** unless you have permission to do so.

You Cannot Build a Home Without a License

You must have specific permission or license to build a home from a copyrighted design, even if the finished home has been changed from the original plan. It is **illegal** to build one of the homes found in this publication without a license.

What Garlinghouse Offers

Home Plan Blueprint Package

By purchasing a multiple set package of blueprints or a vellum from Garlinghouse, you not only receive the physical blueprint documents necessary for construction, but you are also granted a license to build one, and only one, home. You can also make simple modifications, including minor non-structural changes and material substitutions, to our design, as long as these changes are made directly on the blueprints purchased from Garlinghouse and no additional copies are made.

Home Plan Vellums

By purchasing vellums for one of our home plans, you receive the same construction drawings found in the blueprints, but printed on vellum paper. Vellums can be erased and are perfect for making design changes. They are also semi-transparent making them easy to duplicate. But most importantly, the purchase of home plan vellums comes with a broader license that allows you to make changes to the design (ie, create a hand drawn or CAD derivative work), to make copies of the plan, and to build one home from the plan.

License To Build Additional Homes

With the purchase of a blueprint package or vellums you automatically receive a license to build one home and only one home, respectively. If you want to build more homes than you are licensed to build through your purchase of a plan, then additional licenses may be purchased at reasonable costs from Garlinghouse. Inquire for more information.